D1295901

The Psychology of Literacy

The Psychology of Literacy

SYLVIA SCRIBNER

MICHAEL COLE

HARVARD UNIVERSITY PRESS
Cambridge, Massachusetts, and London, England   1981

Library of Congress Cataloging in Publication Data

Scribner, Sylvia, 1925–
  The psychology of literacy.

  Bibliography: p.
  Includes index.
  1. Language and culture—Liberia. 2. Illiteracy—
Liberia. 3. Writing. 4. Psycholinguistics. 5. Vai
language. 6. Vei (African tribe) I. Cole, Michael,
1938–   joint author. II. Title.
P35.5.L5S3   401'.9   81-607
ISBN 0-674-72115-2   AACR2

To David Scribner and Sheila Cole

Preface

If you venture beyond these prefatory comments you will encounter a text that is neither brief nor simple. In this respect, at least, this book is true to our experience. An undertaking as large as "The Vai Project" would have been difficult under ordinary circumstances. The questions we asked required us to adopt methods from a variety of social science disciplines and to submit the information we collected to the kind of statistical analysis appropriate to each method. In these pages you will encounter, side by side, sample surveys and ethnographies, linguistic elicitation, clinical interviewing, and psychological experimentation. Each of these individual pieces requires an adequate level of description and an integrative theoretical framework to contribute to the meaning of the whole.

We remark upon these complexities because they were further compounded by the fact that the Vai project was not conducted under ordinary circumstances. We undertook this study of literacy in a relatively remote part of the world among a group of people whose language we did not speak and of whose literacy practices we had only a schematic knowledge. According to our theoretical perspective—and our practical needs—we needed to secure, as quickly as possible, the kind of detailed knowledge of the people and their literacy activities that is usually available only to an ethnographer who spends a long time in the field. We also needed expert skills in language analysis so that we could understand the relationship between the form of the writing system and the properties of the oral language it represents.

Although we felt competent enough in such matters to know what kind of work needed to be done, we had neither the training nor the time to carry on such a project by ourselves. We needed help, and we got it.

First, and a precondition for everything else, was the cooperation we received from the Vai people themselves. Foreign researchers today are not always welcome in village communities in the Third World. We ordinarily travel to such places pursuing questions that originate in our own cultural and professional settings, questions that may have little relevance or interest for the people we work among. In such cases, the benefits and gratifica-tions of research are entirely one-sided.

In the case of the Vai project the two "sides" to the research bargain may have had different conceptions of the questions that could be asked about literacy, but both shared a genuine interest in the topic. The Vai people are proud of their original writing system and want to see it accorded its histor-ical due. In every village we visited, local leaders and script literates would come to meet us. They taught us the script; they patiently retold tales of its origin and history; they allowed us to read and copy their private note-books and correspondence; and they sat patiently through hours of inter-views and experiments. In a real, not a formal, sense, the Vai people were full participants in this work. They asked that we bring word of their intel-lectual achievements to the wider world. It is a privilege to do so.

The staff roster at the end of the Preface lists everyone who was formally associated with the project for a year or more. Augustus Caine, listed as a consultant, not only introduced us to Vai society but at every step of the way helped us to understand and interpret our experience. His advice was a product of both his scholarly training in anthropology and his insights as a native member of Vai society—a combination of qualifications unusual anywhere and close to unique in Liberia. Stephen Reder and Michael Smith were principal participants. Reder specialized in a linguistic analysis of Vai that served as the basis for experimental work. He contributed key ideas for studies discussed in Chapter 10 and for data analysis programs used in Chapter 13; he conducted his own series of studies and has de-scribed some of them in Chapter 11. Smith furnished much of the ethno-graphic material on which experimental work and data interpretations were based. We have drawn heavily from his field notes and reports. Both Reder and Smith gave us detailed comments and criticisms on the first draft of this book. Mohamed Nyei, our research fellow, is an Arabic scholar, Vai script literate, and college-educated Vai man who was our ex-pert on the indigenous uses of the scripts we studied. He collaborated in studies on segmentation (Chapter 9) and integration (Chapter 10) and wrote most of the Vai script and all of the Arabic passages appearing in this book. Ethan Gologor and Bob Schwartz carried out the difficult task of serving as field director, providing us with two years of care for the collec-tion of questionnaire data. Gail Stewart, a specialist in Vai script, edited passages and reviewed all of the Vai transcriptions in this book to ensure accurate representation of the Vai language.

The staff roster far from covers the case. Jean Lave, whose research on informal and formal learning among Liberian tailors overlapped with ours, was counselor and critic from start to finish. Momulu Getaweh, then earn-ing his doctorate in sociology at Boston University, tutored Reder (and sometimes us) in the Vai language. Judith Orasanu and Ken Traupman helped design and interpret the results of inference studies (reported in Chapter 13); and Michael Pratt collaborated and carried much of the burden of working through an analytic scheme for the communication studies (reported in Chapter 12). Marjorie Martus of the Ford Foundation, which supported this research, kept before us the fact that one of the reasons for going to Africa to study literacy was to bring a new perspective to our own educational concerns.

The list might continue, but specific attribution of personal contributions has its limits as well as its oversights. It leaves out of the picture an important and, to us, indispensable source of intellectual energy—conversations with colleagues where talk runs free and ideas have no name tags. We were fortunate to share corridors at Rockefeller University with members of the Laboratory of Comparative Cognition; the Psycholinguistic Laboratory (George Miller); and the Mathematical Psychology Laboratory (William Estes).

Our look backward is not all a good-humored glow. It was hard to keep Liberia and New York coordinated; five years of field work was more than we had bargained for; some of our grander schemes collapsed; our families grew impatient with our frequent physical—and mental—departures to Africa.

But the work got done, even as many aspects of its nature were discovered in the process. In the last analysis, it was our responsibility to integrate the activities of the scattered participants and the individual lines of evidence. From our early gropings for a functional approach to the psychology of literacy, we arrived in the course of the work at a theoretical framework that we hope will contribute to a deeper understanding of the way in which different kinds of socially organized practices help shape human thought. We offer this framework in return for the resources provided us.

VAI LITERACY PROJECT, 1973–1978

Augustus F. Caine, consultant

Stephen Reder (1975–77), associate, psycholinguistics
Michael Smith (1973–75), associate, ethnography

Ethan Gologor (1973), survey field director
Robert Schwartz (1974), survey field director
Elizabeth Hurlow-Hannah (1975), field director

Mohamed Nyei (1975–78), research fellow

Deborah Malamud (1977–78), data analyst

Field interviewers and assistants:
  Mole Gbese (1973–74)
  Mabu Sambolah (1973–74)
  Budu Sherman (1973–74)

Abraham Bai Paasewe (1973–77)
Hamidu Getaweh (1975–77)
Siafah Fahnbulleh (1976)
Momo Konneh (1973)

Research assistants, data analysis:
Janice Sherman Throop (1973)
Pamela Sutherland (1974)
Joan Macaneny (1975)
Neva Wartell (1976)

Technical consultants:
David Burns (1973–75), computer programs and data analysis
Charles Lave (throughout), multiple regression analysis
Gail Stewart (throughout), Vai script

Contents

Photographs showing uses of Vai script, Arabic, and English follow page 34.

A Note on Orthography

Except when the Vai script is used, the Vai language in this book has been transcribed into a modified form of the English alphabet. Consonants are pronounced approximately like their English equivalents, with the following additions (equivalents from the International Phonetic Alphabet are shown in brackets):

$ɓ$, like English b but with air forced inward [ɗ]
$ɗ$, like English d but with air forced inward [ɓ]
$ñ$, like English ng in hang [ŋ]

The clusters kp and gb are pronounced rather as if the two consonants were spoken simultaneously.

Vowels are pronounced as follows:

i, like i in machine [i]
a, like a in bah [ɑ]
u, like u in rune [u]
e, like $é$ in sauté [e]
$ē$, like e in then [ɛ]
o, like o in bone [o]
$ō$, like o in lost [ɔ]

Double vowels indicate lengthening of the vowel sound. The mark ~ indicates nasalization. Although Vai is a tonal language, tonal marking has been omitted except in instances where it is essential to analysis. High tone is indicated by ´, low tone by `, high to low by ^, and low to high by ˇ.

In some Vai words, the phonetic representations may vary. For example, *kai* and *kali* are two possible spellings of the word for "hoe"; the word for "paddle" may be rendered *laa* or *ɗaa*. Names of places and people in this book are given their customary English-alphabet spellings. Spelling of place names generally follows that appearing on the 1973 geographic maps of Liberia published by the U.S. Geological Survey in cooperation with the Liberian Geological Survey, as approved by the Liberian Board of Geographic Names.

Part I

Framing the
Questions

1

Writing and Thought

Concerns with literacy and thought tap some of our deepest notions about language and human nature. It is an age-old belief that speech distinguishes society from the social organization of other species and thus sets human apart from beast.

In our times this belief has been somewhat shaken. We now know that complex communication systems regulate the behavior of bees, birds, and beasts,[1] and the dividing line does not appear as clear as in the last century when scholars hailed language as a supreme achievement of human intellectual power (von Humboldt, 1863). Yet another belief about language has come to play an organizing role in the way we think about ourselves and society. That belief concerns written language. Writing, we can be certain, is the exclusive possession of the human animal. Its origins are to be found in cultural history rather than in biological evolution. Unlike spoken language, writing is of fairly recent invention (systematic writing systems did not appear until 4,000 to 3,000 B.C.) and it has yet to become a universal feature of all human societies.

As a new device of human communication, writing has often inspired a certain mystique. Travelers and missionaries delighted in reporting the astonishment of traditional peoples when first encountering the use of graphic symbols to convey messages. An anecdote of a Wesleyan missionary in the Fiji Islands is characteristic:

> As I had come to work one morning without my carpenter's square, I took up a chip and with a piece of charcoal wrote upon it a request that my wife should send me that article. [The chip was given to a Fijian chief to deliver] but the Chief was scornful of the errand and asked, "What must I say?" . . . You have nothing to say, I replied. The chip will say all I wish. With a look of astonishment and contempt, he held up the piece of wood and said, "How can this speak? Has this a mouth?" [When the errand had been successfully performed] the chief tied a string to the chip, hung it around his neck and wore it for some time. During several following days, we frequently saw him surrounded by a crowd who were listening with intense interest while he narrated the wonders which this chip had performed. (Clammer, 1976, p. 67)

European scholars have also expressed awe at the "stupefying leap of the imagination" involved in the invention of writing (Diringer, 1962, p. 19). Many consider the introduction of writing systems into social life a watershed in human history. While the descriptive terms differ, the notion that literacy introduces a great divide among human societies runs deep in contemporary social science. Literacy, it is said, separates prehistory from history (Goody and Watt, 1968), primitive societies from civilized societies (Lévi-Strauss, in Charbonnier, 1973), modern societies from traditional societies (Lerner, 1958).

For the most part these judgments have been based on the profound changes in social life which have often accompanied the introduction and adoption of writing systems. We know that remarkable transformations occurred in the ancient Mesopotamian societies during the formative period of the great scripts. Schmandt-Besserat (1978) chronicles the intimate connection between the writing systems and increasing complexity of agriculture and trade. She shows how the rise of rudimentary farming in these societies was accompanied by the invention of crude tokens, used as a means of recording the amount of grains and animals produced. Over the millennia, as cities arose and trade expanded, changes occurred in the tokens which moved them inexorably toward the writing system used by the Phoenicians just prior to the advent of alphabetic writing in Greece.

Studies of the interdependencies between writing systems and the rise of modern political and economic systems have attracted scholars from many disciplines. Most agree that written records provided the crucial technology for elaboration of the arts and sciences that characterize world history in the last 2,500 years. Even Lévi-Strauss, a well-known critic of the notion of historical progress, acknowledges that the invention of writing made it possible to accumulate the knowledge of each generation as "working capital" for the next (Charbonnier, 1973). Literacy has also been held to be instrumental in the development of increasingly complex commercial and administrative networks. Some scholars argue that the very existence of a technology of writing was sufficient to propel the growth of mass production and mass education; others (see Gough, 1968) consider it more appropriate to view literacy as an enabling factor whose effects were constrained by existing social conditions. We will meet these arguments again as they enter into current debates about "modernization processes." Whether literacy is considered a primary or a secondary causal factor, however, few doubt that the printing press and the book, no less than the steam engine and telescope, provided the technological basis for the rise of industrial society (Lilley, 1966; Lefevre and Martin, 1976; Eisenstein, 1979). The social repercussions of literacy in modern history appear self-evident.

Less prominent but of even earlier origin are claims for psychological repercussions of literacy. These underlie deep-seated popular notions equating literateness with intellectual ability. As literacy shapes culture, the argument goes, so it shapes human minds. A simple version of this argument appeals to the growth of the mind that results from the assimilation of knowledge and information transmitted by written texts. More radical is the claim that mastery of a written language affects not only the content of thought but also the processes of thinking—*how* we classify, reason, remember. According to this view, writing systems introduce such basic changes in the way individuals think that we are justified in speaking not only of literate and preliterate societies but of literate and preliterate people.

Since these claims go to the heart of our research, we will sketch here some of the forms they have taken in influential historical and social science writings. Our presentation is selective, intended to highlight different conceptions of the relationship between literacy and thought as well as the type of evidence that scholars in the last few decades have relied upon to support their claims.

COMPARATIVE AND HISTORICAL STUDIES

Post-Homeric Greece provides the setting for the earliest speculations about the relationship between written language and thought, and, as with many philosophical inquiries, Plato was their progenitor. This setting, and Plato's speculations, continue to play an important role in contemporary theorizing about the psychological impact of literacy.

In Plato's day, for the first time in history, a large part of the populace knew how to read and write in an alphabetic script, and the written text was becoming a serious competitor to oral literature as the vehicle for transmitting the cultural store of knowledge. Differences between these two modalities were apparent to Plato, and their implications troubled him. It seemed incontestable that engagement with written materials would affect men's minds, but rational analysis suggested complex, and sometimes contradictory, consequences. Some argued, for example, that letters would give men better memories; Socrates pointed out that, on the contrary, letters might weaken memory and lead to forgetfulness as learners came to rely on external aids for "reminiscence." Would the knowledge available in books help to make men wise? Socrates feared that disciples of the written word would have the show of wisdom (they would know the letters) without the reality (they would not necessarily grasp the true ideas) (Plato, *Phaedrus*, p. 323; for a critical analysis, see Greene, 1951).

On the other hand, Plato did not conclude that wisdom was a necessary outcome of oral learning. He was suspicious of education that relied primarily on the oral mode of the Homeric tradition—the transmission of knowledge through the recitation and memorization of the epic poems. Dramatic poetry as performed by professional bards appealed to the emotions, not to the higher faculties, and thus undermined the role of reason

(Plato, *The Republic*, p. 333). This latter speculation, pitting certain oral modes of discourse against reason, introduces a theme that has never disappeared from critical studies on the psychology of writing.

The classicist Eric Havelock (1963, 1976, 1978), intrigued with Plato's critique of the oral tradition, demonstrated through a comparative analysis of the Homeric poems and Platonic dialogues that Plato's suspicions about differences in thinking associated with written and oral communication must be taken seriously. Each modality has a lexicon and syntax suited to its own requirements. Homeric epics were memorized, and this requirement, together with the recitative conditions under which the poems were learned, gave primacy to attributes of language that would support memory: rhythm, personalistic and vivid imagery, narrative style. Both the language and the setting in which poems were performed promoted emotional identification with the material, not a critical attitude toward it. Because oral language is concrete and imagistic, it is unsuitable to the expression of abstract concepts or logical propositions. Havelock expresses this unsuitability as follows:

> Oral information is likely to be unfriendly to such a statement as "The angles of a triangle are equal to two right angles." If, however, you said, "The triangle stood firm in battle, astride and posed on its equal legs, fighting resolutely to protect its two right angles against the attack of the enemy" you would be casting Euclid backward into Homeric dress, you would be giving him preliterate form . . . Oral storage is hostile to the expression of laws and rules which are stated as such in terms which are connected by the timeless present. It is unfriendly to statements which place cause and effect in analytic relationship. (Havelock, 1978, pp. 42–43)

Written language, however, has an appropriate syntax for the expression of analytic relationships. And in the very course of producing it (Havelock stressed especially the use of the alphabet; see Chapter 14), the writer is forced to engage in abstract operations that provide the basis for the replacement of imagistic representations by true concepts. Alphabetic literacy spawned Platonic ideas.

Note that Havelock's demonstration of different modes of thought associated with oral and written language rests on identification of linguistic differences in the two modalities. Differences in thought are both inferred from and proved by the same language specimens.[2]

In a wide-ranging and influential essay, Jack Goody and Ian Watt (1968) further developed Havelock's line of reasoning from the perspective of the social sciences. Like Havelock, they began with a consideration of the special characteristics of the written modality, specifically language representation through an alphabetic system. They noted that the rise of alphabetic literacy in post-Homeric Greece occurred during the same period in which two new intellectual disciplines took form—history and logic. They argued that alphabetic literacy was the precursor and precondition for these disciplines, and, more clearly than Havelock, they posited changes in individual thought processes as the mediating links connecting these cultural phenomena. While Havelock emphasized differences in oral and written language systems as the decisive aspects of literacy, Goody and Watt stressed the implications of the permanency of language, accomplished through its representation in visual symbols. New intellectual operations, impossible to carry out on transient oral utterances, could be performed on this frozen language. With a written record, for example, readers could systematically compare one set of statements with another, becoming aware of inconsistencies which flourish unnoticed in oral tradition. Special modes of analysis are required to set these straight. One direction led, through Herodotus, to the development of historical criticism and methodology, squaring present accounts with those of the past; and the other led, through Aristotle, to analysis of the relationships among statements, squaring present claims with each other. To writing we owe Aristotle's invention of the syllogism and modern systems of logical inference: "The kinds of analysis involved in the syllogism and in the other forms of logical procedure are clearly dependent upon writing" (Goody and Watt, 1968, p. 68).

Goody and Watt also proposed that alphabetic literacy transformed basic categories of time and space and led to the new ways of classifying knowledge that philologists and historians had identified in their studies of ancient civilizations (Snell, 1953; Frankfort et al; 1972). Subsequently Goody (1968) and other scholars drew on evidence from a wide range of sources to demonstrate the hypothesized links among literacy, logic, and classificatory schemes in other societies and historical periods. This later work emphasized that what had previously been termed the consequences of literacy ought really to be considered literacy's implications, implications that might, or might not, come to fruition in any particular cultural/historical circumstances. This view led Goody to study the factors that control the degree to which the potentialities of writing are exploited. In these analyses, evidence from documents, historical studies, field observations, and oral traditions provides the basis for generalizations about the intellectual impact of literacy.

In this very condensed summary of one line of theorizing we find many of the propositions about literacy and thought that dominate discussion in other scholarly and practical arenas: written language promotes abstract concepts, analytic reasoning, new ways of categorizing, a logical approach to language. It is striking that the scholars who offer these claims for specific changes in psychological processes present no direct evidence that individuals in literate societies do, in fact, process information about the world differently from those in societies without literacy. They simply make assumptions about changed modes of thinking in the individual as the mediating mechanism for the linguistic and cultural changes which are their object of inquiry. This is an entirely appropriate procedure for anthropologists, sociologists, and classicists. Historically, the kinds of observations that can substantiate claims about individual thought processes have been the province of psychology and have rested on theories and investigative methods this science has developed. To support the thesis that literacy makes a difference in mental processes, psychological analysis has to be joined with cultural analysis. The challenge to the psychologist is to turn other social scientists' hypothetical mechanisms into demonstrated mechanisms. Unfortunately, few psychologists have taken up this challenge.

PSYCHOLOGICAL THEORIES AND RESEARCH

At the time we began our work, little guidance was available within psychology for testing speculations about written language and thought. This lack of attention to the possible formative influence of literacy was not accidental. Classic theories of intellectual development have been more concerned with studying universal structures of intelligence than variations in function associated with cultural conditions. Where cultural variations in thought processes were of major concern (as, for example, in the work of Heinz Werner, 1948), little theoretical or empirical effort was directed at identifying the mechanisms by which "culture" could account for intellectual differences.

A major exception to this generalization is the theory of higher psychological functions developed by Lev S. Vygotsky in the 1920s and 1930s. (Vygotsky, 1962, 1978 are the major texts available in English.) Vygotsky set out to overcome the schism between society and mind by constructing a unified account of cultural and psychological change. Entering psychology on the eve of the Russian Revolution, he was profoundly influenced by Marx and Engel's historical materialist theory of society and its potential significance for psychological science. According to Marx, man has no fixed human nature but continually makes himself and his consciousness through his productive activity. In the process of human labor, man transforms physical nature with the use of tools, and in the process of tool use he transforms his own nature. The dialectical and reciprocal nature of these processes of change was captured in Engel's statement that the anatomy of the human hand is as much a product of labor as it is the instrument of labor. As technology develops, human interaction with the environment becomes less direct; it is mediated in increasingly complex ways by the systems of tools that human societies devise.

Vygotsky brilliantly extended this concept of mediated human-environment interaction to the use of signs as well as tools. By "signs" he referred to socially created symbol systems such as language, writing, and number systems, which emerge over the course of history and vary from one society to another. Mental processes always involve signs, just as action on the environment always involves physical instruments (if only a human hand). Changing tools alter the structure of work activity: tilling the soil by hoe and by tractor require different patterns of behavior. Similarly, Vygotsky claimed, changing symbol systems restructure mental activity. According to Vygotsky, basic psychological processes (abstraction, generalization, inference) are universal and common to all humankind; but their functional organization (higher psychological processes, in Vygotsky's terminology) will vary, depending on the nature of the symbol systems available in different historical epochs and societies and the activities in which these symbol systems are used. Language is a universal symbol system, and its acquisition plays a crucial role in the development of higher psychological processes in childen. But other symbol systems are not universal and introduce culture-specific differences in the way higher processes are organized.

Vygotsky considered written language a sign system with significant consequences for the transformation of intellectual processes. In the following passage he speculated about the effect of graphic symbols on memory:

> A comparative investigation of human memory reveals that even at the earliest stages of social development, there are two principally different types of memory. One, dominating in the behavior of nonliterate peoples, is characterized by the nonmediated impression of materials, by the retention of actual experiences as the basis of mnemonic (memory) traces . . . This kind of memory is very close to perception, because it arises out of the direct influence of external stimuli upon human beings . . . We call this *natural memory* . . .
>
> Natural memory is not the only kind, however, even in the case of nonliterate men and women. On the contrary, other types of memory belonging to a completely different developmental line coexist with natural memory. The use of notched sticks and knots, the beginnings of writing and simple memory aids all demonstrate that even at early stages of historical development humans went beyond the limits of the psychological functions given to them by nature and proceeded to a new, culturally-elaborated organization of their behavior . . . we believe that these sign operations are the products of specific conditions of *social* development.   (Vygotsky, 1978, pp. 38–39)

In this example Vygotsky describes the effects of literacy in terms of writing as a material product. Elsewhere he analyzes the special cognitive demands that writing as an activity places on the child or adult who is in the process of becoming literate. In Chapter 12 we will present this analysis in detail because it forms the basis for one of our major lines of research. Here we note only that, while building on different concepts and using different observations, Vygotsky concurred with the speculations of ancient philosophers and the inquiries of modern scholars in viewing writing as a formative influence on higher forms of thinking.

EXPERIMENTAL OBSERVATIONS OF LITERACY EFFECTS

Our story would be simpler if Vygotsky's grand theorizing had initiated a generation or more of empirical research on the cognitive effects of writing systems, or if continuing work had led to the formulation of more specific hypotheses about just how, and in just what ways, writing might make a difference. As far as we know, Russian psychologists initiated only one large-scale investigation for the specific purpose of determining how changes in cultural conditions, exemplified by the introduction of schooling and literacy, affect intellectual functions. In the 1930s Alexander R. Luria (1976) led a psychological expedition to a region in Central Asia that was in a period of rapid social change as a result of reforms introduced by the central government. New machinery and collective systems of ownership were displacing traditional modes of farming, schools were opening up in the countryside, and communication with the outside world was expanding in many directions. Not all residents were equally caught up in these changes, however, which made possible a comparative study of their effects. Luria compared groups of traditional nonliterate farmers with other residents of the same villages who had gone through brief literacy courses or who had participated in short teacher-training programs. He used a variety of experimental tasks dealing with perception, word associations, concepts, classification, and reasoning. On these tasks and in informal interviews he found consistent differences in performance among the three comparative groups, which he interpreted within Vygotsky's theoretical framework. The most traditional and isolated of his populations, with neither literacy nor schooling, tended to respond to the tasks in a concrete, context-bound way, guided by the perceptual and functional attributes of things. The most schooled group, on the other hand, tended to take an abstract approach and be responsive to the conceptual and logical relationships among things. Minimal literacy groups fell in between.

In this series of studies Luria found confirmation of Vygotsky's thesis that sociocultural changes formed the basis for the development of higher memory and thinking processes and more complex psychological organization. But the design of his research limited what could be inferred about the particular effect of particular changes. While the groups could be designated by the amounts of literacy or schooling they had attained, they also differed in age and exposure to other novel activities such as collective management and planning of agricultural operations. Thus, differences in performance could not be attributed to literacy or schooling experience per se. This covariation of literacy with other major changes in life experience—a pervasive condition in almost all settings—is a formidable obstacle to research on educational effects, and a point to which we will constantly return.

After Luria, the thread picks up again on another continent three decades later. Patricia Greenfield, a developmental psychologist from Harvard, studied cultural influences on concept formation among Wolof children in Senegal, West Africa (Greenfield and Bruner, 1966). On many of the tasks presented she found differences in performance between children attending school and their unschooled siblings or counterparts, matched for age and rural or urban residence. This research on school effects is a significant forerunner of our own research on literacy and is discussed more fully below; here we single out one experimental task on which the nature of the children's performance suggested to Greenfield the importance of their knowledge of a written language. The task required classification of familiar objects and was not dissimilar to one used by Luria. Schooled and nonschooled children differed systematically in some of the ways they grouped objects together and how they talked about their grouping. Greenfield interpreted these differences as due to the schooled children's capacity for context-independent, abstract thought. She went on to link this thinking to literacy by a series of propositions about the nature of oral and written language: oral language relies on context for the communication of messages and is, therefore, a context-dependent language. In contrast, written language requires that meaning be made clear, independent of the immediate reference. If one assumes that context-dependent speech is linked with context-dependent thought, and context-dependent thought is the opposite of abstract thought, it follows that abstract thought fails to develop in a nonliterate culture. Societies with written languages, however, provide the means for abstract, decontextualized thinking (Greenfield, 1972).

In recent years David Olson in Canada has followed the strategy of comparing preliterate preschool children with school children of various ages and educated adults to test the thesis that literacy makes possible a unique form of logical competence. According to Olson (1975, 1977), literacy allows people to master the logical functions of language and to separate them from its interpersonal functions. For example, literacy is said to provide people with the ability to listen to the sentence "John hit Mary" and to derive the sentence "Mary was hit by John" simply on the basis of the logical relations among terms in the sentence without any factual information about who was hitting whom. Evidence that preschool children lack this ability, while older school children and adults display it, has been claimed by Olson to provide support for the theory that literacy biases cultures toward the development of formal reasoning systems.

Both Greenfield and Olson have been working within a cognitive developmental perspective described by Jerome Bruner as an attempt to take into account the shaping influence of culture on thought. Echoes of Vygotsky are clearly heard in his general statement of this perspective: cultures provide amplifiers in the form of technologies to empower human cognitive capacities (Bruner, 1966, p. xii); cultures with symbolic technologies such as a written language will thus "push cognitive growth better, earlier and longer than others" (Greenfield and Bruner, 1969, p. 654).

While these psychologists have brought the power of psychological analysis and technique to the problem of literacy and thought, their experiments fail to support the specific claims made for literacy's effects. We will confine our attention here to one outstanding difficulty. No comparisons were ever made between children with and children without a written language; comparisons were made between schooled and unschooled children, and schooling and literacy are not synonymous. The attribution to literacy of causal significance in cognitive development remained, as with Vygotsky, on the hypothetical level.

COGNITIVE EFFECTS OF SCHOOLING

The Greenfield study, while silent with respect to literacy as such, was nevertheless important as one in a series of cross-cultural investigations that were gaining prominence in the late 1960s and were beginning to raise some unsettling questions. Until then, almost all developmental research had been conducted in industrialized societies with universal and compulsory schooling.[3] When researchers made age comparisons to track developmental changes, they were also making concealed grade comparisons. As psychologists in industrialized countries became involved with educational concerns of developing nations, new research opportunities arose. Not all children go to school in poorer countries, and reasons for their nonattendance may have more to do with governmental decisions about where to locate a schoolhouse than with the children's or the families' attributes. Since the starting age is not uniform and progress through the grades is not as lockstep as it is in the United States, there may be considerable age variation at any given grade level. Psychologists of various theoretical persuasions have taken advantage of these opportunities to conduct comparative studies varying age and schooling independently. Over a wide range of cultures and experimental tasks, results have been remarkably consistent: schooled children have generally outperformed nonschooled children on cognitive tasks considered indicative of level of intellectual functioning. (For reviews of school effects see Scribner and Cole, 1973; Brown and French, 1979; Rogoff, 1980.)

The evidence appeared robust and it has continued to accumulate. But what did it mean and how could it be interpreted? Commonly the behaviors that have been shown to vary with age are interpreted within the framework of developmental psychological theories. Although the particular theory may vary, in all such frameworks the child is seen as progressing through successively more complex stages, each building on the other, each characterized by a particular structuring of component cognitive and affective capabilities. It is characteristic of developmental theories that while the individual stages are described in detail in terms of a set of tasks, specially designed to make the properties of intellectual organization visible, the mechanisms of change between stages are not very well specified. Although experiences in the world are universally assumed to be important, the precise ways in which interactions between child and environment produce change remain vague.

The reason for this vagueness is easy to understand when we consider the vast number of candidate experiences in everyday life that could induce more complex intellectual functioning in children. In the face of so many possibilities, it is tempting to fall back on a general principle (such as Piaget's concepts of accommodation and assimilation) as a mechanism for change and then to seek specific examples of situations that will serve as tokens of the general mechanism (the strategy followed in most developmental research). The fact that schooling is in many respects isolated from the rest of the child's experiences, and that it occurs in a distinctive setting, makes it attractive as a place where formative forces of development might be discovered and analyzed.

In order to be maximally useful, however, studies of the effects of schooling on cognitive development need guidance from developmental theories regarding what aspects of schooling will have what effects and why. Here reliance on general principles can become an impediment to research if the principles are never tested. (See, for example, the discussion of this issue in Greenfield, 1976.) More specific mechanisms are preferred.

One of the more widespread ideas is that school, by representing subject matter outside of its normal contexts of occurrence in a symbolic medium, provides the student with practice in abstract, decontextualized thinking (for example, Bruner et al., 1966; Stevenson et al., 1978). Schooling, as we pointed out some years ago (Scribner and Cole, 1973), is also a setting in which children are exposed to large amounts of information organized into subject areas exhibiting common conceptual structures and many examples of problems of the same type. From the work of psychologists such as Harry Harlow (1962) and the anthropologist Gregory Bateson (1972), we would expect such experiences to produce generalized thinking skills within the domains represented by schoollike tasks.

Vygotsky, too, speculated on the ways in which schooling might promote development. Not only does schooling rely on the mediating technology of reading and writing, it does so in settings that fundamentally reorder the motives for carrying out operations on the world. A child masters a spelling list for reasons that are totally extrinsic to the activity, unlike the reasons why she may learn to mend a net, ride a bike, or repair a radiator. All such characterizations of the way that schooling exerts its effects are more or less plausible. But it is extraordinarily difficult to advance our knowledge of causal mechanisms when all candidate experiences are intertangled and co-occurring. Hypotheses about the effects of mastery of a written language, however, can be "untangled." The process of "literacization" is not the same in all countries as the process of schooling; adults as well as children move from preliteracy to literacy in a variety of writing systems and through diversified learning experiences. Studies of the psychological effects of literacy converge with, and can contribute to, the broader area of interest on the effects of education obtained through schooling.

SOME REAL-WORLD CONCERNS

Thus far we have emphasized speculation and scholarly research suggesting that the acquisition of literacy is a watershed in the history of human thought. This is an important topic in its own right, and it will occupy a central role in our work. Evaluating competing theories about a phenomenon that implicates so many personal and social factors is a difficult enterprise that will lead us into the byways of statistical analysis, ethnographic field methods and psychological experimentation.

But the story of literacy and thought involves more than scholarly pursuit of verifiable theories. At least since the end of World War II, governments of the nations of the world, individually and collectively (through the agencies of the United Nations), have pursued an explicit policy of providing all of the world's peoples with at least the rudiments of literacy. The rationale for massive literacy campaigns reveals a strong affinity to scholarly speculations about the cognitive consequences of literacy, and carries this line of thinking into the realm of economic and political development. The description of nonliterate thought in a UNESCO report on literacy may by now sound familiar: "The illiterate man's thought . . . remains concrete. He thinks in images and not in concepts. His thought is, in fact, a series of images, juxtaposed or in sequence, and hence it rarely proceeds by induction or deduction. The result is that knowledge acquired in a given situation is hardly ever transferred to a different situation to which it could be applied" (*UNESCO Regional Report on Literacy,* 1972; see also statements in other UNESCO publications by Maheu, 1965; Rafe-uz-Zaman, 1978.)

Programs incorporating this kind of thinking have had disappointing outcomes in many parts of the world (Harman, 1976). In Liberia, for example, where we had conducted previous research, educational efforts begun by the government in the early 1960s were not yielding evidence of greatly increased individual well-being or intellectual acumen. The programs were an enormous fiscal burden for the Liberian government to absorb, even at a relatively low level of coverage in the countryside. Dropout rates in the schools were high and the standard of education generally low. Discouragement with the combination of expense and low return had generated a good deal of discussion about programs that could reach the same goals with greater efficiency.

In this context, the experience of the Vai people has to be considered remarkable. Although the Vai are a relatively small part of the population of Liberia and have few government or missionary schools in their area, they play a prominent role in the commercial life of the country. This might be considered no more than a local anomaly explainable on any number of grounds, except for one fact: the Vai boast a writing system of their own invention that they use in their commercial and personal affairs.

From a theoretical point of view, the existence of the Vai script (which we were told was not taught in school, but rather in the home) offered an occasion to resolve some of the scholarly disputes about the consequences of literacy. We could separate schooling from literacy. We could look at the acquisition of literacy in a social context radically different from any that had provided the basis for speculations about literacy's effects.

But Vai society also offered a chance to explore a very practical set of issues. Assuming that a significant proportion of Vai people knew their script and used it (a safe assumption, as later research revealed), the Vai represent a case of a rural African people spontaneously engaging in activities that governments have made massive efforts to initiate. What kept them literate? Was there anything in the Vai experience that could be used to improve the effectiveness of educational programs in other parts of Liberia or other parts of the world? These and other very practical questions of the social and economic conditions that promote literate activity also loomed large in our thinking as we began our work. We saw in Vai country an unusual, if not unique, laboratory for the study of many important questions about the nature of human society and individual intellectual activity.

2

Schemes and Designs

Scholars had provided us with a set of intriguing speculations about the psychology of literacy, and the Vai people offered us an unusual setting within which to test them. But grand theoretical speculations have a way of being difficult to pin down. At the outset, we had little information about Vai society to guide our study of literacy there, and no worked-out methods for translating grand theories into testable hypotheses among literate people anywhere. Earlier cross-cultural work, however, provided us with a general framework for the enterprise and a plan for our first information-gathering efforts. In this chapter we describe this plan and the overall logic of the project as we conceived it when we began. How our schemes and designs were modified in encounters with local realities is the subject matter of succeeding chapters.

A CULTURE-COGNITION MODEL

Questions about the behavior and thought of individuals are traditionally the concern of psychologists, and it might be expected that our research would consist almost exclusively of administering and analyzing experimental tasks—the cognitive psychologist's stock-in-trade. We did, of course, plan to use the standard psychological techniques of experimentation and clinical interview to explore cognitive variation among the Vai people, but our research objectives could not be met through methods of inquiry developed within psychology alone. Consequently, we planned to draw upon techniques practiced in other social sciences to accomplish our ends.

To begin with, over a decade of experience in cross-cultural research had convinced us that we could neither construct appropriate experimental tasks nor interpret them accurately without some knowledge of their relation to activities that were meaningful within the culture. Since behavior

)f any kind—and perhaps most important, intellectual behavior—cannot)e completely understood apart from its social context, some study of Vai ociety would, in any event, have been a component of our research. But ,ur objective went beyond this general concern. We were trying to test :ausal hypotheses about particular cultural influences on intellectual skills; his goal moved the study of cultural activities which might otherwise have)een peripheral to a central place in the overall effort.

As suggested in the theoretical speculations about literacy that we re-viewed, the classical way of portraying causal relations between cultural ınd psychological phenomena assumes a direction of movement *from* cul-ure *to* the individual: something about culture (conceived in any way a)articular theory dictates) effects some outcome in some individual (with)utcome again conceived according to theory). The general logic of this :nterprise was clearly laid out by psychologists and anthropologists who mitiated work on culture and personality in the 1940s (see Hsu, 1971, espe-:ially Whiting that volume). With some modification, their model can ,erve to put our theory-testing research about culture and cognition in per-,pective. Figure 2.1 lays out the assumed relationships. The model has hree principal components: social organization and characteristics of the :ulture as a whole (box 1); specific aspects of this cultural matrix which are)resumed to act as causal links (box 2); and individual psychological pro-:esses that are assumed to vary in accordance with variation in the causal nechanisms (box 3).[1] In our version, intellectual skills are the endpoint—ve use the term *consequences* (or, in the context of statistical analyses, *depen-dent variables*) of various lines of determining influences. We were extracting or special consideration the determining influences exercised by educa-.ional practices, specifically those relating to literacy. But we recognized hat these practices were themselves determined by the history, social itructure, and activities of Vai society as a whole. We realized, too, that :ognitive variations, if we should find they occurred in patterned ways, vere unlikely to be wholly attributable to the effects of literacy but were .ikely to be the outcome of multiple causes. (This assumption is represented n the diagram by the arrow connecting box 1 to box 3.)

Our research involved us in data-gathering activities for each of these :hree components. In Chapter 8, we describe in detail how we went about dentifying cognitive tasks that might help reveal literacy's consequences.

Figure 2.1. A culture-cognition model

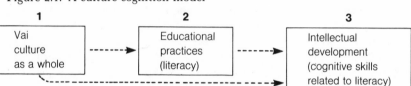

Here we will consider what it is we needed to know about antecedents or determining influences.

We clearly needed a great deal of information about Vai script literacy and other educational practices (box 2). Although some scholarly papers (Hair, 1963; Dalby, 1967) had been written about the Vai script, and one intriguing article (Stewart, 1967) had described it as still an active force in contemporary life, descriptive detail and systematic information about Vai activities involving reading and writing were not available. Yet this information was decisive. No theory, not even the most speculative, would suggest that the mere ability to write a few words (one's name, for example) or decipher some characters in the script should have any cognitive consequences whatsoever. Some level of proficiency would be necessary—but how should proficiency be defined? Increasing skill in carrying out the mechanics of reading and writing is clearly involved, but following Vygotsky we adopted a functional approach and placed greater stress on the active uses to which literacy skills were put. In the prospectus that we prepared to secure support for the project, we spoke of the need for establishing a functional definition of literacy levels among the Vai: "Psychological hypotheses about the consequences of literacy generally view literacy as a set of activities or operations that an individual performs, rather than some static capacity that he has. How much practice a given individual has in these activities would clearly be relevant to whether or not literacy has generalized intellectual consequences."

One of our first tasks, then, was to find out about and describe how individuals used the script. Were uses varied or limited? Did all individuals use the script in similar ways, or were some uses highly specialized?—or secret? How did use of Vai script relate to English literacy and schooling? And what was the nature of the relationship?

It should be immediately clear that describing Vai script literacy also required us to go beyond a mere cataloging of individual activities with the script. We could not hope to achieve even an elementary understanding of the intellectual significance of these activities unless we had an account of their role within Vai society. To what extent did induction of the young into responsible adult roles make use of literacy as a medium for transmitting traditional knowledge and skills? Was literacy a means of acquiring new ideas and information about the world beyond Vai borders? Did knowledge of the script enable literate individuals to engage in any occupations or enterprises that were inaccessible to nonliterates? These questions required us to broaden our information-gathering efforts to encompass aspects of Vai society and everyday life that would help us understand the place of literacy within Vai culture as a whole (box 3).

Thus far we have emphasized our need for *descriptive* information about cultural antecedents, but the model as such is a *predictive* one: we were undertaking to demonstrate an association between antecedent literacy practices and consequent cognitive performance, and to do so under analytic conditions that would clearly establish literacy as a causal factor. For this purpose we had to develop a comparative research design.

A COMPARATIVE DESIGN

The logic of testing for effects of prior experiences always involves some comparison of performance. Performance measures might be secured by testing the same group of people before and after the presumably crucial set of experiences (a longitudinal design) or by testing at one point in time various groups of people who differ in their participation in these experiences (a cross-sectional design); ideally the two methods are used in combination. Under circumstances existing in Vai country, it was not feasible for us to adopt the longitudinal approach. An attempt to follow a group of individuals over a long enough period of time to test consequences would have added an enormous burden to all the difficulties of conducting systematic research in a distant setting. Becoming literate is not like going to school; we knew from the experience of other adult literacy programs that the learning process can be expected to start, stop, and resume episodically, exceeding the constraints of time-limited research. Under voluntary learning programs such as we suspected Vai script literacy to be, there are no guarantees that individuals initially selected for study would aspire to or achieve the level of expertness necessary to justify the assumption of acquired cognitive skills. So we were committed to a cross-sectional comparison of groups differing in literacy education.

We were drawn to Vai society in the first place because we hoped that the existence of an indigenous script, transmitted outside of an institutional setting and having no connection with a Western-style school, would make it possible for us to disentangle literacy effects from school effects. To accomplish this disentangling, we had in mind a basic comparative scheme of analysis involving three population subgroups: school people, Vai script literates, and nonliterates.

As Figure 2.2 illustrates, we planned to make three pair-wise comparisons or contrasts. Comparison 1, schooled versus nonschooled individuals, was a necessary baseline study. While there had been considerable research comparing schooled and nonschooled populations in other cultures, we had no systematic information on possible school effects in Vai society. It would have been foolhardy for us to pursue the effects of literacy-without-schooling without examining whether or not literacy-with-schooling, under the specific conditions obtaining among the Vai, was associated with the particular skills other investigations had disclosed. This aspect of the design was essentially a replication study. Comparison 2, between Vai script literates and nonliterates, is self-evident as the core question of the research. Finally, comparison 3, between schooled and Vai script literates, was intended to take us beyond the simple demonstration of literacy effects (if we

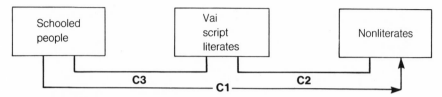

C1 (Replication of earlier cross-cultural work)

Compare schooled individuals to nonliterates

Question: Does formal schooling make a difference to performance on cognitive tasks?

C2 Compare Vai script literates to nonliterates.

Question: Does literacy per se (that is, literacy without schooling) make a difference to performance on cognitive tasks?

C3 Compare schooled and Vai script literates.

Question: Are schooled and nonschooled literates equivalent in performance or does schooling contribute to performance over and above literacy?

Figure 2.2. Initial comparative design

should find them) to some estimation of their quality and magnitude with respect to effects associated with schooling. At the base of this comparison was the question, Is literacy a surrogate for schooling?

Simple as this scheme appears, its logic places a stringent constraint on the comparison groups. Ideally, schooled individuals and Vai script literates should be compared to counterpart nonliterates who are similar in all important respects except that they lack schooling or literacy. If it were the case that schooling and Vai script knowledge were random or chance phenomena—like a blessing showered on one out of every two residents in each town—we could proceed directly to constitute experimental groups and draw conclusions about literacy from their average levels of performance. But this is exactly the assumption we could not make. Studies of literacy within our own and other societies (Hunter and Harman, 1979, for example) have conclusively demonstrated that literacy tends to co-occur with other significant personal and social attributes and experiences. In theory, literacy influences should be tested holding all other characteristics constant; in practice this goal can be approximated but not fully achieved. The rigor of the approximation, however, was decisive to the entire enterprise. We needed to have accurate information about the extent to which schooling or Vai script literacy co-occurred with other significant experiences or knowledge (jobs in the cash economy, travel to major cities) which theory suggested might also be important determinants of particular cognitive skills. We needed that information in a form that could be coded and quantified and used in predictive statistical analyses.

METHODS

Methods for securing precise, quantifiable information on background characteristics have been developed within sociology and are widely used to explore linkages between social phenomena and individual change. These methods typically involve the selection of a representative sample of the population and individual interviews conducted in a standardized format around a fixed set of questions. Multivariate statistical techniques are then applied to questionnaire responses in order to test hypotheses about what goes with what and to examine the independent contribution of co-varying factors to the dependent variable of interest (in our case, cognitive performance).

At the time we undertook the Vai research, these methods had been used in two widely recognized cross-cultural studies: a six-nation study of the experiences contributing to modern attributes and values (Inkeles and Smith, 1974) and Mideastern studies exploring psychological characteristics that promote national development (Lerner, 1958). The standardized questionnaire approach has been severely criticized in recent years (for example, Cicourel, 1964) for yielding problematic data. Two sources of potential invalidity are stressed, both magnified when the research is conducted in a culture alien to the investigator's. First, respondents may color information they supply to sensitive topics or respond to social pressures in the interview session rather than to the substantive items. A second source of invalidity stems from the potential ambiguity of questions. In order to add and compare answers, the researcher must assume that individuals are answering the "same" question, that the question she asks conveys the intended meaning, and that it is appropriate for tapping the domain of interest. Each of these assumptions is highly problematic in cross-cultural research. Respondents, in large numbers, may not share the investigator's interpretation of questions or of the meaning of the interview; worse still, the investigator is less likely to pick up on the warning signals of mismatched understandings when she is not a native to the culture. These ambiguities are compounded by the additional problem that the investigator comes to the field with a variety of expectations that can and do shape the data she carefully records.

Classical anthropological methods for studying culture have been designed to minimize these problems. Typically, anthropologists emphasize the importance of personal participation and detailed systematic observation of people's activities in situ. Interviewing tends to be nondirective in nature, adapted to the individual spoken to, and sensitive to the conversational context. The outcome of these research efforts is generally a detailed and rich description of cultural practices and their meaning to members of the culture (Geertz, 1973). Quantitative methods may be applied to this information to test specific hypotheses about observed relationships (see Naroll, 1970), but not all anthropologists would agree that such techniques are appropriate. While these methods overcome the problems of interpretability that survey interviewing presents, they have their own limitations. A principal shortcoming is that in-depth study of life in one or more communities is limited in the extent to which it can lead to generalizations that go beyond the particular places and people the anthropologist encounters.

Our approach to these methodological dilemmas was an eclectic one: we believed that both systematic survey data and qualitative community studies were necessary for our work and that each had a unique contribution to make to it. We needed the quantitative data that standard interviews provide to measure the independent contribution of literacy to cognitive task performance and to allow us to compare individuals on the basis of the functional uses of literacy. We needed detailed descriptions of Vai social life and practices, especially literacy practices, to verify the interview data, to help us interpret it, to understand the larger social system in which literacy flourished, and, crucially, to help us design sharply focused tests of Vai literacy's cognitive consequences. We therefore combined the survey and ethnographic approaches in the hope that each might check and supplement the other. We decided to conduct a survey of a population sample from which we would select individuals to compose our comparative groups; and we made plans to add an ethnographer to our staff to provide a cultural description of the Vai people, supplanting the only extant—and very outdated—study by Ellis (1914).

This was our notion of how our research would proceed, but the plans we had in mind did not lead in a straight line to our final destination. Our specific activities underwent many changes once we arrived in Liberia and began our work. We confronted conditions we had not planned for, and found some of our assumptions mistaken. But there was a consistent direction to our work, and we could not have ended up where we did if we hadn't started out where we did.

3

Vai People and Their Script

The Vai people live for the most part in an area thirty-five to forty miles wide that spans the border between what is now Sierra Leone and Liberia (see Figure 3.1).[1] The Vai on the Liberian side of the border occupy perhaps seven thousand square miles of land crisscrossed by rivers and streams. Many of the rivers empty into Lake Piso, which is separated from the Atlantic Ocean only by a long spit of sand. Along the coast the earth is sandy and swampy; except for palm trees and some patches of grassland, little grows there. Further inland, the lateritic soil (its rust color signaling the presence of iron ore, one of Liberia's major sources of national income) supports a lush undergrowth, secondary growth of trees, and occasional groves of large trees—reminders of the high forest that once dominated this region of the world.

The climate in Vai country is damp all year round, but especially so in the rainy season beginning in May and extending into November. Approximately 170 inches of rain fall during the average rainy season, which at about 76 degrees Fahrenheit is only slightly cooler than the 80 degree average during the dry season. At all seasons humidity is high, and noontime temperatures are sufficient to discourage heavy outdoor labor.

According to the most recent census (Republic of Liberia, 1974), the Vai living in their home area of Liberia (Cape Mount County) number about twelve thousand. Many Vai live in other parts of the country, either in Monrovia—the capital and the only real center of commerce in Liberia— or at one of the foreign concessions exploiting Liberia's natural resources. A large rubber plantation owned by the Goodrich company is located on the southeastern border of Vai country; a large iron-mining operation is to be found in Bomi hills, some thirty miles to the northwest. Many Vai men work at one or another such enterprise sometime in their lives, often taking members of their families with them. There are also Vai enclaves in concessions and towns in distant parts of the country, where the Vai are prominent as tailors, carpenters, cookshop proprietors, and small businessmen.

The people one encounters in Vai country are almost all engaged in

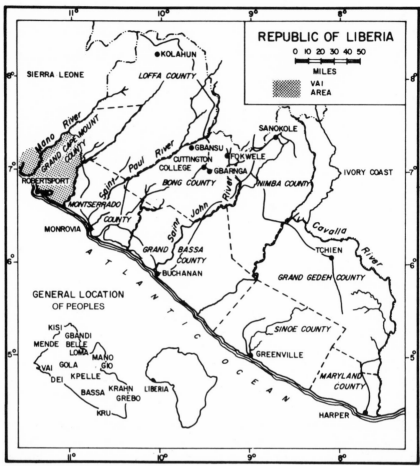

Figure 3.1. Liberia

farming. Although other economic activities supplement this central activity, most features of Vai life that initially impress a visitor are organized around the need to grow enough food to get through the year.

The country seems sparsely populated. Flying over it, one sees a patchwork of small farms, some newly planted, some growing back to bush, interspersed with low jungle vegetation that has recovered during a cycle of inactivity. Larger towns are located along one of the area's four major roads, technically classified as all-weather, although they are impassable for variable periods during the rainy season. The largest town in Vai country is "big" Robertsport (population 2,562), which is large by virtue of its status as the capital of the county and its proximity to the sea. (The sea was the most rapid means of surface travel until the road from Monrovia was completed.) Larger interior towns contain about forty to sixty houses and two hundred inhabitants. Far more numerous are smaller towns which vary in size from two or three to a dozen houses and are usually a walk of an hour or two from a road.

GOHN, A VAI TOWN

Typical of the towns we worked in was Gohn Zodua, where members of our research group lived from time to time and where Mike Smith carried out the first stages of our ethnographic work. Gohn is probably no more than forty miles by air from Monrovia, but it can be reached only after two or more hours' travel by motor road. The town is linked to the main Monrovia–Sierra Leone all-weather road by a small feeder lane, which, bridges willing, can be traversed by car. Relatively few vehicles travel to Gohn. The difficult access road traverses two valleys and climbs a ridge before it plummets down a steep hillside onto a long causeway extending across a marsh and river that separate the town from the countryside surrounding it. During the rainy season the road is often impassable. From the top of the ridge above Gohn one can see far across the high forest to iron-mining country to the northeast. But the road goes no further; from Gohn the trip north is by foot.

After crossing the river, the road rises for a hundred yards or so to the edges of the town, ending in a long, house-lined High Street. The remainder of Gohn's houses are arranged in two semicircles around the central street, which is really no more than a cleared area where cars may park or turn around, and which serves as a sort of village square. On the eastern side of the street are two antiquated iron cannons, relics of an era when Gohn was a center of slave trade and a fortified site. Now the cannons serve as benches for the people who gather in the evening before prayer services in the town mosque. More customary benches are provided by bamboo stalks that are lashed together and arranged alongside the houses lining this part of the square.

Gohn's houses are similar architecturally to those in any other Vai village. They are generally rectangular in shape, with walls seven or eight feet high, topped by zinc roofs that rise to a peak in the middle of the house and provide a catchment device for fresh water in the rainy season. The number of rooms per house and house size varies; some are as small as twenty feet by twenty feet and are divided into two to four small rooms connected by a corridor. Some houses are double that size, with as many as six rooms. Often one room is set aside as a sort of dining-living room. Kitchens are never part of the main house but are separate structures, often open on the sides, where food is cooked over an open fire using wood and charcoal. Toilet facilities and a bathing area to which water is carried are set some yards away from the main living structures.

The houses are constructed for the most part using wooden poles four to five inches in diameter for the main supports, with smaller sticks woven in between. Mud, sometimes mixed with cement, is daubed into the sticks, smoothed over on the surface, and glazed with whitish clay dug from river valleys. Many of the houses have carefully crafted wooden window frames and shutters; these are rare in other parts of Liberia and are a source of the reputation the Vai have gained for their carpentry skills. In addition to these standard structures, Gohn has a concrete shed that belongs to a well-to-do taxi driver who seldom appears in town, and a large religious meeting hall under construction. There are also a few smaller, open-air meeting houses where matters of public interest are discussed or where people simply gather for relaxation.

Four of Gohn's houses are notable for their shape and interior design. They are round and are not subdivided into separate rooms, and they have thatch roofs made from the fronds of palm trees. These houses represent the traditional Vai architectural style. One serves as the headquarters of the women's secret society, the organization charged with the traditional education of Vai girls, which has continued to function (although now on a modified basis) since the earliest accounts of the Vai were written.

The first sign of writing one encounters in Gohn is likely to be seen on the lintels of doorways, where inscriptions in Arabic (most often, the opening line of the Qur'an) may be written in chalk or ink. Just inside the door Arabic is again encountered, this time in the form of a talisman bound in a tight package hanging from the rafter above the door.

Houses vary considerably in the amount of furniture they contain. Some are almost bare except for a table, a few chairs, and beds with straw mattresses; others contain modern furniture carted from Monrovia. The commonest form of wall decorations are calendars of variable vintage depicting Mecca, Liberian political notables, and beauty queens. Family photographs are also common. In homes of people who have spent time in Monrovia or have attended school, photographs from recent magazines may paper the walls.

It doesn't take a visitor long to discover that Gohn has an illustrious history. It was once a great slave-trading center with a large, active population and a ruler who was called a king. Today, its two cannons are all that remain to suggest to the casual eye that Gohn is anything other than the typical Vai village we found it to be. The people earn their basic living by farming, and the cycle of activities that this mode of subsistence entails guides a great deal of what they do day in and day out.

CHARACTERISTIC LIVELIHOOD ACTIVITIES

The distance between towns is made necessary by the demands of farming. For about the past five hundred years, the people in this region of Africa have grown rice on upland plots of cleared land (unlike the swamp rice cultivation that Americans think of as rice farming). Plots of a few to several acres are used for one (or at most two) years, and then must be allowed to lie fallow for about seven years before they will sustain a full new crop. The need to move one's farm constantly, combined with the need to walk to the farm from home every morning, insures that towns will be neither large nor close to each other.

Farming is everyone's work, although not all play an equal part in the farming cycle. The farming year begins early in the dry season when a new plot of land needs to be cleared. This is primarily men's work, as the underbrush and smaller trees are cleared away with machetes (which we will refer to by the Liberian English name "cutlass"). The cut greenery is allowed to dry for a few weeks and then set afire. The ashes that remain provide the fertilizer required by the new crop and rooted stumps that help to hold the soil in place. Left standing are palm trees providing nuts, which are a staple of the Vai diet, as well as very large trees that provide much appreciated shade in the heat of the day. Once the cut underbrush is dry, the men, with help from women and older children, build small A-frames; these serve as camp-style kitchens and as places to spend the night on farms that are a significant distance from town.

With the kitchen built and the ashes cooled, it is time to broadcast new rice seed and pray for rain. The broadcasting is done by the women and children; they first scratch the soil with small hoes and then distribute seed into the irregularly tilled land. The children spend all day on the farm chasing away the birds who come to feed upon the exposed seed. The prayers are led by the town imam, the Muslim religious leader.

At this time, too, the men cut the smaller felled trees into approximately two-foot lengths, drive them into the ground, and bind them with vines, providing a fence to keep out small animals who will come to feed upon the rice shoots once they appear. Weeding is done by the women and children. When the rice is ready to harvest months later at the end of the rainy season, everyone participates in gathering it, tying it in bundles, and storing it under the roof of the kitchen.

While rice is the staple crop, it is not the only crop grown by the Vai. As a rule, the prior year's rice farm is cultivated with cassava, one or more varieties of yam, and perhaps peanuts and other vegetables. In addition, some crops—primarily cocoa, coffee, and occasionally rubber—are grown for cash.

Sources of animal protein are scarce in Vai country. In those interior areas where primary jungle remains, there are still large animals and a variety of antelope, deer, wild pigs, and monkeys. Although they are hunted, such animals are rarely encountered in the more densely populated parts of Vai country where we worked. Fish are also sought in the rivers and streams, but except near the seashore and Lake Piso (which abounds with barracuda and, in some areas, grouper and sea bass), the streams are not plentifully supplied with them.

Although securing a livelihood from the soil, streams, and forest requires a great deal of physical labor, the technology of Vai agriculture and food gathering is relatively simple. The cutlass and hoe are the main tools of farming. In principle, no money is needed, because the seed is retained from the previous year's growth. Fishing is carried on with nets woven by the women. Hunting, which at one time was carried out with traps, bows, and arrows, has long since used the rifle as the standard weapon.

The Vai are considered outstanding for their ability to fashion wood and cloth. At the turn of the century, Vai culinary tools made of wood were a standard item of trade, along with their looms. At present, the Vai are known throughout Liberia as carpenters, weavers, and tailors. In years gone by, items like pots, cutlasses and knives were fashioned by the village blacksmith, one of Vai culture's traditional specialists. Most villages retain a blacksmith as well as a weaver who fashions cloth. Handmade goods from these craftspeople are still highly valued, but in many instances imported substitutes have taken their place.

Although trade in slaves is now long past, trading is still an important feature of Vai life, one that we think is bound up with the continued existence of an indigenous writing system. At the turn of the century, Ellis (1914) commented explicitly on the importance of the Vai as middlemen in a trading network that linked the markets of the modern world with the interior of the Guinea coast of Africa. At that time Europeans did not trade outside the ports of entry, so once the farms were cleared, many Vai men traveled by foot and canoe to the coastal town of Robertsport where they picked up manufactured goods, salt, liquor, tobacco, and gunshot. They sold these goods in the interior in return for raw materials, including gold and diamonds.

Trade may be even more a part of Vai life now than in the past, since the advent of roads has made it possible for a person to play more than one economic role at a time. With the roads linking Vai country to Monrovia and to the large concessions have come a variety of new economic roles which supplement farming and require the mastery of new skills. The automobile is one conspicuous element of contact and technological change. The Vai are extremely active entrepreneurs in a system of transportation that relies heavily on private automobiles and pickup trucks to move goods and people from one area to another. It is not enough to know how to drive an automobile. In a country where spare parts are as scarce as paved roads, every driver must double as his own mechanic.

In trade for cocoa, coffee, and labor, the Vai obtain other modern goods, principally cloth, modern building materials, tools, and occasionally radios. This trade has the effect of increasing the amount of resources devoted to making money, removing people (mainly men) from the countryside to areas where cash labor is more plentiful, and importing new ideas along with new products. There is no question that Vai people are being more and more often exposed to the way of life represented by other tribal people and (primarily) urban Liberians whose national language is English and whose preferred mode of life is modeled in many respects upon Euro-American standards (as an ideal, if not an accomplishment).

EDUCATION

Although Vai agricultural practices and material culture can be described in terms that make it appear rudimentary when compared to the money-based technological economy with which it is in ever-increasing interdependence, learning to be a competent Vai adult cannot be considered a rudimentary matter. Like all other people, the Vai have evolved methods for insuring that their young acquire the knowledge necessary to function as adults. With the exceptions to be noted below, the institutionalization of learning among the Vai, as among many of their neighbors, traditionally resided in the bush school, conducted by men for boys as part of the activities of the Poro society and by women for girls as part of the activities of the Sande society. Much has been written, but little information transmitted, about the content and form of education represented by the bush school.[2] In years gone by, children (alternately boys and girls) would be removed from their homes for a period of four to five years during which they were presumably taught important subsistence skills, the lore of the group, and other knowledge necessary for them to assume adult roles upon returning to their village.

There is little doubt that the Poro and Sande societies continue to play an important role in the life of Vai villages. Important personages are known to the villagers, although this knowledge is not displayed for outsiders. Knowledge of medicine, both in the sense of "medical practices" and in the more general sense of "important knowledge with which one can influence the course of events" (which foreigners are likely to interpret as witchcraft), is a valuable resource of important members of these secret societies. Among Vai men, this power of specialized knowledge is shared in certain domains with knowledge of Islamic versions of similiar practices. Among women, midwifery remains an important role for functionaries of the Sande society.

Almost any weekday morning between the first of February (when the Liberian government's school year opens) and the first of December (when the school year terminates), one can encounter young boys and girls dressed in blue-and-white school uniforms walking by the side of the road, their books perched securely on their heads. If one travels these upcountry roads often enough, it becomes apparent that the sight of children walking to and from school is restricted to relatively few towns. In fact, formal schooling in American-type schools, where instruction is in English, remains available to a small minority of children living in Vai country, despite increased government expenditures on education in the decades of the '60s and '70s.

Until quite recently, education in English was to be obtained within Vai country only by attending a missionary school, of which there were perhaps a dozen in 1945. Since that time, the government has built about twenty-six elementary schools and two junior high schools in the area, enough to accommodate only a fraction of the school-age population. Pay in government schools is low and sporadic. Facilities are minimal or absent, qualifications of teachers match their remuneration, and the product is a rudimentary level of schooling for those who go no further than sixth or seventh grade. For the family with extra means or the child with extra desire, moving to Robertsport, the county seat, or to Monrovia to live with a relative, is the surest way to complete a high school education—the minimum level necessary to acquire the monetary benefits that are the major incentive for this kind of education in the first place. Since many students cannot afford to move to the areas where better facilities are available, and home schools are both limited in levels of available education and temptingly near the farm where work needs doing, village education in English tends to be rather limited.

While the level of English education that the average village child receives may only be sufficient to decipher a brief letter, higher levels of English literacy are made use of in the countryside. At least one person in any town can be expected to be able to read and write more complicated texts; to him will fall the task of reading directives to the town chief from government officials and of writing replies. In most towns one encounters young men who have spent some time in Monrovia and have completed from five to twelve years of schooling. Finding no work to support themselves, or perhaps no work commensurate with their level of expectation, they return home. Some settle down to farm, many commute periodically between village and city, looking for paid labor in one place, helping with the farming and often establishing a household with wife and children in the other.

A third variety of education is audible almost any daybreak. It begins with the murmur of children carrying bundles of sticks to the town meeting place. Here the sticks are piled together and lit, providing light in the predawn gloom for the children, who bend over their individual boards with passages from the Qur'an written on them. For two hours or more the singsong of their chanting can be heard, accompanied occasionally by an admonishment from the teacher, or the snap of a small whip landing on the backside of an erring student.

Starting at age five or six and continuing for a number of years, most Vai boys and a few Vai girls gather under the guidance of the village imam to learn to read chapters from the Qur'an. Unless they are living in a town with an especially advanced teacher (Gohn is one such town), they are unlikely to learn Arabic sufficiently to read or write with comprehension. Depending on their skill and fortitude, however, they learn to decipher Arabic characters well enough so that they can begin at any point in the text to read what is written there. As they progress, the imam will tell them about the general content of the passages they are reading.

As a rule, a few boys from each town go on to become what we think of as Qur'anic scholars. They travel to a town where a well-known teacher resides and live there until they have completed their studies. Completion, as we will see, is a concept of variable meaning. For some it means completing the Qur'an, which can then be recited from beginning to end. For others it means learning Arabic and studying commentaries on the Qur'an. For a few it means induction into the secrets of "Muslim medicine," which, upon return home, will become a mixture of traditional Vai and Islamic practices.

The three forms of education we have described—traditional socialization, English schooling, and Qur'anic schooling—contrast in ways that arrested our attention from the outset of our work. Each is associated with its own language: Vai, English, or Arabic. Each has its own dominant sphere of influence: traditional economic and social activities, the modern economic and government sector, or religious affairs. Both training in traditional activities and English schooling are intended to have direct economic effects. Qur'anic and English schooling are both conducted in languages not spoken at home by most students and (in the case of Arabic) not necessarily understood by the student. In these two cases, education is closely associated with, and, in fact, dependent upon, specific forms of literate skill, while traditional socialization appears to proceed in the absence of any knowledge of written Vai. We think it significant that literacy in Vai script is not only learned independent of schooling but independent of the acquisition of traditional knowledge and skills; we did not, it will be noticed, introduce a discussion of Vai script writing and reading in connection with socialization practices and traditional education.

This does not imply that Vai script knowledge lacks instrumental importance or that it is not valued by the people. On the contrary, Vai people are extremely proud of their original writing system and do not find it in the least surprising that European and American scholars have continually visited their country to learn about "Vai book" and the role it plays in their daily lives. Any visitor to Vai country will be proudly told, as we were, "There are three books in this world—the European book, the Arabic book, and the Vai book; God gave us, the Vai people, the Vai book because we have sense."

VAI SCRIPT AND ITS CHARACTERISTICS

The Vai script ranks high on the developmental scale that Gelb (1963) and other historians of writing (Moorhouse, 1953; Diringer, 1968) have applied to writing systems. According to these scholars, writing systems have progressed over the course of centuries from systems in which symbols directly depict events, objects, or ideas (pictographic and ideographic scripts) to systems in which symbols represent language. (For an opposing point of view, see Hodge, 1975.) It is these systems, representing elements of language by conventional visible marks, to which Gelb applies the term "true writing." Elements of language expressed in symbols may be units of meaning such as words (logographic systems) or elements of sound such as syllables or phonemes (syllabic and alphabetic writing). Sound-based scripts are considered the most advanced, since representation of a limited set of sounds is sufficient to symbolize an infinite number of speech utterances. In the Vai script, graphic symbols represent syllables in spoken Vai, and on this score alone the script qualifies as a major historical achievement.

Development and use of a phonetic writing system such as the Vai script requires segmenting the stream of speech into a set of discrete units (in this case, syllables) which recur in its continual and unbroken flow. Skilled readers, once they have mastered their own writing system, often take this sound analysis for granted. But is is not easily accomplished either by individuals first learning to read (Gleitman and Rozin, 1973) or by entire societies in the process of developing a writing system (Gelb, 1963).

Linguists who have examined the Vai script note how well suited it is to the structure of spoken Vai (see Koelle, 1854; Klingenheben, 1933). The majority of syllables in Vai speech share a common shape; most syllables begin with a consonant (C) and end with a vowel (V). A Vai syllabary, arranged in a matrix of consonants and vowels, is presented in Figure 3.2.[3] The chart contains all the syllables and sound elements represented in the writing system, approximately 210 in all. What is immediately apparent is the systematic nature of the syllabary. With the exception of seven vowels occurring on their own and the syllabic nasal (ñ), a script character represents every possible combination of consonant and vowel. Because of these systematic features, the linguist A. Klingenheben (1933) remarked that the script was so ideally suited to the characteristics of spoken Vai that foreign linguists should use it to learn the language rather than attempt to master it through the Roman alphabet. His overall evaluation was that "the Vais have acquitted themselves by no means badly as phoneticians" (p. 170). The structural fit between speech units and written symbols may be one important factor contributing to the spread of Vai script literacy and its endurance through changing times.[4]

As important as structural linguistic features of the script are the uses to which it is put. To the casual visitor, reading and writing in Vai script are not prominent activities in upcountry communities; still, knowledge and use of the script are manifest in many ways. For one thing, the arrival of a taxi often brings letters written in Vai from relatives and business associates in other areas of Vai country and other parts of Liberia. Funerals are a ubiquitous feature of life in a Vai village, where the infant mortality rate

	i	a	u	e	ɛ	ɔ	o
p							
b							
ɓ							
mɓ							
kp							
mgb							
gb							
f							
v							
t							
d							
l							
ɗ							
nɗ							
s							
z							
c							
j							
nj							
y							
k							
ŋg							
g							
h							
w							
-							

ʕ Syllabic nasal

Nasal syllables

	ĩ	ã	ũ		ɛ̃	ɔ̃	
ɦ							
m							
n							
ny							
ŋ							

Figure 3.2. The modern Vai syllabary

exceeds 50 percent and life expectancy is low; these events attract relatives and acquaintances from many parts of the country, each of whom is obligated to bring gifts that must be reciprocated. Consequently, recording the names of donors and their gifts at funerals, as well as a variety of other administrative activities such as listing political contributions, are features of Vai life in which literacy plays a central and visible role. Some religious and fraternal organizations maintain records in Vai script, and we have documented at least one case in which a Muslim association was governed by a constitution and bylaws written in Vai script (Goody, Cole, and Scribner, 1977). Farmers and craftsmen use the script for business ledgers and technical plans. A few who might qualify as Vai scholars write family and clan histories, keep diaries, and record maxims and traditional tales in copybooks.

As our narrative unfolds, these activities involving the Vai script will play a more central role in our argument. We present this brief sketch of Vai literate activities here so that the reader can place this key area of concern in the larger context of Vai life.

Performers in a traditional Vai ceremony.
Note the Vai script on the headdress.
(Courtesy of Stephen Reder.)

A town chief and Qur'anic teacher, Cape Mount County

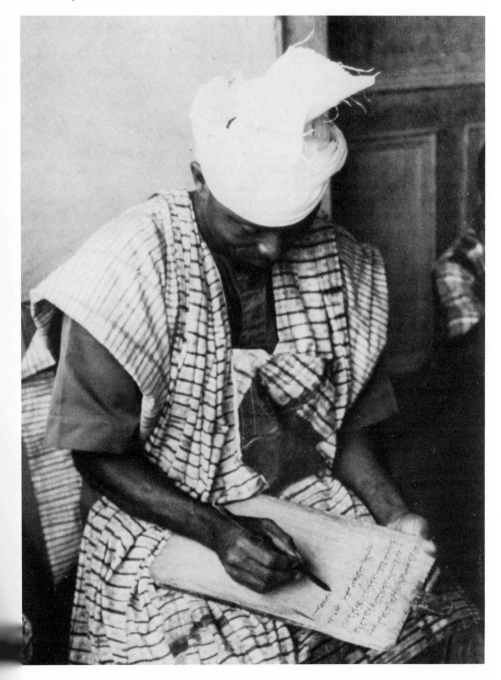

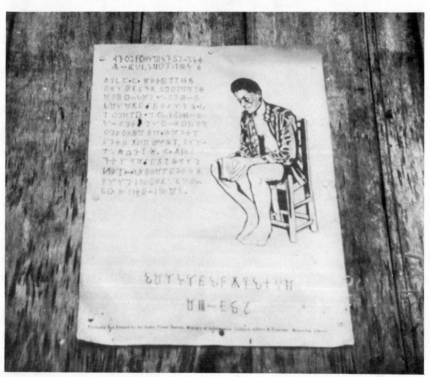

A rare example of Vai script on a government poster in Cape Mount County

/

Welcome to the town of Fandoh in Gawula chiefdom

A welcome sign in English and Arabic

*A multiscript Muslim brotherhood banner at
a Cape Mount County celebration. (Courtesy
of Stephen Reder.)*

A sign outside an upcountry store

A tombstone in a Vai community in
Monrovia

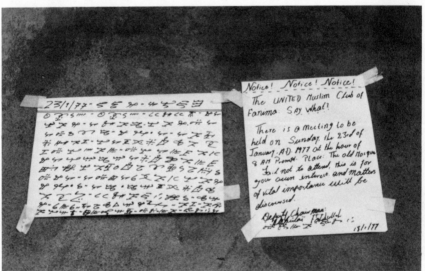

Posters on the side of a building in a Vai
community in Monrovia

Part II

Social Context of
Literacy

4

Doing the Work

During the 1972–73 academic year we mulled over the possibility and advisability of undertaking a major research project to address speculations about literacy and its consequences. Sylvia Scribner had returned from a period of fieldwork among the Kpelle, and was enthusiastic about returning to Liberia to put her ideas about literacy to a test. Michael Cole was engaged in research on the effects of education in the Yucatan, but Don Sharp, who had been a participant in earlier Liberian work, was rapidly taking over direction of the Yucatan work, and the lure of a society where literacy was not synonymous with education seemed too attractive to pass up.

Casual daydreaming turned into serious planning when the Carnegie Corporation agreed to support research on Vai literacy as part of a grant to carry out comparative research on cognitive development in several parts of the world. Armed with what we imagined to be adequate financial backing for such an enterprise, we began preparing in earnest for research among the Vai.

GETTING STARTED

Getting started faced us with many practical problems that were to have deep and long-term effects on our research. To begin with, we had no institutional base in Vai country from which to work. To enter Liberia as anything other than tourists or immigrants we had to obtain resident visas, but to obtain such visas we needed sponsorship. Here we received help from Cuttington College, the institution that served as the base for our earlier work among the Kpelle; the college agreed to sponsor our presence in Liberia.

But Kpelle country is Kpelle country. While our prior contacts could get us into Liberia, they did not provide entree into Vai country, which is only a hundred or so miles from Cuttington College but several cultural groups distant. At this point, our acquaintance with Dr. Augustus Caine, an anthropologist and former minister of education in Liberia, was crucial. Dr. Caine had lived as a boy in the important Vai town of Jondu. Although he had spent many years in the United States, where he obtained his degree in anthropology, he retained not only a fluent speaking knowledge of Vai but some reading knowledge of Vai script as well. Equally important, like other Liberians from traditional backgrounds, Augustus Caine retained strong ties to his hometown, where he maintained a house and acted as patron for various important civic activities. Augustus had recently returned from a teaching position in the United States to head the newly formed government Institute of Public Administration. Familiar with our earlier work, he expressed a strong interest in joining our research enterprise and in contributing professionally to the extent permitted by his competing duties.

With the problems of entry into Liberia and an introduction to Vai country on the road to solution, we began to organize the work. The first task facing us was to secure information about the distribution and social correlates of literacy in Vai society. We planned to do this by conducting an interview survey. Because of competing work and family obligations, neither of us would be able to devote the full three to four years of living and working in Vai country that we considered a minimum requirement for completing the project—so we decided upon a division of labor. Together we would design and set in motion the initial survey, expecting it to take about a year to complete. Implementation of the survey would be placed in the hands of a field director, preferably someone with experience living and working in Africa and trained in social science research. We planned to visit Liberia to participate in the survey work from time to time but to save our main on-site effort for the design and implementation of experiments that could test hypotheses about literacy in Vai country as it revealed itself in the survey.

In the summer of 1972 we advertised for a field director and appointed Dr. Ethan Gologor. Ethan had recently completed a Ph.D. in cognitive psychology at the Graduate Faculty of the New School and had previously served in the Peace Corps in Somalia. From our limited knowledge of that country it seemed likely that anyone who had worked there as a volunteer and still found the idea of working in rural Liberia attractive was a hardy enough soul to be a good risk.

A number of unexpected contingencies delayed the start of fieldwork, but in early December 1972 Ethan and his wife set off for Liberia to scout out housing and begin exploring the area in which we proposed to work. A few weeks later, just after New Year's 1973, we arrived in Liberia to begin the research.

Our destination on this trip was the town of Robertsport. We guessed initially that Robertsport would make a good place to set up our project headquarters. According to the map, it was centrally located with respect to most of the areas we thought we would be covering in our survey. Its location on the ocean would provide a source of fresh fish and relief from the hot, humid weather for which coastal Liberia has been notorious since European explorers first began trading there. At the time of our first trip Robertsport was not accessible by road, but a road was under construction and was completed six months later.

The most important preliminaries concerned housing and introductions to Vai script scholars, people who knew enough of the script and its uses to act as informants in the early stages of our work. Here the good offices of Augustus Caine proved essential. Augustus had attended St. John's Episcopal school in Robertsport for a short while as a young boy. He knew that during the 1920s and 1930s the Vai script had been taught at St. John's and that a man who still taught there, Tamu Diggs, remained active in promulgating the script through his contributions to a mimeographed newsletter published by the Robertsport YMCA, a page of which was devoted to news written in Vai script. He also arranged an introduction for us with Boima Gray, a Vai man who had worked for many years in the Ministry of Education. Mr. Gray provided us with important information about the script, and helped us to find qualified research assistants who could administer our survey and help us get to know Vai country.

After preliminary meetings in Monrovia we headed for Robertsport. With the road still unfinished, the trip first involved a dusty ride by chartered taxi to the town of Bendu, located on the eastern inland edge of Lake Piso opposite Robertsport. When enough people had gathered, a motor launch was loaded with passengers and their gear for the trip across the lake. January is the dry, hot season in that part of the world, and crossing the lake was a pleasant hour's journey.

The Gologors had arranged housing in Robertsport at the Episcopal mission hostel located on a hill overlooking the town, the lake, and the ocean. The hostel's large veranda served as an office.

The work began on several fronts. We had in mind preparation of a survey questionnaire that would provide information about literacy and schooling and how these educational activities were influenced by personal experience and the larger contexts of life in Vai country. But we knew little about any of these matters. We needed to interview knowledgeable people just to find questions which made sense locally and which covered the issues we thought important in terms of our general interest in literacy. We also needed to be on the lookout for questions we hadn't dreamed of, but which could emerge as important for Vai script literacy. Once we had a set of questions in hand, we needed to obtain Vai translations of those questions and find some way to discuss them with country people to see if they were considered sensible.

We also needed to develop appropriate versions of the various cognitive tasks we intended to use as initial indicators of consequences of traditional nonschooled literacy; and we had to devise a usable reading test for Vai script literates. On all these matters we obtained a good deal of help from Tamu Diggs, who acted as a friendly consultant. But Mr. Diggs had his own work to do and it was clear that we were imposing severely on his time. What we needed were younger men who could act as research assistants in the field, who could help us with the arduous task of administering the survey and act as our guides as we went from town to town. Since work of this sort has little precedent in Vai country, we had to train research assistants once we identified men with the necessary qualifications. Here our introductions to Boima Gray and Tamu Diggs proved invaluable. Mr. Diggs, through his friendship with J. Bai Paasewe, a Vai script literate who did the cutting of stencils for the YMCA newsletter, recommended to us a nephew of Mr. Paasewe's, Bai Paasewe. Bai turned up one morning in Robertsport to offer himself as a candidate for research assistant. He could read and write English as a result of a partial high school education, but he could not read or write Vai script. In the ensuing weeks we added three additional assistants, Budu Sherman, Mabu Sambolah, and Mole Gbese. Bai, Mabu, and Budu had all attended high school for two years or more and could read or write English rapidly. Mole had less schooling and could read and write English only a little, but he was an adult. That is, he was an adult in Vai terms, a country man who farmed in the area of Bendu and had traveled throughout the countryside, both in the capacity of a census taker for the government and as an important figure in the Vai men's secret society. He knew people from many parts of the country, and we thought he would be particularly helpful in explaining to leaders in towns we traveled to what it was we were doing in terms they would understand.

GETTING AROUND

A few days after our arrival in Robertsport, we began to conduct pilot interviews with people living in the traditional Vai section called Grassfield. As is true in larger Liberian towns, Robertsport consists of a more modern sector with carpentered buildings and shops and several native "quarters" where traditional forms of housing, cooking, and life are more or less retained by various ethnic groups living there. In Grassfield we met many Vai people who spoke no English and who agreed to answer our questions, which we presented in an extremely informal fashion to explore problems of comprehension, incompleteness, and sources of difficulty. This was a time of training, not only for our assistants, but for us all. After a few days of such pilot work, we decided to leave Robertsport and carry our fledgling survey instrument across Lake Piso to the town of Buluma, a small village a few hours' walk from Bendu.

When we entered Buluma we were introduced to traditional Liberian customs for greeting strangers, procedures that were to play a vital role in the course of our work throughout our stay in Vai land. As soon as a stranger arrives, he goes to find the town chief or the most important person in the town at the time. The traditional greeting is the Vai equivalent of "What news here?" The townspeople then tell the local news. Depending on what has been happening and who the visitor is, they may tell of how the seeding of the crops is proceeding, or the cutting of bush, or the progress with the Sande society school where young girls are being initiated into adult roles. They may tell of a recent death or a recent accomplishment of the town. The visitor thanks the people for their news and is expected, in return, to tell his news. In our case, the news was that we had come to Vai country because we had heard that the Vai people had invented and were using a writing system ("Vai book"). We spoke of our previous work among the Kpelle, who had told us about the Vai book, and how it was a rare accomplishment in human history for any people to have invented a writing system. We explained that we were interested in how the Vai people taught and learned their writing system because we hoped to be able to help children in Liberia as well as in our own country deal with problems of reading and writing in their school work.

Our news was almost always met with politeness and usually with some enthusiasm, especially among the older people in town. The Vai are extremely proud of their writing system, and they know it distinguishes them from other tribal people in Liberia. They also know that from time to time foreign scholars have come to study the Vai script, and this attention has helped to bring the Vai status in the eyes of their countrymen. This kind of reception was encouraging because it signified a point of common interest with the people.

However, there were also points of difficulty. Very often, younger men in the town, or men who had more experience working in foreign concessions or living in Monrovia, knew that when white people come to Liberia they typically come to make money and that the Liberians with whom they work very often stand less to gain than those who come bearing gifts (in our case, gifts of interest in the Vai script and education). Such people were suspicious of our motives and, although they might not have aired their suspicions upon a first meeting, they were not hesitant to do so during the course of our stay in the town. Even those who felt that an interest in the Vai script was legitimate had other reasons for concern. When we began to ask questions about the number of men in town, the number of literates in town, where people lived when they were not in town, we raised suspicions that we might be agents of the Liberian government, concerned more with keeping track of people for purposes of taxation than for our stated purpose. Often we unintentionally raised the hope that we would bring a school or a clinic to the town we visited, and when it turned out that we had only small gifts to offer there was disappointment. The problem of establishing rapport within a town was crucial to our enterprise, and all of these issues greeted us on our visit to Buluma in our initial attempt to do pilot work on the survey.

In the case of this initial visit, the town agreed to accept us. We stayed for two days, interviewing several people, conducting experiments, talking, getting familiar with the conditions of the work, and exploring the appropriateness of the various questions that we had tried out in Robertsport.

By the time this expedition was completed, we were running short of time for our first stay. After returning to Robertsport we collated the information we had received; we modified the survey questions and cognitive tasks. We roughed out a questionnaire to leave with Ethan, who was charged with the difficult tasks of putting the questions together in a format suitable for mass interviewing and of completing the training of the staff. The initial part of our research was now under way.

THE PILOT SURVEY: REORIENTING TO LIBERIAN REALITY

Between the first of February and the end of May, Ethan and the four Vai assistants carried the initial questionnaire to two towns in Vai country, interviewing all the adult residents. Work in Buluma, the first town, was completed in February. In all, forty-nine adults, ten of whom were Vai script literates, participated in the survey, answering all of our questions about life experience and completing the cognitive tasks we set them. From Buluma the crew moved to the major town of Jondu, hometown of Augustus Caine and a major center of Vai script literacy in the nineteenth and twentieth centuries. Jondu is a proud town whose name translates as Slave House. In the nineteenth century, it was a waiting station for men and women who had been captured as slaves in war and were to be sold to slavers coming across Lake Piso to pick them up.

In Jondu we experienced our first major difficulties. Matters began serenely enough. Bolstered by an introduction from Augustus, Ethan visited the appropriate people in town, was officially accepted, and set to work. But after a day and a half the town chief demanded a halt to the proceedings. He called a meeting at which he accused Ethan of taking advantage of the townspeople on the assumption that they were just country people who didn't know any better.

Ethan was aghast. He had taken great pains to explain the various parts of the questionnaire to the assembled townspeople two days earlier. He had agreed to pay interviewees at a rate established as equitable in earlier work. He had, on the basis of his prior experience, told people how long the questioning would take and tried to make the proceedings as public as possible.

The town chief was not impressed. He had been interviewed himself and was unhappy about how long it took. He was perturbed too by the difficulty of the questions. Most of all, he was perturbed that he had not been paid more money.

Ethan had to make the first of many such difficult decisions. The town was renegotiating its bargain, which Ethan had not violated. If he capitulated, they could renegotiate again if they pleased, and almost certainly the news of the events would precede us to other towns. Should he fold up camp and leave, or should he give in? He decided to stay, and in good Vai fashion he renegotiated the renegotiations down to a level of cost that he felt the project could tolerate. To do this meant standing up in a town meeting and delivering a long speech in which he reviewed the history of the Vai script, its uniqueness and contemporary importance, and the special role of Jondu and its citizens in the script's development and preservation. In view of these special circumstances he doubled the rate paid for participation in the survey as a sign of respect for each individual. The town chief accepted this offer on behalf of the town and the work went forward.

Making arrangements to do our interviewing was only one of the problems that faced us as we moved from thinking about a study of nonschooled literacy among the Vai to carrying out actual research operations. In the mundane matter of living—finding a house, food to eat, and a vehicle to get around in—Ethan encountered a series of difficulties that shaped the organization of later work. With the coming of the road, Robertsport ceased to be a workable headquarters town. Workmen occupied the available (and not-so-available) living space. Food was scarce. The road, although passable in most places, was still only partly finished and accidents were frequent. Passable or not, the existence of the road was enough to discourage the operators of the motor launches that connected Robertsport with Bendu and the inland sections of Vai country, and they discontinued their service. The decision of where to relocate our headquarters was complicated by the impending arrival of a Gologor baby; Robertsport's small hospital had lost the services of its only resident doctor shortly before the Gologors' arrival. Considering the driving time between many different points that he wanted to reach and the need for adequate health care, Ethan decided to set up house in Monrovia where his wife and baby could safely stay while he made periodic expeditions to live in towns where he would be conducting the survey.

Extra travel meant that a car would be needed. Ethan purchased a handsome maroon Mazda. The first night he had possession of the car its shine attracted a form of thievery that we had never before encountered. The windshield was neatly removed from the car, leaving no other part damaged. Travel was curtailed until a new windshield was installed, this time with an identifying mark etched into the glass to disturb such entrepreneurship.

While these living and working arrangements were being wrestled with in Liberia, we were beginning to review the results obtained from Buluma and Jondu. We had 119 completed surveys. People had found it possible to answer most of our questions in ways that we felt were interpretable and codable for future statistical analysis. Some questions, however, proved unworkable; on several (for example, "Do you think it's a good thing to be able to read Vai script?") there was little variation in response (in this case everyone answered yes). Because unanimity meant that the question would not discriminate among respondents, we decided to eliminate such items from the questionnaire. We also discovered gaps in the information provided on certain questions and answers too ambiguous to be coded, so we revised the questionnaire accordingly.

We also spent a good deal of time reviewing tasks in the cognitive battery. Performance on certain tasks accorded well with our initial expectations. But on some, performance was so high or responses so uniform that we worried about the possibility that people were telling their friends about the tasks, easing their way. A good deal of Ethan's time was taken up experimenting with these tasks, finding forms that proved neither so easy that everyone got all the items right nor so difficult that everyone failed to get anything right. He conducted a number of pilot studies, helping us to arrive at a set we could be confident of using in the remainder of our work.

These operational and research difficulties, taken together, led us to the conclusion that we had seriously underestimated the amount of time it would take to accomplish the project. The information we had gathered was invaluable as a guide to conducting a reliable survey, but we knew that we would have to begin again with an instrument that reflected the lessons learned in the pilot work. By April 1973 we realized that we needed to obtain special funding and an expanded time frame to carry through on our initial goals. At this point, the Ford Foundation thought enough of the promise of this research that it agreed to finance the project. We decided to make our next trip to Liberia in midsummer, bringing with us a new field director (Ethan had signed up for only a year) and a new survey instrument. By this time we also knew that we needed to engage someone who would get to know Vai society in the less structured, informal way that is characteristic of anthropological research; we arranged to have Mike Smith, a Cambridge University student of Jack Goody's, join us to do an ethnographic study of literacy in a traditional Vai town.

In July 1973 the second wave of Vai research began. Ethan helped to orient us in Monrovia, where he had made arrangements for us to carry on our work in Vaitown, the traditional Vai neighborhood. Mike Smith moved to Diaa, an upcountry town we were to get to know well as time went on, and we were joined by Bob Schwartz, who had just completed a postdoctoral fellowship in psychology at Stanford University. Stephen Reder, a graduate student in psycholinguistics at Rockefeller University, also spent the summer with us, intrigued by the possibilities the script offered to examine linguistic theories about the impact of writing on spoken language and language change. Returning to New York, he joined our staff and studied the Vai language and script in preparation for his own research and as a project specialist in linguistic matters. In the fall of 1974, we began our major survey interviewing—a venture that required a year to complete.

CONDUCTING SURVEY FIELDWORK

Our experience in the pilot survey helped us learn how to lay the proper groundwork for extensive visits in the towns selected for the major survey. We negotiated the conditions of our stay in each new site. The particular quids and quos varied but the pattern of exchange was consistent. The town leadership's obligation was to make housing available to us for rental; provide us with water and, occasionally, cooking services; rent us space for office work and interviewing; and help us secure the cooperation of all individuals selected for the interview sample. We contracted to pay an agreed-upon fee per session to each person participating in inerviews and experiments and to provide the town with help to undertake or complete a needed project: finish a road, set up classes in Vai script, hire a school-teacher. We responded as best we could to appeals for a car ride or cash help when someone in town confronted an emergency; and we lent what support we could to the town's efforts to secure greater government aid for its self-improvement projects.

In each town we began our interviewing with the chief and the elder statesmen, as a courtesy and because they usually requested that we begin in this way. The time and effort it took to complete the interviewing of the sample population varied with a number of factors—season of the year and press of farming duties; degree of warmth exhibited toward the project by the town leaders; the number of Vai script literates and enthusiasm for the script in each particular location.

The final questionnaire consisted of sixty-eight questions, many of them requiring detailed autobiographical accounts. (We describe the major topic areas in the next chapter.) It was administered in a session lasting anywhere from forty-five minutes to an hour and a half, depending on each respondent's style of communication and how much he had to communicate. Every respondent also participated in a second experimental session lasting forty-five minutes to an hour in which we presented the set of cognitive tasks. In additional sessions we interviewed literates about the scripts they knew, how they learned them, and what uses they made of them. These sessions averaged one hour per script. Participation in project work was thus by no means a casual encounter; the time each respondent devoted to it ranged from a minimum of two hours (for nonliterates) to a maximum of five hours (for those few individuals who were literate in English, Vai script, and Arabic and had to be interviewed about their activities with all three).

The four staff members conducted all sessions. To reduce the effects of interviewer and experimenter bias, we organized the staff into working pairs. One member conducted the personal history interview and the other the experimental session for half their assigned sample population, and for the other half they switched roles. In large towns in which all four men were stationed, this plan worked relatively well. In smaller towns requiring only one staff pair, there were slippages. And, over the course of the survey year, other unplanned events—early arrival of the rainy season, a staff member's illness—forced us to redistribute work.

We planned to have interviews conducted individually, and so they were. But individual sessions were not always private sessions. Every effort was made to secure quiet and privacy for the respondent by interviewing inside our rented houses; during especially hot spells, interviewers set up tables and chairs under trees remote from public walk-and-lounge ways. Even with these precautions, the novelty of the proceedings, especially in the first few days after our arrival in a town, tended to attract a fringe of interested observers. Like "sidewalk kibbitzers," onlookers offered comments from time to time on the interview conversation. These intrusions represented little threat to the integrity of the information secured on personal history, but we had to take into account in our data analysis their potential contaminating influence on responses to attitude questions and experimental tasks.

Research assistants recorded responses on the interview schedules directly in English.[1] The field director maintained quality control by observing several interviews in every town, and reviewing all completed interview schedules weekly, checking for inconsistencies, omissions, and ambiguities. After we had trained staff assistants in the basic techniques of interviewing and administering the experimental tasks, we made no attempt to alter their individual styles nor to prescribe one best way to make questions meaningful to respondents or to maintain interest and cooperation. We left these matters to their ingenuity.

Each staff member functioned in accord with his own educational level and past occupational experience, as well as personal interest and ambition; all proved skillful in coaxing respondents through the lengthy and at times tedious sessions, with the result that we had no more than a handful of respondents who broke off and refused to complete the interview program.[2] In all we interviewed 650 people in all parts of Cape Mount County and a section of Monrovia.

Michael Smith, sharing the skepticism of many anthropologists about the appropriateness of standardized interviews in a traditional culture, wrote us about the "unanticipated" response he encountered in Diaa, the site of the ethnographic study:

> I was surprised when I first saw how long it [the questionnaire] was. I didn't think that anyone would sit down for long enough to answer it, or, if they did, that they would answer it seriously ... Well, I was wrong—and it fascinates

me why the Vai should, in the busiest season of the year—during two of the worst farming years one could have picked ... have spent a lot of time answering questions which had little to do with the essential business at hand ... Not only did the majority of people eventually come, but when they got there they answered with great deliberation. How many times does one remember someone saying, "I don't know, but I'll come back and tell you when I've checked with so-and-so." (Smith, personal communication)

The fees we paid each respondent undoubtedly made the work more attractive. Yet we would not do justice to the intellectual curiosity of the Vai people if we suggested that they were motivated to cooperate only by monetary considerations. We like the explanation given by one elderly farmer. The interviewer, afraid the farmer was losing patience, urged him not to "get vexed." "Oh, no," the farmer said, "I won't get vexed, because this is a way for all of us to gain experience, too."

5

Survey Goals and Methods

In this chapter we step outside the narrative framework to describe the interview survey more systematically. First we review the techniques we used to secure a representative interview population; then we discuss the principal topics we covered and our assessment of whether or not respondents understood and answered the questions in the sense we intended.

We engaged in an interview survey to accomplish two overlapping and complementary purposes: description and prediction. In order to make general statements about the social basis and functions of literacy in Vai society (a descriptive undertaking), we needed to supplement ethnographic observations in a few locales with systematically collected information from a representative array of towns and people. We also needed measures of literacy accomplishments and population characteristics that could be quantified and used in various statistical tests to predict possible effects of background influences on cognitive performance. Since our principal interest was in testing hypotheses about literacy's impact on cognition, we needed statistical control over characteristics that might covary with it. Moreover, we wanted an opportunity to test effects of nonliteracy factors such as urbanization and modernity that have been proposed as alternative explanatory mechanisms for cognitive change.

Both our descriptive and predictive goals required that we adopt systematic sampling procedures that would yield as representative an interview population as possible. Representativeness would provide the strongest basis for making general statements about literacy among the Vai people; at the same time, we hoped a systematic sample would give us access to the full range of naturally occurring variations in literacy and other life experiences that were important to our hypothesis-testing analyses.

"Drawing a sample" in a traditional village-based society without demographic records is, as other investigators have noted, a process of continuous compromise between methodological niceties and pragmatic realities (Naroll, 1970). Seeking representativeness, we decided on complete coverage of the four chiefdoms in Vai country. We adopted a multistage sampling procedure to arrive at a specification of the interview population: within chiefdoms we selected towns; within towns we selected households; within households we selected respondents.

Our criteria for town selection emphasized diversity, and we made a special effort to include villages of different sizes and accessibility to main roads. Our plan was to select a large town located on a motor road in each chiefdom, and for each large town to include one or more small satellite towns located off the road.[1] In addition, we decided to include a sample of urban Vai living in the capital city of Monrovia. This way of sampling towns was purposive in that we specified in advance the kind of places we wanted rather than leaving this to chance selection. With the exception of one chiefdom in which we were unable to establish contact with a small off-the-road town, we succeeded in carrying out our design and achieving diversity: survey towns included isolated communities, centers of traditional learning, and larger towns at the hub of rural commercial and political activities.

We initially planned to interview residents in a random sample of households in each survey town, but this completely randomized design proved unsuited to our purposes. We discovered that most towns had relatively few literate households; random selection would not give us large enough groups of literates for comparative purposes. We therefore modified our sampling strategy to maximize the number of literate informants. As soon as we arrived in town, we conducted a complete census, enumerating all households and their occupants and identifying those with a member literate in any script. Every house with at least one literate resident was included in the sample. From the remaining nonliterate households, we randomly selected one out of every two, but in no case did we include less than the number of literate households.[2] Within selected household units we interviewed all members, male and female, who were reported to be fifteen years of age or over.[3]

These procedures, while a departure from strict probability sampling, protected against the intrusion of bias with respect to the critical variables of literacy, knowledge and skill. There was no bias in selection of literate households because all such households in survey towns were included; there was no bias in selection of nonliterate households because these were chosen randomly from our town census enumeration. The Liberian government conducted an official nationwide census in 1974, just at the end of our interview study, making it possible for us to compare our survey population with demographic characteristics of the population as a whole. Our overall count of adults (using the same definition of "adult" as the Census) coincides almost exactly with the Census count for seven of the nine survey towns. Considering the notorious difficulties of census-taking in rural African communities, differences in personnel in the two censuses, and the mobility of town residents, we find the degree of concordance of the two independent survey teams encouraging. We also compared selected characteristics of the Cape Mount County population as reported in the Liberian Census with characteristics of our county *interview* sample. Considering men only (who will become our principal hypothesis-testing group), the two populations are remarkably alike in age, marital status, and school achievement. Thus, we can say with some confidence that although our methods did not follow every rule of probability sampling, we did in fact end up with a survey population rather nicely representative, on several significant dimensions, of the Cape Mount Vai population as a whole.

INTERVIEW TOPICS

Every member of our interview sample received the demographic questionnaire, and everyone reporting some knowledge of a script received literacy questionnaires as well. Table 5.1 summarizes the major categories of information we elicited.

Table 5.1 Principal interview topics, major survey

Demographic characteristics (Part I)	Acquisition of literacy (Part II) (completed for each script)	Uses of literacy (Part III) (completed for each script)
1. Identifying data	1. Reasons for learning	1. Correspondence
2. Family ethnic affiliation and social position	2. Teachers and their relationship to respondent	2. Recordkeeping (personal)
3. Marital and household status	3. Characteristics of teaching sessions (frequency, length, individual/group)	3. Technical plans or diagrams
4. Resources		4. Other occupational/farming uses
5. English schooling	4. Duration of study	5. Diaries
6. Literacy status Vai script Arabic English	5. Teaching methods 6. Teaching materials 7. Self-study	6. Histories and literature 7. Religious purposes 8. Town business (census, minutes,
7. Parental and family schooling and literacy status	8. Completion of learning 9. Opinions on learning the script	records) 9. Scribing 10. Teaching others
8. Residential history		11. Written material in
9. Travel		house
10. Occupational history		
11. Knowledge of languages		
12. Integration in traditional society		
13. Modernity		

The demographic questionnaire (Part I of our survey) required descriptive personal information (age, marital status, and the like) and a complete account of schooling and literacy experiences. In addition, we asked questions pertaining to family origin, occupational history, beliefs, attitudes, and other topics. These questions were motivated by our desire to have this research, unlikely to be duplicated, speak to sociological theories of social change as well as psychological theories of cognitive change. We single out for discussion here the questions and tests we used to measure schooling and literacy achievements and the more theoretically interesting domains of personal history and attitudes that we explored.

Education and Literacy

Measures of schooling and literacy status. It was relatively simple to secure reliable information about the level of formal English schooling. We conformed to the usual convention of using last grade completed as the metric for ordering individuals with respect to amount of schooling. Securing reliable information about Vai script and Arabic literacies, however, was not the simple matter of head counting that it might at first appear. What level of reading or writing in these scripts would justify calling a Cape Mount resident literate? Historical studies of literacy in European nations and in the United States provide no fixed criteria (Schofield, 1968; Laquer, 1976; Resnick and Resnick, 1977). Definitions of literacy continually change with changing social conditions, even within societies having long traditions of schooling and literacy. In the early days of the U.S. Census, for example, a person's ability to write his name entitled him to be classified as a literate; today, the Census requires either a sixth-grade education or reported ability to "read and write a simple message" as necessary qualifications for literacy.

At the outset of our work, we had no information about the minimal functional skills the Vai people thought necessary for literacy status nor whether they emphasized (as U.S. educators did until recently) the importance of reading skills over writing skills. In light of these uncertainties, we adopted two approaches. First, we gave social and personal definitions free play by using self-identification of the ability to read or write a particular script as a measure of literacy status in that script. We counted as literate anyone who answered yes to either of two questions: "Do you *read* (Vai, Arabic, English) script?" "Do you *write* (Vai, Arabic, English) script?" To test hypotheses about psychological consequences, however, we needed some objective measure for evaluating these self-reports, as well as measures that could rank individuals according to lesser or greater literacy skills. We turned to the traditional solution and designed reading comprehension tests for this purpose. Although by this time it was clear to us that each of the three scripts in use had its own learning context and socially prescribed minimal skills, we attempted to achieve some uniformity in our assessment devices. The test for each script followed a standard format; each presented four passages of graded difficulty. We asked the respondent to read a passage aloud and to answer a comprehension question about it. Interviewers assigned scores on a five-point scale, ranging from 0 (could not read aloud or answer a question about the first passage) to 4 (could read all passages aloud, including the final passage, quickly and with understanding).

These test procedures served as more or less comparable devices for assessing reading skills in the Vai script and English alphabet; literacy education in both these scripts follows the learning-to-read model in our schools—decoding visual symbols into comprehensible language units.[4] Presumably even beginning readers are expected to read with comprehension, and increased proficiency is represented by ability to comprehend passages of increasing difficulty. This model, however, does not apply to Arabic learning as we encountered it in Vai country. In the great majority of cases, Arabic literacy begins with memorization of chapters of the Qur'an. Depending on preferred teaching methods, the students may be required to commit passages to heart entirely by rote with no inkling as to their meaning (though we doubt this state of ignorance is maintained over the course of years) or may receive more or less explicit explanation of the sense that particular passages convey. In traditional learning contexts, instruction in the Arabic language itself does not begin until the Qur'an has been completely memorized. Modern methods of instruction in which Arabic is taught as a second language are becoming increasingly widespread in schools in Monrovia and larger towns. Only a minority of those who start the Qur'an, however, go on to complete it; and still fewer go on to becoming Arabic literates in the sense that they can understand the Arabic language as well as decipher its orthographic representation.

Mike Smith's analysis of the problem from his work in Gohn summarizes the various landmarks that one could use to determine Arabic literacy and the difficulty of applying them in a consistent way to individual literates. The following are excerpts from his discussion of levels of literacy:

(i) You have learned to "read" the whole Qur'an in the sense of being able to produce the correct sound sequence in Arabic of any Qur'anic passage presented, without being able to translate it into your own language. You may be able to "explain" what it means (i.e., paraphrase a translation or a summary of a translation given you by the teacher) or you may not.

(ii) You are able not only to read out the Arabic of any Qur'anic passage, but also to write the Arabic from memory without a text—possibly the whole Qur'an. Again, you may be able to "explain" what it means and you may not.

(iii) You are able to "read" the Arabic of any Qur'anic text and recite it from memory; also to recite a translation of the whole Qur'an. Thus, you are able to produce a "translation" of any passage. In addition, you may have studied one or more of the commentaries of the Qur'an in a similar way.

Levels (i), (ii), and (iii) require no systematic knowledge of the syntax and semantics of the Arabic language. In these stages, the individual cannot speak Arabic, apart from a few religious phrases and exclamations, and can write it only from memory or by copying directly from texts.

(iv) You can "read" and translate the whole Qur'an into your native language, since you have been taught Arabic as a language.

(v) Your Arabic is strong enough to read commentaries on the Qur'an—law books, textbooks on how to pray, and so on. Advanced students not only write personal letters in Arabic but are also fluent in modern written and spoken Arabic.

As this analysis suggests, it is extremely difficult to define people's skills in Arabic. Levels (ii) and (iii) are hard to differentiate because the basis for the reader's translation often cannot be ascertained. Differentiations between levels (iii) and (iv) can be made, in theory, by asking whether people have read additional commentaries on the Qur'an and whether they use Arabic productively in letter writing and record keeping, but in practice, it is not easy to check on informants' answers.

In face of these difficulties we adopted a pragmatic approach: we decided to categorize individuals according to large-scale distinctions for the purposes at hand rather than attempt to work out fixed criteria. We constructed our Arabic reading test so that the first two passages (chapters taken from the Qur'an) could be read and answered by memory as well as comprehension; the third and fourth passages required knowledge of the Arabic language and reading with comprehension. We interpreted scores of 1 and 2 conservatively as indicating Qur'anic knowledge by memory, and only the advanced scores of 3 and 4 as indicating comprehension. This procedure gave us the flexibility to segregate memorizers from comprehenders and include or exclude the first category from counts of literates as the sense of our enterprise dictated.

Identical reading scores on tests of different scripts (say 3 in Vai script and 3 in English) thus do not refer to identical skills or knowledge; they are nonequivalent in that sense. Within specific scripts, however, reading tests proved to order individuals reliably according to their relative levels of skills.

Demographic and Attitudinal Topics

Family characteristics. These questions were included to help us situate literacy and nonliteracy within the social organization of Vai society. We distinguished two attributes of special importance: family education and family traditionalism. The first topic reflected our interest in the possibility of intergenerational continuities in schooling or literacy. Even in countries with universal schooling, evidence suggests that the amount of schooling young people obtain is heavily influenced by how much schooling their parents had (Bernstein, 1971; Leichter, 1976; Sharp, Cole, and Lave, 1979). In a nation such as Liberia, in which English schooling is still optional and is only now becoming available in the countryside, one would expect that the educational status of parents would play an even greater role in determining which particular children are enrolled in school. Since we were interviewing an adult population, parents' schooling, in the main, referred to events occurring prior to 1930. This was an era in which the only schools available to Vai people in Cape Mount County were Christian mission schools serving a mere handful of the population.

We had less basis for assuming family influence on acquisition of Vai script literacy. Unlike English schooling, Vai literacy was traditionally obtainable in the countryside; it required no cash investment and occasioned no rupture in living activities. Ease of access might make for more distributed literacy (that is, literacy less concentrated in particular households) than English literacy; on the other hand, it might be that more subtle factors of growing up in a household in which reading and writing occurred would perpetuate "book learning" across generations. In the case of Arabic, we suspected that religious beliefs within the family might be a dominant factor in fostering literate practice. For all three scripts, then, we inquired in some detail about the distribution of schooling and literacy among kin members.

Items relating to family traditionalism were largely inspired by our interest in determining to what extent Vai script literacy was historically associated with a social elite. The only full-scale ethnography available at the time (Ellis, 1914) portrayed Vai society at the turn of the century as involving certain status distinctions among families, with a suggestion that some important chiefships were handed down according to a descent rule. During that period a number of Vai families retained servants or domestic slaves, usually acquired from other ethnic groups.[5] Since 1930, when the Liberian government abolished domestic servitude, those servant families remaining in Vai country were assimilated into the families and towns of their former masters. Older men still occasionally reminisce about these times, but questions about domestic servitude or servant ownership could not be handled directly in today's climate of opinion. Instead we sought indirect evidence about family status through questions suggested by our Liberian collaborators, asking whether anyone served the respondent's family in the "olden days" or whether the respondent's family in those days served another. On a broadly similar tack, everyone was asked the ethnic identity of both parents and whether they would consider their family to be "old Vai."

Resources. Vai society does not divide itself into two classes of the very rich and very poor, but families differ in the amount of resources they command, both those resources pertaining to the traditional economy and those necessary for getting along in changing times. To assign relative standing within the traditional economic sector, we asked about the number of houses the individual owned and counted rooms in his living quarters; we discussed the kinds of farming activities people engaged in, and secured information on number of spouses and children (important human resources in an economy as labor-intensive as Cape Mount County's). In questions about cash income, we sought to capture all possible sources of money flow, from occasional marketing (banana, fish, or soft drinks), to the sale of cash crops (coffee, cocoa, rubber), to fees for service (rarely encountered outside of Monrovia). We also attempted to secure a complete occupational history for each informant, but found that we could only approximate this ideal because of the varied and multiple activities in which many of our informants engaged.

Modernity and traditionalism. A number of influential theories of national development and social change have suggested a strong link between personal literacy and a set of attitudes and beliefs labeled "psychological modernity." (Lerner, 1958, was among the first and most influential sociologists to advance this view.) A large-scale comparative study conducted in six developing countries (Inkeles, 1969; Inkeles and Smith, 1974; see also Schuman, 1967) had demonstrated a consistent and transcultural set of relationships among schooling, knowledge of world events, and values associated with Western industrial society. As a result of these and other findings, some investigators (Schuman, Inkeles, and Smith 1967; Armer and Youtz, 1971; Inkeles, 1973) were proposing that literacy was a precursor of individual modernity, and that, separately or together, they were mechanisms for cognitive change. In all areas where empirical research attempted to test the theory, however, only schooled literacies were studied. We used the occasion of our survey to examine whether the relationship between literacy and modernity would hold up in the case of a nonschooled literacy. We also wanted to avoid a situation in which some global psychological construct such as modernity might operate as an unidentified factor to affect cognitive performance. We therefore incorporated a short version of the modernity scale developed and used by Inkeles and his colleagues into our questionnaire, adapting certain questions as they advise to make them meaningful within Vai society. (These questions are listed in Table 5.2.)

For further probes as to whether literacy among the Vai was associated with traditional or modern tendencies, we included a question about belief in the jinna (water people) that figure so prominently in Vai lore (see Ellis, 1914), and we inquired about special roles in secret-society bush schools.

Items eliciting extent of urban experience and contact with the modern sector were quite straightforward; we worked with each respondent to secure as accurate and complete a chronological account as possible of all res-

Table 5.2 Modernity questions

1. Which is most important for the future of this country? (Have person choose one and circle the one he chooses.)
   A. The hard work of the people
   B. Good planning on the part of the government
   C. God's help
   D. Good luck
   CODE: A, B: modern
         C, D: traditional

2. Two twelve-year-old boys took time out from their work in the rice fields. They were trying to figure out a way to grow the same amount of rice with fewer hours of work.
   1. The father of one boy said: That is a good thing to think about. Tell me your thoughts about how we should change our ways of growing rice.
   2. The father of the other boy said: The way to grow rice is the way we have always done it. Talk about change will waste time but not help. Which father said the wiser words? (Circle one)
   CODE: 1: modern
         2: traditional

3. Have you ever been so concerned about some public problem that you really wanted to help do something?
   A. Frequently
   B. Few times
   C. Never
   CODE: A, B: modern
         C: traditional

4. If you were to meet a person who lives in another country a long way off (thousands of miles away), could you understand his way of thinking? Yes ——— No——— (Check one)
   CODE: Yes: modern
         No: traditional

5. Learned men (scientists, scholars) in the universities are studying such things as what determines whether a baby is a boy or girl and how it is that a seed turns into a plant. Do you think that these investigations are:
   A. All very good
   B. All somewhat good
   C. All somewhat harmful
   D. All very harmful
   CODE: A, B: modern
         C, D: traditional

6. Some people say that:
   1. Men will someday understand what causes such things as floods, epidemics, and droughts.
   Others say:
   2. Such things can never fully be understood by man.
   Which opinion do you agree with?
   (Write any comment or explanation person gives. Encourage him to give one by asking, "Why do you agree with that opinion?")
   CODE: 1: modern
         2: traditional

7. Which of the following reasons should carry the most weight in determining the honor that a man receives?
   1. Coming from an important family
   2. Having a lot of money
   3. Having a high education
   CODE: 1, 2: traditional
         3: modern
8. 1. Some people say that it is necessary for a man and his wife to limit the number of children to be born so that they can take better care of the children they already have.
   2. Others say that it is wrong for a man and his wife purposely to limit the number of children to be born. Which of these opinions is the correct one?
   CODE 1: modern
        2: traditional
9. Which source of information do you trust the most to learn about what is going on in this country?
   1. The word of your friend
   2. What the Paramount Chief tells you
   3. What you hear on the radio
   CODE: 1, 2: traditional
         3: modern
10. How often do you listen to the radio?
    1. Everyday
    2. A few times a week
    3. Rarely
    4. Never
    CODE: 1, 2: modern
          3, 4: traditional
11. Have you ever talked with a government official to tell him your opinion about some public issue such as what the government should do about building schools or carrying the road to your town?
    1. Many times
    2. A few times
    3. Never
    CODE 1, 2: modern
         3: traditional
12. What are the biggest problems facing the town where you live?
    CODE: No or one problem: Traditional
          Two or more problems: Modern
13. Where is the town of Gbarnga?
    In what country is the city of Conakry?
    In what country is the city of London?
    CODE: Less than two correct: traditional
          Two or more correct: modern
14. Do you think a man can be truly good without having any religion at all?
    1. Yes
    2. No
    3. Maybe
    CODE: 1, 3: modern
          2: traditional

idences (defined as a stay of six months or more), major trips, frequency of trips, and purposes served by trips. Similarly, we checked carefully for information on number of languages spoken, keeping in mind that multilingualism might itself be associated with cognitive performance, especially on verbal tasks.

Acquisition of Literacy

Part II of the survey was devoted entirely to questions attempting to secure a retrospective account of the age and circumstances under which each self-reported literate acquired his script knowledge or schooling. A majority of these questions were for factual information: names of teachers, teachers' methods of instruction, study practices, and duration of time spent with a teacher in learning sessions. The same general topics were covered for Vai script, Arabic, and English schooling, with necessary modifications in the specific items.

Uses of Literacy

Part III of the survey inquired about the individual's participation in various literacy activities. On the basis of our informal observations, we prepared a list of principal uses which we knew occurred and supplemented this with potential uses and open-ended questions trying to capture specialized and idiosyncratic exploitations of script knowledge. For high-frequency uses, such as letter writing, we followed up with detailed questions on volume of correspondence and status of those to whom letters were sent (friend, kin, or stranger). We asked for full reports of all written materials people had in their possession (usually limited enough to permit enumeration but in some cases so voluminous as to require broad categorical summary). We encouraged interviewers in this session and the session about script learning to depart from our pre-set question categories and probe for people's own descriptions of their reading and writing activities.

INTERVIEW RELIABILITY

How much confidence can be placed in a procedure as sharply set off from Vai life as our lengthy and, for the most part, highly standardized interviews? In earlier chapters we pointed to the difficulties, both anticipated and unexpected, that attended our efforts to develop survey questions and interviewing procedures. Our own reservations about the suitability of surveys to uncover dimensions of Vai society and literacy had prompted us to employ a dual method of study—survey on the one hand, ethnography on the other. Given this background, our first step on completion of the survey was to apply various tests to questionnaire responses to check their reliability.

Reliability Viewed Subjectively

Our first approach to evaluating the reliability of the written words on the interview schedules was simple and direct. We interviewed each of the interviewers, going over each item, probing for difficulties, and asking for judgments about informants' reactions. We also asked Mike Smith to prepare a detailed analysis of his experience with the questionnaire and to assess its accuracy in the light of his personal acquaintance with the people interviewed in Gohn and Diaa. A consistent picture emerged from these evaluations. Items reported as "no problem" by one staff member generally had that status for others; items flagged as particularly unreliable by one were reported as troublesome by all.

Interviewers felt confident that all questions concerning personal education and literacy were clearly understood and comprehensively answered. They were also confident that basic information on such personal history topics as marital status, family composition, and places lived and visited was generally accurate. Smith told us that in subsequent conversations with former interviewees he confirmed that they had indeed lived where they said they did or took the trips they reported. Critical categories of information relating to occupational experiences and skills were also considered by the men to be reasonably complete and factually accurate, but it was the general consensus that economic indicators such as the amount of cash income earned the past year or the number of houses owned were consistently underreported.

Information on family social status, role in traditional society, and beliefs and attitudes presents a more checkered pattern. Two interviewers believed that questions asking about family servitude ("In olden days did your family work for others?") were unreliable. Smith said he didn't think these questions got at the slavery issue to which they were addressed. No one, however, reported difficulty with the general question "Were your people Vai in olden days?" or with specific questions on mother's and father's tribal affiliations. Individuals readily volunteered information on their belief, or lack of belief, in water people and on whether they had attended bush school, but the more sensitive question "When bush school is in session do you have a special part to play?" aroused resentment.

Most questions on the modernity scale were easy to ask, interviewers said, but our own analysis of transcribed interviews suggested unusual latitude in the way they phrased the questions. People found many of the questions provocative and took a long time to consider them and weigh their remarks. Smith observed that some of the topics are of great interest to the Vai: "For example, whether a rich man is better than an educated man is a topic people can be heard discussing any day." (Ellis, 1914, included a long parable on this very question in his collection of Vai proverbs and folktales.)

There was at least one question on the modernity scale, however, which the Liberian interviewers claimed perplexed people: "If you were to meet a person who lives in another country a long way off, could you understand his way of thinking?" One interviewer reported, "It made people mad. They said, 'If you don't understand the man's language, how would you know his way of thinking? If you get to know a person you can understand him.' They thought I was making a fool out of them by asking this question." Another interviewer said, "People always say things like, 'I've not been living with him before. How do you expect me to know his thinking? If he's a stranger he'll be thinking first about his food and home.' " Summing it up, then, we may say that the majority of the questions eliciting demographic data were strong, but those relating to family servant status, secret-society status, and personal attitudes require interpretive restraint.

Reliability Viewed Objectively

The objective case for reliability in these interviews rests primarily on consistency of replies across related items. Before we turn to an examination of these data, however, we find, in the summaries of actual responses, interesting and subtle evidence of the seriousness with which Vai people approached the interviews and the care they took with their answers.

Confirming the interviewers' reports, we find practically no "missing" or "I don't know" replies on the basic demographic items. Such responses are concentrated in items that appear to justify them. Fine discriminations respondents made among questions are illustrated by a comparison of the items concerning father's and mother's schooling. In parental generations, it was almost unheard of for a Vai woman to have gone to school. When asked whether their mothers had attended school, almost everyone answered no; there were only 6 "I don't know"s. But there were 141 "I don't know"s to the question "Did your father go to school?" Father's schooling was more likely, yet many respondents were not brought up in their father's houses and, lacking positive knowledge, refrained from a positive reply.

The strongest evidence for response reliability is in the pattern of intercorrelations among items that are conceptually related and that our ethnography suggested typically go together. Among the most significant of these correlational clusters are those involving our basic literacy measures. Recall that the interview schedule provided for two methods of ascertaining literacy status: self-identification and administration of a graded reading test. Perhaps the best indication of the honesty and accuracy of interview respondents (and, reciprocally, the validity of our measures) is the fact that only a small handful of people who were self-claimed readers or writers in a particular script failed to secure a minimal score of 1 on the reading test for that script (four among those given the Vai script test scored 0, five on the Arabic scored 0, and three on the English). In spite of our misgivings about the unavoidably ad hoc nature of these tests, scores were highly correlated with all other measures of literacy use and skill.[6] Vai script reading scores, for example, were significantly associated with assignment of expert status in the script (that is, being named by other respondents in reply to the question "Who knows Vai script best in this town?"). Arabic readng score was strongly linked with reported uses of the script requiring comprehension and knowledge of the language, such as writing letters in Arabic or teaching the Qur'an. And, finally, English test scores correlated, as they should, with grade level completed in school.

Although possible underestimation of the number of houses owned and cash income precludes our using these items as indicators of "true" levels of economic status, they nevertheless proved sturdy as measures of an individual's relative standing within the surveyed population. Having many houses, for example, was strongly associated with having many spouses and many children; higher income was associated with higher skill ratings, training, craft experience, and English schooling—correlations that make sense in terms of expected real-life relationships. Finally, in spite of the sensitivity of questions relating to family status, reports that the family in olden days was Vai (rather than, for example, Kpelle) were congruent with reported ethnic affiliations of parents (Vai or some other ethnic group).

This is selective information. But the conclusion that, in general, the survey yielded trustworthy responses is upheld when these responses are subjected to further analysis, and the outcome is an orderly and coherent picture of social dimensions in Vai life and the place of literacy within it.

6

Literacy and Its Characteristics

How literate are the Vai people in terms of numbers engaged in reading and writing activities? How literate are they in terms of the functions which these activities serve? Responses to our survey interviews enable us to answer these questions in an exact rather than impressionistic manner; they also tell us about typical paths to literacy and patterns of literacy activities among the several generations in our survey population. Autobiographical accounts of some men and women we came to know well help to enrich our understanding of the motivation and circumstances that lead individuals to acquire knowledge of Vai script, English, or Arabic and to practice literacy in the countryside.

EXTENT OF LITERACY

Close to one-third of our total interview population of 650 reported themselves as literate, and virtually all of these were men (191 out of a total of 202 literates). Exclusion of women from Qur'anic learning was not unexpected, but the restriction of Vai script knowledge to men was surprising. In many informal discussions, we asked whether some custom or rule prohibited men from teaching women the script or women from learning it on their own. We were repeatedly assured that this was not the case, and from time to time anecdotes reached us about a woman in this or that town who knew the script. Women literates did not come forward in our survey interviews, however. Unfortunately, we can only report and not account for the male-restricted nature of schooling and literacy in Vai society.

Before analyzing how literacy is distributed among the three scripts, we want to consider what the figures tell us about the extent of literacy in Vai society as a whole. As previously explained, our interview population was obtained through purposive, not random, sampling to ensure an adequate number of literates for theory testing, and, therefore, we cannot extrapolate the level of literacy found in the survey to the total population of Vai communities. By making a few assumptions, however, and by using 1974 Liberian Census data to supplement survey data, we can arrive at a reasonable estimate of the total number of literates among the Vai in the towns we surveyed. Since these towns were selected to be representative of all chiefdoms in Cape Mount County, we have a basis for extrapolating estimated literacy rates to the county at large.[1]

Table 6.1 presents these estimates. The Liberian Census, which counts only reading knowledge of English as literacy, reports a county-wide literacy rate of 11.6 percent (Republic of Liberia, 1974); our inclusion of Vai script and Arabic literacy boosts this rate to 19.1 percent. Even this statistic, spread as it is over the entire population including children, may underestimate the extent of active literacy. Since literacy functions in Vai society are primarily carried out by men, an alternate approach to assessing their impact is to compute percent of literates for the adult male population. This approach enables us to view literacy practitioners against their own social base. Again, using estimates based on Liberian Census reports, we find that approximately 28 percent of Vai men have some knowledge of some script. Literacy in the traditional Vai script is dominant (20 percent), followed by Arabic literacy (16 percent), and, in third place, English (6 percent), the official literacy of the Liberian government.[2] These estimates add up to more than 28 percent since knowledge of the scripts is often overlapping—an exceptional feature of literacy among the Vai which requires further analysis.

In our own culture we tend to think of literacy as knowledge and use of a single writing system. We take it for granted that many people are multilingual (speak more than one language), but we typically assume that they are, nevertheless, monoliterate (represent all languages they speak in one script—in our case, the Roman alphabet). While we were attracted to Vai society in the first place because of its variety of writing systems, we assumed that different individuals would know different scripts. We did not

Table 6.1 Estimated percentages of literates in Cape Mount County survey towns

	Percent of total population (including children)	*Percent of total adult male population*
Vai script	6.6	20.3
Arabic	5.0	15.7
English	11.6	6.2
Total literacy[a]	19.1	28.4

a. Because of considerable overlap of Vai script–Arabic literacy, total percent of all literate individuals is less than the sum of the three scripts.

Table 6.2 Script knowledge among Vai men (major survey respondents, $N = 290$)

Scripts known	N	Percent of male literates
Total number of literates	191	
Vai script only	53	27.7
Arabic only	38	19.9
English only	32	16.8
Vai-Arabic	47	24.6
Vai-Arabic-English	5	2.6
Vai-English	6	3.1
English-Arabic	6	3.1
English-other (e.g., French)	4	2.1
All Vai script	111	58.1
All Arabic	96	50.3
All English	53	27.7

anticipate the extent to which multiscript knowledge would be characteristic of individual literates and represent a personal intellectual accomplishment.[3] Table 6.2 classifies male survey informants by script knowledge according to their performance on our reading tests. The greater number are monoliterate, in descending frequency from Vai script to Arabic to English; close to one-third are literate in two scripts; and a few individuals have achieved mastery of all three writing systems. Biliterates overwhelmingly represent the combination of Vai syllabary–Arabic learning. Considering all Vai script literates, better than 40 percent know Arabic as well; or, considering all Arabic literates, nearly one-half (49 percent) also know Vai script. In contrast, co-occurrence of either Vai script or Arabic with English is rare. Going to English school seems to represent a cutting point, an educational choice that turns the individual away from participation in learning either of the two traditional scripts. Exclusivity of English and Arabic is understandable, since both literacies require extended daily study during roughly the same age period. The rupture between English school and Vai script rests on less apparent factors. Vai script does not require an extended period of study and is customarily learned in adulthood. Our conjecture is that youth who attain English literacy in school are drawn to pursue opportunities in the cash economy, thus cutting themselves off from available Vai script tutors as well as the cultural supports fostering interest in the script.

PATHS TO LITERACY

For each literate and each kind of literacy, we had inquired into the process of becoming literate. Our questions were selected to tell us as much as possible about the social organization and context of learning and teaching processes, as well as the criteria people used to judge a "finished product." As we shall see, each of the three literacies is distinctive with respect to major features of the process of becoming literate.

Becoming Literate in Vai Script

Becoming literate in Vai script is not child's play; it is an activity generally reserved for young men in their late teens and twenties. Some respondents reported that they had begun to learn Vai script at fourteen or fifteen years of age (for many, beginning age represents an estimate); 20 percent were thirty years old or older when they began.

As one might expect of people who become literate as adults, learning to read and write Vai script is almost always a voluntary activity, although many say they were encouraged to study it by friends or male relatives. Momokai Paasewe, one of several people whom we asked to recount their life stories, described his motivation for learning Vai script, and many accounts we heard were quite similiar:

> As for the Vai script, I knew it through many things, especially when we were young men and we used to invite friends from other towns to come and have big feasts and dances. We became very friendly with the people from Mavema, and Mr. Kromah was the leader who helped us get together. I had a friend then named Swary; he lives in Sierra Leone now. He was the one who knew the Vai script in our dance group. He taught me and I learned it. We used it to arrange our dances. If he was interested in a girl, he wrote to someone in Mavema to make sure she would come. Also, he was a friend of my father's and they used to write to each other in the script. I used to see the letters and see them talking and I became interested in learning too.

Mr. Paasewe learned Vai script in order to meet young women in a manner that was not public knowledge; letters were his vehicle. Another informant reports that he began to learn the script at the urging of his family because his father, who was losing his eyesight, could no longer read. The father had to ask someone outside the family to read letters he received, and his mother became upset because personal matters could not be kept within the family under such circumstances. As it happened, this informant was working with a carpenter who was literate in the script, so he asked his boss to teach him. Other people tell of working alongside someone who received a letter at his farm, and starting to learn out of curiosity or because they were away from their home village and received, or wanted to send, a letter whose contents they preferred to keep to themselves.

It is striking how transmission of the Vai script occurred in such a way as not to transform the social relationships among individuals into a formal teacher-learner relationship. A definite accent lies on teacher and pupil living and working together. One informant reported, for example, that he began to learn when he went to work at a sawmill in the high forest of the

Vai Koneh district, where a fellow sawyer was able to read and write Vai script: "All of us were living together . . . Every time he received letters he read and answered them, so I too got encouraged and decided to ask him to teach me." Over several months, as they worked together, they would have a session, "sometimes five minutes when we met, because we never used to stay too long talking about it." Very few of our informants reported that they learned the script entirely on their own or that they learned it in an organized school setting. Almost everyone learned it from an individual; a few informants reported that they had two teachers but always at different times. As a rule, the student met with his teacher from three to five times a week in lessons that could be as short as ten or fifteen minutes and as long as one or two hours, with an average lesson time of about forty-five minutes.

Learning Vai script also seems to be a personal affair—it is learned by the student acting as an individual. Very few of our informants had lessons with more than one other student present; only four said they studied with as many as seven or eight others.

The period necessary for learning Vai script well enough to be considered literate is exceedingly short by comparison with those reported for adult literacy programs throughout the world (for example, Gray, 1969). Many informants told us that they studied for less than a month, and some claimed to have learned sufficient Vai script for correspondence purposes in a week. On the average, it was reported that two to three months of lessons were required to achieve some functional literacy, although some people admitted to needing more time, even a year, to complete the process. Of course, it is not entirely clear what "completing the process" meant to our informants, who were virtually unanimous in telling us that if they found a particular letter or document difficult to understand they routinely consulted with an acquaintance reputed to be especially knowledgeable. Some students do not complete the process. Various reasons were cited for this failure, including the verdict that learning the script was too hard.

When asked how long it should take a good student to learn Vai script, people estimated that it required about two to three months—the same length of time they reported for their own learning. Poor students were estimated to require several years to learn the script, but no one admitted to being such a poor learner.

The single most salient basis for judging someone fully literate in Vai script is ability to read, a criterion suggested by almost every literate to whom we spoke. Some informants referred to a man's reputation, or his knowledge of individual characters, but a criterion that we thought might be selected as important—skill in communicating in the script—was mentioned by less than 5 percent of our informants.

Very early in our pilot work we discovered that several methods were used to teach reading and writing in Vai. In some cases an individual was given a letter by a friend who explained in detail exactly what the letter said to the point where the learner knew the letter by heart and could identify each character in it. After a few such letters had been mastered, the student attempted a letter of his own. When asked about specific methods their teachers used to help them learn the Vai script, respondents described four teaching strategies:

1. Names of things were listed on the page and the student copied them over, memorizing them as he went.
2. Individual character names were listed, often with the particle syllable *mē*, corresponding to *this is*, appended to it.
3. Strategy 2 was combined with a constraint which listed characters according to their sound. For example, in an early interview, Mike Smith was told that every person should begin by learning the characters that occur very frequently (the basis for this frequency judgment was not explained); among the characters listed were *kpo, lo, ndo, gba, sa, la, nda,* and *ga.*
4. Characters were taught according to their visual form.

Teachers often combined two or more strategies. Names of things and character names were reported by almost every informant as the basic lesson materials. Teaching of characters by form was also mentioned frequently, with somewhat fewer people reporting that their teachers had given lessons emphasizing the sounds of characters as in the third strategy.

In several towns we set up classes in which a resident with advanced knowledge of Vai script taught it to interested townspeople. We knew these classes could not be used as a model of how teachers taught individual students informally, but we hoped to observe different kinds of teaching strategies, types of difficulties students experienced, and the rapidity with which they learned. We knew that Vai script had been taught in schools not dissimilar to those we set up at various points in its history, so what we were arranging, while not the contemporary norm, was not outside of Vai experience entirely.

Our experimental classes produced, at one time or another, all of the strategies for teaching Vai script that our informants had told us about. Classes met for about an hour four to five times a week. In general, lessons were graded in difficulty, beginning with some simple version of one of the strategies, and proceeding to the point where people could read and write letters drawing on a basic set of thirty to forty characters. In some cases, the first session at Vai class was the first time that people had ever held pencils in their hands or made marks on paper; simply learning to manage these writing materials raised initial difficulties. Learning to read the script proceeded rapidly, however, and in one class four of eleven students learned to write sophisticated letters within a few weeks.

In the classes we observed, reading and writing were inextricably linked; in our survey as well, people who indicated that they could read Vai also reported that they could write it. However, several informants, especially older people, told us that they learned to read before they learned to write. One reason for greater facility in reading among the older generation was the difficulty of finding writing materials. A century ago, writing was done on leaves using dyes from local plants as ink. We heard reports of individuals who had learned to read and write from teachers who scratched characters in sand or clay. At present, paper is reasonably accessible in Vai country in the form of school children's copybooks, which are a major medium for use of the script.

Learning Arabic: Qur'anic Literacy

If learning Vai script is more or less an invisible activity that fills the interstices of people's work lives, learning Arabic, or at least that aspect of learning Arabic which involves learning to read and recite from the Qur'an, is a visible and audible part of everyday life in almost every Vai village.

The following description, taken from Mike Smith's field notes of June 1, 1974, when he was in Gohn, describes one session that is not atypical, except that few teachers are as well versed Arabic scholars as Alihaji B. or possess such a fine copy of the Qur'an.

> I was ready at 7:30 when Alihaji called and said he was about to start teaching. Surprised, I said I thought I was late, but he explained that students get up at 5:30 and read over their lessons until 7:30 or 8:00—when he begins teaching. The school is held in the mud-and-wattle palaver house beside his house at the north end of town. It's open on four sides, though the entrance is away from the road. Around the walls are stacked the boards inscribed by Alihaji and Qur'anic texts. All the chapters are different, and some texts have lists of single letters written below them, presumably for the beginners.
>
> Alihaji himself lies in a hammock strung lengthwise, while the fifteen or so students, all small boys aged from five to ten, sit on the dusty floor or squat against the walls, each clutching a board. Most of the boys are dressed in short trousers alone and their bodies are smeared with dust and ash. In one corner is a heap of firewood. In the center of the floor, the ashes of a fire. Alihaji begins by reading a whole chapter from his magnificent huge green Qur'an, gold-embossed script on the cover. He reads, half chanting, and all the boys follow him, phrase after phrase. This is purely oral recitation, for they squat leaning on their boards, the inscribed face turned away from them.
>
> Two of the older boys sit next to the teacher, holding Qur'ans;—the latter reads a long passage and one of the two, his own son Usmaana, repeats it after him reading each phrase from the Qur'an and following the text with a finger. At various points Alihaji explains difficulties of meaning in Vai—"Abraham is now speaking to his son, 'I saw you in the dream, I will kill you, I will cut your throat! Do what ever you wish,' says Ismaila . . . the time Abraham got ready to kill his own son, they told him he's already made the sacrifice—'That will be a blessing on you forever.' " In between, Alihaji reads the sentences in Arabic, the students after him. Then they continue just with the Arabic.
>
> All of the students are at different chapters. Alihaji moves with a Qur'an

from Usmaana who's at the next chapter to the other students. Alihaji: "God brought us in the world for a purpose and sent his book for us to read so that we should go on the right path . . ." That finished, a youngster brings us his board; Alihaji recites from memory, still trying to find the place in his Qur'an. And so on for most of the other students who recite their texts phrase by phrase after him in turn. Then the two older and more advanced students go to teach the younger ones from their boards. Some of the youngest ones haven't been here a year and are still learning the letters.

. . . During the afternoon the pupils help Alihaji on his farm and Alihaji's wives with the housework—notably in fetching water and firewood. A lot of the students' apparent "free time" is devoted to rehearsing the lessons given the day before, so that the number of hours devoted to study each day may well total four, five, or more.

Our survey results confirm the impression that children begin to learn the Qur'an at an early age; a majority of children begin their training a few years before or after their tenth birthday. As might be expected from this early starting age, adults are more heavily involved in the decision to learn the Qur'an than in the decision to learn Vai script. In general, children are *sent* to learn the Qur'an. Sometimes this means no more than attending classes held within their town; the level of expertise available from local teachers is often limited, however, so a great number of our informants traveled to other townships in Liberia and Sierra Leone to continue their studies.

Our observations suggested two major ways in which Qur'anic teaching was organized in Vai country. The first, which we found more common, consists of a teacher and six to twelve students meeting around a bonfire; the chants of the children, interrupted from time to time by a comment from the teacher or an older, more knowledgeable student acting as the teacher's assistant, go on for about two hours. Teachers emphasize recitation; they provide little explanation of the meaning of the texts being read, and the children have virtually no knowledge of the meaning of individual words or phrases.

The second kind of Qur'anic school is more formally organized. In Gohn, at the school described by Mike Smith, a special classroom is used by the Arabic teacher, and the children have been divided into four or five "grades" according to their proficiency. The children work from blackboards. In addition to learning to write, they are being taught some Arabic along with the decoding skills necessary to pick up the Qur'an and begin reciting.

People were almost unanimous in maintaining that learning Arabic was a difficult and time-consuming job, but one that most could accomplish if they were obedient and followed their teacher's directions. Although religious practices are at the heart of learning the Qur'an, informants rejected the notion that God had anything to do with success in learning to read; interest and cleverness were the two characteristics most often mentioned, following obedience, as important determinants of success.

Becoming Literate in English

In certain respects, becoming literate in English is similar to the process of becoming literate in Arabic. In both cases it is necessary to master an alphabetic orthography of a foreign language. In both cases individuals are most likely to begin learning while they are less than ten years old, and the process of becoming literate requires years of work in a relatively formal setting in which a single teacher instructs a large group of children. Unlike learning the Qur'an, becoming literate in English is a secular activity that is motivated largely by pragmatic concerns. English is the official language of the country, the language of commerce and government affairs. Government officials—tax collectors, surveyors, elected representatives, judicial authorities—are required to conduct their official business in English (in practice, a good deal of the oral communication is in Vai, but Vai has been forbidden as a medium of official written communication, so it is important that every town have at least one person literate in English to act as town clerk for purposes of dealing with the government). It is also considered a distinct asset to have one or more family members complete enough school to be able to obtain work in the modern sector of the economy, especially government. Educated relatives can act as buffers between the relatively powerful authorities in Monrovia and the relatively powerless rural inhabitants of Vai country.

All English literates in our survey had attended government or mission schools for varying periods of time. The availability of schooling is sparsely and unevenly distributed within Vai country, and its quality varies as well. Even today, many village towns do not have their own elementary schools; only four public junior high schools and one high school serve the county. Students who want to finish their education often have to leave home, relying on relatives in Monrovia or larger towns to board them while they go through the higher grades. For most students, becoming literate in English means attending a school in their own village or nearby town until family demands to help on the farm or participate in village life preclude further attendance (when, for example, girls are given in marriage sometime after age twelve). The dropout rate is high, with the result that many people who have attended school have not become "educated," in the standard American use of the term. One-third of the schooled men in our survey had a sixth-grade education or less; 21 percent had some junior high school education, and 28 percent had attended high school. As one might expect, not all had achieved a firm grasp of reading and writing; 32 percent tested on the beginning levels of our reading test (levels 1 and 2).

Several of the English literates we met were unusual in having begun their schooling later than the norm (in effect, when they were young adults). While they stayed in school just long enough to acquire elementary skills in reading and writing, they taught themselves fluent literacy on the basis of this brief period of attendance. These men remained in Vai country, using English literacy for many of the pragmatic purposes others meet with Vai script literacy skills, but their knowledge of English also permitted them to open up new channels of communication with non-Vai English literates. In contrast, youngsters now attending school intend to achieve the status "being schooled." Mike Smith says of this situation: "They started on a school program which is based on time elapsed in the institution and is therefore, as in Euro-American societies today, an elaborate and lengthy *rite de passage,* rather than a simple context for the transmission of technical skills." A significant feature of the *rite de passage* represented by current English schooling, in contrast to either Qur'anic learning or learning to read and write Vai script, is that it represents a passage out of traditional Vai society rather than a route to status and security within the society. In terms of the problems which are of central concern to our research, it is significant that English school through its curriculum requires students to master a wide variety of concepts without counterparts in traditional Vai society; the effect of this experience on individuals' future social status and ways of thinking will be a question of central interest, because in this respect English education contrasts sharply with both Vai script and Qur'anic learning.

USING LITERATE SKILLS IN VAI COUNTRY

The third section of our major survey questionnaire represented our attempt to catalog systematically the applications of the three literacies known to the Vai. Results are summarized in Table 6.3. The first set of questions concerns letter writing, which we knew to be a dominant use of the Vai script. The second set of questions probes other personal, occupational, and civic writing activities, and the third, the values people ascribe to script knowledge—that is, how they think literacy makes a difference in their personal lives. We will begin with a description of the functions of each script and then make some comparative observations about the distribution of functions across scripts.

Using Vai Script

Letter writing. Of the 107 respondents literate in Vai script (and for whom we have complete interviews), 94 percent reported that they wrote letters. Among those who wrote, only 21 percent reported having written to strangers; 79 percent reported that they wrote exclusively to friends and relatives. As one informant put it: "How can you write to someone you don't know?

Table 6.3 Uses of scripts

	Percent reporting		
	Vai script (N = 107)	Arabic (N = 85)	English (N = 47)
1. Correspondence			
Writes letters	93[a]	31	87
To friends, relatives	72	26	64
To strangers	21	5	23
Has written a letter for someone else	61	4	51
Reads letters	97	33	96
From friends, relatives	71	29	74
From strangers	26	4	22
2. Record keeping (personal)	78	32	53
Family events	71	29	47
Work/business/financial	52	11	30
Legal	10	4	0
Other	15	7	13
3. Town records, business	63	26	21
4. Technical plans, diagrams	38	26	19
5. Literary and historical material	53	22	53
6. Religious uses	55	100	77
7. Writes other language in script	54	19	19
English	50	2	—
Vai	—	13	13
Arabic	47	—	11
Other tribal	11	4	2
8. Has taught script	44	19	17
9. When last wrote			
Within past week	64	45	79
More than 1 week up to 1 month	21	24	23
1–2 months	14	17	9
Over 2 months	7	4	2

a. Numbers in literacy groups are somewhat less than those reported in Table 6.2 because some respondents failed to complete literacy interviews. Numbers in the left-hand columns under each script refer to percentage engaging in the designated categories. Numbers in the right-hand columns refer to percentages in relevant subcategories.

... How can you possibly have any business with someone you don't know?" There was considerable variability in reported frequency of letter writing. On the low side were those who corresponded only once or twice a year; most people reported writing one or more letters every few weeks, and a good number wrote more than a letter a week. A great deal of letter writing is performed for nonliterate kin and neighbors, 61 percent reporting they have functioned as letter-writing scribes. Reports about letter reading match the answers we received to questions about letter writing almost exactly, reflecting the close correspondence between these two activities in Vai script correspondence.

Central to our concerns is the content of Vai letters. We attempted to gather evidence on letter content by an examination of the large corpus of letters that we collected during our project, supplemented by letters made available to us by Gail Stewart, amounting in all to more than one thousand letters spanning a number of decades.

Overwhelmingly, the subject matter of these letters is best described as personal business: family and town news, requests involving deaths, plans for visits, and financial matters. Representative examples are the following:

> This letter belongs to my in-law, Mole. My greetings to you. This is your information. My grandmother is dead. This is a *waa* for you. [Note: Traditionally, *waa* is an enclosed envelope that is formally sent to an in-law asking him for a special contribution toward the ceremony for the deceased individual in question.] The feast has been scheduled to be held on the 18th of the lunar month. So that is your information. My greetings to you.
>
> > I am M.K.
> > Bendu

> This letter belongs to my brother, M.S., at Sinje. My greetings to you.
> I told you some time ago that I was going to send your money very shortly, but it happens that I became sick, so I beg you to be patient. Secondly, I am still thinking about what I told you; I will come to discuss it with you on Friday. Please try to think of it too and tell me which one is better.
> Tell your wife, A., that I have bought her dresses and will bring them along. Extend my greetings to her.
>
> > I am A.B.

> Pa Lamii,
> My greetings to you. This is your information. I have arrived here so if the sheep has been bought, please send the money tomorrow morning. I am waiting to receive it. Tomorrow I shall be going up to Kle.
>
> > It's M.S.

These letters, and countless others like them, share several characteristics. They all presuppose that the recipient knows the writer and a good deal about his affairs. But they are by no means impossible for us, as total strangers, to understand. To be sure, there may be a reference we cannot interpret ("I am still thinking about what I told you"), which is clearly intended to remind the recipient of something that the writer does not want to discuss in the letter. But the main message is almost always understandable, even though we do not know the actors involved. Letters are also short and written to convey a specific message. We found no examples of chatty letters to the family. Vai script letters exhibit a businesslike tone over and above the content of the news they transmit.

Occasionally we came across letters that appear to place strong communicative demands on both writer and recipient. In the following letter, a rather complex "death business" is transacted by someone acting on behalf of the person whose traditional role is to see to the distribution of the deceased's possessions.

This letter belongs to Uncle Boakai. My greetings to you. This is your information. Your niece, H.M., died. Everything she left has been put on record. Here is a copy of the record.

When I went to Salala I demanded that everything should be shown to me to have a look at them; Momolu made them available to me. Your nephews, Momolu and Ambulai, asked me to divide them. But brother Seku asked me to tell him who must be present before we can divide them up, and I told him that you and the aunts have to be present. He then asked me to appoint someone to take care of the property until I wrote to you to come. This is the reason why this letter is written. Please come and divide the property.

However, if you yourself are unable to come please do send someone to represent you. If you are to send a representative please do send one whom you trust; someone like you yourself, to come and divide out this property for us.

You should find out among yourselves how to handle this matter, and whatever conclusion you might arrive at, please do inform me in writing. Please do not delay or ignore this message.

Since you are the head of the family, we have waited until we hear from you. If there is any information which I do not offer in this letter, brother Seku will tell you himself.

I am looking forward to hearing from you as early as possible.

I send my greetings to everybody.

I am V.K.

Table 6.4 Contents of Vai script letters (sample of 50)

Whose affairs are involved	
Writer and nonfamily person	26
Writer and family	19
Town business	5
Function	
Requests only	18
Information only	20
Requests and information	12
Topics (duplicated count)	
Requests	
Money	10
Death-related	3
Materials/medicine	6
People (help)	5
Queries and miscellaneous	5
Information	
Plans for visits	15
Illness/deaths/births	7
Reasons for not repaying debts	4
Miscellaneous	6

We made a rough content analysis of fifty letters gathered from a heterogeneous sample of Vai script literates living in upcountry towns. Table 6.4 classifies letters in this corpus according to function and content. Three-fifths of all of these communications contain a request of some sort; better than half are written for the sole purpose of asking the recipient to do something, almost always to provide some assistance in the way of money, goods, or people. Information is also communicated; the most common category of news involves announcements of forthcoming visits or reports of family events (births, illnesses, and deaths). Some informational letters tell the recipient why the writer has not yet repaid money or other goods due. Considering requests, apologies for not meeting requests, and visit plans, the great majority of letters can be said to be transactional—they involve movement of money, things, and people, usually between family members and friends. In spite of its popularity and obvious pragmatic value, letter writing is circumscribed in the sense that it is restricted to known correspondents and to highly familiar personal business; no missives are written "To Whom It May Concern."

Record keeping. Table 6.3 also contains information on non-letter-writing activities involving Vai script. Record keeping is almost as ubiquitous as personal correspondence and is reported by 78 percent of Vai literates. Among those who keep records, the leading topics are family business and financial transactions—two domains that often overlap. Sometimes family records consist of no more than mere registration of children's birthdates or other important events in a family album style. But in several instances we found men who kept detailed records of money spent on kin, especially their wives—a hedge against the possibility of divorce, at which time the husband may have to repay the bride-price given him by his wife's father (minus, these records suggest, special outlays that the husband has provided). The following is one such record, collected from a middle-aged man in a remote Vai village.

1968

Masaa—this is what I spent on her.

I tied rope on her hand	$ 1.00
I engaged her (as a friend)	8.00
I engaged her parents (as friends)	16.00
I asked for information concerning her	.05
I asked for her to visit me	4.00
And I gave Masaa two bed sheets	3.00
I bought two lappas for her in Jene	
The two lappas worth	2.00
I gave her three pairs of slippers	3.00
Ma Gasa brought cloth and I bought some for her	2.00
I gave her four panties (2 for 25¢ each and 2 for 50¢ each)	1.50
I gave her three headties	15.00

I gave her two towels	2.00
I gave Ma Satu one cloth	15.00
I gave Momolu one shirt	1.00
I gave Bai one shirt	1.00
And I helped my in-law, Gohni, against the house	2.00
I gave him one long trousers which he gave to the man who thatched the house. It costs	12.00
I gave him two shirts	2.00
She borrowed money from some people and her mother sent her to me to refund it. She came and I paid the money. .05 [actually $5.00]. One day they spent time here and her mother said that they did not have any food, I should therefore give them food and I gave the food.	5.00

Records, more or less systematic, are commonly used for trade and business purposes. Some farmers report keeping records of amounts of seed planted and harvested, so they can compare crop yield over the years; those who participate regularly in commodity markets for products such as coffee, cocoa, and rubber may keep track of sales and prices received; craftsmen will occasionally list goods and supplies they have on order and maintain lists of customer purchases. In addition to records that have some permanency, script literates report diverse notational uses of the script, especially for occupational purposes: tailors use it to record relevant measurements and masons planning trips to Monrovia make up shopping lists of materials they need.

Recording town business is a prominent use of the script. This record keeping is in the spirit of individual accounts, except that it is a public process designed to reduce disputes among neighbors, who, given the kin structure of Vai towns, are also relatives. Until the 1940s, when English replaced Vai by government decree, the script was used to record court cases; today it is still used for personal note taking on the proceedings, although not for official purposes. Chief Lahai Siimoh Zodua of Gohn described public business uses of the script succinctly when he told Mike Smith: "The Vai script is used for town business principally to list contributions whenever the town is making a collection. Sometimes to record what is said at meetings. In court you would write down only the principals involved and sometimes the crime—but never a summary of the proceedings. English script is not used in town business."

We collected many interesting examples of town records and related documents, including several that were formal and contractual in nature. A Muslim "friendly society," whose members were widely scattered, was regulated by a set of bylaws written in Vai script (described in Goody, Cole, and Scribner, 1977), and we found an example of town bylaws in the script as well.

A more typical use of town records is to account for money collections that accompany special occasions. These records tend to be more complex than those kept for personal reasons, and often consist of tables of information arranged in orderly classification systems. One such account of monies collected at a funeral feast impressed us with its expert use of a hierarchical classification scheme.

The account was recorded in a copybook of the kind used by children attending government elementary schools. The facing page of the booklet has the inscription, "When all this money was collected (and used) there remained $4.00." The first page begins a listing of contributions made by the older women, subdivided by town quarter. The entries are labeled according to quarter and the name of each woman within the quarter is listed along with her contribution. Each new quarter is marked off from the preceding one with extra space. The entries continue in this manner for three pages of the notebook. Entries for older men begin on the fourth page. Thirty-four men are listed, ordered again by quarters but without any marked space between quarters. These entries are followed by a list of thirty-nine younger men. The next page lists the quarter chiefs in a section by themselves. Then follow four pages labeled at the beginning as "younger women" and containing their names and contributions. The next page of the notebook summarizes this information; it lists the number of people contributing from each population category and provides a grand total for the entire town ($202.75). But this is not the end of the record. It continues with the names of people who are visitors to the town and are not expected to pay toward the proceedings. The first such group are men from Monrovia, then women from Monrovia, and, finally, women visitors from miscellaneous locations—a fine example of classes within a class.

Records such as these, while they are by no means common, provide everyday evidence for links between literacy and tasks involving higher-order intellectual activities that psychologists tend to describe as abstract.

Our next category of script use involves technical plans and diagrams, a literacy function reported by 38 percent of Vai script literates. The nature of these schematic plans varies considerably from one individual to another and their use is concentrated among craftsmen. Weavers use a matrix plan to diagram the black and white patches needed to complete different blanket or tunic designs; masons lay out the number of bricks needed for houses; and carpenters sketch rough plans on which they note dimensions of the structures they are building. One carpenter's plan is shown in Figure 6.1, in which the script is used to label the rooms (for example, "sleeping room") of the projected dwelling—a grand edifice by usual standards.

Other uses of Vai script. The next category of literate activity, *writes literature,* requires further elaboration. When we first included this question in the survey, we sought to find out whether the informant wrote textual material, either fiction or nonfiction, intended primarily to be read by someone else. We knew of the existence of such written material—a circular giving one side's account of a land dispute, a historical account of the migration of

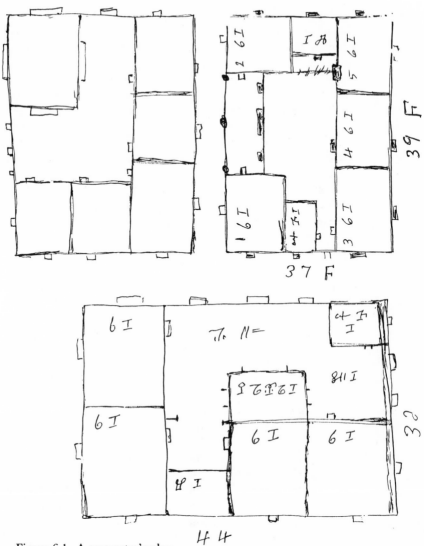

Figure 6.1. A carpenter's plan

the Vai people to Vai country. From Ellis's 1914 ethnography of the Vai we had one example, in the Vai script, of a traditional Vai story. But we could not tell from the text if the story was written in Vai script at Ellis's request, or if it was simply a copy of a story that Ellis collected along with other stories he reproduced in his book in English.

We believed that at least some people wrote down stories and maxims because the "Book of Ndole," which was written sometime before 1850 (and which Gail Stewart had begun to study at the time we began this work), contains a lengthy parable in addition to accounts of the invention of the script and events early in Ndole's life. But when we came to investigate such texts, we found them to be relatively scarce and very much the property of the people who owned them. Certain books are greatly valued and very private property. Most of these books, like the "Book of Ndole," are not continuous texts on a particular subject; rather, they are large (and sometimes expensively bound) volumes with blank pages on which the owner, or one of his forebears, has made entries. As with diaries, events of major importance to the writer are recorded. Entries might include marriages, births, and deaths of family members, as well as local, national, or even international events. Within a single volume one can also find family genealogies, historical accounts of the founding of a clan or a town, parables, proverbs and stories we thought of as fables. The variety of written content to be found in one individual's book is illustrated below in documents provided by Mambu Paasewe, a middle-aged weaver whose forebears founded the town of Wuilo, where we did a good deal of work in the later part of our project.

Example 1

I am Mambu Paasewe (wrote) 1961.
This is a history in this book.
The Lofa War was fought in 1871. The white people took over the country in 1885. The Kohnkundu War was fought in 1898. The Kouza War was fought in 1914. The collection of the hut tax war began in 1918. Boima Koi war was fought in 1919. Firestone came in 1928.
Hitler war was fought in 1939.
War broke out (Talah) in 1942.
Chief Mana died in Gendema in 1872.
Kaamo Alihaji died in Failoh 1937.
Kaamo Boakai Kiawu died in 1958.
Kibaa died in 1927.
Freedom came about across the river in 1928.
The locusts came in 1930.
The freeing of the slaves came about in the same year.

Example 2: A History of the Settlement of Wuilo

This is a history on this side. Our great-great-grandfather's name was Bai Zina. He married two wives; and these are their names. Grandma Bolowu Gbese and grandma Gasa Mgbofo. Grandma Bolowu Gbese bore the following children by grandpa Bai Zina.

1. Grandpa Bile Siyaa
2. Grandpa Bai Tapuvu
3. Grandpa Wusumani
4. Grandpa Jaa-Bgana
5. Grandpa Tawe
6. Grandpa Kai Kpale

These are grandma Gasa Mgbofo's own.

1. Mama (grandma) Kona
2. Mama (grandma) Fatimata
3. Mama Fata

4. Mama Guwa-Nyamagbe
5. Mama Koba

These are grandpa Bai Zina's brothers.

1. Grandpa Fah-Sandaa
2. Grandpa Yowu Ngowo

Grandpa Sandaa was the one that bore grandpa Sasi, grandpa Fole Bila, and grandpa Ja Siafa.

This is the history about the coming of our great grandfathers. Grandpa Kohule-paa and grandpa pa-Kpomgbo were the ones that immigrated, but they brought war into this country. They were Gbandi people. When they started their journey, they began with war. When they came they landed at a place called Ngali-Nga. Grandpa Kohule-paa was the elder and grandpa pa-Kpomgbo was the younger brother. However, both of them were war heroes. But no matter what you do, your elder can treat you just like a small boy. While they were in Ngali-Nga grandpa Kohule-paa often told his brother that he was indolent. At that point, grandpa pa-Kpomgbo told his brother, "I want to go across the river to settle there. When I settle there, no man will ever pass by me to bring war to you. There I will be and make my (rice) swamp." His brother then agreed. When he came, the first place that he settled was Bo near the river. He left there and came to Sawoi, from Sawoi they settled at Suhe, from Suhe they settled at Wuilo. They were in Sawoi for a long time, but the water problem was very difficult there. One day grandpa pa-Kpomgbo's hunter went in the bush to hunt. He reached the waterfall, and stepped up to one of the largest rocks. He sat down on that rock and rested. He then went down the river and came to a place that was all rocky ground. He went on for a long distance and reached to a junction—where the river branched out. He then left the main river and followed the branch. He went up to its source. He then went inside the bush, making a trail until he again reached to the water-fall and the same place where he sat on the rock in the morning. He said, "This is the same place where I got to this morning." There he stopped and went back to Sawoi. When evening time arrived he told grandpa pa-Kpomgbo; he said, "The place that I saw today is good for building a town because the place is surrounded by water. And also, there is a waterfall there near the river." When morning came grandpa pa-Komgbo gathered together his warriors. He then told them his hunter had said that he had seen a certain place that was good for a settlement. "Water problem is not hard there at all," he said. "Therefore, let us go there and see." They went there and saw the place. The place was good for a settlement, and they built a camp there. They sat and picked out a place to brush. They brushed the place. The place where grandpa sat is where our foundation stone is now today. He then said, "The name of this place is Wuilo."

Example 3: A Moral Parable

This is a story about a chief and his two children. One day during the dry season, the chief told his son to go to the farm and bring home some firewood. The boy got up, took his cutlass, and went to find the firewood for his father.

As the son was preparing to leave, his young brother got up to follow him. But the old chief said, "Don't take that boy with you; if you do, I will beat you when you return."

"OK, pa," the boy said to the chief. But when the older boy was walking along the path, the younger son began to follow him. The older son did not send the younger son home, but allowed him to follow along.

The boy and his younger brother walked a long distance from the town to an old farmsite. They began collecting firewood. While the older boy was gathering the wood into a bundle to tie it, a snake came out of the bark of an old log and bit the little boy, who died. The older boy let the wood drop and fell to the ground, crying. He cried and cried and cried; "My father told me today not to let this boy come with me to collect wood." At this time he became very frightened, not only because his brother had died, but at the thought of what his father would do when he returned home.

The snake had not moved. He was not dead, but lay still on the ground. At last the boy turned to look at the snake. He said to it, "Look, snake, my father told me today not to bring this boy with me. He said he will beat me if I do. And now you, snake, have bitten him and killed him on account of me."

The snake just lay quietly beside the log while the boy talked to it.

"You, snake," the boy said. "Please, I beg you, bring this little boy back to life so that I may take him back to town with me."

The snake still lay motionless, but he was not dead.

"You may come with us to town and you can bite him there in the presence of my father, the chief. That way he will not beat me," the boy suggested.

The snake agreed to bring back the younger boy's life. He brought some medicine and wrapped the little boy in it. The little boy came back to life and the two boys started for home. The older boy carried the wood and the snake followed along behind, because it was part of their agreement. As soon as they arrived in the town, the older boy put down the wood and the snake bit the younger boy, killing him once again. Everybody in the town was shocked by this terrible deed and they all began to mourn.

While the people were mourning, one old man came. "Stop crying," he told the people. "Let's find out if anything strange happened while these two boys were at the farm collecting wood." All the people stopped to listen, and the older boy reported all that had happened on the farm.

When the boy was through reporting, the old man said to the snake, "You, snake, take a took at me and then look at this young child (referring to the older brother). See how young he is." The old man thought for a while, and then he said to the snake, "This little boy asked you a favor and you complied and you made a bargain with him; all the more reason you should do so with me. As old as I am, with my head white, let me make a bargain. Do what I am going to ask of you. You listened to a small child, you should therefore listen to me. Please, I beg you, heal this little child for me and bring him back to life as you did before."

The old man made no bargain, but the snake once again stretched itself out and brought forth medicine to put on the dead little boy; the little boy woke up and sneezed—he had come back to life.

* * * *

And so, anybody who listens to a child should also be expected to listen to the elders. You should respect what the elders say and not let them be ashamed.

What impresses us about these Vai books is their strongly personal flavor. Like diaries that are a part of our literate tradition, the Vai book is generally intended for the writer himself. But there are certain times when parts of the Vai diaries, unlike ours, are brought into a public discussion. Mambu Paasewe reported to us that on occasions when the town elders felt that their young folk were becoming unruly, he would give a public reading of the moral tale we have included here and of similar stories. One of us witnessed another occasion in which a dispute arose over an event many years in the past; a Vai script literate who had recorded the event brought out his book to demonstrate his record of the proceedings; and that record was considered definitive.

These relatively rare occasions notwithstanding, Vai books, including those containing literary contents, are not intended for general distribution. They are a private affair, compiled by individuals for their own use and pleasure, and for that of their close friends and kin. Vai books are not used as a part of the process of teaching Vai script, nor are they produced in any quantity. The few exceptions to this generalization occur, significantly, among people who are close to the Americo-Liberian culture that dominates the capital city of Monrovia and that uses formal schooling in English as its literate base. Thus, we found multiple copies of biblical stories translated into Vai, occasional government posters advocating a policy or candidate for public office, and a section of a newsletter produced by the YMCA office in Robertsport devoted to local news, all written in the script.

The category of writing activities that we have labeled "religious" might be considered literature, except that it consists almost entirely of using the Vai script to represent Arabic verses from the Qur'an. We encountered cases where the Qur'an was represented phonetically (which allowed the copier to recite prayers and memorize them) as well as cases where a biliterate who knew the meaning of a verse in Arabic, or a monoliterate in Vai script who had access to a translator, wrote a translation of the meaning of a verse. We also collected examples of instructions for proper religious observances.

Almost everyone felt that knowing the Vai script was useful in one or more ways, as indicated in Table 6.5. Vai literates are often called on to write for others and to read letters for others, mechanisms by which literacy is spread throughout the community. Conducting one's personal affairs is the leading advantage claimed for literacy by most informants, consistent with everything we have said about the practice of Vai script thus far. Some people, alluding to the use of Vai script for conducting business transactions at a distance, point to making money as another worthwhile outcome of script knowledge. Direct usefulness in work is a surprisingly low-frequency justification for learning the script, but it is possible that the question was narrowly construed. Virtually everyone engaged in a craft who knows the script uses it for work-related purposes, even if in minimal ways.

Using Arabic

The first major contrast between uses of Vai and Arabic is discernible in the first line of Table 6.3: letter writing is an activity engaged in by only a minority of Arabic literates. This observation is consistent with our asser-

Table 6.5 Advantages of literacy (responses to question, "Has knowing (Vai, Arabic, English) script helped you?")

Script	Percentage giving this reason[a]
Vai script	
Keeping track of own affairs (privacy)	89
Money	16
Job	6
Help to others	14
Arabic	
Prayers	66
Money	36
Future life	31
Morals	10
Prosperity	8
English	
Write letters	70
Job	45
Prosperity	11
Speak better English	16

a. Based on duplicated count. Informants often gave more than one reason.

tion that for most informants in our sample "Qur'anic" is a more appropriate description of their literate activities than "Arabic," but some know enough Arabic to correspond in it. (Those who write letters all had reading scores of 3 or 4 on our reading test.) Unfortunately, we were not able to collect enough letters in Arabic to ascertain the nature of this correspondence, so we cannot contrast its contents with those of our extensive collection of Vai script letters. People's reluctance to show us letters in Arabic contrasts with their relative willingness to give us letters in Vai script, leading us to suspect that Arabic letters involved matters of secrecy.

Among those who know how to read and write, almost all keep family records. From inspection of several such records we know that they consist mostly of the listing of important dates: births, deaths, and marriages. In fact, many Vai books contain entries in Arabic for these events if the book's author is also an Arabic literate. Financial records are less important than in Vai script, but religious uses are universally practiced. In virtually all cases this category refers to writing out prayers.

In two respects Arabic makes possible activities that are not generally undertaken as a result of Vai script literacy. An Arabic teacher in a more formal, larger school can earn a living from a combination of money paid for teaching and the labor that students provide on his rice farm. Many Arabic literates also expound on Muslim law and belief, to which various practices, referred to in Liberian English as "Muslim medicine," are added. A Muslim doctor is generally considered a wise man who can give good advice and set people straight if they are having difficulties. This advice may be similar to what we would consider appropriate to a priest or a rabbi, but the practitioner is also often called upon to discover facts about the world, past and present, practices that could be glossed as occult. A Muslim doctor might be asked, for example, to help determine the best place to begin a new farm or to help convince a reluctant girl to marry a supplicant. Practitioners make small charms, usually containing a fragment of the Qur'an, which can be found in almost any house in Vai country above the front door; other charms are used on the farm or are carried on the person.

Some Arabic scholars are to be found in upcountry towns where they carry on an active intellectual life, teaching and studying Islamic religious, legal, and other kinds of texts. A few have extensive libraries with Arabic dictionaries, histories, and general science texts as well as theological works. From time to time these scholars will travel over the countryside to visit with each other and engage in textual commentary and disputation. Thus, Arabic literacy relates individuals to text on both the "lowest" (repetition without comprehension) and "highest" (analysis of textual meaning) levels—but the lowest levels predominate for the overwhelming majority of Arabic literates among the Vai.

Comparing Vai and Arabic Script Uses

Among biliterates, especially those with a reasonably high level of reading skill, we can get a direct look at the division of labor accomplished by differential use of Vai and Arabic scripts. Sixteen biliterates in our major survey had reading scores of 3 or 4 on both scripts. For these people we found that nine used both Vai and Arabic in their letter writing and record keeping, but that if one script dominated in these activities, it was always Vai. The opposite was true for religious uses: seven people used both Vai script and Arabic for religious matters, but in the nine cases in which the individual used only one of the scripts, it was Arabic. Here we see an intrapersonal division of labor corresponding to the social division of labor we have reported, Vai script literacy dominating in practical matters and Arabic literacy in religious matters. But the separation is by no means complete. Special studies of Arabic literacy, an enterprise we were not in a position to undertake, would have been necessary to tell us more about the practical applications of Arabic.

A fascinating feature of the multilingual, multiscript configuration is that different scripts are not only deployed for different functions but are sometimes deployed across languages as well (see Table 6.3). About one-fifth of Arabic and English literates, but better than one-half of Vai script literates, reported that they used their script knowledge to write another language. The Arabic alphabet was used almost entirely to represent the Vai language—in most cases, to transcribe prayers. Literacy in the vernacular (Vai) script had the greatest range and flexibility; practically everyone had tried his hand at rendering English in the script and nearly as many had used it for Arabic. It is unlikely that these cross-language script uses are particularly varied. We know that the Arabic rendered in Vai script consists primarily of prayers or other religious items; we suspect that the English is heavily represented by nontext uses (places or person names, for example). Nonetheless, the use of a vernacular script in this way suggests a high level of sophistication with respect to the sound-representational rules of the Vai writing system in addition to the pleasure literates take in playing around with writing. It suggests as well that the potential social and educational functions of literacy in an indigenous script may be greater than they at first appear.

Using English Literacy

In view of the implicit and explicit contrasts we have made between Vai script literacy and English literacy (the latter being the official language of the country, government, and commerce), one might expect that uses of English would contrast strongly with those of the indigenous script. For example, English literates might engage in more letter writing to strangers, since they would be able to conduct business with non-Vai readers, and legal record keeping might be more prevalent. We would also expect a greater production of textual material from those who, in the course of schooling, were exposed to a wide variety of narrative and didactic material.

Interview findings, however, disappoint these expectations. Uses of English literacy, especially in the countryside, are very similar to those of Vai script literacy; letter writing and record keeping that focus on family and business affairs are the most prominent activities. To be sure, English literates are less likely to record town business and more likely to report that knowing the English alphabet helps them with their work. But similarities in the functions of the two scripts overshadow the differences.

Such similarity is not a superficial result of tallying noncomparable answers to noncomparable survey questions. Mike Smith, who lived in Gohn and acquired information through observation and personal conversations as well as interviews, reported that all English literates in town corresponded regularly with friends. One man wrote about twice a week to friends and relatives in distant towns and in other parts of Vai country. This same person also wrote once to a government official asking for a job. The other English literates in town carried on similar correspondence. All of the English literates in Gohn kept records which, like Vai script records, noted births and deaths of family members, money owed by and to various people, goods ordered from Monrovia, and even contributions to a traditional funeral feast. One of Gohn's English literates kept a diary whose contents were identical in kind to those of the diary we excerpted in our discussion of Vai script literacy. The principal, and by no means trivial, difference between English and Vai script literates is availability of reading material from newspapers, books, and magazines brought upcountry from Monrovia. The world at large can be found in the homes of English literate Vai people, at least as the world is reflected through the pages of *Time, Newsweek,* and the *Liberian Star.*

The reason for the rather close match between Vai and English uses is to be found in the nature of our sample of English literates—particularly the level of schooling they achieved, the occupations they engaged in, and their geographical location. The majority of English literates in our major survey were traditional upcountry Vai people who had less than a junior high school level of education. Even those living in Monrovia were not living in a dispersed downtown area or the more affluent suburbs—they resided in the Vai quarter where the routines of domestic life are very much like those upcountry. (Cooking is generally done in a separate building on a wood or charcoal fire, electricity is rare or nonexistent, extended family networks share "quarters" of the district, an area chief has nominal authority, and so on.) Perhaps most important, the level of schooling attained by these men, although sufficient to teach them how to read and write, had not secured them jobs in the technological/bureaucratic sector of the Liberian economy. On the average they were more likely to have engaged in jobs in the modern sector of the economy, but they did not hold high positions and rarely had continuous enough employment to keep them in the capital; as a result, we encountered English literates engaged in rice farming in the interior. For these people, English literacy seems to function in a manner similar to Vai literacy.

This is not to say that written English in its capacity as the official national literacy does not penetrate to the village level. It does, but for the average person this penetration comes in the form of a few government circulars which one of the English literates in town is likely to read and interpret for other townspeople or in letters from friends and relatives. Official uses of English affect very few people directly in their status as English literates.

SUMMARY

It is apparent that Vai people have developed highly diversified uses for writing, and that a host of pragmatic, ideological, and intellectual factors sustain popular literacy. As in other multiliterate societies, the primary functions of literacy tend to be distributed in regularly patterned ways

Table 6.6 Characteristics of literacies

Characteristic	Vai script	Arabic	English
Script	Syllabary	Alphabet	Alphabet
Language	Native	Foreign	Foreign
Teacher-student	Personally selected, one to one	Family selected, group	Assigned by school location
Dominant teaching method	Decoding-encoding	Memorization	Decoding-encoding
Social context	Home and every-day settings	"Class" setting	Class in orga-nized school
Related knowledge transmitted	No systematic knowledge trans-mission	Religious knowl-edge—Islam	Systematic secu-lar subject mat-ter
Cultural orientation	Traditional	Traditional	Modern

across the scripts. Each script not only has its own central functions, but represents a different language, involves a different writing system, and presents would-be literates with a different course of study. We have summarized these distinctive features in Table 6.6. As the table demonstrates, the literacy we came to study among the Vai people turned out to be pluralistic in form and highly varied in its uses and combinations.

In spite of the many functions the three scripts serve, certain literacy activities that occupy a central place in our own and other industrial societies are not prominent among the Vai. With the exception of a small number of Arabic scholars and secondary English school literates, literacy rarely leads to acquisition of new bodies of knowledge. At the same time, traditional (non-Islamic) institutions continue to function without reliance on the written word or transmission of culturally valued information through textual means. These restrictions on the role of literacy among the Vai should be kept in mind when we test hypotheses about its intellectual consequences.

7

Social Correlates of Literacy

As a result of the first two years of work we had gathered information about the personal attributes, social roles, and everyday activities of the Vai people from many different sources.

The primary source was the questionnaire that we call the demographic survey; another was the ethnographic record made by Mike Smith during his extended stays in Vai country. These two classes of information were unusually well linked in our research. In a departure from orthodox ethnographic inquiry, Smith's descriptions were initially guided by the interviews conducted in and around (but not restricted to) the questions in our survey. He found the questionnaire a useful way to elicit and organize information about the histories and current lives of the people among whom he lived. Conversely, we found Smith's familiarity with the people and their culture an important resource in interpreting the survey responses. We will first feature the quantitative results of the survey, but as the exposition unfolds, we will turn to the ethnographic information to supplement the statistical analysis. Our task is made easier by the convergence of the two approaches: the description of Vai literates that emerges from our counting operations is the same in all essential respects as the picture that emerges from our observational records.

BACKGROUND CHARACTERISTICS

A tabulation of questionnaire responses provides a useful starting point for our examination of life experiences associated with each kind of literacy. Since all but a handful of literates are men, our discussion of survey outcomes is based on analyses performed on a population of 290 male respondents. We have divided this population into five comparison groups according to literacy status: nonliterates, Vai script monoliterates, Arabic monoliterates, Vai script–Arabic biliterates, and English schooled. Literacy status is determined here by affirmative answers to survey questions about reading and writing knowledge. Our description is selective and is intended to draw attention to differences in life experience associated with literacy and to those dimensions of living that are of special theoretical interest.

Age and family status. Our suspicion that there might be large age differences among literacy groups was confirmed. Average age of nonliterates is close to that of the population as a whole, but the respective literacy groups are nonrepresentative. Vai script monoliterates are older than all other groups, underrepresented in youngest age brackets and overrepresented in the fifty-year-plus range. English literates are concentrated in the under-twenty group, reflecting the recently increased availability of English schooling and the student status of many; Arabic monoliterates are the next youngest group and also include a number of Qur'anic students still with their teachers. Since our survey procedures called for exhaustive interviewing of all literates in the survey towns, these age differences cannot be the result of a sampling bias. Other evidence shows that they reflect the differential patterns of transmission of each of the literacies, English and Arabic being acquired in childhood and youth and Vai script customarily being acquired in adulthood.

Head-of-household status is claimed by 37 percent of the sample. But 58 percent of Vai script monoliterates and 64 percent of Vai-Arabic biliterates report this high-status position. We might suspect that status is merely a byproduct of an age differential; older men have more of an opportunity to achieve it. Multiple regression techniques permit us to test this hypothesis, since they allow the analyst to hold certain factors constant (such as age, in this instance) and determine whether other factors make independent contributions to the variable of interest. Applying these techniques, we find that Vai script literacy contributes to the probability of being head of household, in addition to and independently of age. Becoming literate in Vai script is an act of personal choice, and, as we have seen, a learning activity that is typically undertaken in adulthood. Mike Smith saw the association between script knowledge and family status in this way: "Becoming literate . . . is a sign of one's respect for Vai leaders, language, and history. It's no accident that a lot of men decide to learn the Vai script just as they're settling down permanently, taking on a farm, raising a family, making known their voice in communal affairs."

Occupations. A useful introduction to a review of occupational status and its possible relationship to literacy is provided by Lévi-Strauss's remark (1966) that in traditional communities men must be *bricoleurs*—jacks-of-all-trade. A person's principal activity is not necessarily captured by the title of his major subsistence-producing enterprise. Mike Smith observed: "To say 'I am an accountant' tells one more about an American than the hypothetical equivalent 'I am a farmer' would tell about a Vai person. Actually, one does not say in Vai, 'I am a farmer,' although this is grammatically possible. Instead, a Vai person would say 'I make farm,' this convention signify-ing that the person is not thereby excluded from pursuing a number of other occupations at the same time." A majority of people in our survey re-ported more than one occupational activity (town chief plus Qur'anic teacher plus farmer, for example).

Survey results portray a society in which the principal activity is still farming, although diversification and upgrading of job skills is now in progress (as skill is conventionally measured; we used the U.S. Census of Occupations and the Liberian Census). The relationship of literacy to pro-duction role can be summed up in the generalization that literates are less likely than nonliterates to be subsistence rice farmers only. More of them work in the crafts and other occupations; when engaged in farming they are more likely to get some cash from it. Each literacy group, however, re-veals its own characteristic occupational pattern. The English literate group is the only one in which the majority depend on paid work rather than farm income for their living. Vai script literates often combine farm-ing with the practice of a craft, and 40 percent report that at some time they served an apprenticeship to a master artisan. Principal crafts in Vai country are, in order of frequency, carpentry, masonry, and tailoring; car-pentry and tailoring are sometimes practiced by the same individual, con-currently or sequentially. Arabic monoliterates, in contrast, are an identifi-able cluster in what we have called "traditional professions"—Muslim doctor, Muslim teacher, town chief.

As we have seen, literacy is useful in craft occupations and instrumental in certain lines of Muslim practice. Leaving aside those vocations requiring some knowledge of the Qur'an or Arabic alphabet, the overrepresentation of nonschooled literates in cash-producing activities is of more than passing interest, especially with respect to Vai script. It seems plausible that men with some script knowledge should be attracted to engage in market activi-ties or to enter the crafts; it is equally plausible, however, that those already in such pursuits might decide to learn how to read or write to maximize their gains. We have no evidence allowing us to make inferences about the direction of influence, but simply as a pairing of facts, the association be-tween occupational diversity and Vai script literacy has general implica-tions. Occupational choice and skill level are known to be strongly related to English schooling in many developing countries; whether literacy skills per se are associated with special occupational patterns has not been empir-ically investigated, although the expectation that literacy education will lead to economic advancement has motivated a number of government-sponsored mass literacy programs (Hunter and Harman, 1979).

Some sixty-odd principal occupations named by respondents in the sur-vey were submitted to a panel of ten Vai informants who were asked to rate them as "traditional" (activities engaged in by Vai people in olden days as well as today, such as weaving); "transitional" (traditional occupations carried out with modern means, such as carpentry); or "modern" (jobs introduced by imported technology with no antecedents in the culture, such as automobile driving). Resulting ratings were applied to survey responses. Nonliterates, Arabic monoliterates, and biliterates cluster in traditional occupations; Vai script literates in transitional occupations; and English literates in modern occupations.

Language knowledge. Monolingualism among the Vai, as among West African people generally, is virtually nonexistent. Of those men who speak more than one language, a majority speak more than two. An interesting feature of the distribution of language knowledge is the extent to which all groups, including nonliterates, report some ability to speak English. English is the lingua franca in Monrovia and other large towns, and some English phrases or expressions are commonly heard even in remote hamlets. Biliterates and English literates show some superiority in number of languages spoken, the latter group reporting English more often than others (a natural concomitant of their having participated in formal instruction in English as a foreign language in school); in contrast, biliterates' language skills are concentrated in other African languages.

Residences and mobility. In a stereotypical view of the West African countryside, it appears as jungle or bush, dotted with isolated communites whose residents' world is bounded by hometown horizons. The history of the migrating Vai makes us skeptical that such a characterization was ever applicable to their society, and Mike Smith reported that a hallmark of contemporary village life is the constant undertaking of journeys and visits, from an hour or two to months or years in length; at least two or three people arrive or depart every day, often many more.

Such constant migrations and movements are reflected in survey residence and travel statistics. Almost all our respondents had lived outside their hometowns at one time or another. This fact is not antithetical to stability or integration in a single town. Vai script literates show at least the same level of multiple residence as the rest of the population, but their long-term residency in a single town is much greater than that of other groups. Two-thirds of them report having lived twenty years or more in the town in which we met them. Is this simply a matter of Vai script literates' more advanced age? For the population of Gohn, Smith was able to calculate the length of time each adult spent there as a proportion of his life span. He concluded that Vai script literates spend proportionately more of their lives in their home areas than Arabic and English literates, who travel, among other possible reasons, to pursue their learning.

Tallies of number of trips within the year appear to support the propensity of Arabic literates to travel as compared with Vai script literates; for sheer frequency of trip taking, however, nonliterate men prove the most peripatetic—71 percent report trips several times a month.

Among a people generally on the move, meaningful distinctions are likely to be found in the occasions for travel and places reached, rather than in the mere fact that trips are made. A first trip to the capital city of Monrovia for a small-town farmer undoubtedly has a different psychological impact from a trip made by a tailor who has negotiated Monrovia since he was twelve and has been back and forth dozens of times. Upcountry travel often covers well-worn routes and is generally undertaken for mundane purposes. In his summary of his second trip to Vai country, Mike Smith reported:

> Altogether 73 percent of our sample population [in Gohn] have traveled only on the routes of heaviest population movement in Liberia . . . Usually they go to visit relations, to go shopping or to work. Sometimes it's young people simply traveling around "to see the area" as their counterparts hitch about Europe and the U.S.

However, some journeys are rather special:

> One Arabic-only literate went with his Qur'anic teacher to Freetown [Sierra Leone] for a few days, while three women went to visit relatives in the eastern part of Sierra Leone . . . Vaanii Z. spent two and a half years helping to survey the Liberian-Guinea boundary in 1928–31.

And some spectacular:

> Chief Boakai sailed as a deckhand on an Italian freighter in the West African coastal trade for six months in the 1920s and traveled as far as Lagos. Momo G. toured the then Belgian Congo for two months with his paternal uncle; Bendu, the only literate woman in the town, spent nine months in the capital of Mali, visiting her mother; and Alihaji has, as his title indicates, made the *hajj* [pilgrimage] to Mecca.

Thus, a general concept such as "mobility" will not be useful for following up hypotheses about effects of experience on cognition. Indices such as "size of place furthest traveled" or "purpose of travel" will provide the richest information. According to our interviews, much of the going and coming is in the service of family business (illness, celebration). Traveling for work-related purposes is undertaken by all groups, but least by Vai-Arabic and English literates; in contrast, English literates and Arabic literates are the only groups reporting travel for educational purposes.

One aspect of residence and travel history of special theoretical interest is the extent of urban experience, linked in many sociological theories with higher rates of literacy, and in some psychological theorizing with higher levels of thinking (Lerner, 1958). Except for English literates forced to move to larger towns to secure postprimary schooling or jobs in the modern sector, literate and nonliterate groups do not appear to differ in extent of urban experience. Similarly, exposure to life in a foreign-run mining or plantation enclave is approximately the same for all male groups except Arabic monoliterates, among whom a number, at the time of the survey, were still studying Qur'an with local teachers.

Beliefs and attitudes: traditionalism. We turn now from practical affairs of living to ideology, and examine whether attitudes and beliefs vary systematically with knowledge of any script. Early in the survey we found almost everyone reporting their adherence to Islam (some mission-educated Vai are practicing Christians but few in the countryside avowed it), and we therefore dropped a question about religious affiliation. On a question probing belief in water people, opinion was divided. Nonliterate, Arabic monoliterate, and biliterate groups split evenly for and against belief in water people. English literates, reflecting either skepticism in the old lore or greater circumspection in the interview situation, voted nonbelief in a 6:4 ratio. Vai script monoliterates composed the only group breaking the pattern, with an overwhelming affirmation of belief in water people.

Almost everyone reported having been to bush schools of the Poro and Sande societies, with somewhat lower proportions of initiates among English and Arabic monoliterates. A question with more discriminating power is whether or not the respondent played a special role in bush school, an allusion to functions within the secret societies carried out by individuals especially knowledgeable in rituals and traditional practices. Vai script monoliterates again stand out as a group in the greater frequency with which they acknowledge such roles. Questions of causal direction are tantalizing but unanswerable with the information on hand: Do special roles call on literacy knowledge, suggesting that Vai script may have certain functions in bush school, or is the relationship a manifestation of the greater all-around integration of Vai script literates into the traditional culture?

In each survey town, respondents were asked to identify "elders"—respected individuals who constitute something like a council of advisers to the chief. High agreement about the identity of these people enabled us to assign elder status to individual respondents in our survey. A greater proportion of elders was found among Vai script monoliterates than among any other subgroup of the population.

Beliefs and attitudes: modernity questions. Just as observations and survey data reveal constant movement in a population often depicted as stationary, replies and comments on modernity questions show a variety of opinions flourishing within established communities, covering the spectrum from traditional to modern.

We analyzed determinants of modernity in terms of three subsets of questions. One set was treated as a modified short form of the modernity scale and was scored by the conventional method developed by the scale's designers. A question probing knowledge of the location of three major cities was analyzed separately because it alone could be said to have a correct answer based on fact instead of opinion. We also separated out for special analysis a question referring to religious affiliation, which we knew to

Table 7.1 Performance measures, modernity questions (major survey respondents)[a]

	Overall modernity (12-question short form)	Location knowledge score	Religious attitude score
Nonliterate	17.7	1.2	1.5
Arabic monoliterate	17.2	1.0	1.3
Vai script monoliterate	18.7	1.3	1.3
Vai-Arabic biliterate	19.1	1.5	1.3
English schooled	19.8	1.9	1.3

a. If all questions were given modern replies, total scores would be as follows: 12-question short form, 24; location knowledge score, 3; religious attitude score, 2.

be an issue of special relevance to the Vai; their Muslim faith might be thought to predispose them to be disdainful of nonbelievers.

Table 7.1, which displays average response scores for these question classes, suggests a modernizing effect of English schooling and some possible influence of Vai script literacy. Because of our theoretical interest in sociological theories of modernity, we decided to test these apparent differences by multiple regression techniques in order to identify specific experiences contributing to increased modernity. We explain these techniques and our use of them in Chapter 8. We will discuss results separately for each performance measure.

Modernity scale. Scores were predicted by two classes of variables. First were factors associated with schooling—how far a person went in school (last grade completed) and competency in reading English (score on English reading test), each of which contributed independently to increased modernity.[1] Second were factors associated with literacy in Vai and Arabic scripts. Greater proficiency in Vai script (Vai reading score) and being biliterate boosted modernity scores, while a Qur'anic school variable (years studying Qur'an) depressed them. We did not secure a significant effect of urbanization, an important component of modernity according to Lerner's original conceptual model (1958). There was some indication that the number of years a person had lived in larger towns affected modernity when we considered only the simple correlations, but the relationship was weak compared with effects of schooling. Schooling and residence in larger towns were correlated in our sample, and the outcome of the regression analysis suggests that schooling rather than urban experience mediated modern attitudes.

Overall modernity = 17.8 + .30 Vai script reading score + .19 last grade
$(R^2 = .22)$ (3.5)   (2.7)
          + .38 English reading score − 1.25 in school now
                (2.3)   (2.5)
          + 1.0 biliterate − .12 years Qur'an
             (2.3)   (2.6)

Knowledge of locations. When we turn to question 13, the information question, schooling's effect is attenuated. Ability to speak English is a stronger predictor than last grade in school. English reading score (presumably a reflection of school experience) makes an independent contribution to knowledge. Number of years of urban living exerts a direct and positive effect over and above the other factors. The contribution of number of spouses is more difficult to interpret; we can only speculate that access to information made possible by a knowledge of English is associated with resources that may permit travel or purchase of a radio.

Location knowledge = .83 + .41 speak English + .14 English reading score
$(R^2 = .21)$ (4.3)   (3.7)
          + .12 number spouses + .04 years urban living
             (2.9)   (2.8)

Religious attitude. Since the Vai are Muslim and were converted to reform sects within Islam, we were interested in their opinions about the possibility of a nonbeliever being a good person despite his lack of faith. The average group scores in Table 7.1 indicate that there was little variation in response to this question, and the outcome of the regression equation confirmed that scores were only weakly related to demographic variables: Vai script monoliteracy, years studying Qur'an, and prior status as a school student each contributed small decrements to modernity of response, whereas extent of urban living was positively related to a modern answer.

Modern religious attitude = 1.39 + .02 years urban living
$(R^2 = .06)$ (2.5)
          − .21 in school before − .03 years Qur'an
             (2.7)   (2.9)
          − .18 Vai script monoliteracy
             (2.5)

Thus, our results tend to confirm findings in earlier studies (Inkeles, 1973) that English schooling is an important determinant of modern attitudes, and that urban experience is related to knowledge of the larger world and to open-mindedness about religion. They give a mixed message with respect to the more general hypothesis that literacy per se functions as a modernizing influence. Learning associated with mastery of the Qur'an and achievement of Arabic literacy appears on the whole to be a retarding influence, while Vai script literacy exerts a modest positive influence on modern attitudes. Before we restate these results in the general form "Vai script literacy is related to modernity," we need to remember that we have also found Vai script literacy to be associated with traditional beliefs and roles as well. Tradition as tapped in our questionnaire and modernity as measured in this internationally used scale do not emerge as opposites, an outcome with intriguing implications for theories of both social and psychological change.

FACTOR ANALYSIS

Comparative data on age, urban residence, and other background characteristics are useful in highlighting commonalities and differences in life experiences associated with each kind of literacy. But this average picture, taken one variable at a time, yields no more than an unconnected set of facts about each literacy; it does not reveal whether particular experiences or social attributes go together in patterned ways and whether certain patterns distinguish literates from nonliterates, or one literacy group from another. The idea that culture represents patterned configurations of experience is central to all modern studies of society, and since we set out to examine the impact of culturally organized activities on thought we could not rest with a simple listing of disconnected attributes. We therefore turned to factor analysis to help us identify possible underlying patterns in Vai social organizations, and to determine their relationship to literacy.

We were concerned with patterns of relationship for still another reason. We planned to test causal hypotheses about literacy's influence on cognition, and in this enterprise we confronted an analytic problem that bedevils all social science research. Insofar as literacy might vary with other life experiences, how are we to know—if we should find that literate and nonliterate groups differ with respect to a cognitive performance—that a specific literacy experience, and not some other associated experience, underlies the difference? Suppose, for example, that we found English literates applying a different classification scheme to the grouping of objects than others. It could be plausibly argued on the basis of earlier research that classification strategies are influenced by experience in modern occupational activities (Scribner, 1974; Luria, 1976); if schooling and these activities go together in Vai life, we would need to take special steps in our analysis to control for occupational differences in order to assert that it is English schooling, and not occupation, that affects classification performance.

We also have to be concerned with covariation resulting from selection of certain individuals into one of the literacy groups. In our society, for example, success in school is correlated with performance on intelligence tests, a fact that has led some social scientists to argue that students in the higher grades of school in developing countries have been "selected" by their higher IQ. If this were true, differences in performance between college students and those in lower grades, or individuals with no schooling at all, could not be attributed solely to experiences the college students had encountered in school, without taking into account possible preexisting differences in scholastic ability.

Selection problems that produce covariation are not completely solvable unless we set up an experiment in which we randomly assign individuals to groups (in this case, Vai people to literacy groups). That is a patently absurd idea. Instead, following in a long social science tradition, we attempted to evaluate the possible influence of literacy's covariates using the statistical techniques of factor analysis and multiple regression.

Although factor analysis is well grounded in statistical theory, it is not a problem-free technique. Its output—patterns of responses to questionnaire items—is dependent in the first instance on the particular items used as input. Our coding of questionnaire responses yielded a possible 180 items of information about each respondent. Some of these items were clearly uninformative either because everyone answered them in the same way, or because data were missing, or because they were almost completely redundant with other items. Our first task, therefore, was to select from this pool a set of useful items to enter into the analysis. A second problem with the factor analysis technique is describing what the output shows and interpreting its meaning. Factor analytic solutions yield information about patterns in the set of responses, but they do not simultaneously provide a set of rules for mapping those patterns back into the reality of everyday activities. Analogous problems arise in the conduct and interpretation of multiple regression analyses. We claim no special insight into the process of interpretation; rather, we have tried to be consistently conservative in our attribution of importance to factors that emerge from the analysis, selecting for further comment only those that seem to map clearly onto information gathered in the ethnographic part of our research.

We knew as we started this analysis that few women were literate, so we performed three separate analyses: one for the survey population as a whole (including women), one for men alone, and one for women alone. Although some details varied, comparisons of factor analyses for the three populations presented us with a consistent pattern. Because the all-male analysis brings literacy-related factors into the sharpest focus and is consistent with our method of presentation up to this point, we use this analysis as the basis for our discussion here.[2]

The factor solution produced thirteen factors or independent clusters of items accounting for nearly half of the variation (47 percent) in the survey responses (see Table 7.2). A feature of this method of analysis is that the first factors extracted from the data represent the most general relationships—whatever is most common among items—while later factors represent remaining "commonness" among these or other items resulting in more specific patterns. The first factors, therefore, are the most important

Table 7.2 Summary of Factor Analysis, demographic questionnaire (major survey)

Factor 1 *(Traditional status)* *(Vai script literacy)*		*Factor 2* *(Urbanization)*	
Head of house	.63	Town size	.82
Number of rooms in house	.51	Town road rating	.80
Age	.69	Birthplace	.33
Number of children	.82	Years lived in towns of 2,000+	.41
Number of children at home	.62	Years lived in towns of 10,000+	.45
Ever a farmer	.33	Modernity of occupation	.38
Ever married	.59	Occupational training	.36
Number of spouses	.76	Ever farmed	−.55
Number of houses	.70	Farmed last year	−.53
Number of children in school	.67	Total income	.71
Educational level of children	.54	Ever in bush school	−.32
Read Vai script	.62	Speak English	.33
Read Vai in alphabet	.42	Subsistence farmer	−.37
Who invented Vai script	.33	Income × town size	.88
Family boss in old days	.35		
Elder	.51		
Vai script reading score	.67		

Factor 3 *(English schooling)*		*Factor 4* *(Arabic literacy)*	
Ever work	.49	Traditional-professional	−.32
Modernity of occupation	−.38	Religious travel	−.34
Son-pa occupation compared	.34	Educational travel	−.47
Modernity of pa's occupation	−.39	Years Qur'an	−.65
Ever farmed	.39	Part Qur'an finished	−.76
Farmed last year	.39	Arabic reading score	−.80
Ever married	.38		
Who invented Vai script	−.34		
Speak English	−.34		
School status	−.78		
Last grade	−.84		
Pa schooling	−.37		
English reading score	−.70		

Table 7.2 (Continued)

Factor 5		Factor 6	
Tewo chiefdom	.61	Birthplace	.40
Years lived in towns of 2,000+	−.32	Kind of places lived	.56
Years lived in towns of 10,000+	−.35	Number of places lived	.78
Traditional-professional	.33	Ever live in a concession	.50
Size of farthest place of travel	−.33	Years lived in towns 2,000+	.55
Ever in bush school	.38	Years lived in towns 10,000+	.45
Number of tribal languages spo-		Gawula chiefdom	.31
ken	.40		
Gawula chiefdom	−.53		

Factor 7		Factor 8	
Birthplace	−.30	Tewo chiefdom	.42
Father's tribe	.55	Travel for family reasons	−.53
Mother's tribe	.46	Travel for work reasons	.51
Belief in water people	.31	Vai Koneh chiefdom	−.58
Read Vai script	.32		
Number of male relatives know-			
ing Vai script	.31		
Vai script reading score	.31		
Tombe chiefdom	.41		

Factor 9		Factor 10	
Skill rating	.58	Cash farming	.70
Years at skill rating ≥ 2	.74	Subsistence farming	−.80
Modernity of occupation	.37		
Occupational training	.68		
Son-pa occupation compared	.40		

Factor 11		Factor 12	
Size of farthest place traveled	−.43	Head of house	−.57
Years studied Qur'an	−.30	Number of people in house	−.69
Father studied Qur'an	−.61	Number of rooms in house	−.67
Brothers write Arabic	−.37	Vai Koneh chiefdom	−.30
Pa's script knowledge	−.38		

Factor 13	
Number of trips taken	.37
Special role in bush school	−.32
Know history of Vai script	−.42
Family boss in olden days	−.37
Family servants in olden days	−.40

in that they account for the largest proportion of shared variation. In our solution, the first four factors accounted for 28 percent of the total variation.

Before we describe the result of the factor analysis, our attention is drawn to an absence: there is no factor that includes all three types of literacy. "Literacy in general" does not emerge from this analysis as a dimension of Vai life. Each of the three literacies is represented on a different factor and there is no overlap among them.

The first factor (representing nearly half of all the variation in our data) is a Vai script–related factor, striking evidence of the importance of script knowledge in Vai life. We describe this factor as "status in the traditional culture." Variables contributing most heavily to this factor are those we had included as indicators of substance in the traditional economy—such material and human resources as numbers of houses, spouses, and children. Being head of household, having a larger house than others, carrying the socially prominent role of elder, and being a member of a family that was boss in olden days are all aspects of being a well-rooted, high-status up-country person. The discovery that Vai script literacy, not Arabic or English, is a component of traditional status arose in our ethnographic observations. Smith reported the greater involvement of Vai script literates in the life of Diaa, and described script literates in Gohn as "more solidly located within Vai country and culture." The factor analysis extends these observations to establish the rootedness of Vai script literates as a general feature of Vai society rather than one restricted to the social structure of selected communities.

Another interesting aspect of factor 1, linking traditional culture and Vai script literacy, is that knowledge of the reputed inventor of the script is represented here. Reading Vai in the English alphabet, an uncommon skill exclusive to a few men in the sample, is also represented. The traditionalist aspect of Vai script literacy is further specified in factor 7, the only other factor on which Vai script reading knowledge appears. Here, literacy in Vai script is prominent in families in which both father and mother were Vai (father's tribe, mother's tribe); it is associated with espousal of traditional beliefs (water people) and is centered in Tombe, a chiefdom historically associated with promulgation (and, some say, invention) of the script.

A more detailed analysis of groupings of variables on this factor draws attention to what at first appears an anomaly: traditional parents have more children attending nontraditional modern educational institutions (number of children in school). To determine whether this is an artifact of having larger families in general (number of children), we used multiple regression analysis to see what items on the factor would predict the number of school children if total number of children was held constant. Only one variable entered as a predictor: knowledge of Vai script. This outcome confirms our initial interpretation that nonschooled Vai script literates send a proportionately greater number of their children to school. But the factor itself gives only clues as to possible causes. Since English school costs money (and loss of child labor), one is tempted to consider the link between traditionalism and schooling to be affluence. This may be the case, if affluence is measured in terms of property (houses) and human resources (spouses). Cash wealth (total income), however, contributes to another factor in association with nonfarm occupations and urbanism. We believe that status may be a component of this factor, but that it is passed from generation to generation differently at different times. Long ago high status meant that others worked for you; then it was reflected in being the head of a large family and using the script; today it can also mean being educated in English schools. Mike Smith contributed an independent piece of information confirming the link between Vai script literacy and English schooling. In a census of all children attending the Diaa elementary government school he found that more children came from households in which there was a Vai script literate than would be expected from their proportion in the town population.

Factor 2 represents urbanization. Sociological theories notwithstanding, it is independent of and unrelated to literacy of any kind. This is a bipolar dimension represented at one end by rural traditional elements (farming for subsistence only; playing a special role in bush school) and at the other end by modern elements. Dominating the urban pole is the size and accessibility of the town the respondent is presently living in and total cash income. Long-term residence in cities is also featured, together with its expected accompaniments: more modern occupations, job training, and lack of participation in the agricultural sector (never farmed). Ethnographic accounts tracing individual careers suggest that living in the Vai section of Monrovia represents personal mobility rather than uprooting and relocation of older family generations. Consistent with this observation, we find only own-generation attributes and no family-related characteristics on this factor.

English schooling is the dominant item on factor 3. This again is a bipolar factor—at one end farming and the personal status attributes that go with this life activity; and at the other end, schooling, which, as we might anticipate, is related to earning a living in a modern occupation. Here intergenerational continuities reappear: a respondent's schooling is related to his father's having been in school. At the time of parental generations, access to English schooling was considerably more restricted than today. Those who succeeded in achieving some schooling often went on to occupy posts in administrative, military, and commerical organizations. This fact of history is represented by two other items on this factor: modernity of father's occupation and personal upward mobility (Son-pa occupation compared). Personal mobility is a measure of the respondent's occupational skill rating compared to that of his father and it is associated with the farming, nonschool end of the continuum. Here is another piece of evidence that men in our survey who had attended school had fathers of high skill status—they were following in father's footsteps, as it were, rather than changing their family's orientation and occupational pursuits.

An interesting story of different paths to English schooling emerges from a comparison of factor 1, featuring Vai script literacy, and factor 3, featuring school attendance. Imagine three generations: respondent, respondent's father, and respondent's children. On factor 3, a tiny handful of older generation men who succeeded in getting to and through English mission schools or schools in Monrovia set their sons (our respondents) on the same path; in another pattern of transmission (factor 1), families with no history of English schooling but investment in Vai script literacy in the present generation (our respondents) are now sending their children off to school to give them access to power in the modern economy. They are transmitting status in an acculturative way.

A similar pattern of continuity between parental literacy and school attendance emerged in Smith's work. He was able to map kinship structures and prepare a more complete family history for offspring in his residential towns than we could accomplish for the survey as a whole. Of total number of "born offspring" in Gohn, he determined who had been or were attending English schools and found that 70 percent of schooled children had at least one literate parent—largely English literates and Vai script monoliterates and biliterates. He attributed this association as much to parental attitude toward schooling—"parental encouragement"—as to availability of money resources.

Arabic literacy is represented on factor 4 both in terms of performance on our reading comprehension test and the educational experience which made it possible (years studied Qur'an and chapters completed). Travel for educational purposes and practice as a traditional professional (Qur'anic teacher, Muslim doctor) are also represented. Not shown is a marginally associated item—whether or not any of respondents' brothers write Arabic—which supplies a missing piece enabling us to conjecture that Arabic literacy, like the other two literacies in Vai society, is family-linked. No personal attributes or particular patterns of occupation or experience are linked to Arabic literacy, as opposed to either Vai script or English literacy; whatever the social patterning of Arabic literacy might be, our 180 questionnaire items failed to capture it.

Finally, occupational experience relates strongly only to schooling. Skill rating appeared with Vai script in factor 1 (traditional status) but was below our statistical criterion of significance, while it was a high-loading item on a nonliteracy related factor (factor 9); income and training appear in the urban constellation (factor 2), which also lacks a specific literacy element.

Remaining factors organize more specific clusters of items which supply interesting details but do not change the larger picture summarized here.

TWO PERSONAL ACCOUNTS

Our discussion of factors accompanying literacy has thus far relied on numbers. Two outstanding people—one literate in English, the other in Arabic—gave us a different way to think about the social context of literacy. Each was asked to narrate a personal life story, to tell us whatever they chose or thought would be of interest about themselves; comments about their educational experiences were not specifically requested but were offered as part of this general account.

Wokie Fahnbulleh

An extraordinary example of early schooling in English and its continued influence within a single family in a single area is provided by the autobiographical account of Victoria Wokie Fahnbulleh, who was the school teacher in Diaa during the period in which members of our project were guests in Cape Mount County. Wokie Fahnbulleh's story begins with her mother Victoria Kinii, the oldest inhabitant of Diaa, where Mike Smith worked in 1974 and again in 1976–1977. At the time of our earliest visits, Victoria Kinii Fahnbulleh was ninety years old, a frail and venerable old lady whose children were counted among the most influential people in the area.

The elder Victoria had been born in 1884, in a small hamlet a few miles away from the town of Diaa near the Mano River, which now separates Liberia and Sierra Leone. When she was a young girl, the Vai were almost constantly warring with the people around them, towns were raided, and the area was considered unsafe for children. During one period when there was strife with people from Sierra Leone, the children from the area were evacuated to Robertsport, then the major outpost of the Liberian government in the area. Robertsport, then as now, was the home of St. John's Episcopal Mission. Victoria Kinii was enrolled at the mission school and completed high school there. At the turn of the century, the number of tribal Liberian women who could boast such an education could almost certainly be counted on the fingers of one hand.

Upon graduation she returned home, accompanied by her mother, who saw to it that her English-educated, Christian daughter was married to a proper Vai man—which in this case meant an important hunter-blacksmith-farmer with several wives in the Vai-Muslim tradition. Victoria Kinii lived in the area, making a farm and raising her family. At some time which her daughter dates as prior to World War I, she began teaching local children English, and in 1930 she was asked by an American missionary to set up a school in Diaa. Her son, Ismaila, built her a house and she became head of the Diaa school, a post that she still held in 1950 when the government took over responsibility for the school from the Episcopal mission. It was not until some time in the late 1950s that Victoria Kinii retired. After a long interval, the government got around to appointing a successor: in 1968 the Minister of Education named daughter Victoria Wokie to be principal of the Diaa school, a post she has held ever since.

Victoria Wokie Fahnbulleh tells her story this way:

When my mother decided it was time for me to go to school, I was living on my grandmother's farm. My mother didn't tell my grandmother that she wanted me to go to school; she just came and visited at the farm. One day she told me to come along with her for a walk on the road. And I followed her. She told me she had come to take me to the Bethany mission to go to school. She explained that she had not told my grandmother, who would not have agreed for me to go, and she asked me if I agreed. I said yes. I wanted to go to the mission to learn. So right then and there we set out for Robertsport and she brought me to the mission. She brought me to the baker, who took care of me, and to the school's headmistress, who had asked her to open the school in Diaa long ago. I stayed at the mission all year until vacation time when I went home.

When it was time to return to school, I was living again with my grandmother. I asked my little sister if she would like to go to the mission too. While we were playing I said, "I am going to steal you and take you to the mission so that you can be an educated person too." Hawa agreed, and on the day it was time for me to go back to school, she accompanied me to the road. I took her with me to Robertsport. Today she is a nurse at Kennedy Hospital in Monrovia.

While I was at the school, the doctor in charge of the hospital asked if any students wanted to come to work in the hospital. I did, and after training in Robertsport I was sent to my own clinic. But while I was there I heard that my mother was ill. I went straight home without asking permission and I took care of her. When I returned, the doctor said that I could no longer work in the clinic because I had left without telling anyone.

For a while I did nothing but doing fancy crafts work and selling it. But after a while the people where I was staying asked the government to make me a teacher in their town. The government said that if the people built a schoolhouse, I could be the teacher. So I taught there from 1958 to 1964. Then they moved me to another town, but the people did not support the school and they were always taking their children out. I complained about the situation, and in 1968, I went to Feweh Caine and put the matter before him. I said I want to go to Diaa and teach my own people and he agreed. So I came back to Diaa and I have been here ever since.

I teach the children their ABC's and some of them as far as fourth or fifth grade. Now most of the children go from here to the higher grades in the school in Gbesse [where a large government school is located—about five miles' walk from Diaa]. There is no complaint about them; they do well there.

We have arranged it so that the children go to Arabic school in the evening with Suleimana Fahnbulleh after they have studied with me in the morning. I say that learning is good. If you learn you can do anything. I am trying for my children in Diaa to get things in the future. I am standing in Mama Kinii's shoes. I will not allow this school to fall down.

Wokie's autobiography brings to life some of the correlates of English literacy we identified—intergenerational continuity, (in this case mother-daughter), and relationship to modern occupations (teaching and nursing); but it reflects as well the affinity between some aspects of English schooling and Vai culture's history and tradition forecast in the "traditional status" factor (factor 1) of our factor analysis.

Suleimana Fahnbulleh

Family influences on Qur'anic learning are illustrated in the autobiographical account of Suleimana Fahnbulleh, who was an admired scholar and the Qur'anic teacher in Diaa when members of the project were stationed in that town.

One of the first things that I remember, an event which marks the beginning of my self awareness as a person, is wanting to know my birthday. I went to my uncle. "Uncle," I said, "other people my age know when they were born. They know how old they are. I want to know when I was born."

My uncle told me he had it all written in a book. He said I was born in 1920 on December 20th.

At about this time I saw that there were boys who were learning Muslim book [the Qur'an] and I asked my father to let me join them. He told me I was too small, but he was pleased, and he asked my uncle to begin teaching me. That was when I began. I started reciting *al-hamdu*. My uncle wrote it and I learned it. I learned several chapters, but still I did not go to school. My father told me that he had promised to give me to his brother to learn the Qur'an. My uncle was a famous teacher and I studied under him for two years.

I also saw my friends going to [English] school. I asked my uncle if I could go to school. He agreed. but I couldn't get into the school because it was crowded. So I got the children to teach me my ABC's at home. They brought home the Primer I Book. I kept after them and they taught me. I did Primer I and Primer II. The children who taught me were very advanced. Some were in seventh or eighth grade. They taught me the times tables and addition at home.

Then I went to school. It was in the town of Bomi in Sierra Leone. [Note: at this time, presumably in the 1920s, Vai people moved more or less freely across the Liberia—Sierra Leone border that divided their country.] They put me in the first grade, but when they gave an examination, I came in second in the class of thirty-one children. So they put me in the second grade. So, I was quickly promoted to third grade and then fourth grade in the same year.

At this time, I was sent here to Diaa. I was not certain what would happen. There was some chance that I would be sent on the Mission, but there was no money. My father said that he had promised to give me to his brother for learning the Qur'an, so that is how I came to Diaa. I lived here and studied in Pujehun [a small half-town near Diaa]. I studied the whole Qur'an and I learned it. I learned two or three additional books.

While I was there studying I was sent to work on my teacher's farm. It was forest there. I considered it my own farm because it was for my teacher, and everyone is supposed to be connected with someone. I was there with the wife of my teacher.

At the farm a tree fell on me while we were working together. I bled from the mouth for two days; on the third day it stopped bleeding because our country medicine is very strong. They put medicine on the cut in my head and took out the stick that had cut me. I got better and they brought me back to Pujehun.

While I was away, one of my grandfathers asked my teacher if he could send me on an errand for him to do his business. I went to the town of Jenne Wonde [about a two-day walk from Diaa] where I worked for my grandfather. There I got married and had children. When the business was finished, I went to Monrovia where I lived for seven months. Then I went to a place in Lofa county to look for diamonds because there was nothing to live on in Monrovia. I never found any diamonds. While I was looking my brother sent for me and said I should return to Diaa. I went to a sand-cutter [diviner] who said I would never find diamonds. That is why I am here now.

When I returned I sometimes taught small children the Qur'an, but it was not my work. Then I had a dream. I dreamed that I was in a big field. There were so many people all around me; young people, old people. I was teaching them the Qur'an. I told my teacher from Pujehun about the dream. He said that it meant I was to be a teacher. He said, "Even if you are not highly educated, even if you do not want to do it, the people will make you. That is the meaning of your dream." I was here and people began to send me their children. And it was so. I teach them Qur'an and I send them to English school. That is what they are living on today. The children do not help me on the farm. They no longer know how to use the cutlass, so it is a struggle.

So that is what I can tell you. All I have passed through. May God give us luck.

Suleimana Fahnbulleh's narrative illustrates many themes that recurred in our discussions with people about becoming literate. As a teacher of the Qur'an he interprets the request to tell about his life in terms of the role by which he is primarily recognized. At the outset, he indicates that his uncle was a Qur'anic teacher who kept records of family births in addition to teaching children the Qur'an. Exposure to English as well as Qur'anic learning was a part of his early experience; the two potential forms of education competed for Mr. Fahnbulleh's allegiance. It appears that family preferences led to his early induction in Qur'anic rather than English literacy, but throughout his life he has pursued both types of learning.

The narrative illustrates as well the mobility of a Vai man, and the multiplicity of activities he can engage in while continuing to "make farm" in some locale where he has family ties. Finally, it illustrates the recognized nonexclusivity of the different kinds of literate training, with schooling in English assigned the role of giving children "what they are living on today."

The statistical techniques we applied to our survey data resulted in an organized representation of significant aspects of life in Vai society. It is a bare bones representation, but one that is entirely compatible with the richly detailed accounts available from ethnographic descriptions and recorded life stories. Although neither the survey nor the ethnography could succeed in capturing all the intricacies and dynamic processes in Vai life, the two sets of data proved not only to complement but to enhance each other. And their convergence puts us in a stronger position for our theory-testing experimental studies.

What have we learned of a substantive nature?

We quickly discovered that the Vai defy description in stereotypical terms as a traditional closed society. As indicated by the factor analysis and responses to many of our questions, Vai people travel widely within Liberia and are likely to engage in occupations other than farming at some time in their lives. Their traditional crafts are adjusting to new technologies. Almost everyone speaks two or more languages and will spend some time living in an urban center. Acceptance of English schooling and endorsement of positive evaluations of science and personal knowledge has not resulted in displacement of traditional practices and beliefs.

One of our purposes in examining correlates of literacy was to test popular propositions in social science writings that link literacy to urbanism and modern attitudes. We secured support for earlier findings relating these social and psychological conditions to English schooling, but results with respect to Vai script and Arabic were too complex to be aggregated into statements about literacy per se. This observation brings us to one of the more important outcomes of our combined survey and ethnographic studies—we failed to find a discrete dimension of Vai life that could be labeled "literacy." With nearly 30 percent of our male respondents having some reading or writing skill in some script, we were nonetheless unable to discover any attribute other than sex which related to all types of script knowledge. The common core of literacy, to the extent that we feel comfortable in using the phrase, refers only to family status in Vai society at large; all other aspects of background and current experience are related only to specific scripts.

These results converge with our data on the acquisition and use of literacy. All our information points toward the specificity of literacy. Just as each script has its own course of learning and carries a special segment of the larger social system's literacy functions, so each group of script literates is part of a somewhat different social network and participates in occupational and other cultural domains in a somewhat different manner.

The literacy group differences, of course, are not a complete surprise. We knew from the outset that Vai script literacy and English literacy were distinctive with respect to their functions and their acquisition processes; but we did not know that they were almost entirely exclusive of each other. Nor did we have much knowledge of Arabic literacy and its distribution. Our evidence for the specificity of literacy knowledge among the Vai has several consequences: one, primarily theoretical in nature, suggests the need to revise some of the leading speculations about literacy and its social basis and functions; these issues will be considered in the last chapter when all the results of our work are before us. But a more immediate consequence was a major change in our plan of investigation.

Recall that when we began our research we planned to compare three groups: nonliterates, schooled English literates, and nonschooled Vai script literates. The literacy and schooling patterns disclosed in the survey did not fit this scheme. One modification was made necessary by the differential sex composition of literates taken as a group and nonliterates taken as a group, and our first revision of the comparative design was to restrict it to men only.

The discovery of the considerable heterogeneity of the Vai script literates—four out of ten also qualifying as some kind of Arabic literate—posed another problem. Vai script literacy and Arabic literacy differed in too many ways to be grouped together and glossed simply as "traditional literacies" or "nonschooled literacies." "Arabic literacy" was also too simple a gloss for the extremely varied kinds of reading and writing activities among the Vai that made use of the Arabic script. It would have simplified our studies if we could have temporarily set aside Arabic literacy and concentrated on the Vai script/English school/nonliterate comparisons we had in mind at the outset. But the extensiveness of Vai-Arabic biliteracy made that simple solution impractical. Not only would we have drastically reduced our potential subject population in terms of total numbers of Vai script literates available, we would also have introduced a selection bias. We had discovered from an analysis of reading scores that Vai-Arabic biliterates had a higher concentration of top scores on the Vai script reading test than their monoliterate counterparts. We needed that range of skill as part of our studies. Keeping the Vai-Arabic biliterate group in the comparisons, however, pushed us one step further—for then we needed the other half of that combination to disentangle which of the script knowledges might influence cognitive processes within the biliterate group, and we needed to study Arabic monoliterates as well.

Therefore, we decided to maintain separate experimental groups for each script and each naturally occurring script combination. Our modified comparison scheme, with five major subgroups rather than three, is diagramed in Figure 7.1.

The five groups arrayed across the bottom of the diagram form the framework for analysis of the cognitive consequences of literacy as indexed

Figure 7.1. Population subgroups for comparative cognitive studies

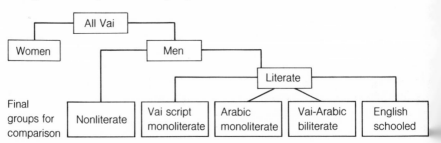

by performance on the cognitive task battery that was a part of our survey. As was true for the factor analysis, we exclude women from the major analyses because they were, by and large, precluded from engaging in literate activities.

Survey evidence also poses serious issues of interpretation when we turn to causal hypotheses linking literacy to cognitive consequences. As we suspected, even careful literacy group distinctions will not protect us against covariation problems. For example, the fact that Vai script literates are older than average, or that English literates engage in more modern occupations, or that Arabic literates have traveled widely, raises the possibility that these experiences may distort literacy group comparisons or be the real agents of cognitive change, should it be found.

In the chapters that follow, our analyses will be shaped by these considerations and by other survey results. As a communicative convenience, we will present summary performance data in tables arranged by literacy groups. Statements about the influence of literacy will depend most heavily on multiple regression analyses which permit us to test covariate hypotheses. In the set of variables we will include literacy measures, demonstrated literacy correlates (such as age, modernity of occupation), and other variables that are candidate causes of cognitive change (for example, extent of urban experience). If a literacy variable enters an equation, we will try to substitute other variables for it (for example, if last grade in school is a predictor, we will ask if modernity of occupation will displace it). Only when a literacy variable remains in an equation after attempts to substitute for it will we claim a genuine literacy effect. We recognize the conservatism of this course, but the temptation to capitalize on chance relationships in order to show literacy as a causal agent is too great to let our predilections and the computer rule our choices.

Part III

Testing Consequences: Developmental Paradigms

8

Does Literacy Substitute for Schooling?

We first attempted to determine whether literacy induces cognitive change by administering a set of experimental tasks to all survey respondents. Two considerations guided our selection of tasks. First, we wanted tasks that had produced significant differences between schooled and nonschooled populations in prior cross-cultural research. And of this set we wanted to select those that bore as close as possible a relation to the hypothetical cognitive changes literacy has been said to produce or promote. In its simplest form, our strategy was to determine if the kinds of changes associated with school education would be observed as a consequence of experience with either of the two literacies that flourished outside Western schools.

HISTORY OF THE EXPERIMENTAL TASKS

A number of tasks met our criteria and all of them had a common history. Since most had been used to demonstrate school effects in traditional societies, one might surmise that they were the outgrowth of theoretical or empirical analyses of the nature of schooling and its potential significance for intellectual operations. This was not the case. We located no tasks specifically designed to test theory-derived hypotheses about either schooling or literacy. All the experimental paradigms in common use were invented in the laboratories of experimental and developmental psychologists for quite another purpose than the study of cultural differences in thinking. Whether dating from the turn of the century (one of the classification tasks we used) or American learning laboratories of the 1950s (a free recall task we employed), these paradigms had been designed to analyze basic cognitive processes of the general human mind. Most had also been widely used within the United States and overseas to map developmental change in children and had come to be seen as reliable diagnostic indicators of levels of intellectual development.

The key phrase here is "developmental change." The history of our Vai research is, in some sense, an extended effort to analyze various kinds of intellectual change and to specify what makes them different kinds. What do most psychologists mean by the developmental kind of cognitive change? Different theorists make somewhat different uses of the construct, but the term "development" typically implies the occurrence of basic transformations in the way the mind operates—changes that are thought to represent increases in the general mental capacities of individuals similar to increases in physical capacities brought about by biological maturation. For our purposes, it is sufficient to characterize the distinctive aspects of developmental change as including (1) emergence of new, qualitatively distinct intellectual capabilities, and (2) availability of these capabilities for performing many tasks in a variety of content domains. Developmental changes are often contrasted to changes produced by learning, which are typically considered to involve specific skills and limited, specialized content. Illustrative examples of each type of change have been popularized: the capacity to engage in hypothetical reasoning or abstract thought is taken to represent a developmental phenomenon; acquiring reading skills is an achievement of learning.

The tasks available to us, then, came trailing connotations as indicators of lower and higher levels of thought. We did not view this fact as disabling to our initial hypothesis-testing venture. Most speculations about the effects of schooling and of literacy have indeed been couched in just such developmental terms. As we noted in the first chapter, the Greenfield-Bruner thesis explicitly maintained that schooling pushes cognitive growth to new levels; and Luria, Goody, Havelock, and others claimed that literacy is linked to abstract and logical reasoning—processes that are at the high end of the developmental continuum. It made sense, then, for our first pass at experimental studies to press into service tasks that psychologists, by tradition and theoretical persuasion, accepted as indicators of change in general mental abilities. However, in adopting the tasks, we did not commit ourselves to a developmental interpretation of the results. We were especially wary of such a course because, unlike most other psychologists conducting comparative research, we were working with adults rather than children, and we had major reservations about the applicability of developmental interpretations to fully mature populations. However, inasmuch as the experimental tasks all presumed to tap general mental abilities, we adopted the term "general cognitive change" to represent the phenomena we were studying with these measures. We refer to this phase of our experimental research as "testing for general consequences of literacy."

The cognitive battery we put together sampled five domains of intellectual activity that have figured prominently in speculations of literacy effects: abstract thinking, taxonomic categorization, memory, logical reasoning, and reflective knowledge about language. In several domains we used more than one task to minimize the danger of general conclusions on the basis of results that might only indicate situation-specific performances. We experimented at length with the format of tasks and analyses of performance measures.[1] We were not so much concerned with comparing total scores as we were in identifying characteristically different operations that might be brought to bear in accomplishing any given task. Toward this end, we built into our tasks both behavioral and verbal measures: we asked people to do something (to group items, to recall words) and we evaluated the way in which they did it (number of categories discovered, number of words remembered). We also asked people to tell us how they had gone about the task and to explain their reasons for responding in a certain way. This distinction between doing and talking-about-doing is as old as the developmental tasks themselves and is explicitly included in a number of theories as a crucial marker of level of intellectual development. We believed it especially important to include this distinction in our comparison of school-based and nonschool-based literacies because our previous research and that of others had implicated schooling in the ability to describe the principles underlying performance (Scribner and Cole, 1973).

METHODS OF ANALYSIS AND RULES OF INFERENCE

We selected multiple regression analysis to assess the independent contributions of literacy, schooling, and other experiences to performance. We represented our crucial variables—literacy and school factors—by multiple measures. Although reading test scores and reports of functional uses of literacy were highly correlated for each script, we avoided any presupposition that they would substitute for each other as predictor variables. We used both reading scores and a variety of measures of script usage in the regression equations. English literacy was represented by the same variables as Vai script and Arabic literacy, and was entered into equations alongside variables depicting school experiences. As for school itself, we not only used the conventional measure of last grade completed, but made further distinctions between rural and city schooled populations and between student and ex-student groups. Finally, to maximize the chances of finding educational effects, we took account of possible erosion of schooling or literacy learning by computing the time elapsed since each literate had concluded his course of instruction.

On the basis of survey analyses, we selected for inclusion in our equations age, modernity of occupation, travel, type of farming, and other variables shown to be highly correlated with one or another of the three literacies. And we included, as theoretical variables of interest, measures of urban experience, occupation, income, and multilingualism. Because we were concerned about possible drift in the way our experimental tasks were presented over time and potential biasing effects of individual experimenter styles, we used both experimenter and date of test as control variables. We report results here without the control variables, but in all cases equations with controls were composed of the same variables and produced results consistent with those reported.

As we have already pointed out, we were well aware at the outset of this work, and our survey confirmed, that different literacies are associated in varying degrees with other life experiences. In testing hypotheses about literacy effects, therefore, we tried to rule out all other sources of variation to see if any literacy-related variable would survive as a statistically significant factor. One important element in this conservative strategy was our "within-group" test: if a literacy-related factor appeared to make a difference in performance for the population as a whole, we checked to see if it affected performance in the same way within the specific population to which it applied. For example, if level of schooling (last grade completed) increased number of correct answers to logic problems for the entire population, it should function in the same way for the schooled population itself: twelfth graders should outperform those in the lower grades. We applied the same logic to variables such as Vai script reading score or years studied Qur'an. If we failed to find literacy variables affecting performance within the appropriate literacy group, in addition to the population as a whole, we could not rule out the possibility that group differences were due to literacy covariates and not literacy itself. All literacy-related effects we report in this chapter meet these within-group tests.

As for the performance measures, we methodically devised and tested alternative forms for coding and ranking responses, using both traditional and specially constructed measures. In addition to analyzing performance task by task, we factor-analyzed all measures across tasks and computed individual factor scores for the various dimensions emerging from this analysis. As a test of our own procedures, we carried out all our basic predictions twice—once using single values on the independent variables and raw scores on the performance measures, and a second time using factor scores for the independent variables (described in Chapter 7) and factor scores for task performance measures. Results of both analyses—on raw scores and factor scores—corresponded in all major respects.

TASKS AND THEIR OUTCOMES

We will report results task by task, presenting the theoretical rationale behind each experiment, describing our procedures, and summarizing regression equations. As a reference guide, we present in Table 8.1 vital statistics for the basic comparison groups, calling special attention to average levels of schooling, literacy, and age. Performance measures are summarized in Table 8.2.

Table 8.1 Background characteristics, major survey (group averages)

	Nonliterate men (N = 104)[a]	Vai script Monoliterate (N = 53)	Arabic monoliterate (N = 36)	Vai-Arabic biliterate (N = 44)	English schooled (N = 53)	Nonliterate women (N = 349)
Literacy measures						
Vai reading score (1–4)	—	2.87	—	3.25	—	—
Arabic reading score (1–4)	—		2.31	2.57	—	—
English reading score (1–4)	—	—	—	—	2.94	—
Last grade completed	—				7.20	
Nonliteracy measures						
Age	33.70	49.15	31.11	47.73	29.23	36.20
Number places lived	3.3	3.3	2.6	3.3	3.4	2.8
Years urban residence (coded)	2.8	3.0	1.7	3.0	4.5	2.4
Work in concession (no/yes)	.3	.3	.1	.3	.2	.1
Size, farthest travel (coded)	2.0	1.7	1.7	1.5	2.1	2.1
Skill rating (1–6)	2.1	2.3	1.7	2.7	2.4	1.6
Modernity of occupation (1–3)	.6	.6	.5	.4	1.2	N.A.
Farmed last year (no/yes)	.7	.7	.6	.9	.2	.5
Special role in bush school (no/yes)	.1	.2	.1	.1	.0	.2
Speak other tribal languages (no/yes)	.6.	.6	.8	.8	.8	.5
Speak English (no/yes)	.6	.5	.4	.5	.9	.4

a. Numbers in comparison groups differ slightly from those reported in Table 6.2. Assignment to group in the present analysis was based on reading score. Eleven literate women are not included here.

Abstraction

All psychological theories rest heavily on the proposition that the ability to classify things and events that vary in myriad ways among themselves is a basic function of the human intellect. But many also hold that radical changes occur in ways of classifying as a result of maturation or of specific life experiences. These shifts are commonly described in terms of a transition from concrete to abstract thought patterns. Psychologists have traditionally investigated these processes by presenting various arrays of stimulus materials to individuals, instructing them to find things that are similar or to group together those things which are alike or belong together. (Classic references include Ach, 1905; Goldstein and Scheerer, 1941; Vygotsky, 1962.)

A fuzzy concept in psychology, the notion of abstract thought has been

Table 8.2 Performance measures, experimental tasks, major survey (group averages)

Tasks and measures	Population groups						
	Nonliterate men (N = 104)	Vai script monoliterate (N = 53)	Arabic monoliterate (N = 36)	Vai-Arabic biliterate (N = 44)	English schooled (all) (N = 53)	grade 10+ (N = 16)	Nonliterate women (N = 349)
Abstraction							
(Geometric sorting task)							
Number dimensions sorted (out of 3)	1.6	2.0	2.0	1.9	1.7	1.9	1.7
Form/number selected (max 2)	1.1	1.1	1.1	1.4	1.2	1.3	1.1
Verbal explanation (max 12)	5.3	5.1	5.8	5.6	5.6	9.3	4.9
Taxonomic categorization							
(Constrained classification task)							
Number categorical choices (out of 6)	3.4	3.5	3.0	3.5	3.8	3.9	3.4
Verbal explanation (max 42)	31.5	31.2	29.0	29.5	32.5	34.6	30.5
(Free sorting task)							
Taxonomic cluster score (D)	.10	.08	.11	.11	.07	.06	.09
Memory							
Amount recalled, task 1 (max 24)	16.2	16.0	16.2	16.2	17.1	14.9	16.5
Amount recalled, task 2 (max 24)	16.9	16.8	17.2	17.9	17.7	17.7	16.7
Cluster score, task 1	2.1	2.2	2.7	2.4	2.4	2.1	2.2
Cluster score, task 2	2.5	2.3	2.5	2.8	2.1	1.8	2.2
Logic							
Number correct (max 6)	1.6	1.3	1.7	1.5	3.0	3.9	1.7
Theoretic explanations (max 10)	6.1	5.7	6.2	5.7	7.6	7.9	6.2
Language objectivity							
Total score (out of 3)	.7	.5	.9	1.2	1.3	1.3	.7

used to designate a variety of behaviors observed on these classification tasks. These include the following aspects of behavior:

1. Ability to single out a particular attribute (say, size) shared by a set of objects in order to subsume them into distinct, mutually exclusive classes (literally, to *ab-stract* one feature from many as a basis for classification.)
2. Ability to shift flexibly from one attribute to another (say, from size to shape) as a basis for constructing classes (to be relatively unconstrained by preexisting organization and to envisage other possibilities, sometimes equated with context-free thinking).
3. Ability to give a verbal label to a class (name it) and to explain the basis for class membership (sometimes designated as verbal-logical thinking).

All these operationally defined notions about abstraction have been claimed as specific effects of schooling in cross-cultural research, and they are consonant as well with speculations about the cognitive implications of literacy. Havelock (1963) maintained that ordering events and doings to "topical groupings and categories" (p. 189) is contingent on the development of a written language which identifies and names the headings and categories (aspects 1 and 3 above). More generally, he conceived of literacy as the precondition for the emergence of universal concepts, as opposed to those based on images. As we have seen, Greenfield's claims (1972) that written language promotes context-independent abstract thought relied on observations that school children would shift flexibly from one attribute to another in a classification task (aspect 2) and explain the basis for their groupings (aspect 3); and Luria (1976) similarly used such classificatory behaviors as evidence for the shift to abstract thought accompanying literacy and education.

The task designed to examine abstraction required subjects to categorize and recategorize the geometric figures depicted in Figure 8.1. These figures are classifiable by form, color, and number. We were interested in determining how successful people would be in grouping together cards that contrasted on one dimension only, form or color or number (aspect 1 above), and how facile they would be in reclassifying them according to other dimensions (aspect 2 above). We also secured verbal explanations of the groupings (aspect 3). Demands of the task were comparable to those of Greenfield's study (1966) described in Chapter 1, except that she used common objects rather than geometric figures. In addition to her findings, other cross-cultural studies using geometric figures had found that school-

Figure 8.1. Sorting and resorting geometric stimuli

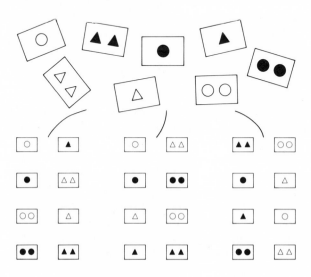

ing improved ability to classify and reclassify such stimuli and also biased individuals to pick form rather than color as an initial basis of classification. (For reviews, see Cole and Scribner, 1974; Sharp, Cole, and Lave, 1979.)

Performance on this card-sorting task was rather poor.[2] On the average, different population groups achieved only 1.8 dimensional sorts—that is, they did not readily reclassify the cards. Contrary to previous findings, schooling did not increase the average number of successful classifications, nor did any other of the more than twenty-five variables we examined in regression analyses predict how many successful sorts individuals would achieve. Other aspects of performance were predictable.

$$\text{Sorting on form or number} = 1.05 + \underset{(2.2)}{.11} \text{ teach Vai script} + \underset{(3.2)}{.28} \text{ biliterate}$$
$$(R^2 = .08) \qquad + \underset{(3.2)}{.36} \text{ in school now}$$

$$\text{Overall verbal explanation} = 5.41 + \underset{(3.8)}{.04} \text{ (last grade)}^2 - \underset{(3.0)}{2.52} \text{ in school before}$$
$$(R^2 = .05)$$

$$\begin{aligned}\text{Verbal explanation} \\ \text{(with number classif.} \\ \text{held constant)} &= -.21 + \underset{(15.1)}{3.14} \text{ number classif.} + \underset{(4.5)}{.03} \text{ (last grade)}^2 \\ (R^2 = .47) & \quad - \underset{(3.6)}{2.25} \text{ in school before}\end{aligned}$$

Because such equations will be found later in the text, we digress briefly to give the reader unaccustomed to such data summaries a working grasp of how to interpret them.

Taking the equation for sorting cards according to form or number as an example, the first thing to notice is that relatively little of the variance (8% indicated by the square of the multiple correlation coefficient, R^2) is accounted for by our predictor variables. However, three variables do predict this measure of categorizing performance. There is a positive contribution of experience in teaching the Vai script. (The number in parentheses below each variable name is the t ratio calculated for that variable; see Cohen and Cohen, 1975, for an explanation of how this test of significance is calculated. Only variables with a t value greater than 1.9, indicating a .05 level of significance, are reported.) The positive coefficient of .11 in front of "teach Vai script" indicates that this kind of experience will contribute an expected increase of .11 points to the form-number score for the average individual, all other things held constant by statistical means. Although we report regression coefficients to two decimal places, it should be understood that regression coefficients are subject to sampling variability and may be sensitive to the specific regression model used as well. They should be treated as useful estimates of the amount of change, positive or negative, contributed by the variables in question to the performance in question. For our example equation, we see that status as a Vai script–Arabic biliterate increases performance by about .28 points, and being presently enrolled in school increases performance by .36 points. All three effects are statistically significant, although not particularly large.

With respect to the second equation involving proficiency of verbal explanation, we see that only schooling affects performance. The higher one's last grade, the better the performance by a very small amount, while being out of school for some time quite markedly lowers one's score.

These conventions of interpretation, when applied to the remaining equations, represent a reasonable translation from "regression language" into English. The only additional convention that needs to be kept in mind concerns interactional variables that represent the joint action of two primary variables. In later equations we will encounter such interactions as "age × Vaitown," indicating that the conjoint effect of these variables in a multiplicative way influences performance.

Based on the outcome of the regression analyses, we see that all three kinds of literacy enhanced the tendency to sort the cards according to form or number, an outcome consistent with the notion that literacy focuses attention on these aspects of graphic symbols (as compared, for example, to the nonrelevant attribute of color). Specialized script functions such as teaching Vai script or using Arabic for letter writing (found within the biliterate group but not represented in the overall regression analysis reported above) were the strongest literacy predictors. When it came to explaining the principle by which a dimensional categorization had been achieved, only amount of schooling distinguished itself as a factor influencing performance. Separate analyses indicated that ten or more years of schooling were needed to produce an effect. A decrement was associated with being out of school at the time of our survey. In a separate analysis, we controlled for number of successful classifications and found amount of schooling contributing directly to explanation score, over and above sorting score.

In summary, all groups, including nonliterates, could achieve at least one successful abstraction (dimensional sort) and all were equally good or poor at breaking up one classification and achieving another. All literacies affected dimensional preferences, but only schooling enhanced ability to formulate verbally the basis for preferential selections.

Taxonomic Categorization

Despite their wide use in comparative studies of mental performance, we did not want to restrict our studies of classification to geometric figures. Such figures are unlikely to play much of a role in the lives of traditional rice farmers who may never have been exposed to regular geometric shapes.

Nor is it likely that they had encountered experiences in which such shapes were invested with meaning or important instrumental functions. Therefore, we included two tasks which required classification of objects familiar to people from their everyday experience. Both were concerned with preference for using taxonomic class membership rather than perceptual or functional properties of things as the basis for similarity groupings. One of the more robust findings in developmental research with Western-schooled children is that as they advance through the grades they shift their basis for similarity judgments from how things look or how they function to the semantic classes they can be subsumed under. Extensive cross-cultural research has found taxonomic classification to vary markedly with task and materials except for those with higher levels of schooling (Cole and Scribner, 1974; Scribner, 1974; Rogoff, 1980).

Constrained classification. Our first task, constrained classification, was modeled after procedures invented by Luria. He had used this task as an indicator of literacy's facilitating effect on the development of verbal-logical thinking. Among the Kpelle, we had found, using our version of the task, that formal schooling at the secondary level was associated with greater reliance on taxonomic grouping principles.

In this classifying task, fifteen objects were spread out on the table in front of the informant. The objects were examples of three Vai categories: foods (bitterball, kola-nut, eggplant, cassava, onion), farm implements (hoe, hammer, cutlass, file, knife), and kitchen utensils (cooking stick, glass, sifter, bowl, spoon). Two of the fifteen objects were selected according to a prearranged schedule. The informant was then asked to choose from among the remaining objects one that belonged in the same group as the two selected by the assistant. He was asked to place the best-fitting object between the two preselected objects and explain why the three belonged in the same group. (We conceived of the preselected objects as constraints within which the categorization had to be made—hence our term "constrained classification.")

As in the previous categorizing study, we were interested in two classes of response. First, when two pairs of objects from the same category were presented as constraints, we wanted to see if subjects would choose another item from that same taxonomic category; second, we were interested in the adequacy of verbal explanations for the choice, especially the explicit use of category names ("These are all foods," for example, or "These are all cooking things").

Results can be easily summarized: in our population of informants, the only factor consistently associated with taxonomic choices was urban living. Vai script and Arabic literacies slightly improved categorical choices (not explanation) for some object pairs, but their inconsistency from one set of items to another suggests no solid effect of literacy on this kind of categorizing. Here, too, contrary to expectation, we failed to find an overall effect of schooling. When we checked carefully, however, we found that those few subjects in our sample who were roughly equivalent in amount of schooling to the high school subjects studied by Cole et al. (1971) did in fact outperform all other groups, both in number of taxonomic choices and in verbal explanations. The basic predictive equations are:

Number of categorical
choices (food pairs) = .80 + .15 frequency of Vai letter writing
$(R^2 = .17)$ (2.6)
+ 1.16 live in Vaitown
(7.7)

Number of categorical
choices (utensil pairs) = 2.23 + .22 teach Arabic − .03 years studied Qur'an
$(R^2 = .05)$ (2.3)   (2.2)
+ .05 years urban living
(3.2)

Verbalization (food)
(with no. of categorical
choices held constant) = 10.80 + 1.01 number of categorical choices
$(R^2 = .16)$ (6.0)
− 1.63 special role in bush school
(3.1)
+ .17 years urban living
(2.8)

Verbalization (utensils)
(with no. of categorical
choices held constant) = 8.42 + .99 number of categorical choices
$(R^2 = .12)$ (4.5)
− 1.70 special role in bush school
(3.3)
+ .15 years urban living
(2.6)

Free classification of objects. As an unconstrained sorting task we asked subjects to group together items from a set of twenty-four common objects representing four taxonomic categories: food, clothing, tools, and utensils. Here again we had prior evidence that educated and uneducated Liberian tribal people differ in the way they respond to this request: educated subjects are more likely to use taxonomic categories. Under some circumstances we found evidence that both schooling (Cole et al., 1971) and exposure to the modern sector of the Liberian economy (Scribner, 1974) could enhance taxonomic categorizing performance. Among our Vai survey population, only minimal school and no nonschool literacy-related differences were detectable; all groups used taxonomic relations as a grouping principle at an above-chance level. Consistent with this picture of little variation in scores, taxonomic grouping behaviors were unpredictable in multiple regression analyses.

Overall, these results discourage conclusions about a strong influence of literacy on categorization and abstraction. The absence of strong effects of formal schooling may appear surprising to those familiar with the developmental and cross-cultural literature on this issue, but it should be kept in mind that for the first time we were gathering data entirely from adults, many of whom had experienced rather little education, and that often years ago. It is equally important to note that where levels of schooling and current school attendance were similar enough to warrant comparison, the influence of formal schooling among our Vai informants followed the same pattern obtained in earlier work using these tasks.

Memory

We have already had occasion to review the long history of speculation linking literacy to fundamental changes in the way humans remember. This speculation is particularly interesting because it leads in several somewhat contradictory directions. The main line of speculation, which can be traced all the way from Plato down into the mid-twentieth century, is that literate people depend upon the cultural artifact of writing to remember and so are out of the practice of committing large bodies of information to memory. While this argument may have been plausible in the social context of Athenian society, it hardly applies to the conditions of formal school-based learning in contemporary societies—and certainly not in Liberia, where successful passage through the grades requires memorization of quantities of subject-matter facts. Such practice ought to yield increased skill in memorizing material for later testing. Because Vai script literacy, on the other hand, does not involve such memorization, it is a useful case for investigating whether use of writing for mnemonic purposes (records and the like) contributes to a decrease in memory skills.

Another line of speculation suggests that the existence of written texts preserving sanctified or culturally valued knowledge encourages literal retention of the words of the text. Lord (1960) makes this point by contrasting the rote performance of a literate balladeer with the more constructive memory processes that Parry had documented for epic ballads. In the case of the Vai people, this hypothesis would predict that Qur'anic learners would make fewer transformations in their recall (stick more closely to the original order and recall more) than other groups.

Finally, a large body of developmental and cross-cultural research has shown that schooling is related to use of sophisticated memory strategies involving taxonomic organization that are themselves associated with superior recall. In one previous study among the Vai, conducted many years earlier, we obtained evidence that Vai script literates on a free recall task made greater use of taxonomic categories built into the list than nonliterate counterparts—that on this task they were, in fact, like schooled populations. (For a review, see Cole and Scribner, 1977.)

Realizing that we could not follow up on all these possibilities in our survey (we continued throughout the project to examine relationships between literacy and memory, as discussed in Chapter 13), we settled on two versions of a recall task involving categorizable items. In the first, individuals were asked to recall the twenty-four common items used in the free classification task described above after they had finished classifying them. The names of these items were then read out in random order, and individuals were asked to recall them in any order they chose.

Each task was analyzed separately. The amount recalled on the first task was influenced by age (which produced a decrement) and knowledge of other tribal languages (which contributed to improved recall). Schooling produced complicated effects—both positive and negative—depending on where it took place. On the second recall task following oral presentation of the list, the total amount remembered was increased by both schooling and biliteracy. Age again contributed to a memory decrement.

Moderate levels of taxonomic clustering were exhibited by all groups on both tasks; but no literacy or population factors were associated with degree of memory organization. We found little evidence for preservation of serial order even for Qur'anic literates, who we predicted might resort to this memory strategy. The basic predictive equations are:

$$
\begin{aligned}
\text{Amount recalled (task 1)} \;(R^2 = .08) = {} & 16.4 + \underset{(3.1)}{.30 \text{ last grade}} \times \text{live upcountry} \\
& - \underset{(2.5)}{.02 \, (\text{last grade})^2} \times \text{live in Vaitown} - \underset{(2.7)}{.0004 \, \text{age}^2} \\
& + \underset{(2.0)}{.84 \text{ speak tribal languages}}
\end{aligned}
$$

$$
\begin{aligned}
\text{Amount recalled (task 2)} \;(R^2 = .05) = {} & 17.6 + \underset{(2.4)}{1.27 \text{ Vai-Arabic biliterate}} \\
& + \underset{(2.1)}{.00001 \text{ age}} \times (\text{last grade})^2 - \underset{(3.2)}{.0004 \, \text{age}^2}
\end{aligned}
$$

Amount of clustering (task 1) = not predictable
Amount of clustering (task 2) = not predictable

These results have to be considered perplexing. We had obtained some population-linked predictors of level of recall, but our two "process" measures, clustering and serialization, were unpredictable. Yet theoretically the process measures should have been most closely associated with differences in experience. We also did not anticipate the fact that biliterates' level of recall on the second task would stand out among the nonschooled literates. It might be that these men were reflecting some common experiences associated with biliteracy, but we did not know what these might be, and we had no theory of how such experiences would operate on *level* of recall in the absence of any differential performance on either clustering or serialization. More work was needed.

Logic

The association between literacy and logical thinking appears, as we have seen, in scholarly works as well as in discussions among public leaders and educators. Goody and Watt (in Goody, 1968) considered writing the precondition for Aristotle's invention of the syllogism and the emergence of the discipline of logic. In recent years, Olson (1977) has developed a body of research around the proposition that writing makes possible a separation of the logical and rhetorical functions of language, and that the process of becoming literate involves learning the separability of these functions. Thus the literate person is able to attend to logical relations between the propositions of a syllogism without getting involved with, or misled by, their content. At the time we conducted our Vai research, we had before us only our own cross-cultural research on verbal reasoning and Luria's studies on syllogisms conducted in the 1930s. Luria found that when nonliterate informants had no personal knowledge of the facts alleged in the premises, they were likely to refuse to admit the possibility of drawing any conclusion at all. When the content of the problem concerned local conditions, subjects often based their answers on their own experiences, ignoring the premises and concentrating on the empirical adequacy of the conclusion.

This work is of direct relevance to our research because the mode of reasoning with syllogisms that Luria first documented disappears under the influence of schooling (Scribner, 1975, 1977). Luria reported that as little as six months to a year of literacy training and involvement in collective farm work were sufficient for this change from experience-based to premise-based reasoning to take place. Cole at al. (1971) and Sharp et al. (1979) showed increases in premise-based responding as a consequence of one to three years of formal schooling.

On the basis of extensive pilot work, we constructed a set of six problems that varied in their content. All had simple logical structures and were routinely answered correctly by children in the United States (Hill, 1961). Problems are presented in Table 8.3. We constructed the problem list in such a way that for three problems, the correct logical answer coincided with the factual state of affairs. In problem 1, for example, the correct answer is, "Yes, this school is built in a town." It is also the case, as numerous informants took care to advise us, that schools in Liberia are always built in towns: "Otherwise, who would attend them?" Because of the congruence between logical necessity and social truth, different routes could lead to a correct solution: accepting the problem premises and drawing an inference, or matching the propositions to one's knowledge about the location of

Table 8.3 Logic problems

1. All the schools in Vai area are built in towns.
   The government is building a school in Vai area.
   Is this school built in a town?

2. All houses in Liberia are made of iron.
   My friend has a house in Liberia.
   Is my friend's house made of iron?

3. All people who own houses pay house tax.
   Boima does not pay a house tax.
   Does Boima own a house?

4. All women who live in Monrovia are married.
   Kemu is not married.
   Does Kemu live in Monrovia?

5. All government officials are wealthy.
   All wealthy men are powerful.
   Are some government officials powerful?

6. Some of the people we know are not in school.
   All of the people we know are in Liberia.
   Are all of the people in Liberia in school?

schools and answering on the basis of that knowledge. In other problems, correct logical answers involved acceptance of premises running counter to life experience, or of ambiguous factual status. Problem 4, "All women living in Monrovia are married," created considerable controversy both in individual administration and in group discussion.

After each person provided a yes or no answer to the problem question, we asked for an explanation of the answer. We scored reasons that were given as either *empirical* (justified in terms of real-world knowledge and belief) or *theoretical* (justified in terms of the information contained in the premises). Examples of empirical responses (using problem 4 for illustration) are: "I don't know Kemu"; "Kemu could live with her mother in Monrovia." Theoretical reasons given to the same problem would include the following: "You said all women who live in Monrovia are married"; "That is what you said."

Of all the survey tasks, logic problems proved the most predictable and demonstrated the strongest effects of schooling. Not only did amount of school increase the number of correct answers, but it contributed to the choice of theoretical explanations, over and above correct answers. Schooling was the only background characteristic to improve performance; neither Vai script nor Arabic literacy had an effect on either measure. Experiences reflecting isolation from modern Liberian life (such as farming only or playing a special role in bush school) were associated with poorer solution performance. The basic predictive equations are:

Number correct = 6.83 + .36 English reading score − 1.03 farmed last year
$(R^2 = .12)$ (3.4)   (3.8)
                         − .68 special role in bush school
                                    (1.9)

Explanation score = 2.42 + .01 (last grade)^2 + .61 in school now
$(R^2 = .25)$ (4.7)   (2.1)
                    − .52 special role in bush school − .69 farmed last year
                           (2.4)   (4.3)
                    − .16 travel large city
                           (2.3)

Explanation score
(with number correct
  held constant)   = − .63 + .36 number correct + .01 (last grade)^2
    $(R^2 = .52)$ (13.9)   (5.0)
                    + .52 in school now
                      (2.2)

LANGUAGE OBJECTIVITY

One theory about the cognitive effects of literacy assumes that the critical feature of writing is its objectification of language. Making language an object by representing it in graphic symbols is considered an aid to understanding that language exists as a separate system, independent of the things it denotes or references. Goody (1977) speaks of the way in which the act of writing down words may change an individual's concept of the relation between words and their referents: "Words assume a different relationship to action and to object when they are on paper than when they are spoken. They are no longer bound up directly with 'reality'; the written word becomes a separate thing, abstracted to some extent from the flow of speech, shedding its close entailment to action" (p. 46). Scribner's earlier work on literacy (1968) speculated in similar vein.

The problem we included as part of the survey to test these ideas was taken from Piaget (1929, repr. 1960):

> Suppose that everyone in the world got together and decided that from now on we will call the sun the moon and the moon will be called the sun. All we are going to do is change the names. Could we do that if we wanted to?
> Now, when you go to bed at night what will you call the thing that you see up in the sky?
> What will the sky look like when you go to bed if this is so?

We had no prior experience with this sort of problem in research with nonliterate adults, but at the time we began our survey, we had a preprint of an article by Osherson and Markman (subsequently published 1974–1975) in which they reported that young children (up to approximately the third-grade level, or ten years of age) experienced difficulty correctly describing the night sky after they had been coached to agree that the moon could be called the sun and the thing up in the sky at night would then be called the sun.

We took a slightly different approach to the problem. We were interested in whether nonliterate adults would agree that the names attached to referents (in this case, the names "sun" and "moon") were, in fact, arbitrary. On the basis of anthropological discussions of word magic (for example, Horton, 1967) we thought it entirely possible that nonliterate adults would refuse to agree with the first question, or that agreeing with the first, they would still fail to apply that agreement to the second question. Therefore, we did not coach people but simply asked them to justify their answers to each of the questions. We assigned points, depending upon how fully individuals could answer each of the sun-moon questions. Because we had only developmental data from the United States and Europe to go on, this item in the survey was clearly more of a fishing expedition than the other cognitive tasks.

No group responded in a particularly impressive fashion. English literates and biliterates were the only groups in which a majority agreed to the possibility that names for the sun and the moon could be exchanged. But even these groups averaged less than two correct answers out of three. Detailed analysis showed that both schooling and biliteracy improved performance on the task, but the relationships were by no means straightforward: the effect of schooling depended on the informant's age and place of residence, and we could not identify the specific literacy functions responsible for elevating biliterates' scores. The basic predictive equation is:

$$\begin{array}{l} \text{Language} \\ \text{objectivity score} = 6.98 + .65 \text{ writes letters for others in English} \\ (R^2 = .08) \hspace{5em} (2.2) \\ \hspace{4em} + .50 \text{ Vai-Arabic biliterate} \\ \hspace{7em} (2.9) \\ \hspace{4em} + .01 \text{ (last grade)}^2 \times \text{live in Vaitown} \\ \hspace{7em} (2.9) \\ \hspace{4em} + .54 \text{ out of school now} - .00001 \text{ age} \times \text{(last grade)}^2 \\ \hspace{5em} (2.4) \hspace{9em} (1.9) \end{array}$$

From people's explanations it was clear, however, that their answers reflected a Vai view of the world, rather than confusion between words and things. A common reason for denying the possibility of exchanging names was a practical consideration, "You will never get people all over the world to agree to that," or an ideological conviction, "Humans should not interfere with God's work." Genevan children responded to Piaget in quite a different manner, offering accounts such as, "No, because the sun shines hotter than the moon"; "Because the moon must be the moon and not the sun and the sun must be the sun" (Piaget, 1960, p. 81). Some explanations of this kind were offered in our interviews but they constituted a small minority of the negative cases in all groups.

Realizing the complexities involved in trying to assess people's understanding of language properties, we made plans for follow-up studies.

MODERNITY AND COGNITIVE CHANGE

One of the important reasons for including the modernity questions in our survey was the speculation by various sociologists of a link between modernity and modes of thinking. The causal direction of these hypotheses usually runs from prior experience (education) to cognitive change to modernity, although it seems plausible to consider the possibility that becoming modern may itself induce cognitive change. Whatever one's intuitions, the data we collected on the precursors of modernity, when compared with data on the precursors of improved performance on our cognitive tasks, represented an unusual opportunity to determine what relationship, if any, obtains between modernity and cognition.

For our sample of 290 men, modest but significant correlations were obtained between the short-form modernity score and such cognitive tasks as responses to the logical syllogisms, reversing the names of the sun and the moon, and free recall (these correlations varied between .17 and .24). Several variables that predicted cognitive test performance, most notably education, were among the predictors of modernity as well. Consequently, these first-order correlations do not help us to determine if modernity predicts cognitive performance over and above predictions from demographic independent variables. The answer to this question, obtained from a series of regression analyses, was no. Adding modernity scores to the prediction equations for our cognitive dependent variables did not improve prediction and they did not enter significantly into equations. When we used cognitive variables in the equations that predicted modernity, we also failed to obtain significant changes in our prediction equations. In short, we found no evidence of a direct relationship between modernity and cognitive performance; performances on modernity attitude questions (see Chapter 7) and on cognitive tasks were predictable by various combinations of past experience, of which education was a major variable in common, but they were not predictive of each other.

THE FACTS IN REVIEW

What did we learn from our mass administration of cognitive tasks? Provisional answers are available from a review of regression analyses. School effects are fairly consistent; effects of nonschooled literacies are spotty and appear on only a few performance measures. Of the many classes of nonliteracy experiences examined, urban living and its converse—involvement in the traditional sector—prove to be the only factors affecting what people said and did in the experimental situations.

The most impressive finding is that formal schooling with instruction in English increased ability to provide a verbal explanation of the principles involved in performing the various tasks. Justifications given by schooled individuals were more task-oriented and informative than those given by others; they more often made use of class and attribute names. While these results are consistent with those of previous studies, for the first time we have shown that schooling affects verbal explanations over and above any influences it may exert on successful execution of the task itself. Our methods of analysis also move us a step further in pinning down these effects to some aspect of schooling other than the fact that it involves knowledge of the English language or English literacy. Speaking English never substituted for school variables, and on verbalization measures, school—not English reading scores—was the best predictor.

So much for the positive contribution of schooling. Since all the tasks were chosen initially because they had demonstrated school effects in other traditional cultures, it is reassuring to see this distinction emerging in our findings. Yet the exceptions—tasks and measures on which we failed to reproduce school effects—are equally important and instructive. We did not, for example, find schooled individuals demonstrating a more flexible abstract attitude in the geometric sorting task, nor a greater tendency to use taxonomic organizations in the free sort and recall tasks. One explanation for these discrepancies with earlier studies may lie in the low level of schooling represented in our sample. In earlier research involving reclassification of geometric stimuli (Gay and Cole, 1967; Sharp, Cole, and Lave, 1979), schooled and nonschooled populations drew apart at the third-grade level and above. (Greenfield also obtained her greatest contrast at upper grade levels.) Separating scores by level of schooling also enabled us to find some school effect on the constrained classification task. But unequal amounts of schooling is only a partial explanation. No grade or school effects could be brought to the surface for the free sort and recall tasks. It appears that school influences in this part of our study are too complicated to ascribe to a "last grade completed" construct—although this is the way schooling variables are ordinarily discussed. Because we were dealing with an adult population whose experiences with Western-type schooling were quite diversified, we were forced to attend to variations often neglected. Place (Vaitown versus upcountry) and the era in which schooling occurred played a role in some analyses. One of the most important distinctions turned out to be school status at the time of our survey—whether individuals still engaged in schooling as their primary pursuit or whether they were out of school and occupied with daily activities that might or might not call upon the skills they had acquired there. Our results raise a specter: even if we were to accept as a working proposition that school produces general changes in certain intellectual operations, we might have to qualify the conclusion to refer only to students, recent ex-students, or those continuing in schoollike occupations.

What about the effects of nonschooled literacies? These surely disappoint the grand expectations and lofty theories that inspired us to undertake this line of investigation. Under conditions obtaining in Vai society, neither syllabic Vai script literacy nor Arabic alphabetic literacy was associated with what are considered the higher-order intellectual skills. Neither literacy enhanced the use of taxonomic skills on any task designed to test categorization. Nor did either contribute to a shift toward syllogistic reasoning. Nor did the traditional literacies improve the adequacy of verbal explanations or foster greater use of category labels. Any influences that we found were local and selective. Both Vai script and Arabic literacy (but only among biliterates) contributed to preference for form and number in the geometric sorting task. But they failed to affect any other aspect of performance on this task that would warrant statements about abstract attitudes. Arabic reading scores contributed to recall when a word list was orally presented and when reading scores were associated with biliteracy. While biliteracy contributed to more correct answers on the language objectivity (sun-moon) problem, we are at a loss to account for the specific literacy-related experiences behind this effect.

MID-COURSE CONCLUSIONS

Despite the unresolved questions and ambiguous findings this eperimental assay may leave behind, there are several conclusions about which we believe there can be little argument. In our opinion, they help lay to rest some misconceptions about the psychology of literacy that went unchallenged in the past for lack of empirical data. First, it is clear from the evidence we reviewed that nonschooled literacy, as we found and tested it among the Vai, does not produce general cognitive effects as we have defined them. The small and selective nature of Vai script and Arabic influences on cognitive performance precludes any sweeping generalizations about literacy and cognitive change. At best we can say that there are several localized literacy-specific effects on certain task specific skills.

Implicit in the foregoing discussion, but worth stating explicitly, is the fact that there is no evidence in these data to support the construct of a general "literacy" phenomenon. Although many writers discuss literacy and its social and psychological implications as though literacy entails the same knowledge and skills whenever people read or write, our experimental outcomes support our social analysis in demonstrating that literacies are highly differentiated. Arabic and Vai script do not trade off for each other in predicting cognitive performance, nor do they (singly or in combination) substitute for English literacy.

Thus, neither Vai script nor Qur'anic-learning-and-Arabic-script act as surrogates for schooling. They do not produce the range of cognitive effects that schooling does, nor do they always act on the same tasks. Discrepancies between effects of these literacies and schooling challenge the hypothesis that schooling affects thinking by equipping children, in Greenfield's terms, with a "written language." Men literate in Vai script qualify as having a written language but they do not (behaviorally or verbally in the experimental tasks) "look like" their peers with schooling. Whether literacy in the English language acts as a surrogate for schooling could not be tested definitively for the very reasons that motivated this research. There is an almost complete confounding of English literacy and schooling. In any event, claims about the mediating effects of written language that are restricted to particular languages lose attraction as well as explanatory power.

While not the center of our attention, the effects of urban experience and its converse (traditional life) also suggest that generalizations about literacy's psychological impact in developing nations may be overstated. In Lerner's model (1958), literacy and urbanism were linked. That model may still apply in nations where school-created literacy preempts literacy programs. As an "exceptional case study" our Vai observations are valuable in showing that neither modernizing experience (literacy or urbanism) may be entirely subsumed under the other. The effect of urban living on classification tasks seems reasonable, but a moment's reflection shows that it is neither self-evident nor trivial. Why should adults living in Vaitown show a stronger preference for taxonomic relations than their relatives upcountry? What are the mechanisms behind such a switch? The survey experiments provided a reasonable starting point for probing literacy's effect on cognitive processes, but they were flawed by the fact that, even if successful in demonstrating literacy effects, they could tell us very little about how these consequences were generated.

9

Literacy and Metalinguistic Knowledge

Our survey results made it clear that nonschool literacies practiced among the Vai do not have the same cognitive effects as Western-type schooling. Yet we were unwilling to abandon the possibility that there might be some form of pervasive intellectual changes related to literacy per se. Turning away from developmental theorizing about higher-order thinking and memory skills, we decided to examine cognitive change in domains more closely related to acquisition and use of written language.

One such domain is language itself. A theme encountered throughout the psychological and linguistic literature is that becoming literate profoundly changes what people know about their language and how they think about it. A competent member of any language community must command a vast amount of linguistic knowledge to participate effectively in the speech events required in that community. Two kinds of linguistic knowledge are commonly distinguished: implicit knowledge underlying speech activity, and reflective, explicit knowledge about language that the individual can formulate and talk about. Because this latter knowledge builds on already established (implicit) linguistic competence, it is commonly referred to as metalinguistic knowledge or metalinguistic awareness. How to distinguish metalinguistic knowledge from other kinds of language knowledge conceptually and how to investigate it empirically are still matters of active debate among psychologists and linguists (see Mattingly, 1972; Savin, 1972; Cazden, 1974; Ehri, 1979).

One line of theorizing assumes that metalinguistic consequences arise from the material properties of writing.

Several hypotheses have developed from a consideration of written language as an object. One claim, with which we dealt in Chapter 8, is that writing distances language from the things it denotes. A symbol in a script does not stand directly for anything in the environment but rather for some linguistic or semantic unit which in turn symbolizes an aspect of reality. It follows that becoming literate should diminish the tendency to confuse properties of words and properties of things, or, in Piaget's terms, dispel nominal realism.

Another claim is that the written form of a language may define or make salient certain linguistic units that are not marked off in speech. For example, in ordinary speech we may pause between phrases but not after each word, yet we write English in the alphabet with spaces after each word. If we did not follow this writing convention, would we have the concept of a word as a constituent element of English? (For early consideration of this topic in anthropology, see Sapir, 1921, pp. 33–34, and for a comprehensive treatment in psychology, see Ehri, 1979.)

A second line of theorizing about metalinguistic consequences of literacy emphasizes the mental processes involved in writing. From the outset, the individual learning how to write confronts the machinery of his language. In a famous passage to which we will refer in several contexts, Vygotsky (1962) describes the writing process as a "deliberate structuring of the web of meaning" (p. 99). Through processes of self-conscious composition, a literate person should gain a greater understanding of the systematic nature of language, its regularities, or, in general parlance, its grammar.

Olson (1977) has further extended the view that written language involves specialized linguistic operations. He maintains that experience with reading or producing texts promotes skill in attending to logical relationships in statements, independent of the way they map onto the reader's notion of reality. Literates should therefore be skilled in handling the implications of verbal statements regardless of their content (Olson and Nickerson, 1978).

While various theorists may stress one or another of these components, metalinguistic knowledge is usually conceived as embracing all of them and constituting a general orientation to language. If that were the case, one would expect to find that these different aspects of linguistic knowledge are highly correlated with each other. We designed our studies with this possibility in mind.

RESEARCH IN OVERVIEW

When we decided to pursue this line of work, we knew it would involve mainly exploratory activities rather than experimental proofs. Few investigations of metalinguistic skills had been conducted at that time, and well-tested tasks and methods were not on hand. Research involved only alphabetic literacies and Indo-European languages. What little was known about the developmental course of metalinguistic skills concerned children, not adults with mature competencies in spoken language.

In our tests of general cognitive effects, we had available a battery of tasks on which psychologists had reached a general (if shaky) consensus about the processes underlying performance and the behaviors that might be considered reliable indicators of those processes. In contrast, research on metalinguistic skills was still heavily dependent on interview methods (Downing and Oliver, 1973; Papandropoulou and Sinclair, 1974; Osherson and Markman, 1974–1975). Most investigators made inferences about children's understanding of language on the basis of their talks with them about language. A presupposition in this procedure is that questioner and respondent mean the same thing when they use the same words. But it is exactly this assumption that metalinguistic research seeks to test, and it is one assumption that cannot be taken for granted in situations like ours where investigators and informants come from different cultures and language communities. Because of these difficulties, we adopted a conservative course: we decided to cast a wide net for metalinguistic effects, to replicate observations, and to try to reproduce promising outcomes under changed experimental conditions.

Our metalinguistic investigations began immediately after the conclusion of our major survey and continued until the end of our fieldwork. In the main, they were carried out in the format of survey investigations modeled after our major survey. We collected background information by means of a questionnaire and administered a set of tasks. Background information always included items identified as important covariates of the specific literacies in our major survey as well as characteristics (such as modernity or multilingualism) that theoretically could exercise direct effects on metalinguistic knowledge. While all surveys involved members of our basic literacy subgroups, the number of groups represented and their literacy characteristics differed somewhat from one survey to another because each survey had a different central interest. The first study, which we refer to as the metalinguistic survey, was devoted entirely to exploration of metalinguistic skills and concentrated on the effect of the traditional, non-schooled literacies. Five tasks sampling components of metalinguistic knowledge were presented to 50 respondents in small rural towns in Cape Mount County; none of them had attended school.[1] Our two interviewers were college students, one of whom was skilled in all three literacies and one of whom knew both Vai script and English. Following completion of this study, we conducted a replication survey with 105 men to test the sturdiness of the results of several independent lines of investigation on memory and communication as well as outcomes on the metalinguistic tasks. This study was conducted in other small and isolated towns in Cape Mount County by an interviewer from the staff of the major survey who had only a partial high school education. It included individuals who had once attended English school as well as a number of young men and women still in school in upcountry locations. Finally, the third survey investigation incorporated two metalinguistic tasks in a battery that was designed to test for component skills involved in reading Vai script. This investigation, which we call the integration survey, was conducted among 100 men in these groups: nonliterates, Qur'anic and Arabic literates, men of novice and ex-

Table 9.1 Comparison of metalinguistic tasks across surveys

	Metalinguistic survey (N = 50)	Replication survey (N = 105)	Integration survey (N = 100)
Experimenters	Mohamed Nyei Hamidu Getaweh	Bai Paasewe	Hamidu Getaweh
Populations	Nonliterate men Vai script monoliterate — Vai-Arabic biliterate —	Nonliterate men Vai script monoliterate Arabic monoliterate Vai-Arabic biliterate Schooled	Nonliterate men Vai script monoliterate Arabic monoliterate — Schooled
Tasks	Language objectivity Longest word Word definitions Grammar Logic	Language objectivity Longest word — Grammar Logic	Language objectivity Longest word (forced choice) — Grammar —

Table 9.2 Background characteristics of metalinguistic survey population (men only)

	Nonliterate (N = 18)	Vai script monoliterate (N = 13)	Vai-Arabic biliterate (N = 19)
Age	47.44	47.54	51.63
Number of years lived in urban towns[a]	8.50	6.92	5.63
Farm only (no/yes)	.33	.46	.21
Lived in foreign concession (no/yes)	.22	.38	.21
Modernity of occupation (1–3)	1.56	1.39	1.58
Speak English (degree 0–3)	.94	.69	.84
Number of tribal languages spoken[b]	1.11	1.00	1.00
Vai script reading score (1–4)	—	3.39	3.21
Number of years knew Vai script	—	24.69	31.68
Arabic reading score (1–4)	—	—	2.68
Number of years studied Qur'an[c]	.89	—	13.32
Last grade English school	—	—	—

a. "Urban town" here and in following summaries refers to a town with population of two thousand or over.

b. Number of tribal languages here is in addition to Vai.

c. A few individuals who had once studied Qur'an for two years or less but whose current reading score was 0 are included in this group.

Table 9.3 Background characteristics of replication survey population (men only)

	Nonliterate (N = 22)	Vai script monoliterate (N = 22)	Arabic monoliterate (N = 19)	Vai-Arabic biliterate (N = 24)	Schooled (N = 18)
Age	42.77	41.09	35.84	41.13	22.78
Number of years lived in urban towns	2.14	4.59	3.00	4.38	14.39
Farm only (no/yes)	.41	.32	.32	.21	.00
Lived in foreign concession (no/yes)	.27	.27	.32	.21	.50
Modernity of occupation (1–3)	1.23	1.23	1.68	1.54	1.94
Skill rating (1–6)	1.77	2.32	2.05	2.79	2.39
Speak English (degree, 0–3)	.64	1.00	.95	.96	2.56
Number of tribal languages spoken	2.18	2.46	1.74	1.54	1.56
Vai script reading score (1–4)	—	2.59	—	3.04	—
Number of years knew Vai script	—	9.23	—	14.04	—
Arabic reading score (1–4)	—	—	2.00	2.33	—
Number of years studied Qur'an	—	—	5.21	6.63	—
Last grade English school	—	—	—	—	9.78
English reading score (1–4)	—	—	—	—	3.50

pert status in Vai script, and senior high school or college men. One of the interviewers from the metalinguistic survey carried out this work. Traditional literates were from Cape Mount County communities; the students all attended school in Monrovia. In none of the studies did we attempt to secure a random sample of the population as a whole; instead, we elicited cooperation on a voluntary basis from members of literacy subgroups we wanted to compare.

The major features of these surveys are summarized in Table 9.1. Background characteristics of survey populations are given in Tables 9.2, 9.3, and 9.4. As can be seen, the many differences in critical population characteristics, experimenters, and (in some cases) tasks preclude comparing absolute levels of performance from one survey to another. However, this method of linking surveys by overlapping tasks provided, as we intended, a strong test of metalinguistic hypotheses. Replicating an outcome under these conditions gave us some confidence that performance differences among groups may have been more than the happenstance of sampling procedures or fallout from the instructional styles of individual interviewers.

We can report at the outset that results of this work discourage the no-

Table 9.4 Background characteristics of integration survey population (men only)

	Nonliterate (N = 20)	Qur'anic only (N = 10)	Arabic (N = 10)	Beginning Vai script[a] (N = 20)	Advanced Vai script[a] (N = 20)	Schooled (N = 20)
Age	38.65	28.20	32.10	41.45	42.65	23.95
Number of years lived in urban towns	5.45	8.10	4.20	4.50	5.40	7.50
Lived in foreign concession (no/yes)	.00	.30	.00	.20	.15	.25
Skill rating (1–6)	2.35	1.80	1.80	2.35	2.40	2.50
Speak English (degree 0–3)	1.00	1.00	.80	1.05	1.00	2.10
Number of tribal languages spoken	1.25	1.00	1.00	1.55	1.35	1.05
Vai script reading score (1–4)	—	—	—	1.60	3.45	—
Number of years knew Vai script	—	—	—	8.55	15.75	—
Vai script use score[b]	—	—	—	2.90	7.15	—
Extent of Vai script teaching (0–2)	—	—	—	.40	1.20	—
No. years studied Qur'an[c]	.35	4.60	8.80	.55	2.80	1.15
No. years wrote Arabic[c]	—	—	9.80	—	1.70	—

a. Vai script literates scoring 1 and 2 on reading test were classified as beginners; those scoring 3 and 4 were classified as advanced.

b. Each reported use scores 1 (for instance, letter writting, keeping diary, etc.)

c. A few individuals in nonliterate, schooled, and beginning Vai script groups briefly studied Qur'an. Because many advanced Vai script literates are biliterates, this group included four men who had learned some Qur'an and two who had finished it. One of these also knew Arabic as a language. We took these variables into account in regression equations.

tion that metalinguistic knowledge, as exemplified in our tasks, can be considered a unitary phenomenon. If it were a unitary ability, we would expect people who scored well on one task to score well on the others; performances would be correlated. We tested this hypothesis of general metalinguistic skills both for the entire population in the metalinguistic survey and for each of its literacy subpopulations separately (since we considered it possible that one or another of the literacies might make a difference to general metalinguistic skills while others might not). Some significant intertask correlations were obtained, but no more than we would expect by chance. No consistent pattern of intercorrelations among tasks emerged in either analysis. Similar correlational analyses applied to the replication survey produced the same outcome. Finding no evidence for general metalinguistic abilities, we turned to the weaker hypothesis that literacy among the Vai might promote specific metalinguistic skills.

It will simplify our exposition if we handle our research vertically, following a single metalinguistic issue over time and through a series of studies, rather than organizing it horizontally by describing studies addressed to a variety of issues. Unless otherwise specified, all performances were analyzed by regression equations according to procedures substantially the same as those described in Chapter 8. When we report that literacy is a significant factor it means that a script-related (or school-related) variable survived all attempts to displace it by covariates or other predictor factors.

LANGUAGE OBJECTIVITY: NAMES AND THINGS

In the preceding chapter, we reported the results of our probes about the interchangeability of the names of the sun and the moon. No groups in our initial survey, not even the schooled populations, had performed in a particularly impressive manner. This task, however, had a long enough history and seemed to speak so directly to theorizing about metalinguistic awareness that we decided to continue working with it.

Results for the language objectivity problem in the two surveys using this task are presented in Table 9.5 in terms of average levels of performance. Looking across the rows of the table, we see no compelling reason to think that literacy increases ability to understand the arbitrary relations between names and things. This generally negative conclusion is somewhat modified when we submit the data to multiple regression analysis. The final equation predicting answers to the sun-moon question in the metalinguistic survey is the following:

Language objectivity = 2.5 + 1.9 biliteracy − .03 age × biliteracy
$(R^2 = .16)$ (2.1)   (1.9)
               − .88 farming only
                   (2.7)

In the replication survey, the comparable equation is:

Language objectivity = .53 + .19 Vai reading score
$(R^2 = .12)$ (2.1)
            + .80 speak English × Arabic monoliteracy
                     (2.4)
            + .25 English reading score
                   (2.5)
            + .20 number of places lived
                   (2.5)

These results are tantalizing. All three literacies are implicated to a modest degree but they do not meet our conditions for cross-task consistency.[2] Vai reading score, for example, appears only in the replication survey, and biliteracy in the metalinguistic survey; Arabic monoliteracy appears only in common with another language variable, speak English, which might have a direct effect in its own right. A residential variable, farming only (which has the effect of keeping one in the countryside), and number of places lived (the opposite pattern of experience) both point toward wider contact in the world as a factor promoting this kind of performance.

To understand the complexity of the task as it appeared to our informants, we organized a discussion with a group of men who had participated in survey interviews. All of the men were literate in either Vai script or Arabic. We pointed out that some people had answered the sun-moon

Table 9.5 Group means for language objectivity (sun-moon) question

	Nonliterate	Vai script literate	Vai-Arabic biliterate	Arabic literate	Schooled literate
Metalinguistic survey	2.2[a]	2.1	2.6	—	—
Replication survey	1.3	1.9	1.5	1.5	2.1

a. Maximum possible score, 3.0.

question one way and some the other. We asked them to give their replies and discuss which answer might be better.

The first man to volunteer a response said, "Oh yes! We can change the names of the sun and the moon." The conversation proceeded as follows:

Sembe: The reason is this. The man we used to call the president was Tubman, right? When the man died, we put in a man there called Tolbert. So we can change the name of anything. But I can't make myself like you. You hear? And yóu can't make yourself like me. But you can take my name. And it will suit you.

Momolu: I can't agree. Maybe I can say that I will call the sun the moon and the moon the sun but they will not change their work. So I will call them by their own names.

Aamah: I agree with Momolu. Anything that God creates we cannot change. We cannot change a man into a woman.

Sembe: They are not going to change a man into a woman. They are going to change the name.

Aamah: I can't agree. You have never named a woman "Sembe" and I cannot change the name of the moon to the sun.

Sembe: But they didn't say you must change the sun. They changed its name.

Aamah: That's what I am saying! They say we must sit down together and change the sun and the moon. But I myself, I am not with them.

The discussion continued. In support of the notion that names are arbitrary, one man pointed out that by government decree, Liberia had changed its way of recording time to coincide with Sierra Leone's. Another claimed that if he wanted to, he could call the table they were sitting at a chair, and the chair a table. This example pleased almost everyone, especially when the proponent stated that this suggestion was an "amendment" (using the English term, and referring to amendments of government laws). But Aamah stood fast. His parting comment was the following:

There are two things in the world. A thing can be, and a thing can be talked about. The thing that is cannot be changed. Anything that God created, His talking, the names He gave to things, cannot be changed.

In effect, Aamah is arguing that things named by God cannot be changed because both names and things were created by Him and none of God's creations can be changed. But note that the argument takes account of names and things as independent concepts!

The discussion took up the question of whether the name "bird" has feathers. This time Aamah disagreed:

> There are names called birds that have feathers; other names called birds do not have feathers. When they name a person "Bird," he does not have feathers.

When the discussion moved to the question of whether or not you could buy a soft drink with the name "dime," Aamah was particularly clear:

> I can buy a soft drink with the money itself, but not with the name.

These excerpts do not adequately capture the spirited nature of the discussion from which they have been extracted. Aamah was an influential man in Vai society, a Vai script and Arabic literate who could knowledgeably dispute interpretations of Liberian law and Qur'anic commentary. In responding to the possibility of changing names, he distinguished between man-made and God-created (natural) objects, maintaining that names created by God are not arbitrary because God created them. At the same time, he understood the argument about changing names, rejecting it on theological grounds. From his answer to the question "Can you change the names of the sun and the moon?" one might conclude that he is a nominal realist who does not distinguish words and referents. This conclusion appears faulty not only on the internal evidence of the ensuing discussion, but also because he maintained stoutly that names and objects could not supplant each other in the remaining test questions.

CONCEPTS OF A WORD

Many psychologists and linguists take it for granted that all adults have some concept of a word; they also agree that this concept is acquired and that young children's understanding of what a word is does not match that of the literate adult in our society. Children have difficulty distinguishing a word from a nonsense syllable (Ehri, 1979) and recognizing that functional units such as "or" and "to" belong to the linguistic category "word" (Karpova, 1966; Holden and MacGinitie, 1972). They find it hard to separate common English phrases such as "I do" into word units (Huttenlocher, 1964) and define a word (Papandropoulou and Sinclair, 1974; Litowitz, 1977). Some psychologists consider increasing lexical awareness to be part of the general process of cognitive development, but others maintain that learning how to read is a prime factor in enabling children to distinguish words as units of language and to understand their function (Ehri, 1979, for example).

As we have pointed out, awareness of words may be promoted by conventions of orthographic representation which mark word boundaries with spaces. Alternatively, the forms of language analysis required in learning how to read and write may draw attention to words as basic language building blocks, even in the absence of their separation on the written page. These alternative explanations were potentially testable among Vai script literates. Vai script does not segment words; if word awareness primarily relies on the existence of distinguishable units in the script, Vai script literates should have no more developed concepts of wordness than nonliterates. If learning how to read or write heightens awareness of words as building blocks, Vai script literates should be superior to nonliterates on tasks tapping this knowledge, even though the script does not segment words.

We began our study of concepts of a word with a simple task borrowed from Papandropoulou and Sinclair (1974). We asked respondents to say the longest word they could think of. Very young children (preschoolers) sometimes respond to this request with a phrase, or a series of words, or even repeated words ("Mary, Mary, Mary"). When giving a single word, they might pick one in which the referent is long but the word itself short (for example, "snake" or "road"), or interpret word length to be the time it takes to say the word rather than the number of its constituent parts (for example, elongating vowel sounds such as in "craaaacker" or "oraaange"). By mid-elementary school years, children in the United States and other industrialized countries use the number of sublexical units making up a word (syllables) as the criterion for length (Holden and MacGinitie, 1972; Liberman et al., 1974). For the reasons already discussed, we had no specific predictions as to whether Vai script literates would be more prone than others to give a single word. But we hypothesized that if Vai script literates responded with a single word, they would correctly give one with a large number of syllables. Since in Vai script every character stands for a syllable, it is reasonable to suppose that number of syllables might become the dominant criterion for word length in literates' judgments.[3]

Deciding to use such a task and constructing a usable version of it turned out to be two very different issues. Questions about words presuppose that the Vai language has a word for "word." We quickly discovered that there is no lexical item that can be unequivocally identified with the English word "word." The Vai expression closest in meaning is *koali kulē*, which translates roughly as "a piece of speech" or "an utterance." The English equivalent of *koali kulē* varies depending upon the linguistic context in which it is used. In the following sentences, *koali kulē* can be substituted in all of the slots occupied by the italicized words. Each sentence was taken from instructions used in one or another of our metalinguistic tasks and was translated cooperatively into Vai by several Vai informants with some training in linguistics.

1. The Vai language has many *words*.
   I am going to ask you some questions about *words*.

2. I am going to read you two *statements* that you must assume are true.
3. Please take this letter and put a mark between each *utterance*.

As these examples make clear, *koali kulē* may at times be interpreted as "word," "sentence," or "phrase." At other times, it is interpreted as "voice." For example, in a task to be described shortly, people were asked to define *koali kulē* in their own words. Some people replied, "You mean that which comes from your mouth that you make with air?"

In our first serious attempt to obtain judgments on word length, we used instructions that employed the term *koali kulē* in the following context: "Some Vai words (*koali kulē*) are short, some are long. Tell me the longest word (*koali kulē*) you know." We experimented with different forms of the question, substituting "small/big" for "short/long" but found that the first version was more consistently understood as we had intended.

We coded responses in two stages. First, we determined whether the utterance contained a single word or several words. If it contained a single word, we counted the number of syllables composing it.

As with the sun-moon problem, levels of performance in the metalinguistic and replication surveys differed considerably. (See Table 9.6). In the metalinguistic survey, nonliterate and traditional literacy groups offered words in the majority of cases; in the replication survey, however, no more than half the people in any group offered single words.

Following our standard procedure of regression analysis, we tried to find variables that would predict performance for each measure of interest, beginning with the likelihood that an informant would offer a single word in response to the request to name a long word. The small difference among scores in the metalinguistic survey (first line of part A) is reflected in our regression analyses; no population characteristic predicted this kind of performance. In the replication survey (second line of part A), some difference between groups was apparent, but no simple pattern of literacy experience emerged in the analyses. Two interactive variables reflecting various combinations of literacy and Vai script reading scores worked in opposite direc-

Table 9.6 Concepts of a word

	Nonliterate	Vai script monoliterate	Vai-Arabic biliterate	Arabic monoliterate	Schooled literate
A. Gives a single word (maximum score, 1)					
Metalinguistic survey	.72	.69	.79	—	—
Replication survey	.45	.55	.38	.37	.50
B. Number of syllables in word					
Metalinguistic survey	3.1	3.1	4.0	—	—
Replication survey	1.3	1.6	1.3	1.2	1.6

tions. According to our operational rule, "no effect without a replication," we prefer to conclude that the complicated equation of the replication survey did not indicate any reliable effect of literacy.

The equation was as follows:

$$\text{One word score} = .33 + .04 \text{ Vai monoliterate} \times \text{Vai reading score 3, 4}$$
$$(R^2 = .16) \qquad\qquad (2.7)$$
$$- .13 \text{ (biliterate} \times \text{Vai reading score 1, 2)}^2$$
$$(2.2)$$
$$- .23 \text{ farming only} + 1.8 \text{ speak English}$$
$$(2.2) \qquad\qquad (2.0)$$

If we ask whether literacy influences the length of words offered in those cases where the informant responded with a single word, some suggestion of an influence of literacy emerges. In the metalinguistic survey the biliterate group outperformed the two contrasting groups, and results are tied directly to reading ability in the two scripts. In the replication survey there is a positive contribution linked to years of Qur'anic study, and knowledge of two or more tribal languages. This is one of the few cases where we see a hint of experience of Arabic literacy in our data. School status also contributed, but the anticipated superiority of Vai script literates in analyzing words into syllabic components failed to materialize.

The equations in these cases hold constant the possibility that a single word is given.

Metalinguistic survey:

$$\text{Number of syllables} = - .12 + 4.49 \text{ one word}$$
$$(R^2 = .74) \qquad\qquad (11.0)$$
$$+ .08 \text{ Vai reading score} \times \text{Arabic reading score}$$
$$(2.1)$$

Replication survey:

$$\text{Number of syllables} = - .60 + 2.99 \text{ one word} + .22 \text{ speak tribal languages}$$
$$(R^2 = .82) \qquad\qquad (2.10) \qquad\qquad (3.7)$$
$$+ .05 \text{ years Qur'an} + .26 \text{ school status}$$
$$(3.2) \qquad\qquad (2.1)$$

Spotty results with respect to Vai script literates' concept of "word" are difficult to evaluate. They might mean that the guiding hypotheses are invalid, but they might merely testify to the inadequacy of our research techniques. Our experiences led us to believe that linguistic and procedural matters might be at fault. We were trying to study factors that influenced people's concepts of a word through a Vai expression, *koali kulē*, whose meaning was not only ambiguous to us with respect to its equivalent in English, but whose meaning to our Vai informants was extremely sensitive to linguistic and task contexts. The variability, or lack of variability, we encountered in people's performance might reflect their varying interpretation of *koali kulē*. Our interpretation of their performances foundered on our inability to specify their interpretation of our instructions.

To overcome this impasse, we changed our procedures. We initiated follow-up studies in which we used a physical object to provide a common context for discussions about *koali kulē*. We had initiated one such line of work in the early days of the project but could not carry it out systematically at that time because of our inadequate knowledge of the Vai language and script. In this work we made use of an objective referent to which it seemed natural to turn in our queries about the effects of literacy—written samples of the Vai script itself. In effect, we sought to probe Vai literates' knowledge of wordness using script materials in the way theoreticians claim they exert metalinguistic effects, by making language a thing. With a piece of writing in hand, both interviewer and respondent have a common object to which to point in conducting their conversation about language. In the next study we asked literates to show us the units they thought were appropriate referents for *koali kulē*.

SEGMENTING VAI SCRIPT INTO UNITS

Fairly early in our investigation of Vai script reading and writing, we undertook a study of the way in which skilled literates segment their language when asked to take an example of a letter they had recently received and make a mark between each of the *koali kulē* that they found there. In our initial work we deliberately refrained from giving more explicit instructions. Everyone agreed that a letter could be segmented into *koali kulē*; we simply took each person's production and analyzed the segments. We immediately saw that the segments most commonly produced were larger than those we would identify as words.[4] Sometimes people would include in a single segment entire sentences ("They say there is oil" or "I know it"); particles were virtually always attached to words that preceded or followed them.

On the basis of the kinds of segments we encountered in these haphazardly gathered materials, we constructed a model letter, mundane in content to simulate the kind of letter that circulates widely in Vai country. We included various kinds of grammatical constructions that our pilot materials had suggested would produce interesting variability. The model letter was given to ten men, all of whom were skilled script readers and writers, and several of whom were Arabic literates as well. (Unfortunately, we did not collect a large enough sample of segmented letters to permit us to distinguish the performance of these two groups.) Figure 9.1 is a copy of the sample letter on which we have indicated those points where virtually all of the literates agreed in their segmentation. (To convey the sense of the letter, English translation does not follow the Vai exactly; it is close enough, however, to indicate the meaning of the phrases and the significance of the points at which there is wide agreement on segmenting.) Note that possessive pronouns are usually grouped with nouns that they modify ("my big brother," "our health"); subject pronouns in subject-verb phrases tend to be grouped with the verb ("I want"). There is also a distinct tendency for adjectives to be grouped with the nouns that they modify ("big farm"); we had few examples of adjective-noun phrases in the model letter, but this clumping practice was ubiquitous in the pilot materials in which there were many such phrases. Set expressions ("this is your information"), while sometimes segmented, were most often treated as units.

Further examination of Figure 9.1 indicates, however, that we have to temper these generalizations. For example, although "big farm" is part of a single segment (in fact, part of a segment that included "I prepared a big farm"), the elements "three" and "dollars" are kept distinct in the phrase "three dollars." Similar discrepancies can be found for other word combinations which to us appear to be examples of the same kind. An important aspect of the word segmenting data is that in only a few cases did anyone divide a unit we considered to be a word into smaller elements corresponding to anything like a syllable. While this fact may seem trivial, it represents rather strong evidence that literates were attending to meaning while segmenting the text into *koali kulē*, and that units we would classify as words represented minimal units.

With these results in hand, we were interested in getting some idea of the criteria that people applied in their segmenting practices. As one approach, we worked extensively with Adama Swary, an expert Vai script literate who was also literate in Arabic. We began by giving him the standard instruction to segment the letter into *koali kulē*, and he, like other informants, produced units that seemed to us to range from single lexical units to phrases. Then we asked him to go back over the units he had marked off to determine whether these could be divided into *koali kulē* differently. On these passes Mr. Swary broke down some initial phrase units into their components, but on several occasions he combined smaller units to form larger ones. For example, in one section of the text he came upon two characters comprising the English word "book" or "letter," *kpolo* in Vai, which he first kept separate but later combined with three characters representing *mēē la*, to produce the phrase "this letter." In his discussion of Mr. Swary's work, Mohamed Nyei, our Vai research assistant, described the process quite nicely: "I think he grouped units together because of their interrelated meanings in reference to the context in which they occurred."

As a second approach to discovering criteria for segmenting written language in units we interviewed people in a group session. We conducted one such interview in the town of Misila, which has a long tradition of Vai script literacy with a strong admixture of Arabic scholarship as well. We asked the assembled men to segment the standard letter into *koali kulē* using our regular instructions, and then, after a particular segment had been completed, we asked them to explain the basis for the given segment; in

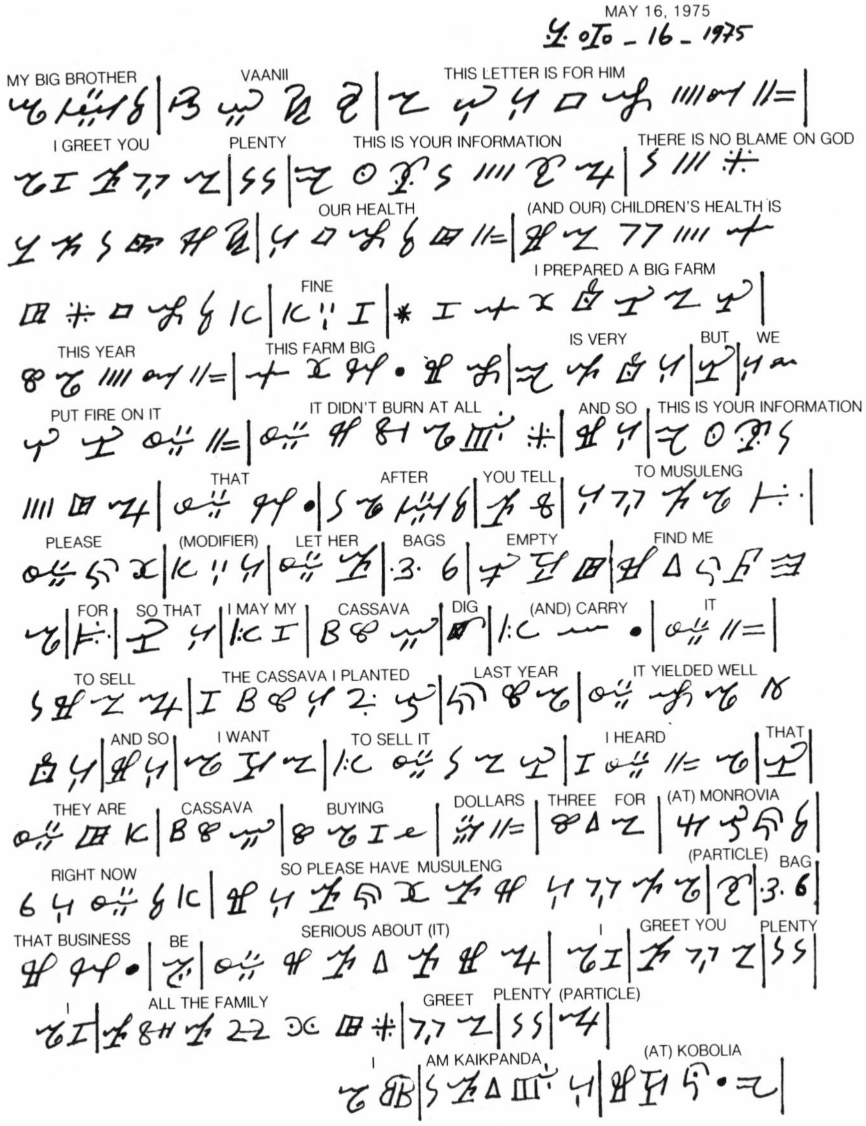

MAY 16, 1975

MY BIG BROTHER   VAANII   THIS LETTER IS FOR HIM

I GREET YOU   PLENTY   THIS IS YOUR INFORMATION   THERE IS NO BLAME ON GOD

OUR HEALTH   (AND OUR) CHILDREN'S HEALTH IS

FINE   I PREPARED A BIG FARM

THIS YEAR   THIS FARM BIG   IS VERY   BUT   WE

PUT FIRE ON IT   IT DIDN'T BURN AT ALL   AND SO   THIS IS YOUR INFORMATION

THAT   AFTER   YOU TELL   TO MUSULENG

PLEASE   (MODIFIER)   LET HER   BAGS   EMPTY   FIND ME

FOR   SO THAT   I MAY MY   CASSAVA   DIG   (AND) CARRY   IT

TO SELL   THE CASSAVA I PLANTED   LAST YEAR   IT YIELDED WELL

AND SO   I WANT   TO SELL IT   I HEARD   THAT

THEY ARE   CASSAVA   BUYING   DOLLARS   THREE   FOR   (AT) MONROVIA

RIGHT NOW   SO PLEASE HAVE MUSULENG   (PARTICLE)   BAG

THAT BUSINESS   BE   SERIOUS ABOUT (IT)   I   GREET YOU   PLENTY

ALL THE FAMILY   GREET   PLENTY (PARTICLE)

AM KAIKPANDA   (AT) KOBOLIA

Figure 9.1. A sample letter in Vai script with segmentation indicated

cases where segments marked off complete phrases, we attempted to obtain more fine-grained segmentations.

The opening of the letter provided the occasion for the first discussion. Mr. Swary took the first three syllables (ññgōlō, "my big brother") and initially treated them as a single koali kulē, thereafter separating them in two units ñ and ñgōlō. The interviewees in Misila segmented the letter such that ññgōlō was made a single unit. The following discussion ensued:

Interviewer: What idea guided you in dividing the letters[5] into words this way?

Respondent: The idea I used to separate this into words is this: If you want to address somebody, ñ ñgōlō, my big brother, you only have to write this and stop.

Interviewer: O.K., so the first koali kulē is "my big brother." Fine. Do the others agree?

Others: Yes, ñ ñgōlō is one word [koali kulē].

Interviewer: But ñ is added here. What does this word [koali kulē, referring to ñ] mean?

Respondent: ñ is a pronoun, so ñ ñgōlō is one word.   [Note: At this point the respondent used the Arabic term damir, "pronoun," for ñ, yet he applied his original criterion of a single idea unit to affirm that ñ ñgōlō was a single word.]

Interviewer: Fine. Here is another expression, kpolo mēē la. Is it also one word?

Respondent: Yes, kpolo mēē la is one word.

Interviewer: Why do you say this?

Respondent: My reason is that when I am speaking to somebody I just have to join these letters. If you do not join the letters of kpolo mēē la together it will not make sense to the person I am addressing.

Interviewer: I agree, but remember that we are not trying to rewrite the letter. We are trying to segment the letter into words.

Respondent: According to our language you may want to say kpolo and stop. That makes a word. But since you have included for him you cannot simply write kpolo and make sense. You must add mēē la because kpolo mēē la refers to the person who is receiving the letter.

This inquiry procedure was followed for all segments of the letter which Mr. Nyei considered multiword phrases. In each case, discussion began with the given phrase and respondents were asked if it contained koali kulē within it. This question readily evoked further segmentation down to the level we would call a word or a word-plus-particle. At this point, interviewees indicated that further segmenting would destroy the sense (jilimasō) of the expression.

This interview, together with the written letter samples, indicates that Vai script literates *can* analyze the written language into semantic units as fine-grained as the units we call words. If metalinguistic skills are considered to involve analytic operations on texts such as those required to segment written language into meaningful units, Vai script literates amply demonstrate such skills. At the same time, all of the evidence suggests that basic units for Vai writers are meaning-carrying phrases (which sometimes consist of only one word) rather than words in our sense. (See Basso and Anderson, 1973, for a study of concepts of script units among Apaches.)

WORD DEFINITIONS

Ability to give information about words by using other words is an index both of metalinguistic skill ("ability to talk about language") and of the conceptual level an individual has attained with respect to particular verbal concepts (Litowitz, 1977). Vygotsky (1962, pp. 52–53) considered word definition to be one of three principal methods for studying concepts, and Luria (1976) used this method in his clinical interviews with Central Asian peasants. Luria expected to find that experience with literacy or formal schooling would foster the use of abstract categories, but he did not assume these influences would be uniform in all concept domains—they should be greater when defining what Vygotsky called "academic concepts" (those embodied in organized theories and bodies of knowledge, typically transmitted in school) than when defining mundane concepts (those concerning common objects, for example). In fact, Luria found that few of his subjects consistently defined either category of words through reference to membership in a general class. Most used examples or descriptive attributes in their definitions, responses which he believed reflect functional/graphic, rather than conceptual, forms of thought.

Following Luria, we incorporated a word definition task in our metalinguistic survey, selecting words representing various categories of concepts. Words referring to things encountered in everyday life (chair, deer) were included, as well as words referring to language elements (name, word). After considerable experimentation, we coded each definition on a binary basis. If the response included an essential feature of the object or a class name it was scored 1; otherwise it was scored 0. In effect, we made a crude distinction between "something resembling a definition" and "nothing resembling a definition"—a conservative course we thought was warranted by the fact that our more detailed scoring schemes were unreliable. On this measure we obtained no noticeable population differences, but there was striking evidence that definitional adequacy was controlled by the semantic properties of the words being defined (see Table 9.7). Words that were more familiar or concrete in meaning elicited the most adequate definitions, while level of description dropped for words at a greater distance from concrete experience. In attempting to define "name" and "word," respondents were rarely able to state essential features or to relate these terms to a general class. This outcome is consistent with our evidence for the ambiguity of *koali kulē* and the apparently several classes of "name" in Vai. And it is also consistent with Luria's distinction between mundane and academic concepts—a distinction that literacy in Vai script or Arabic does nothing to diminish.

Table 9.7 Mean scores on word definitions (all subjects, metalinguistic survey)

Traditional concepts (objects)		Modern concepts (institutions)	
deer	.9[a]	government	.1
chair	1.0	country	.3
sea	1.0		
Modern concepts (objects)		Language concepts	
car	.6	name	.00
newspaper	.6	word	.07

a. Maximum score, 1.0.

GRAMMATICAL KNOWLEDGE

In his extended essay on typography and literacy, McLuhan (1962) said, "It is presumably impossible to make a grammatical error in a nonliterate society for nobody ever heard of one" (p. 246). This statement reflects the common opinion that grammar, in the sense of rules of correct usage, is peculiarly related to the uniformity of expression imposed by the technology of writing. In this view, members of communities with only oral language will recognize speech varieties but not speech errors. On the other hand, linguists' theoretical concept of grammar as the set of underlying rules generating speech assumes that speakers in all language communities are competent grammarians and will easily distinguish grammatically nonpermissible sentences from correct sentences (Hymes, 1963).

For purposes of our research, we specified two levels of grammatical knowledge: first, the ability to make judgments about grammaticality; second, the ability to state the basis for these judgments in terms of particular rules of grammar exemplified in the test sentences. We had no leanings for or against the McLuhan view with respect to literate-nonliterate differences in judgments, but we did expect that Vai script literates would be superior to nonliterates and Arabic monoliterates in making explicit the grammatical basis of their judgments. This expectation followed straightforwardly from Vygotsky's notion that experience in deliberate composition (writing one's native language) will increase understanding of formal properties of the language.

The initial grammar task incorporated in our metalinguistic and replication surveys consisted of three problems. In the first two, informants were read a pair of sentences, one grammatical and one ungrammatical. They were asked to choose the grammatically correct sentence and explain why the other one was not good Vai. In the third problem they were given phrases demonstrating the proper use of a grammatical rule and were then asked to state the rule.

1. Transposed word order
   Wrong: *Aa ñ kē bu la.* (He shot me at the gun.)
   Right: *Aa bu kē nda.* (He shot the gun at me.)

2. Subject-verb agreement
   Wrong: *Deñ mēnunu a tōē?* (These children, what is its name?)
   Right: *Deñ mēnunu tōē?* (These children, what are their names?)

3. Phrases illustrating a rule
   "People say 'my (*ñ*) father,' but 'my (*na*) book'; they say 'my (*ñ*) sibling,' but 'my (*na*) wife.' Why do people sometimes say *ñ* and sometimes say *na*?" [Vai language has two pronoun forms for indicating possession. One (*ñ*) refers to what is yours naturally or what you come out of (parts of body, blood relations, home, birthplace, name); the second (*na*) refers to possessions gained.]

After some experimentation with a unified coding scheme for all explanations, we found that differences in problem structure made it necessary to score each problem using criteria specific to the problem. In all cases, however, a score of 0 was assigned to explanations that made no reference to linguistic features of the sentences or phrases; these included such observations as "The old people say it like that" (a common response); "Bad Vai"; "Not a good Vai speaker"; "Must be a Kpelle man who said it." Explanations disputing the semantic appropriateness of incorrect sentences were assigned a score of 1, while higher scores were assigned on the basis of completeness of explanation in grammatical terms. Analysis of explanations is reported for total scores on all problems.

In contrast to the spotty performance when informants were asked to make judgments about lexical units, results of grammatical judgment of sentences were clear-cut. All groups, including nonliterates, were virtually perfect at identifying ungrammatical phrases. Group differences emerged, however, when we asked people to explain the basis of their judgments; these are shown in Table 9.8.

Table 9.8 Explanations of grammatical errors

	Nonliterate	Vai script literate	Vai-Arabic biliterate	Arabic literate	Schooled literate
Metalinguistic survey	3.9[a]	4.6	5.6	—	—
Replication survey	2.3	2.9	3.2	2.5	2.7

a. Maximum score is 7.

In regression analyses of the metalinguistic survey, Vai script reading score was the only variable to predict the adequacy of explanations. In the replication survey, Vai script reading score again made a positive contribution, this time with a decrement for script literates whose only occupational experience had been farming; in contrast, English schooling produced mixed effects.

Equations were:
Metalinguistic survey:

Grammar explanation score = $3.17 + 4.25$ Vai reading score
($R^2 = .12$)   (2.7)

Replication survey:

Grammar explanation score = $2.38 + .32$ Vai reading score
($R^2 = .19$)   (3.3)
        $- 1.20$ Vai monoliterate $\times$ farming only
        (2.2)
        $+ 2.82$ in school before $- .01$ (last grade)^2
        (3.8)   (2.2)

Encouraged by this evidence of Vai script effects and by the fact that script variables repeated themselves as predictors in the two independently conducted studies, we went on to explore other kinds of grammatical knowledge. The integration survey incorporated a task in which respondents had to point out what was wrong with the sentences presented and to correct them. Six sentences were given, embodying three classes of error: violation of tense, transposed noun-modifier order, and incorrect pronominal reference. Each sentence contained one kind of error; the subject's task was to correct the error by producing a grammatical Vai sentence using the same words ("Say it in proper Vai"). This is a more difficult requirement than the simple recognition of ungrammaticality that was involved in the earlier studies.

The following are approximate English equivalents of the ungrammatical Vai sentences:

1. My child is crying yesterday.
2. This house is fine very.
3. I don't want to bother you (plural) because you (singular) are working.
4. This is the chief's child first.
5. These men, where is he going?
6. They have planting the oranges.

After correcting the sentence, each person was asked to explain the nature of the error. Explanations about what was wrong with the sentence were rated for adequacy on a scale from 0 to 5. The top score was given for any explanation that mentioned both aspects of the mismatch in the sentence. In sentence 1, for example, an explanation was scored 5 if it mentioned that

Table 9.9 Correcting and explaining grammatical errors (integration survey)

	Nonliterate	Arabic monoliterate	Vai script monoliterate	Schooled literate
Number correct (out of 6)	5.1	4.5	5.0	5.6
Explanation score (out of 30)	6.9	8.1	9.9	15.7

one term ("yesterday") refers to the past while another ("is crying") refers to the present.

Average scores are given in Table 9.9. These suggest some literacy group–related variation in ability to put the sentence into correct Vai. The regression analysis confirmed the facilitative effect of schooling and the poorer performance of Arabic literates, and localized this decrement among those who had studied the Qur'an but who could not read with comprehension. The equation was:

Number of sentences corrected = 5.01 − .72 Qur'anic only + .46 last grade
$(R^2 = .10)$ (2.2)   (2.4)

Sizable differences linked to literacy appeared in people's explanations for their corrections. Formal schooling had by far the biggest effect, but it was followed by an effect of Vai script literacy for the beginning Vai group but not for the advanced.[6]

Grammar explanation = 8.0 + .62 last grade + .82 Vai reading score 1, 2
$(R^2 = .25)$ (5.8)   (2.0)

In a final study, we gave a set of grammar questions to eighteen Vai script literates and eighteen nonliterate men in scattered towns in Cape Mount County. Our purpose was to bridge the variations in materials and procedures in the previous grammar studies. We selected some sentences from each set of materials used earlier, presenting these in two task formats ("Which is the correct sentence?" versus "Make this sentence a correct sentence") in a counterbalanced design. Vai script literates outperformed nonliterates in both versions of the task when asked to explain their answers; none of the variations in sentence materials or responses affected the outcome.

ATTENDING TO LOGICAL RELATIONS BETWEEN PROPOSITIONS

In the major survey we found that responses to logical syllogisms were often justified in terms of the individual's experience or belief. English literates who attended school, however, tended to shift away from this response mode and answered the problems on the basis of what the propositions stated, regardless of whether these statements were factually true or plausible. Today most psychologists would agree that the tendency to respond empirically to syllogisms (and thus often give incorrect answers) is not so much a sign of inability to reason logically as it is an indication of how people understand this particular verbal form. So, while we first introduced these problems as a task in logical reasoning, evidence that most Vai people did not respond to them as we intended suggests that we are dealing here in the first place with a language-understanding or metalinguistic skill. Learning how to respond to these problems appropriately (confining one's answer to the information given in the problem) may be a matter of particular language experiences. As we have previously pointed out, Olson (1977) maintains that the crucial experiences are related to analysis of written materials. On the other hand, one of us (Scribner, 1977) offered the explanation that familiarity with certain modes of discourse, rather than literacy per se, might account for a shift in performance on these problems.

Our follow-up studies consisted of four problems. To emphasize the metalinguistic rather than the logic demands of the task, we selected two of the simplest problems from the major survey. We experimented to see if we could induce a theoretical set by preparing new problems using material for which the Vai had no fixed beliefs or personal knowledge. We settled on syllogisms parallel in structure to those of the first study but describing conditions found on the moon. Virtually everyone had heard that astronauts had been to the moon but no one knew much about what they had found there. The problems were:

1. (Old problem) All houses in Liberia are made of iron.
   My friend has a house in Liberia.
   Is my friend's house made of iron?
2. (New problem) All stones on the moon are blue.
   The man who went to the moon saw a stone.
   Was the stone he saw blue?
3. (Old problem) All women who live in Monrovia are married.
   Kemu is not married.
   Does Kemu live in Monrovia?
4. (New problem) All men living on the moon have three heads.
   This one man does not have three heads.
   Does he live on the moon?

As in the major survey, problems were scored both for correct answers and for type of explanation (theoretical versus empirical). Results are presented in Table 9.10.

For this set of materials, correct answers and theoretical explanations occurred with high frequency in both the metalinguistic study and its replication. All groups achieved a level of performance attained only by schooled

Table 9.10   Performance on logical syllogisms

	Nonliterate	Vai script monoliterate	Vai-Arabic biliterate	Arabic monoliterate	Schooled literate
Number correct (max 4)					
Metalinguistic survey	2.9	3.3	3.4	—	—
Replication survey	3.2	3.5	3.6	3.3	3.6
Theoretical explanations (max 4)					
Metalinguistic survey	2.7	3.0	3.2	—	—
Replication survey	3.2	3.4	3.5	3.2	3.6

groups in the major survey. The theoretical mode was not confined to the moon problems: a constant high level of performance was maintained for both the mundane and the fantastic syllogisms. Perhaps because of ceiling effects, solution performance was not predictable in either survey. As for the more sensitive measure of theoretical explanation, we had an unexpected finding. Following the practice applied in our major survey, we tried to predict this measure by entering number of correct answers into the equation as a control. In the metalinguistic survey, no background variable functioned as a predictor, but a procedural variable did influence performance. The variable in question was the order in which the tasks were given: in one sequence, logic tasks came at the beginning before conversations about grammar or words; in the other, they came at the tail end of the interview. When logic problems followed all other tasks, the rate of theoretical responses was significantly higher, seeming to confirm the notion that the discourse context affected how the logic task was understood.

Taken together, these studies of logical-verbal problem solving cast doubt on hypotheses that implicate literacy directly in the acquisition of metalinguistic knowledge about the properties of propositions. In moving from one study to another we found greater variability arising from differences in materials, procedures, and experimenters than in literacy or other background factors.

DISCUSSION OF METALINGUISTIC KNOWLEDGE TASKS

Our efforts to get hold of the fluid indicators of metalinguistic knowledge took us in many directions. What conclusions seem to emerge?

The checkered pattern of performance confirms our initial skepticism that it is not especially useful to think about metalinguistic knowledge as a general orientation to language or a unitary set of skills. Each task we devised, ostensibly to tap some particular aspect of metalinguistic knowledge, turned out to involve a highly diversified array of knowledge and skills. The longest-word task demonstrates this nicely. Among other things, it called for knowledge of words as constituent units of language, knowledge of syllables as constituent units of words, and awareness of the independence of linguistic units from the material world. Answers to the sun-moon question required not only an understanding that names and their referents are independent entities, but an acceptance of the proposition that names are arbitrarily affixed to things by human convention (as opposed to God's or old people's wisdom). With each task tapping not one but an assembly of knowledge and skills, the sensitivity of performance to variations in materials and procedures is not surprising.

Our results furnish little support for speculations that literacy is a precondition or prime cause for an understanding of language as an object. We failed to find literacy exerting an effect on nominal realism as standard tasks measure it. Dominant figures in anthropological theory (for example, Malinowski, 1965) and linguistic theory (Ogden and Richards, 1923) claimed that traditional people have a magical attitude toward words and believe that there is a direct, even causal, relation between the word and the thing it denotes. A decade ago, a scholar of culture and cognition challenged what he called this "cavalier attitude of investing the savage with linguistic pathology" (Tambiah, 1968, p. 187). Our studies support Tambiah's skepticism. Extended conversations about the names of sun and moon demonstrate that the Vai can easily distinguish between word and referent. But acceptance of the notion that names are arbitrary is another matter. During the course of our research, we came to learn that certain classes of names among the Vai are in fact nonarbitrary. These include personal names, which are often selected to reflect individual characteristics ("firstborn," for example), and names of towns ("by-the-waterfall"). Consideration of these Vai naming practices and theological beliefs suggests that people's attitudes toward names need to be assessed in the wider context of cultural belief systems and the rules by which new words enter the lexicon, and not simply as an index of cognitive development.

We could obtain no evidence that literacy in Vai script (or other literacies)[7] led to an understanding of "word" differing in any noticeable way from that of nonliterates. This conclusion is based not only on the outcomes of our ambiguous conversations about words but the evidence in our letter-segmenting tasks that a word is not a primary unit for Vai script literates and the inability of Vai script and Arabic literates to define "name" and "word" in the definition task more adequately than nonliterates. These results cast doubt on the notion that learning to read and write in any writing system will heighten awareness of lexical units akin to the grammarian's; the relationship between word concepts and rules of graphic representation (segmentation of script into word units) merits further exploration.

Applying the strict criteria we set ourselves, we have at least one candidate for literacy effects on language knowledge. In spite of the restricted range of educational functions of the Vai script, the lack of texts as reading material, and the absence of formal instruction, Vai script literates consistently outperformed others when talking about good or bad sentences. We found this result especially provocative because we knew it was not attributable to a general ability to explain things. On experimental tasks in the major survey (Chapter 8), Vai script literates were indistinguishable from nonliterates in clarity and completeness of verbal explanations. In the metalinguistic survey, they showed no special skill in explaining why they answered a syllogism in a certain way. Their expertise appeared only when the topic was how the Vai language is put together.

Why did hypotheses about grammatical knowledge prove more supportable among the Vai than other hypotheses we were at such pains to test? On a post hoc basis we came up with a ready explanation. All of us knew that a common activity among Vai script letter writers was disputation about whether certain expressions were or were not "correct Vai." And we had also heard teachers of the script trying to instill in their students an appreciation of the importance of writing "correct Vai." It seemed natural that such an emphasis on talking about proper speech should be reflected in the ability to explain grammatical features.

But this kind of post hoc interpretation highlights the general weakness of the research strategy we have reported up to this point. Tasks discussed in Chapters 8 and 9 were chosen not because an analysis of Vai script literacy indicated their relevance, but rather because general speculations and theories suggested that literacy *should* have such general effects. Yet our results indicated that literacy affected performance only on tasks whose requirements were linked directly to requirements of specific literacy activities among the Vai.

A SHIFT IN STRATEGY

By the middle of 1976, we knew the major results of the survey experiments and of several early metalinguistic studies. We became convinced that continued pursuit of general cognitive consequences of literacy among the Vai would be no more productive in the future than it was in initial stages. We had entertained this possibility at the outset. Now, in our third year of work, we had amassed a considerable body of knowledge about the distinctive characteristics of the Vai writing system and its major functions. We found ourselves modifying our expectations of experimental results and our interpretations of outcomes because of what we had learned about actual literacy practices among the Vai. Hypotheses derived from general abstract characterizations of literacy, or from historical cases whose applicability to Vai life was problematic, lost their power of attraction.

We were dissatisfied not only with the empirical results of our tests of developmental hypotheses but with their unsatisfactory theoretical status. Most hypotheses we had been testing made assumptions about mediating mechanisms linking literacy experiences to cognitive outcomes, but little evidence was available from our own or other research demonstrating that the presumed mediating mechanisms were actually involved in experimental outcomes. Working with child populations, other investigators have often fallen back on appeals to general mechanisms of "intellectual growth" when discussing performance differences for different age groups. We were barred from such general appeals by the many different lines of evidence we had secured that Vai adults, nonliterate or literate, did not perform tasks like American or European children. We concluded that, at best, continuing this line of research might allow us to support a hypothesis here or there but was unlikely to help us uncover the mediating mechanisms linking literacy to cognitive consequences (should these be demonstrable). Yet pursuit of such mechanisms was our central goal.

Studies of grammatical knowledge were an exception to this general picture. They had produced consistent results indicating that Vai script literates are better conversationalists about formal features of sentences than their nonliterate neighbors. These results were not only reliable but were reasonable in terms of what we knew about the social conditions of reading and writing in the Vai script. We had often overheard or participated in conversations similar to those occurring in our experimental sessions when several literate men in a village were engaged in reading or composing a letter. We knew it was commonplace for them to maintain a running commentary on whether or not a particular piece of language was good or correct Vai. The knowledge we had of Vai literates' talk about the Vai language in naturally occurring situations provided clues to the source of their expertise in grammar explanations in our experimental tasks. We had not set up our grammar studies initially to test the implications of everyday conversations about language, but after the fact we found they had provided such a test. What investigative procedures might these studies suggest for fitting experiment and observation together *before* the fact? They pointed strongly to the need for tasks that would tap not just knowledge or skill in general, but specific knowledges and skills that were actually implicated in literacy activities. From the beginning of our work, we had firmly believed that cognitive consequences of literacy, should they be found, would be closely tied to the functional uses of literacy among the Vai. But in the early stages we had only a very general picture of these functions; we lacked the detailed knowledge necessary to judge whether our experimental tasks bore any close resemblance to the tasks literates confronted in everyday life. After several years of survey and ethnographic observation, we were in a better position to let our knowledge of existing literacy practices guide our experimental work.

In each of the following chapters, this functional approach is applied to a particular linguistic or cognitive domain. In every instance, we used observations of particular literacy activities to formulate hypotheses of specific effects. Then we made functional analyses of the skills involved in these activities. On the basis of these analyses, we designed experimental tasks with different content but hypothetically similar skills to determine if prior practice in the targeted activities enhanced performance.

We began with a series of studies designed to model certain aspects of Vai reading practices. Some of these studies required a sophisticated knowledge of the Vai language, which Stephen Reder brought to the field in 1977. Others built upon observations of reading-aloud activities and theoretical speculations about the processes that might underlie them. This work is reported in Chapters 10 and 11.

We were also intrigued by Vai letter writing, the most frequent use of the script. As soon as the surveys were completed, we began pilot work on procedures to model processes important in letter writing—work leading not only to experiments, but also to interviews on Vai criteria for "good communication." These studies are summarized in Chapter 12.

One of our earliest practice-linked hypotheses, pursued to the end of our fieldwork, grew out of our speculations about the impact of Qur'anic learning on memory. The way Qur'anic learning proceeded in the countryside made it seem like an exercise in graphic figure-sound memory training of an unusual kind. We began testing our ideas, modifying them as we gathered more information about actual teaching practices and the results of pilot studies; this work is reported in Chapter 13.

Part IV

Testing Consequences: Functional Paradigms

10

Making Sense of Sound and Symbol

As a first step in exploring the generalization of skills entailed in reading and writing Vai script, we asked a simple question: Does knowing how to read the script make it easier to read another unfamiliar system of graphic symbols? In effect, we were asking, Does reading help reading? We extended this inquiry to include writing—here defined as the production of statements through manipulation of graphic symbols.

While these questions were an obvious point of departure, their answers were neither foregone nor trivial. To our knowledge, no systematic studies had been conducted among any population to test the commonsense proposition that experience in linguistic interpretation of one set of symbols will facilitate interpretation of another. More important, if such facilitation should be shown to occur, how could we explain it? What specific skills did literates bring to bear on tasks requiring that they make linguistic sense out of graphic symbols?

From these questions probing transfer of reading skills to a very closely related domain of language activity we moved on to a more distant domain and asked a novel question: Do skills entailed in reading Vai script affect language interpretation under conditions when language is not graphically represented (when, for example, language is produced orally)? In other words, does reading help listening? This question was prompted by more than a spirit of curiosity. The notion that learning to read Vai script might affect comprehension of oral language arose as a real possibility in the course of our field observations. Studies tackling this question, like the other studies reported in this chapter, were suggested by our analysis of naturally occurring reading activities and were designed to simulate or model some of the component processes we had identified. As background for the description that follows, we will summarize here some features of Vai script reading that we sought to capture in these experiments.

SCRIPT READING AS A PROBLEM-SOLVING PROCESS

Our studies focused on an assembly of skills that we call skills of semantic integration. Some of these skills are common to reading in any phonetic script; others are related to the distinctive properties of the Vai writing system. At this point in our research we already knew that reading Vai script involved much more than the ability to read off character names one by one. Our observations of Vai script literates deciphering letters from friends, backed up by Reder's controlled studies of the reading process (Chapter 11), had so impressed us with the complexity of the skills involved in reproducing spoken Vai from the written page that we considered it a complex search for meaning and likened it to a problem-solving process.

All phonetic scripts have in common the fact that they represent the stream of speech by symbols for discrete units. These units may be phonemes, as in our alphabet, or syllables, as in the Vai script; but, in any case, to arrive at meaningful language, the reader must put together these elements into larger, higher-order units.

In reading English, the putting-together process may first occur on the word level. As the child or adult sounds out the phonemes c-a-t, they have to be said in such a way as to constitute a word. Reading teachers often refer to the processes required here as "blending" and have identified difficulties some children have with blending as a source of reading retardation. But words also have to be put together into higher-order units such as phrases and sentences, in order to reproduce meaningful language from the printed page. Different skills are tapped here and are typically referred to as skills in semantic integration (Keeton, 1977) or cognitive synthesis (Farnham-Diggory, 1978). In saying aloud from the printed page the words "JUMP OVER THE BLOCK," is the reader able to reconstruct the action commanded in the sentence? Farnham-Diggory, in a long series of studies (1967, 1970; Farnham-Diggory and Simon, 1972), found that when young children were asked to *do* what this sentence *said,* some would jump in the air, make a gesture for "over," and point to a block on the floor, rather than walking to the block and jumping over it.

As Farnham-Diggory points out (1978), many comprehension mechanisms are involved in the accomplishment of a correct interpretation of this string of words. She suggests that two broad classes of integration processes can be distinguished; this distinction is particularly useful for our comparative research purposes. Some of the comprehension processes involved in integration are "top-down processes" or general interpretive processes brought to language; others are "bottom-up" processes by means of which elements (words or syllables) coalesce into higher-order semantic units. We assumed that Vai script literates and literates in Arabic and English alphabets might call upon some common core of top-down skills when they tried to make sense out of written representations of language, but that bottom-up processes would more closely reflect the distinctive representational features of each script.

There are many ambiguities in the way the Vai script represents spoken Vai. Some of these ambiguities arise because the script does not incorporate standard symbols or conventional marks for displaying phonological features that are crucial in comprehending spoken Vai, such as vowel tone. In addition, as we have pointed out (Chapter 9), the higher-order units that carry meaning are not set off in the script. A string of syllabic characters runs across the page without division into words or phrases. A single character on a page, depending on its semantic function, may represent a one-syllable word (many Vai words consist of a single syllable), or it may be the initial, middle, or final syllable of a polysyllabic word. Just as there are no divisions into words, there often are no divisions into utterances or sentence units. For these reasons, Vai readers have had to elaborate special techniques for discovering higher-order semantic units. One common technique, which we heard over and over again, consists of "recycling"—saying strings of syllables aloud repeatedly, varying vowel tones and lengths until they "click" into meaningful units.

While recycling can best be illustrated by audiotape, some sense of it can be captured by the following phonetic rendering of a Vai script literate reading a text aloud to us. In this instance, the text was his own written narrative of his family history; the handwriting was his own; and the narrative content was familiar. But a particular passage was troublesome.

Dudu a ta ɓa kpa lō ē̄ē
mu/
ja we/
a ta ɓa kpa lō ēē/
a ta ɓa kpa lō ēē/
mu/
ja/
a ta ɓa kpa lō ēē/
Dudu/
a ta ɓa kpa lō ēē/
mu/
ja we/
ja we fo lu/
Dudu ata ɓa kpalōēē tōñ jawefolu

Translation: Dudu's mother came from a place called Jawefolu.

In these renditions, the reader varied tone and vowel length as he went over the passage. Finally, he replaced the syllable *mu,* which apparently interfered with interpretation of the sentence, with the syllable *tōñ,* and achieved an acceptable reading.

RESEARCH DESIGN

Our examination of Vai script–specific skills began in each instance with a line of experimentation devoted to particular questions and carried out with different population groups. We then moved on to combine these experimental strands in an interview survey referred to as the integration survey because of its emphasis on these skills. (See description in Chapter 9.) We selected somewhat different comparison groups for this survey because we were especially interested in moving beyond a global Vai script literate/nonliterate contrast to examining script skills against other literacies. If our model tasks succeeded in capturing some of the specific skills involved in reading the Vai syllabary, Vai script literates should differ in their performance not only from nonliterates but from Arabic and English literates as well. Both the latter literacies involve languages other than the native Vai; as alphabetic scripts, both require mastery of different sound-symbol relationships from those involved in use of the Vai syllabary. We expected to find that some aspects of performance on our model tasks would be uniquely characteristic of Vai script while others might be common across literacies.

To test these propositions, we carefully selected members of various literacy subgroups to reflect, as far as possible, knowledge of one and only one script. In our Arabic subgroups, we differentiated between those who knew Qur'an only and those who knew Arabic as a language and could read and write with comprehension (ten men in each group); English literates were all students with an average twelfth-grade level (twenty men). In this line of research we also wanted to implicate, as directly as possible, proficiency in the Vai script as a determinant of superior performance, so we built a novice/expert contrast into our Vai script literacy populations: we set up two groups of twenty men each, one group consisting of beginning readers (those scoring 1 or 2 on our reading test) and the other of advanced readers (those with scores of 3 or 4). Nonliterate groups consisted of separate groups of men and women (twenty in each). All lived in upcountry towns except the students and none of them had participated in previous studies. The interviewer-experimenter was a teacher and University of Liberia student who had worked previously in the metalinguistic survey.

PILOT READING STUDY

The objective of our first series of studies was to determine whether script-reading integrational skills would be displayed on a simulated reading task, using a different set of visual symbols to represent language. An initial— and difficult—problem was to devise appropriate materials. First of all, we had to be sure that the symbolic material used would call on the skills whose generalization we were trying to test—both the general interpretive processes of integration and the processes specific to Vai script integration. Second, they had to be suitable for nonliterate as well as literate men and equally familiar, or unfamiliar, to both groups. Our solution was to adapt a symbol-decoding task that has long provided sport for American readers— the rebus.[1] Principles of the rebus are illustrated in Figure 10.1, reproduced from a book of children's games. In this version the rebus combines pictures, numbers, words, and letters to represent a meaningful sentence—an admonition that may protect the reader from getting stung. In our studies, we were restricted to using pictures but we still could incorporate some of the different types of symbol-sound relationships exemplified in the figure. In certain symbols (the picture of the flower, for example), the object is the intended referent: "In *flower* beds . . ." This kind of picture-referent relationship functions as a pictographic writing system, in which meaning can be directly apprehended from the visual symbol alone. However, the pic-

Figure 10.1. A rebus puzzle

ture of the watch does not stand for a timepiece (noun) but for a certain kind of looking ("watch," verb). Meaning here is mediated by language sound through the principle of homonymity: when words sound alike, the meanings of both can be represented by the picture of one. Picture-referent relationships of this kind model a phonetic script, since the route to meaning is through sound.

Our materials also made use of this principle of sound similarity to model the phonetic Vai syllabary. They consisted of ten black-and-white drawings depicting eight familiar objects and two arbitrary symbols representing a predicate verb ($\Box = \bar{b}\bar{e} =$ "is") and a negation or preposition, depending on linguistic context ($* = ma =$ "not" or "on"). The sentence displayed in Figure 10.2 illustrates some of the processes involved in going from picture naming to "reading" with these materials. The first picture— "hoe" (*kai*)—stands for "the man" (*kaie*). Unlike the example cited earlier for the English rebus, in which the two meanings of "watch" are conveyed by one pronunciation, the Vai words for "hoe" and "the man" are not pure homonyms. "Hoe" requires one tonal and one vowel change to become "the man."[2] *Ta* ("fire")—requires elongation of the vowel to become *taa*, "cooked," and so on. In the sentence shown, seven tonal and vowel length feature changes are required to convert the sequence of picture names into a semantically and syntactically acceptable Vai sentence. All sentences required feature changes of this sort in a manner analogous to the feature changes involved in translating the written page into spoken Vai. Sentences and stimulus pictures are displayed in Table 10.1.

Having settled on materials, our second problem was to determine what behaviors could be used as indicators that the respondent had not only succeeded in naming the pictures (that is, decoding them) but had integrated these names into a meaningful statement. We used two measures for this purpose.[3] The first was a judgment as to whether the informant "read off" the pictures in a meaningful way, or whether he named them one by

Figure 10.2. Reading task, "The man cooked a big chicken"

a. Picture names:	káí	làà	tíyé̌	ɓá	tá
b. Sentence:	kálě̌	lá	tíyé̌	ɓà	táǎ

Table 10.1   Reading task sentences

Practice phrase:

Pictures:	CHICKEN	PADDLE	
Names:	*tíyé*	*làà*	
Phrase:	*tíyé là*		
Translation:	waterside		
Question:	What place is this?		

1.
Pictures:	GOAT	FIRE	CHICKEN	PADDLE
Names:	*ɓá*	*tá*	*tíyé*	*làà*
Sentence:	*ɓá tà tíyé là*			
Translation:	Goat goes to the waterside.			
Question:	Where is goat?			

2.
Pictures:	LEAF	FIRE	CHICKEN	PADDLE
Names:	*jámbá*	*tá*	*tíyé*	*làà*
Sentence:	*jámbâ tà tíyé là*			
Translation:	Jamba goes to the waterside.			
Question:	Where is Jamba?			

3.
Pictures:	ROPE	□ TABLE	*	
Names:	*júlú*	*ɓɛ̀ másá*	*mà*	
Sentence:	*júlú ɓɛ̀ másàà mà*			
Translation:	Rope is on the table.			
Question:	Where is the rope?			

4.
Pictures:	HOE	□ TABLE	*	
Names:	*káí*	*ɓɛ̀ másá*	*mà*	
Sentence:	*káìɛ̀ ɓɛ̀ másáǎ mà*			
Translation:	The hoe is on the table.			
Question:	Where is the hoe?			

5.
Pictures:	TABLE	ROPE	CHICKEN	GOAT	*
Names:	*másá*	*júlú*	*tíyɛ̀*	*ɓá*	*mà*
Sentence:	*másàǎ júlú tíyɛ̀ ɓáǎ mà*				
Translation:	Masaa cut the rope from the goat.				
Question:	What happened to the goat?				

6.
Pictures:	HOE	PADDLE	CHICKEN	GOAT	FIRE
Names:	*káí*	*làà*	*tíyé*	*ɓá*	*tá*
Sentence:	*káìɛ̀ lá tíyé ɓà táǎ*				
Translation:	The man cooked a big chicken.				
Question:	Is the chicken dead? What happened to it?				

7.
Pictures:	LEAF	ROPE	*	CHICKEN
Names:	*jámbá*	*júlú*	*mà*	*tíyé*
Sentence:	*jámbá júlû má tíyɛ̂*			
Translation:	Jamba is not disappointed.			
Question:	Is Jamba happy about what happened?			

one as discrete units. This was not a difficult judgment since, as we have pointed out, a number of sound transformations had to be made in the picture names to incorporate them into a meaningful Vai utterance; our Vai interviewer appeared to have no problem in deciding on the spot when an expression was read in an integrated manner. We also used the time-honored technique of asking comprehension questions. These were always simple, requiring only retrieval of information explicitly stated in the sentence.

Because of the novelty of the task, we set it up as a tutorial session. The interviewer-experimenter acted as a teacher, working individually with each person and taking whatever steps were necessary to help him understand the task and learn to do it. Everyone first learned to name the pictures quickly and without error. (Picture naming continued until our criterion of two errorless trials was reached.) Then the interviewer said, "I am going to put these pictures down so that their names tell something in Vai. Name each picture as I put it down." The first practice set consisted of a picture of a chicken (*tiyĕ*) and a paddle (*laa*). After they were on the table and the person named them, he was told, "These names can tell us where we go to wash clothes. What is that place?" The correct answer—*tiyĕ la*, "waterside"—results from the integration of the two names. As one way of encouraging integration, we asked people to say the names out loud in such a way that the spoken Vai would make sense to anyone. After this practice, seven sentences were given, each followed by probe questions to determine whether the person understood what he was reading.[4] All sessions were tape-recorded.

The first study included ten nonliterate men and twelve Vai script literates from a community near Monrovia. Since this was a pilot study intended to test the suitability of the task, we made no effort to exclude biliterates from the Vai literate sample; several individuals were expert in both scripts while several more knew the Qur'an by memory. All sessions were tape-recorded and each person's utterances were phonetically transcribed.

COMPONENT TASK SKILLS

Observations and transcripts yielded evidence of the many different decoding and integration skills involved in this task. Some men, particularly nonliterates, had difficulty naming pictures systematically without skipping any or changing their order or supplying new names. When the naming sequence was disrupted among Vai script literates, it tended to be because they assigned a single *syllable* to each picture instead of the whole name, suggesting that on this aspect of the task, prior practice with the syllabic script might interfere with, rather than facilitate, performance.

Some of these skills and difficulties in applying them are illustrated in the following transcript of a nonliterate farmer who unsuccessfully spent five minutes on the sentence illustrated in Figure 10.2, *Kaiē la tiyē ɓa taa,* "The man cooked a big chicken." (Omissions are indicated by the number sequences.)

1.1. *Kaiē laa ta ɓa.* (*tiyē* omitted; *ɓa* and *ta* reversed; vowel errors)
1.4. *Kaiē laa tiyē ɓaa a taa.* (*a* inserted; vowel errors)
1.5. *Kai laa tiyē ɓa a taa.* (*a* inserted; vowel and tonal changes)
1.6. *Kai ɓa tiyē a taa.* (*ē* and *laa* omitted; *ɓa* in wrong place; *a* inserted)
1.8. *Ɓaa taa tiyē la.* (*kaiē* omitted; other words out of sequence)
1.12. *Ɓa la taa tiyē la.* (*kaiē* omitted; other words out of sequence)
1.16. *Kaiē laa tiyē ɓa ta.* (all names in correct sequence but read as syllables)

Protocols supply many instances of recycling similar to recursive processes in Vai script reading: subjects first read names as discrete units and varied their pronunciation until the sentence emerged. The following illustrates an efficient performance by a tailor, a Vai script literate, on the sentence "Masaa cut the rope from the goat."

Names: *masa julu tiyē ɓa ma*
Sentence: *Masaa julu tiyē ɓaa ma.*
1.1. *Masa.*
1.2. *Ma sa julu tiyē ɓa.* (nonintegrated)
1.3. *Masaa julu tiyē ɓaa ma.*

Quite another set of skills was involved in answering comprehension questions. Table 10.2 presents selections from a transcript of a Vai script literate who could read the pictures quickly and correctly but had difficulty displaying comprehension of the interviewer's comprehension question. Some informants grasped these questions immediately; the majority learned during the course of practice sentences what this particular testing discourse was all about.

As a conservative measure, we counted a sentence as read correctly only when it was spoken aloud in an integrated fashion and the comprehension question was answered correctly. In spite of the unfamiliarity of the task, nonliterates read and understood 53 percent of the sentences (on the average, 3.7 out of 7). No one had to be dropped from the study for failure to understand what was wanted or inability to "read" at least one practice sentence. The expected superiority of Vai script literates was equally clear; they read 79 percent of the sentences correctly. (The average difference between literate and nonliterate groups is significant: $t = 1.96$; $df = 20$, $p \leqslant$ .05.) These results were sufficiently encouraging for us to undertake two additional studies: a small replication study upcountry using more standardized procedures and a less sophisticated population (in the first study, most nonliterate informants were young men in trades or in semiskilled and skilled occupations in Monrovia); and a major study, conducted as part of the integration survey, in which we compared effects of different types of literacy and different levels of literacy skills.

Table 10.2 Comprehending comprehension questions

Informant:	*Ba ta tiyē la.* (Goat went to the waterside.) [Since this statement was said in a natural speech manner, Interviewer Hamidu Getaweh went on to ask the comprehension question:]
Hamidu:	We're here now, and from what we know being here and I ask you, Is the goat in town? How will you answer it?
Inf.:	I will say it is fine.
Hamidu:	But if we are here and you read this sentence, and I ask you, Where is the goat? What will you say?
Inf.:	I will say, The goat is at the waterside.
Hamidu:	Then it is not in town, not so? Suppose I ask you again, Where is the goat? What can you tell me?
Inf.:	I will say goat is in town when I have not seen this sentence.
Hamidu:	But suppose you have seen this sentence?
Inf.:	I will say, It is at the waterside.
Hamidu:	Then read the sentence again. Say it.
Inf.:	*Ba bē tiyē la.* (The goat is at the waterside.) [Note: The subject has substituted the verb "is" (*bē*) for the verb "goes" or "went" (*ta*). He "read" what he gave as the answer to the comprehension question. The experimenter notices this.]
Hamidu:	Is there any *bē* there?
Inf.:	*Ba tiyē la.* [Note: This time he drops the verb altogether. He recovers.] *Ba ta tiyē la.* (The goat has gone to the waterside.)
Hamidu:	Have you understood this?
Inf.:	Yes. [Note: New pictures are put down and the subject reads them quickly in a natural speaking manner.]
Inf.:	*Jamba ta tiyē la.* (Jamba has gone to the waterside.) [Note: "Jamba," a girl's name, is represented by the picture of a leaf, which is called *jamba.*]
Hamidu:	Where is Jamba?
Inf.:	In the bush. [Note: Unclear whether leaf or name of girl is intended.]
Hamidu:	You have to tell me what the sentence is saying.
Inf.:	Oh hoo! *Ta tiyē la* (has gone to the waterside).
Hamidu:	If I came and asked, Where is Jamba, and you knew already where Jamba is, what will you tell me?
Inf.:	I will say, Jamba goes to the waterside.
Hamidu:	[making sure] Suppose I ask again, Is Jamba in the house? What will you tell me?
Inf.:	No, she has gone to the waterside. [Note: Now the third sentence is presented, and again the subject reads it accurately and quickly.]
Inf.:	*Julu bē masaa ma.* (Rope is on the table.)
Hamidu:	Do you understand what is said?
Inf.:	Yes.
Hamidu:	Where can I find rope?
Inf.:	In the bush.
Hamidu:	The phrase or sentence says that? It says that rope is in the bush?
Inf.:	No. The phrase says that rope is on the table.

A REPLICATION (STUDY 2)

The replication study was conducted in small isolated towns in Cape Mount County. A second interviewer worked with eighteen Vai script monoliterates and eighteen nonliterates using a format similar to that of the pilot study. In the present case, however, coaching was not continued throughout the task: three practice sentences were followed by four test sentences in which the subject had to accomplish the reading on his own. At the conclusion of the reading task, we added new pictures of common objects to the set (checkerboard, spoon, snake) and gave a sentence construction (writing) task developed as part of the pilot study. To specify what we meant by making a sentence, we gave two examples of picture sequences with a missing "word." The informant was asked to pick a picture from the remaining pile, and add it to the series in such a way as to make a meaningful Vai sentence; we also presented two picture sequences in which a picture had to be removed in order to make a meaningful sentence. After this practice in picture manipulation, we asked each person to select as many pictures as he wanted and use them to make up his own sentence. He was then asked to read the sentence aloud: "Put down any sentence that you want to put down in correct Vai so that you can read it for people to understand." Each person had three opportunities to construct sentences in this manner. As before, each sentence read aloud was scored for both integration and comprehension and considered correct only if the two criteria were met. The interviewer recorded the pictures selected for sentences and after the session judged whether each sequence constituted a meaningful Vai sentence.

As Table 10.3 shows, results on the reading task almost perfectly reproduced the outcome of the pilot study: nonliterates accomplished about half the tasks correctly, while script literates performed at a significantly higher level; discrepancy between the two groups was even greater for the writing task.

Table 10.3 Integration skills, replication (study 2)

	Vai script literates (N = 18)	Nonliterates (N = 18)	
Percent sentences read correctly	80.5	54.1	$t = 2.86, p < .01$
Percent sentences constructed correctly	87.3	41.6	$t = 2.82, p < .01$

REBUS TASK IN INTEGRATION SURVEY (STUDY 3)

Incorporation of a rebus reading and writing task in the integration survey enabled us to accomplish two objectives. The first, as in other lines of research, was to check out the apparent effects of Vai script literacy by holding constant the background variables which we knew might influence performance. The second was to distinguish those aspects of Vai script literates' superior performance which might be attributable to reading experience in general, and those attributable to practice with the script.

Pictorial material and sentences were those of Study 2 and procedures were similar, except that only one opportunity was given to write a sentence. Scoring and analysis conformed to more stringent rules. Mohamed Nyei, working from the tapes, checked integration and comprehension scores for a sample of the reading sentences. On the writing task, the interviewer not only recorded the pictures used but wrote in phonetic Vai the informant's reading of the sentence. Mohamed Nyei analyzed the protocols in conjunction with the tapes to judge whether constructions were meaningful sentences; if so, he determined how many tonal and vowel length changes were necessary for the pictures to be understood as the sentence intended.

Results

Ability to read pictures with comprehension differed markedly across literacy groups, as shown in Figure 10.3. Regression analyses, performed on scores of the 100 men in the survey, confirmed selected literacy effects. Schooling contributed to reading comprehension; advanced Vai and beginning Vai, when entered as group identifiers, each made a substantial independent contribution. This outcome suggests that the entire range of Vai script proficiency helped men interpret the picture symbols and translate them into their phonetic equivalents. This interpretation was supported when Vai script reading score substituted in the equation for the two Vai literate groups and increased the total amount of variance accounted for. When Vai reading score was used as a predictor, an experiential variable—number of tribal languages spoken—also contributed to better reading. The summary equation is:

$$\text{Sentences correctly read} = 1.72 + .31 \text{ Vai reading score}$$
$$(R^2 = .32) \qquad\qquad (5.5)$$
$$+ .16 \text{ number tribal languages} + .08 \text{ last grade}$$
$$(2.2) \qquad\qquad\qquad (5.3)$$

For evidence of Vai script–specific integrational skills, we conducted a post hoc analysis. We counted the number of tonal and vowel length features that had to be changed in the transition from picture naming to the use of names in a meaningful utterance. Two sentences required three feature changes, one required four feature changes, and another seven changes. We then compared mean differences in performance on sentences

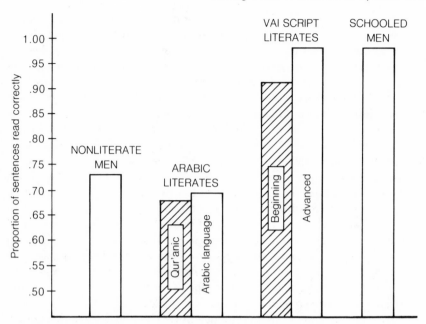

Figure 10.3. Reading task: proportion of sentences read correctly

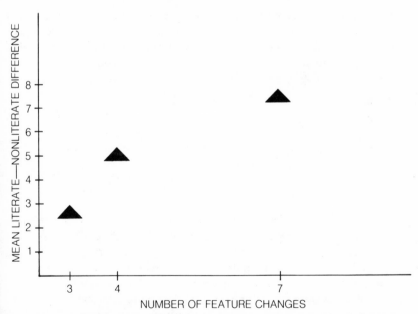

Analysis is across three reported studies for experimental sentences 4–7. Sentences 4 and 7 require three feature changes; sentence 5 requires four feature changes; sentence 6 requires seven feature changes.

Figure 10.4. Mean difference in number of Vai script literates and non-literates reading picture sentences correctly, by type of sentence

at each of these levels of feature change for our two extreme groups, nonliterates and advanced Vai script literates. Figure 10.4 plots these differences, summed across three studies (the pilot study, the present study, and a subsequent replication study). As the number of required feature changes increases, the spread between nonliterates and Vai script literates increases—just what we would expect if Vai literates were applying their skills in sound analysis and semantic integration to the pictorial materials.

This interpretation of the underlying processes contributing to superior reading performance of Vai script literates is further strengthened by an independent piece of evidence from the writing task. Figure 10.5 presents the proportion of men in each group who succeeded in putting together a string of pictures to make up a sentence. The pattern of performance is similar to that in the reading comprehension task with one interesting exception—the two Arabic groups move apart, such that those literates who read Arabic for comprehension are more successful at sentence construction than the Qur'anic literates, who again are virtually indistinguishable from nonliterates. The picture is nicely confirmed in its entirety in the regression analyses. The best equation accounts for 24 percent of the variance and consists of a positive contribution of each of the Vai script literacy groups, a positive contribution of Arabic language literacy, and an age decrement. Again, we can implicate literacy as the force behind group performance: Vai reading score will substitute for both beginning and advanced Vai status, bringing a positive contribution of knowledge of tribal languages with it; and a combination variable measuring experience in writing and teaching Arabic (practices engaged in only by those who understand Arabic language well) will substitute for the Arabic literacy group marker.

The equation using literacy measures (rather than nominal group membership) predicts more of the variance:

Sentences correctly written = .74 + .15 Vai reading score + .03 last grade
$(R^2 = .28)$ (5.0) (3.7)
+ .03 years write Arabic × teach Qur'an
(2.6)
+ .09 number tribal languages − .001 age
(2.4) (2.7)

But there are several ways that sentences can be produced in this task, some more closely related to processes involved in reading Vai script than others. For evidence that skills specific to use of the Vai script were at work, we analyzed the number of feature changes involved in making a meaningful sentence out of the picture elements. (This is analogous to our analysis of feature changes involved in reading.) As Figure 10.6 shows, the number of feature changes moves up group by group, generally paralleling the overall level of performance on sentence construction. On this measure, advanced Vai script literates outstrip all other groups, including beginning script readers.

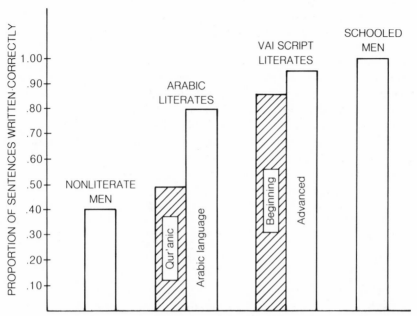

Figure 10.5. Writing task: proportion of subjects writing sentence correctly

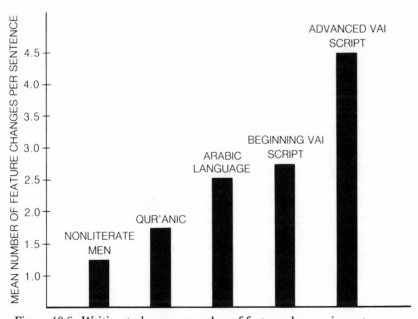

Figure 10.6. Writing task: mean number of feature changes in sentence

To insure that the greater number of tonal changes in the sentences of advanced Vai script literates reflected differences in the properties of the sentences they made, not simply the fact that they made more sentences, we ran regression equations partialing out the variance attributable to the formation of a sentence. Given that a sentence had been constructed, we asked, were there any background subject characteristics that were significantly related to the number of tonal changes involved in the sentence? The one characteristic contributing to this criterion score was whether or not an individual was an advanced Vai script literate. Sentences composed by advanced Vai script literates involved more departures from literal picture naming, a greater number of transformations from picture names to sentences—in short, more constructive efforts after meaning.

The equation for written sentence complexity was:

Number feature changes
in written sentence $\quad = .003 + 2.55$ wrote sentence
$\quad\quad (R^2 = .48) \quad\quad\quad\quad\quad\quad\quad (8.3)$
$\quad\quad\quad\quad\quad\quad\quad\quad\quad\quad + .93$ advanced Vai script
$\quad\quad\quad\quad\quad\quad\quad\quad\quad\quad$ (or Vai script reading
$\quad\quad\quad\quad\quad\quad\quad\quad\quad\quad$ scores 3 and 4)
$\quad\quad\quad\quad\quad\quad\quad\quad\quad\quad\quad (2.9)$

Looking over the entire series of rebus studies, we see some facilitative effects that appear common to prior reading experiences in all three scripts, as well as some attributable to specific features of Vai script reading. Both Vai script literates and English schooled literates were better at reading than nonliterates, and better than both groups of Arabic literates as well. The near-equivalence of nonliterates and Qur'anic literates on a task involving decoding with comprehension is understandable; but the rather poor showing of true Arabic literates is somewhat puzzling. It may be that our routine of requiring picture naming from left to right inadvertently interfered with their routine of reading Arabic from right to left. Be that as it may, the low standing of Arabic language literates disappeared on the writing task, which also called for complex and constructive efforts after meaning. Beyond these general facilitative effects of the three scripts, we succeeded in pinning down particular phonic and semantic integration skills required by the Vai syllabary and showing that they made a qualitatively distinct contribution to performance. It is especially useful for our case that on tasks most dependent on these specific skills (sentence-writing tasks), Vai script literates at high levels of reading proficiency stood out as a group in their ability to work flexibly within the sound system to construct meaningful sentences.

INTEGRATING AUDITORY INFORMATION

Our next studies pushed the question of the generality of Vai script-related encoding and decoding skills a step further: Would these skills be displayed in a task requiring integration of linguistic units in an auditory modality without the support of visual materials?[5]

These studies concentrated on the fact that written Vai does not mark lexical divisions and that syllables may function as constituents of larger word units. To construct meaning out of a chain of syllables, the Vai script reader must often hold a sequence of syllables in working memory until the unit of meaning is determined. Recycling of the sort we have presented in this chapter, as well as examples taken from actual reading performances, have shown what we mean by "contents of working memory." In reading, the Vai script literate has visual symbols available to him. But since these are discrete and not chunked graphically into meaningful units, it seemed to us that chunking might rely heavily on auditory-articulatory processes involving short-term memory. The overwhelming majority of script literates we met read aloud or subvocally; even when reading silently, their lip movements suggested that the articulatory-sound system of language was actively engaged. If these suppositions were valid, Vai script literates should show a special facility for integrating and remembering syllables presented in an auditory mode.

The experiment used a sentence repetition task. Each person listened to a tape in which a Vai speaker read ordinary, meaningful sentences that were decomposed into their constituent syllables. There were two practice strings and five test sentences, each consisting of nine syllables. A sample sentence was:

A nu ma ta ku nu mu ti na.
As spoken meaningfully:
Anu ma ta kunu mutina.
(They didn't visit us yesterday.)

There was a two-second delay between syllables, and syllables were recited in a monotone—that is, without variation in vowel tone or length. As a baseline for interpreting possible group differences in memory for a sentence parsed into syllables, we prepared another set of sentences in which the discrete units were whole words. Each of the five sentences included nine units, as did the syllables sentences. They were read by the same Vai speaker at the same rate and in the same nonemphatic, noninflectional tone of voice. Finally, a third set of materials was prepared using the same words as in the word sentences, but scrambling their order so they did not make sense. These nonsentence word strings were also read on tape by the same Vai speaker. The number of units recalled on this task gave us a measure of memory span for nonmeaningful word sequences. Since the words in these sequences were identical to those in the meaningful sentence, a comparison of the scrambled-order and sentence-order words would allow us to isolate the effect of meaning on recall. A comparison of the word sentences and syllable sentences permitted us to differentiate the effects of different-size linguistic units on the ability to achieve meaning and remember the sentences. We expected that Vai script literates would

---

Table 10.4 Sentences used in auditory integration task

Set I. Syllable sentences
  a. (Practice) *kpo wo mē ma nyi.*
             This lock is not good.
  b. (Practice) *a ɓē wuñ de ma na.*
             She is cooking.
  1. *a nu ma ta ku nu mu ti na.*
     They didn't visit us yesterday.
  2. *jē ɓē kpo lo lō ɓē ɓē lē na.*
     Jebe is feeling fine.
  3. *ɓo lo ma nja a ɓe le ni nyē.*
     The paramount chief has passed here.
  4. *ɓō a ka i ma jañ ha wa la.*
     Boakai did not say goodbye to Hawa.
  5. *ñ ke ñē lō ɓē kpō sō kpō sō.*
     My house is very messy.

Set II. Word sentences
  [Same practice sentences as in Set I, spoken in word units]
  1. *Mui wowa i taa mu fē hī i kunda.*
     We want you to go with us if you are able.
  2. *Mua mēiyē wola lō taayēē lakoa ama ɓēñ wēlē.*
     The upcountry trip we planned for today is not possible.
  3. *Hī koenu mawa ɓēē kē i kōnē mu kundōka.*
     Please let us know if things went well.
  4. *Mbe kunda na ɓēima ɓōima kpolo lō ɓele ɓēlēna.*
     I won't be able to come because Boima isn't well.
  5. *Mbē na i tina woi jēima mui liyambo sa.*
     I shall come to you this evening for us to have a talk.

---

outstrip nonliterates on the syllable strings, since the two groups were most disparate in their experience with phonic analysis and synthesis on the syllabic level. We had no clear-cut expectations with respect to the other sets of materials. (Table 10.4 lists syllable sentences and word sentences separated into units, and followed by free translation into English.)

We first experimented with this auditory integration task in a pilot study involving twelve Vai literates and twelve nonliterates.[6] Early on, we discovered that people did not have the patience to sit and listen to three sets of taped material (syllable sentences, word sentences, and scrambled words), so we decided to give everyone the syllable sentences; then half the Vai script literates and half the nonliterates received the word sentences, while the other half received the scrambled words. For each set of materials, we had two orders of presentation (sentences 1 to 5 or 5 to 1). The syllable set was given last.

Since this task involved the novel activity of listening to a tape recorder, the interviewer always began by demonstrating how the recorder worked, likening it to "a radio you can listen to" and playing back a small portion of the prior recorded conversation. If an informant appeared uncomfortable with the tape recorder or indicated difficulty in hearing, the interviewer read the material aloud, mimicking the tape. This was rarely necessary. Instructions for the meaningful material were:

> You are going to hear a Vai man speaking. He is Mohamed Nyei from Vaitown. He is speaking very slowly but he is talking correct Vai speech. Listen carefully and try to get the sense. When he is through saying a phrase I will ask you to repeat correctly what he said. Repeat it in your own natural way of speaking. If you don't remember all of it, say as much as you can remember. Then I will ask you a question about it.

Comprehension questions were similar to those used in the reading task. For the scrambled words condition, subjects were told that they would be hearing lists of Vai words, and that they should repeat the lists correctly.

Results are presented in Table 10.5. To enable comparison across all sets of material, including scrambled words, we scored each respondent by number of units recalled rather than sentences. A person remembering all five sentences perfectly could receive a maximum score of 45. Consider first performance on the scrambled word sentences (line 1). Literate and nonliterate recall is virtually identical for this meaningless material. This outcome is useful in demonstrating that comparison groups are similar with respect to certain factors affecting memory performance (ability to encode, store, and retrieve words from memory, for example) and nonmnemonic factors as well (orienting to the task, attending to the tape recorder, following instructions, and the like).

Now let us turn to performance on the two sets of materials in which semantic integration could facilitate recall. Looking first at the sentences composed of words arranged in a meaningful order (line 2) we find that both literates and nonliterates show a striking gain in recall. Both groups benefited from the meaningfulness of the material—an indication that when they heard the words, even in their slowed-down rate of presentation, they were able to integrate them into a comprehensible sentence. Vai script

Table 10.5 Mean number of units recalled in auditory integration pilot task

Experimental condition	Vai script literates	Nonliterates
(1) Words, scrambled	15.67[a]	16.80
(2) Words, sentence	34.83	28.33
(3) Syllables, sentence	30.25	21.80

a. Maximum possible score, 45.

literates do somewhat better here than the nonliterates, but the difference between the two groups is not nearly as large as the distance of each group's own recall from the scrambled word condition. This outcome informs us that nonliterate people in the study were able to bring language integrational skills to bear under the conditions of the experiment, working with artificial and nonrepresentative material.

When we turn to memory for the sentences composed of syllables (line 3) we find the two groups showing markedly divergent performances: Vai literates' recall of syllable sentences is near their recall level for word sentences, but nonliterates' recall of syllable sentences is closer to their recall of the meaningless scrambled word list than to word sentences.

With these results in hand we designed a similar listening task for inclusion in the integration survey which also included the reading task. Our principal interest shifted now to exploring the apparent interaction between literacy status and the materials to which auditory integrational skills are applied. Since scrambled word lists had produced no literacy-related difference, we restricted ourselves to the word and syllable sentences. In all other respects, procedures and materials were the same as in the pilot study. Sessions were tape-recorded, and tapes were analyzed and scored by the interviewer and Mr. Nyei.

Analyses to be reported are based on more holistic recall measures than on the number of units recalled, since we wanted to capture subjects' ability to interpret the material as meaningful sentences, and all materials used were meaningful. We scored each recalled sentence for its preservation of the original material as presented. If the subject repeated the original sentence with no more than one lexical substitution and no change of meaning, we scored it as *same sentence*. We also scored whether the comprehension question to each sentence was answered correctly. If the sentence was recalled as the same sentence *and* the comprehension question had been answered correctly, we designated it as a *correctly recalled* sentence; our measure thus taps both memory and comprehension processes, and virtually requires errorless performance.

Table 10.6, which compares mean group performances on word and syllable sentence recall, shows a striking interaction of literacy group with task. On sentences containing word units, the two groups of Vai script literates and two Arabic literate groups recall the material equally well; on sentences containing syllable units, both Arabic groups and the beginning Vai script group drop to the level of nonliterates, considerably below the advanced Vai script level of performance. The performance of school students is especially interesting: they turn in the best comprehension-memory performance for word sentences, but they, too, drop below advanced Vai script literates on the syllable sentence memory task.

These observed group differences are reproduced in regression equations that hold background factors constant. Memory for word sentences is predicted by a negative contribution of nonliteracy and a further decrement

Table 10.6 Mean scores on auditory task, integration survey

Literacy group	Word sentences perfectly recalled (max 5)	Syllable sentences perfectly recalled (max 5)
Nonliterate men	1.45	.90
Arabic literates		
Qur'anic only	2.50	1.00
Arabic language	2.60	1.10
Beginning Vai script literates	2.80	1.10
Advanced Vai script literates	2.85	2.40
English literates (students)	3.45	2.00

attributable to age. We can also get an equation accounting for more of the variance in which literacy factors relating to each script contribute positively to word sentence memory. This equation adds to our knowledge of the particular literacy-associated variables that function as the best predictors on this task. For Vai script, it is reading score; for English literacy, last grade in school; and the best Arabic predictor is a composite variable reflecting years of experience in writing Arabic and teaching Arabic—two activities that only expert Arabic literates perform.

Memory for
word sentences = 2.99 + .44 Vai reading score + .11 last grade
(R^2 = .20)   (3.5)   (3.0)
      + .13 years write Arabic × teach Qur'an − .034 age
            (2.8)   (2.3)

Equations predicting syllable sentence memory also show an age decrement, but apart from this, the only other variable that will enter the equation is the group identifier advanced Vai. The top range of Vai reading scores (levels 3 and 4) will substitute for advanced Vai status for a higher total amount of predicted variance and thus firmly links this group's superior performance to the hypothesized practices that the study was designed to simulate. English schooling makes no contribution here.

Finally, when we perform our most stringent test and enter each person's score for word sentence recall as a control for general memory factors, we find that only advanced Vai script reading scores enhance performance over and above scores on word sentences.

Memory for
syllable sentences = .02 + .51 memory for word sentences
(R^2 = .46)   (8.0)
     + .08 Vai reading score 3, 4
        (3.8)

This outcome provides the cleanest and perhaps most compelling evidence that ability to understand, remember, and reproduce sentences parsed into syllables reflects expertise in reading Vai script; no other literacy or nonliteracy factor examined in our analyses appeared to offer an alternative route to these skills.

Studies discussed in this chapter present a consistent picture supporting the interpretation that specific skills involved in reading and writing Vai script transfer to tasks implicating these same skills. Tasks on which script-specific skills were in evidence represent a continuum of similarity with the original practice: from rebus reading, in which the task transformation consisted primarily of substituting pictorial representations for script characters; to rebus writing, which involved the further change of working with these pictorial representations in a simultaneous display; to the auditory integration task, in which the support of graphic symbols was entirely removed. On each of these tasks, we were able to demonstrate qualitative or quantitative features of Vai script literates' performance that distinguished them, not only from nonliterates, but from members of other literacy groups.

We can claim "common literacy" facilitation on some aspects of the tasks—that is, performance aspects that seem to be enhanced by several (or all) literacies—as well as facilitation that is clearly specific to Vai script literacy. We will consider first how the various literacy groups compare to nonliterates, our baseline population.

Rebus reading and writing tasks suggest that prior experience in constructing meaning from graphic symbols in all scripts is helpful in semantic interpretation of other symbols. This "common literacy" effect is especially clear in the writing task in which the various literacy groups—Arabic, beginning and advanced Vai script, and English schooled—were all about equally able to construct sentences (near-perfect performances) and all much more skilled than nonliterates. Qur'anic students, lacking experience in decoding Arabic into meaningful language, were no better than nonliterates on this task—an outcome that strengthens the case for true literacy effects here. On the reading task, the one anomalous outcome is the failure of true Arabic literates to surpass nonliterates. While we can only give ad hoc explanations of this exception, we believe that our procedures may have interfered with their normal reading routines.

It is perhaps not surprising that prior experience in decoding and encoding operations in any script should give individuals an edge on tasks involving some of the same operations in a substitute symbol system. Perhaps more surprising is the statistical nature of literacy's facilitative effect. In all the studies we undertook—both in Monrovia with more "sophisticated" urban populations and in upcountry hamlets—nonliterate men showed some capability in "reading" and "writing." With little tutelage, they managed to catch on, to read some of the sentences correctly, and occasionally to construct a meaningful sentence from assorted pictures. Their performance is important to any psychological theory of literacy. In this case, it seems to indicate that skills tapped in these two tasks (at least at the level of difficulty at which they were tapped) are not exclusive to or wholly dependent on literacy, although they are enhanced by it. We are inclined to wonder whether nonliterate child groups would have performed as well, and regret that we could not pursue the many intriguing questions our rebus game raised about possible conceptions of graphic symbols that may provide a foundation for adult literacy learning.

Turning to the auditory integration task, we again find effects common to all literacies in ability to make sense out of, and to repeat, a "degraded" (that is, slowed down) sentence composed of words. Because we had designed this task to simulate specific auditory integration processes implicated in Vai script reading, our attention was concentrated on the comparison between word-unit and syllable-unit sentences. Nonetheless, the demonstrated superiority on word-unit sentences of all groups with prior experience in reading text aloud—and Qur'anic students certainly fall into this group—suggests that auditory integration may be enhanced by literacy in general, provided the units are semantically meaningful. Further work is needed here to verify this observation.

Against a background of effects common to literacy in all scripts, the distinctive and predicted effects of Vai script literacy are impressive. Script-specific skills were clearly in evidence on qualitative features of performance in the rebus tasks—the ability to read and write sentences requiring a number of steps in the translation process from picture names to Vai speech. In the auditory integration task, advanced Vai script literates pulled away from all other groups in their ability to handle syllables as the unit of communication. We find the performance differential between advanced Vai script and beginning Vai script groups on this task especially helpful in supporting a causal interpretation of script literacy. As we have often pointed out, even within Vai society there are problems in trying to make a case for literacy-related skills entirely on the basis of between-literacy comparisons. We are in a better position to implicate prior experience when we find systematic and consistent differences among individuals of different levels of proficiency within a single literacy group, as we do here between beginning and advanced Vai script literates. With respect to age, knowledge of languages, and other demographic features except skill rating, the two groups resembled each other closely. (See Table 9.4.) They differed considerably, however, on measures of experience with the Vai script. Advanced Vai, although they were the same ages as beginning Vai, had known the Vai script twice as long—sixteen years compared to eight. They also reported using their script knowledge more often and in more highly diversified writing activities than did beginning Vai. They wrote more letters, kept more records in the script, used it more extensively for religious purposes. And, perhaps most important, almost every advanced Vai person in the sample had taught Vai script, whereas only one-third of the beginning Vai had ever taught it.

The possibility that skills involved in processing written language may affect comprehension and memory of *spoken* language under certain listening conditions is not self-evident and has important implications (but see Sticht et al., 1974). All Vai people in these studies were, of course, native speakers; no group had more or less experience listening to naturally spoken Vai than any other. Vai script readers, however, also "heard" their language in syllabic form during the reading process. Perhaps on that account they were better equipped to hear and understand their language when it was presented in syllabic form during a purely auditory task.

A considerable amount of reading research has been devoted to specifying the nature of phonic skills required in decoding particular scripts, and the best ways of training skills in sound analysis and synthesis. The present studies suggest there may be some utility in reversing the input-output relationships of the customary research paradigms. Practice in reading may promote the development of specialized skills for linguistic analysis in the auditory mode, and these skills may differ for readers in different scripts.

11

The Written and the Spoken Word: Influence of Vai Literacy on Vai Speech

Stephen Reder

Studies of the relationship between oral and written language, though carried out by researchers in many different disciplines, have at least one thing in common—they have been predominantly concerned with examining the influence of speech on writing. Yet, in the auditory integration task, we found evidence suggesting that influences may operate in the other direction: knowing how to read Vai script affected how sentences in spoken Vai were heard and understood (at least under the conditions of the experiment). In this chapter we extend this line of inquiry to examine whether knowledge of a written language influences how literates speak.[1]

Many supposed effects of literacy have been tied to complex communicative skills and uses of language (these speculations are explored in Chapter 12). But here we are concerned with literacy's impact on such characteristics of speech as the way words are pronounced and the way they refer to objects in the environment.

Our work on pronunciation builds on the observations of historical linguists (von Humboldt, 1971, for example) that written language tends to preserve certain phonological features that, over time, become infrequent in, or vanish from, colloquial speech. But we go further in making a theoretical argument for how writing might exert its conserving effect. Specifically we make a case here that changes in word pronunciation and word reference are both due to the same underlying mechanism—namely, that literacy alters individuals' internal representations of language, and these representations mediate the differences we observe in speech characteristics.

We began our work with intensive study of the Vai script and language, and an analysis of letters and documents that we had collected. A comparison of old and recent written materials helped us identify one language feature that seemed to be changing over time. Informal observations suggested that there were systematic differences in frequency of occurrence of other features in current-day Vai writing and naturally occurring Vai speech. We decided to examine some of these features in detail and selected two features as tests of our theory. One feature is a consonant /l/ which occurs frequently in the middle of polysyllabic words. In these lexical contexts, the /l/s are often deleted by Vai speakers: for example, a word such as /kalo/ ("moon") may be pronounced with the /l/ or without it, as in /kao/. Written forms of such words also occur with or without a medial /l/.

The second feature concerns word reference. Vai language has a suffix which, when added to a noun, makes the reference definite rather than indefinite, roughly analogous to the distinction between the English particles "a" and "the" ("the book" denoting a particular specimen of a book, a definite something; "a book" denoting any member of the class of things called "books.") On theoretical grounds, we expected that occurrence of both these features would differ in speech and writing when we applied counting procedures to comparable bodies of language data in these two modalities. Writing is claimed to be less elliptical than speech so that more /l/'s should occur in writing. Moreover, Vai people often told us that in olden days certain Vai words, now often spoken with deleted /l/s, were characteristically pronounced with the /l/ included. According to von Humboldt's thesis, we should find this older form more preserved in writing, especially in the writing of older Vai script literates. As for the definite suffix, if writing demands more abstract terms of reference than does spoken language (because the two communicants do not share a common environment which defines definite things such as which book is meant by *the* book), we would expect to find a greater occurrence of indefinite nouns in writing.

To test our claims we needed two classes of evidence. We had to demonstrate greater frequency of occurrence of the test features in writing than in speech, thus necessitating a comparison between Vai literates' writing and speech; and we had to demonstrate greater frequency of occurrence in Vai literates' speech than nonliterates' speech. The basic data were the occurrences of the test features in samples of oral and written language. Some samples were individual words, others were sentences. The language samples were elicited in a specially designed interview so that the two probe features (and other features not considered here) occurred in a concentrated way; if we had restricted observation to naturally occurring instances we would have had to sample long hours under quite varied conditions to obtain sufficient data for analysis.

The same body of language materials was elicited in two closely coordinated studies. In both, instances of the probe features were produced in two or more tasks. In the first study, 80 literate men, representing a broad range of ages (from eighteen to eighty-three) and regional districts of Vai country, produced language samples in both written and oral versions of the same task. We will term this the literate study. In the second study, which we will term the literate/nonliterate study, a total of 162 people participated: 78 women, 66 nonliterate men, and 18 literate men. Writing was not included in the tasks in this second study. The two studies were run concurrently in the same villages using different subjects.

THE EXPERIMENTAL TASKS

Two tasks incorporating the phonological feature (L) and the morphological feature signaling the definite/indefinite distinction (ID) were used in both studies. In the picture identification task, subjects named each of twenty-seven objects, hand-drawn in ink on 3″ × 3″ white cards by a native artist. These, like most objects, could be named in either a definite or an indefinite form. To give some idea of the variations in word representation produced by variations in L and ID, Table 11.1 shows examples of items with and without these features. The definite form is seen in the figure as the suffix $\bar{e}$ in the word for "hoe" and the suffix e in the word for "moon." (The particular vowel used to mark the definite suffix depends on the phonological structure of the base noun.)

The second task utilized in these studies involved sentence repetition. Five sentences, with a total of eighteen contexts in which /l/ might occur, were used. Two different morphological contexts for L are represented in the five sentences. (See Table 11.2.) First, there are the kinds of cases we gave as examples in Table 11.1: the /l/ occurs in the middle of a multisyllabic word (for example, *kalo*). But there are also cases where the /l/ does not occur in the context of an independent word (a lexeme) but as the ini-

---

Table 11.1   Examples of L and ID items

	L items			
Speech			Vai script	
L−	*L+*		*L−*	*L+*
/kao/	/kalo/	"moon"	〈Vai〉	〈Vai〉
/kei/	/keli/	"egg"	〈Vai〉	〈Vai〉
/jaa/	/jala/	"hammock"	〈Vai〉	〈Vai〉

	ID items			
Speech			Vai script	
ind.	*def.*		*ind.*	*def.*
/kai/	/kaiē/	"hoe"	〈Vai〉	〈Vai〉
/kao/	/kaoe/	"moon"	〈Vai〉	〈Vai〉
/kalo/	/kaloe/	"moon"	〈Vai〉	〈Vai〉

Table 11.2   Sentences showing lexeme (L) and particle (P) contexts for L

---

1. *kiimu deñē da lō bē duñna i dōñē doñ a da dēē wa*
     P

   Because the child's mouth is hurting, (you) put the food in his mouth.

2. *ya jiē tiēlee i daa sa dēndēē mai wa dumaa*
     P

   When you have "cut" (i.e., left) the water, put the paddle on the ground beside the canoe.

3. *bilaima la a fō nje kē ai taana wa fali kalo mēē tele sooluē ma*
     L P   L L   L L

   Braima told me that he's going to Fali on the fifth day of this month.

4. *kpolo mu bē salō masaa kōlō i bi i na a la*
     L   P   L   P

   Bring me the book which is under the table.

5. *andō mō ya tolee bundō jendia lō anda bele jagba bē bendia la jēlēē wayē i bila*
      P   P   L   P L   L

   They say that if you are in a window and someone passes by with a bowl and flag, you will become bald.

---

tial element of a monosyllabic morpheme. We will call these contexts "particles." For example, L-as-particle occurs in the word *tiēlee* where it is attached to the stem *tiē*. It occurs in isolation in the particle *la*. This distinction between L in lexemes and particles will be important in later analyses, because the feature behaves differently in the two contexts, giving us additional information about how variations in writing influence variations in speaking.

In the literate study, each subject carried out both oral and written versions of the picture identification and sentence repetition tasks. First he was shown a picture and asked to name it. Then he was asked to write the name of the object. Then the next item was presented, spoken, written down, and so forth. In the sentence repetition task, each sentence was spoken aloud by the native Vai experimenter and then repeated by the subject. In the literate study, the written version of this task was conducted in a separate session. Each sentence was again recited by the experimenter and written down by the subject in a notebook.

Subjects participating in the literate/nonliterate study took part in only the oral versions of these two tasks. Thus, in the identification task, they were shown a card, named the object, proceeded to the next card, and so on.

RESULTS FOR THE LITERATE STUDY

The test feature L in the identification task. The spoken and written forms of the nineteen items in the naming task differed quite markedly in the extent to which L was in fact produced (hereafter we denote the presence of /l/ as L+ and its absence by L−; by analogy, words produced in indefinite and definite forms will be denoted ID+ and ID−). L+ occurred on 46 percent of its possible occurrences in the written response mode and 26 percent of the time in speaking. Although individual subjects varied widely in their use of L+, and individual words varied in the percentage of L+ they evoked, the difference between written and oral responding is consistent across individual subjects and vocabulary items.

The generality of the written-spoken difference can be tested in a theoretically interesting way. We separated the words which occur often in Vai letters (they were rated by a panel of Vai literates as words encountered frequently in script) from words which were uncommon in the script. Percentages of L+ elicited were higher for written than for spoken forms of both the frequent and the infrequent words. It is reasonably certain that few if any of the subjects had encountered the infrequent words in written form prior to the experiment. This invariant relation of L with respect to word frequency suggests that the difference between writing and speech did not depend upon specific experience with particular written words, but reflected the fact that different processes are at work when people are writing than when they are speaking.

The direction of the difference conforms to the notion that writing is a fuller and less elliptical system than the spoken word. But the bare fact of the differences doesn't give us much information about why they occur. In particular, it doesn't allow us to discriminate among various theories about the impact of writing on speaking. Some assistance comes from the observation that use of L is positively correlated between spoken and written forms of particular words. A word written with an /l/, for example, is more likely to be pronounced with an /l/. Such correlation, of course, invites us to speculate about how subjects' written and spoken forms are influencing each other. Unfortunately, from the data presented so far, we could plausibly argue that speaking is influencing writing instead of the other way around. More information is required to support a causal influence of writing on speech.

One of the first sources of additional information comes from examination of the population characteristics that influence L+. All subjects had been asked the basic demographic questions found to be important in our survey work. They had also been carefully chosen to sample a broad age range, since there was reason to suspect that older Vai individuals use L differently than Vai youth. The correlations between individuals' age and their use of L+ in speech and in writing ran counter to our intuitions (based on expectations about the declining use of L+ in contemporary speech) and provided important evidence that these literate men's knowledge of written Vai was influencing the way they spoke.

As shown in the top panel of Figure 11.1, there is a very modest correlation between literates' age and L+ scores for speech, but quite a sizable correlation between age and L+ for writing. There is also a large correlation between use of L+ in the two modalities, as we noted earlier. The correlation of .20 is of borderline statistical significance ($p < .05$) and accounts for 4 percent of the observed variance in scores. The correlation of .52 accounts for 27 percent of the age-L+ variance. In order to control statistically spurious influences that might be working indirectly to inflate some of these correlations, partial correlation coefficients among the three variables were calculated. The results of these calculations are diagramed in the bottom panel of Figure 11.1. The partial correlation between age and L+ vanishes for the speech data, whereas it remains large for writing. From these results (buttressed by the assumption that age may influence L+ but use of L+ cannot modify one's age), we can conclude that older people are more likely to write L+ and that the written form influences the way they speak.

Armed with this evidence of writing's influence on speech, we sought further evidence about how writing influenced speech production. Here a very close examination of what people did during the course of the picture identification task was necessary. As soon as a card was shown, the subject pronounced its name; then he wrote the name. But a subject sometimes pronounced the word additional times just before starting to write, during the process of writing, or even after he had written the word, as he surveyed his handwriting.

Figure 11.2 shows the proportion of L+ in the spoken pronunciations at

Figure 11.1. Relationships among age, speech, and writing (literate study)

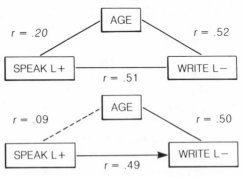

The raw correlations between age and L+ for speaking and writing are given in the top panel. The bottom panel gives the partial correlations; the age-speaking partial correlation is not significant.

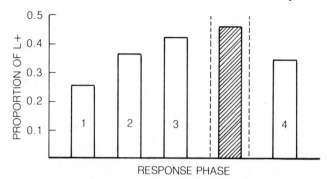

Each bar represents the proportion of L+ in responses. Bars 1–3 are data for successive pronunciations of a word as the subject prepares to write it down. The cross-hatched bar is the proportion of L+ in the actual writing, and bar 4 represents the proportion of L+ on those occasions when the word was pronounced after it had been written.

Figure 11.2. Changes in pronunciation of L during writing (literate study)

different points in the picture identification task. The first column on the left of the figure is the L+ for speaking as soon as the picture was shown, data we reported before. The cross-hatched column is L+ for writing. In between we see that the probability of L+ increases as the person gets ready to write, further increases while he is engaged in writing, and then decreases once the word has been written. The graph makes it appear very much as if the written form "pulls" the spoken form toward it as the person begins the act of writing. The fact that L+ decreases after the word is written is significant because it rules out the idea that mere repetition increases L+ or the idea that L+ is higher in writing because it follows speaking. Rather, these data support the idea that writing actively enhances literates' access to a form of words that includes L+, a form that mediates their prior pronunciation of the word in this task.

We pursued this line of evidence by looking closely at quantitative details of contingencies in the co-occurrence of L in pairs of spoken and written forms produced on individual trials of the identification task. The results of those analyses all supported the idea that literates in the identification task produce speech forms derived from written models. This conclusion would not be as surprising had the literates first written the word and then pronounced it (with their handwritten representation on display), but the procedure here was, in fact, reversed. The literates appear to use an internalized model of their writing to guide their speech. The important point here, of course, is not the specific dynamics of L production, but the evidence that internalized representation of written activity can mediate and thereby change speech activity.

The test feature ID in the identification task. One phonological feature does not a theory make. Questions remain about how general an impact literacy has on Vai speech and whether other such influences arise through similar mediation. The test feature L represents a relatively superficial aspect of language, reflecting variant pronunciations of a particular class of words. Linguists often cite "spelling pronunciations" (for example, pronouncing the *t* in "often") as evidence of the "minor" influence writing has on speech. But variations in L do not change the *meaning* of utterances, only the formal explicitness or completeness with which they are *expressed*.

In order to see whether literacy also affects aspects of language meaning, we examined the use of the test feature ID in the spoken and written language people produced in the identification task. Use of ID in the context of this task reflects the manner in which language refers to the objects being identified. This feature was considered because we had observed a substantial difference in the relative frequencies of definite and indefinite reference in naturally occurring Vai speech and writing. The details of this distribution are not fully worked out, but appear to reflect differences in the use of the referential functions of language in written and spoken communication. In oral face-to-face settings, abundant nonverbal cues and a common physical environment help establish a referential framework not usually available for written communication. Written language thus may need to draw more on abstract terms of reference than speech, including more use of indefinite noun forms.

Use of the feature ID showed the same relations between speech and writing as L; more indefinite responses were elicited in writing than in speech. In fact, nearly twice as many definite responses were given in speaking as in writing. Following the line of inquiry developed in the analysis of the L data, we also considered characteristics of the joint production of ID in spoken and written forms. As found for the test feature L, occurrences of ID in spoken and written forms were positively correlated. The trial-by-trial contingency pattern for joint production of ID in speech and writing was found to be similar to that observed for L.

These results, implicating a common mediational process underlying production of both test features, strengthen the case that writing has a general influence on speech. Both the content and the surface expression of speech elicited in the identification task are influenced by characteristics of subsequently produced writing. But are they separate phenomena? To answer this question, we examined the pattern of co-occurrence of the two test features, L and ID. The two features represent different levels of language structure and may co-occur in particular words in all combinations (for example, the Vai word for "moon" may appear in either of the definite forms /kaoe/ and /kaloe/ or indefinite forms /kao/ and /kalo/). But the absence of formal constraint on the co-occurrence of these features tells us little about processes which may determine their realizations in the identification task. Results of our analyses established that the two test features occur independently of each other, both in literates' writing and in their speech. Since the same production model (specifying that literates' writing mediates their speech) was found to describe data for both features, and productions of the two test features were found *not* to be linked, the mediational model of literacy's influence on speech applies independently to features of meaning and phonology in Vai; it is not a narrowly localized phenomenon.

The test feature L in the sentence repetition task. Oral sentence repetition followed picture identification in the battery of tasks. The five test sentences were recited one at a time, and the subject had to repeat them. Written sentence repetition occurred in a separate session in which the experimenter dictated each sentence to a small group of literates who transcribed it into notebooks.

In moving from pronouncing individual words to repeating sentences, we faced the problem that the experimenters, like other Vai people, sometimes pronounce optional /l/'s as they speak and sometimes do not. The experimenters recited the sentences from memory. We asked them to speak as naturally as possible and they did not always recite a given sentence uniformly with respect to L. All of the oral repetition sessions were tape-recorded, making it possible to verify the relation between the experimenter's pronunciation and the subject's use of L. Only one of the written sessions was recorded. As a consequence, comparative fine-grained analysis of the written and spoken results is not possible. However, overall comparison of L usage in written and oral repetition tasks is possible; individuals' overall level of L+ is used to compare oral and written sentence repetitions and to compare use of L in this task and the identification task.

A second expectation about the production of L derives from its relation to age for the spoken and written versions of the task. On the basis of the results of the identification task, we expect older people to use more L+ than younger people when writing, but not when speaking. Exactly this result emerged from analysis of the sentence repetition data; age is significantly correlated with use of L+ only in writing, and apparently only for words, not for particles.

Confirmation that patterns of L usage are similar in the picture identification and sentence repetition tasks comes from correlations of performance across the two tasks: individuals' spoken use of L+ correlates .31 across the two tasks, while their written use correlates .51. Both correlations are quite reliable statistically, giving support to the notion that the factors which control L+ usage are general across the two tasks.

COMPARING THE SPOKEN LANGUAGE OF LITERATES AND NONLITERATES

Thus far, analyses of literates' spoken and written language suggest that knowledge of the Vai script gives literates a special way to represent their language, one which can influence the way they speak. We next ask whether this mediating mechanism can differentiate literate from nonliterate speech in the same ways it differentiates literates' spoken and written language.

The picture identification and sentence repetition tasks were again the vehicles for collecting language data, although in this case only the oral versions of the procedures were used. While this restriction is obviously essential for nonliterate subjects, we must also be mindful that the presence or absence of writing in the experimental settings might influence the speech performance of *both* literates and nonliterates.

Although nonliterates do not themselves know the Vai script, they frequently share its use with their literate associates (for example, when dictating a letter), and their behavior generally takes into account the existence and functions of writing in Vai society. In the first study, writing was very much a part of the general setting, even when the person was not being asked to write: in the picture identification task, the subject alternatively wrote and spoke; in the sentence repetition task, speaking followed other writing tasks. Writing was not physically present in the experimental setting of the second study. Thus comparisons of literates' speech from the first study with nonliterates' speech in the second study may confound effects of literacy on individuals' speech with the contextual effects of writing present in the experimental setting.

In order to overcome these difficulties, eighteen literates who did not participate in the first study were included in the present study. Comparison of literates' speech across the two studies assesses the extent to which the procedures "set" literates' speech toward their writing. Comparison of literates' and nonliterates' speech in the second study indicates the extent to which literacy promotes this special language "set" even in the absence of writing.

As in the previous study, the experimental session began by asking subjects questions about their past histories which previous research suggested might be relevant to performance. The picture identification and sentence repetition tasks were then conducted.

Results

The picture identification task. Basic results for the picture identification task are shown in Figures 11.3 and 11.4. Each figure graphs the frequency of realizations of a test feature (L+, ID+) in the spoken picture identification responses. The open bars on the left are the data from the present literate/nonliterate study. For comparative purposes, data from the first study are included in the figures as solid bars on the right. In each figure, the bar furthest to the left is for nonliterate women, the next bar for nonliterate men, the next for literate men. The solid bars on the right are the data from

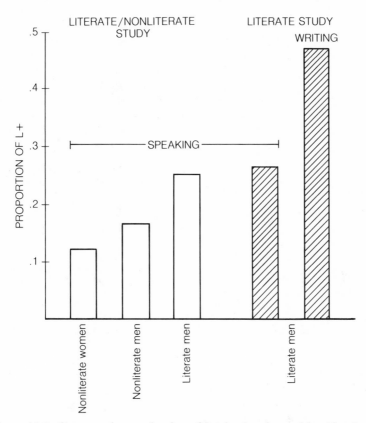

Figure 11.3. Comparative production of L+ in the picture identification task

the first study in which a single group of literates both spoke (second bar from the right) and wrote (rightmost bar). Figure 11.3 shows that the proportion of L+ increases as we scan from the left to the right side of the graph. Statistical analyses of the four sets of spoken data revealed that the only significant contrasts in the figure are between women and men and between literate and nonliterate speakers. Literate men did *not* differ in their use of L+ depending on whether writing was a part of the data collection setting.

The same general picture emerges in Figure 11.4 for the ID data. As we scan the data from left to right, we find systematic increases in the use of indefinite forms. Statistical analyses indicate that men use more indefinite forms than do women, and literates more than nonliterates. In the case of this feature, unlike L, literates' increased use of ID+ is further enhanced when writing is part of the task (the first study).

The sentence repetition task. Analyses of L were carried out for the sentence repetition task, contrasting each of the major groups considered above. The

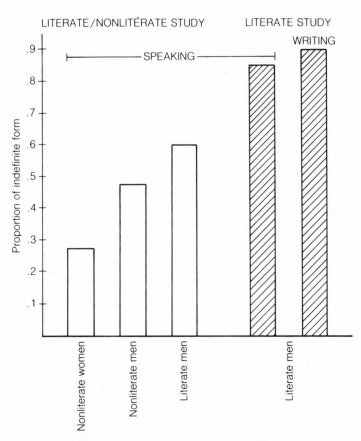

Figure 11.4. Comparative production of indefinite form in the picture identification task

pattern of effects established in the identification task reasserts itself here;
the use of L+ increases as we go from nonliterate women to nonliterate
men to literates. The data collection setting influences Vai literates' use of
L+, which is more likely to occur when writing is present during the experimental session. The nonliterate men use L+ more than the women, and
the literate men (in both studies) use more L+ than the nonliterate men.

A number of additional analyses were carried out to determine if variations in experimenters' use of L or some covarying feature of subjects' past
experience could account for the regular pattern of group differences in test
feature usage. With these factors statistically controlled, the basic results
evident in these graphs remained solid.

This evidence shows that speech is mediated by internal representations
of Vai script writing (see also Reder, 1977). In general, the degree to which
literacy affects speech depends on the test feature under consideration and

the context of language use. Relevant aspects of the context included in this research were the task, the presence or absence of writing as a part of the activity, characteristics of the particular lexical item, and the use of full sentences instead of isolated words. These represent only a tiny fraction of the factors which could control the way written Vai influences the spoken language.

Yet to be explored are the factors that lead nonliterate Vai men to use more L+ and ID+ features in their speech than nonliterate women. One possibility is that written Vai influences the speech of nonliterate men (more than women) because they participate more often in settings where written language is used. The fact that men write to other men and that a nonliterate man is likely to ask another man to read for him would be compatible with this view. But the present results indicate that knowledge of the Vai script influences literates' speech even in settings where writing is not present. Nonliterate men are in closer contact with literates' speech in these settings, too. Vai men are generally somewhat socially segregated from Vai women—men normally eat together, work together, and so on, but men and women normally do not. Until we know more about how literates' and nonliterates' speech is influenced by the presence and absence of the script in a variety of natural settings, it is difficult to pinpoint how the impact of literacy on speech is socialized from literates to nonliterates.

We should bear in mind, too, that there is no direct evidence linking observed male-female differences with literate-nonliterate differences. Separate factors may be involved. One possibility along this line is that the male-female differences are closely tied to interview settings in which the men, more accustomed to engaging outsiders in discussion, adopt a formal style of speech (which likely includes L+ but not ID+) appropriate to such occasions.

These uncertainties should not detract from the central achievement of this work: the demonstration of an influence of writing on the speech of literates. While this influence may vary with contexts of use, it is very surely evidence of one way in which acquisition of Vai script literacy affects individuals' mental performance.

12

Communication: Making Meaning Clear

According to Koelle (1854), Dualu Bukele was inspired to create Vai script at least in part because of his personal experiences with the power of the written word. Bukele, employed by traders on the coast, was often sent to distant places from which he brought back letters to his employers. In these letters, recounts Koelle, employers would be told about Bukele's behavior in the places to which he had been sent: "Forcibly struck" by this experience, he determined to have a means by which Vai people, too, "could speak with each other, though separated by a great distance" (pp. 236, 237).

The story has a colonialist ring, but the notion of letter writing as speaking at a distance is consistent with other information we have about early Vai script use. Reder discovered in informal conversations with elderly Vai script literates that in olden days letters opened with expressions such as the following: "You go from me to ——— [addressee]. You tell him for me ———." These phrases suggest that the letter was conceived as bearing the communication from writer to reader, somewhat as a live messenger would. Discourse with the reader is indirect; the writer speaks to the letter (message bearer) as he would to a messenger; and the communication is referred to in terms of talking (for example, "tell him"). Although we can only speculate about the origins of this practice, it may have arisen because of the frequent use of scribes. Senders of letters may well have told scribes what to say by employing the same forms and expressions they customarily used in giving instructions to messengers. Today the expressions that frame messages in letters no longer reflect the oral modality, but "speaking through someone"—giving a letter to a scribe—remains one of the common ways that adult Vai men and women participate in the literacy subculture. (See Chapter 6, where we reported that almost all Vai script literates in our survey claimed to write letters for others.)

However speculative our ideas about its origins, letter writing over the years has evolved into a distinctive genre of communication among the

Vai. Even the most abbreviated and mundane letters display stylized forms of salutations, introductions, and closings. Here are two examples that illustrate recurring features:[1]

Eddo letter

This letter belongs to Vaanii B. of Wuilo, Tewo. My greetings to you. Old man Fakaman sends greetings to you. Now this is your information.

If you have eddo, please send some. I beg you to bring it to Diaa and give it to Boima B. He is the young man who has the launch. I told him about it and he has agreed so please try to do it so he will bring it to me free of charge; please, we are looking forward to receiving it. I am finished. I am Fakaman's son.

Momo J.

Loan letter

This letter belongs to Pa L. in Vonzuahn. My greetings to you and my greetings to mother. This is your information.

I am asking you to do me a favor. The people I called to saw my timber charged me $160.00. I paid them $120 and $40 is still needed, but business is hard at this time. I am therefore sending your child to you to please credit me the amount of $40 to pay these people. Please do not let me down.

I stop so far.

I am Boakai D.
Fanima

Our collection of hundreds of letters, spanning four decades, shows considerable uniformity in the stylistic and structural features that are prominent in our examples. Letters are well formed and follow a tripartite pattern of conventionalized openings, messages, and conventionalized closings. In both of our illustrative letters, the opening has three elements: a stock line, "This letter belongs to ——— [addressee]"; a greeting; and another formulaic line, "This is your information." This last expression, as we saw in our discussion of word segmenting (Chapter 9), is typically treated as a unitary phrase, and, as far as we could determine, is unique to communication by letter. In light of the historical evidence concerning "oral messenger" types of letter openings, we find it especially interesting that in the present era openings explicitly refer to the communication as a letter.

Closings typically have two elements—a statement that the end has been reached ("I am finished," "I stop so far") and an identification, frequently with name of town accompanying name of writer.

For a comparative perspective on these stylistic features, we analyzed a sample of letters written in the Cherokee syllabary (Kilpatrick and Kilpatrick, 1965), with which Vai script has sometimes been compared. This sample consists mainly of letters written in the last half of the nineteenth century with some from the twentieth. Here is one letter:

Here in Goingsnake District, Cherokee Nation
December 1, 1897

Now! Digu:hl (e)di:sgi Wa:dh(k), my friend, I will write a few words for you to read.

Today Ne:n(k)si Utsi:tsadh(a) came and asked what is to happen. You extended the late E:lini credit. We all knew—it was evident—that she had nothing. You lent her money and now she is dead. Even if E:lini had left anything in the way of possessions, the law does not permit reparation. But Ne:n(k)si herself simply wants to feel right about it. Her soul is much troubled . . .

Somewhere, somehow, you two should sincerely forgive each other. That is what she wants, and I want it too. All I want is for you two to make this right. Now! That is all I have written.

Diga:sa:gwalv Di:ni:nv
Judge, Goingsnake District

With few exceptions, Cherokee letters also display stylized openings consisting of a salutation ("my friend") and a reference to writing ("I will write a few words" or "It became necessary for me to write this"). Letters close with statements such as "That is all I have written" or "I have just stopped writing." These expressions, like those in Vai script letters, indicate that the communicative exchange is framed in conventions of writing rather than speaking, and that writing is viewed as a special form of discourse. Missing from Cherokee letters, however, is any identifiable parallel to the formulaic expression "This is your information" found in Vai script letters.

Still another type of statement crops up frequently in Vai letters as a communicative device. In the loan letter is the sentence "I am asking you to do me a favor." We call this kind of statement a characterization of the communication. It contextualizes the message; it tells the recipient what the topic of the letter is and provides a frame within which the reader is to interpret the specific information that follows.

We reported earlier (Chapter 6) that the overwhelming majority of Vai script letters are transactional in nature—that is, they communicate information intended to lead to some action on the part of the recipient. Money may be involved (purchase, sale, loan or gift), or organization of family gatherings or town events, or arrangements for visits and trips. What distinguishes transactional letters from others is that they are directed toward some desired outcome, not merely dissemination of interesting news (although, of course, some letters do fall into the news-of-general-interest category). The eddo letter we reproduced is a fine example of a transactional letter. A closer reading reveals that the text, apart from openings and closings, efficiently pursues a single objective. The writer had already made arrangements through a third party to have the eddo transported to him, and he has to communicate these arrangements clearly and in detail if he hopes for a successful outcome to his plea. First, he directs the recipient to carry the eddo from Wuilo to Diaa; he then tells the reader to give the eddo to a particular person in Diaa who was preselected as the transporter. The writer identifies this person by name, Boima; but, in addition, he provides another identification: "the young man who has the launch." This information might appear sufficient, but the writer also guards against possibly troublesome contingencies. By telling the recipient that Boima has already agreed to do the job and to do it free, the writer communicates to the recipient the assurance that he will not be hassled if he complies with the writer's request. Although the letter is brief, it contains explicit directions, descriptive material, and statements of enabling conditions. From an expository point of view (if not from a rhetorical one), it appears to fulfill its purpose admirably.

Thus we have found that letter writing constitutes a distinctive communicative genre among the Vai, recognized by them as such; that letters are well structured (they have openings, messages, closings); and that they employ certain stock phrases and stylistic devices (for example, framing statements). Since most letters are prompted by practical needs, their composition puts a premium on the writer's ability to get across what the reader must know in order to carry out his end of the arrangement.

PSYCHOLOGICAL ANALYSIS OF WRITTEN COMMUNICATION

With the knowledge we accumulated about Vai letter-writing practices, we turned to psychological research for analyses of cognitive skills entailed in written communication. A general consensus has arisen that written communication puts a heavier mental burden on a writer than face-to-face oral communication does on a speaker (Higgins, 1977; Schallert et al., 1977; Bruce et al., 1978). In writing, meaning is carried entirely by the language of the text. In oral communication, speaker and listener share the same physical and social contexts and the meaning of their verbal exchange is often dependent on nonlinguistic information available in the environment. For example, a statement such as "Put the cup there," accompanied perhaps by a pointing gesture, is an adequate instruction for a listener but may be uninterpretable if part of a written instruction. Spoken messages also have certain prosodic features (pitch and stress, for example) which help the listener select the intended message from alternative possibilities. Unlike written communication, oral dialogue is interactive. A speaker often knows from the listener's response ("Whom are you talking about?") that his message has been unclear and he has an opportunity to repair and clarify it ("Moley, Bokai's uncle"). Interactive features of oral communication establish the conditions for each participant to monitor and check what the other participant knows.

Recent studies on the development of children's writing (Bartlett and Scribner, 1981; Gundlach, 1981; Scardamalia, 1981) have begun to identify some of the cognitive and linguistic skills required in the production of written texts. A writer must be able to appraise what the potential reader already knows, and what she needs to be told about background and context that will help her understand the message. The writer must also know how to organize the communication so that the reader can build up an organized representation of the information to aid in interpretation of the text (see Anderson, 1977; also Anderson, Spiro, and Montague, 1976). And the writer must be able to employ appropriate linguistic devices to make sure the message is unambiguous. (In referring back to two same-sex characters in a story, for example, use of "he" or "she" in English would not signal which one was meant—"Harry and Joe went to the races. *He* lost a lot of money.") Vygotsky (1962) drew out the implications of this "speech without an interlocutor": "In written speech we are obliged to create the situation, to represent it to ourselves. Written speech must explain the situation fully in order to be intelligible" (p. 99; see also Vygotsky, 1978, chap. 7).

If such skills are required in written communication to a greater extent than in oral communication, it follows that they might be more advanced among individuals with substantial letter-writing experience. Vai script literates appeared a promising candidate group among whom to test this hypothesis. Analysis of our letter collection made it clear that Vai letters are more than talk written down; they are a new, written form of discourse. On some occasions, at least, the purposes to be fulfilled by letters require fuller explanation of a situation to make it intelligible than would face-to-face communication with the recipient. Insofar as elaborating on the here and now to an absent recipient is required by Vai letter-writing practices, Vai script literates ought to be more skilled at constructing well-organized, informative messages.

The crucial notion here is "required by Vai letter-writing practices." Our content analysis of Vai letters (Table 6.4) emphasized that most correspondence was carried on between individuals who knew each other as relatives or friends. Rarely have we found Vai letters in which it is not assumed that sender and recipient share a great deal of background knowledge. Nevertheless, the volume and variety of letters led us to conclude that the majority of script literates are likely to encounter at least some occasions where there is a need to make messages explicit and self-contained. We set out to test consequences of this pressure for elaborated meaning by conducting studies of communication in both experimental and naturalistic situations.

For experimental purposes, we needed a task that implicated the same kind of communication skills that we attributed to letter writing but did not confer an undue advantage on literates over nonliterates. Our solution was to present a task that was equally unfamiliar to both groups. We wanted a task that adults would enjoy doing, and in which the exchange of full information made sense and had consequences. We also required a task producing information that could be analyzed into discrete units and thus measured. After some piloting, we adapted an instructional task developed by Flavell et al. (1968). (See Asher, 1978, for a review of tasks used in referential communication studies.) We taught individuals to play a simple board game with little verbal explanation, and then asked them to explain it to another person so that he, too, could sit down and play it. Board games are popular among the Vai; the structure of the experimental game was simple and similar to a game called *ludo,* an upcountry favorite that resembles Chinese checkers. We conducted several studies varying information requirements and modalities of communication. To validate performance on this game as an indicator of communication skills, we also elicited communications in an everyday context. We commissioned informants to write (or dictate) letters giving directions to their farms—a topic we could safely assume involved knowledge equally familiar to all. We devised our own scoring systems for the instructions people produced, but we worried that these might reflect merely our biases as Western psychologists and not criteria Vai literates use to evaluate "good communication." To check this possibility, we arranged interviews with individual Vai script literates to secure their judgments about the adequacy of farm directions, and to determine whether their criteria for judgment coincided in any way with our own.

A PILOT COMMUNICATION STUDY

We designed our first study to test the usefulness of the game format as a means of examining communication skills and to check out our anticipation of superior performance by Vai script literates. We selected high-contrast groups—the target group of Vai script literates and English students on the one hand, nonliterate men and women on the other. An experienced member of our major survey staff conducted the sessions and transcribed the tape-recorded communications, which he translated into English. Within the single session, we arranged for game instructions to be given in somewhat different contexts and at different stages of participant familiarity with the material. This procedure was motivated by our desire to secure a range of performance (from lesser to greater expertise) and help us select the optimal context for future studies involving a larger number of subjects. Procedures were accordingly somewhat complex.

Speaker-listener pairs were set up within each population group. Each session began with the experimenter leading one member of the pair (selected as speaker) through a complete game. He gave very little verbal instruction but made sure that all rules were exemplified during the game, and that the speaker acquired all the essential facts needed for instructional purposes (speaker's knowledge was assessed in an informal question-and-answer period after the game).

After the speaker learned the game in this fashion, the second member of the pair was brought into the room. The speaker explained the game (oral production 1) to this person as they played it, and then gave a complete, uninterrupted verbal explanation with the game materials present (oral production 2). Finally, the speaker was asked to write a letter to someone who had not seen the game so that "if a board is brought to him, he can play it." Literate subjects wrote their letters, and nonliterates dictated their letters to the experimenter, who tape-recorded them. Game materials were not present while the letter was being written or dictated. Thus, for each speaker, we had three productions: oral instructions as the game was played, a second set of oral instructions after play, and an instructional letter. We coded protocols of each production to capture features of instructions that our analysis of letter writing suggested might distinguish performances of Vai script literates from those of other groups.

We present below our description of the game, followed by transcripts of two oral instructions from informants representing the extremes: skimpy, nonintelligible communication and full, explicit communication.

The game as we describe it

Two contestants play the game by racing counters on a board. Each player has a small plastic animal, a lion or a leopard, as a counter. Players alternate turns moving their counters up a board of black, white, and yellow stripes and then back again. The first one to return to the starting point is the winner. A counter's movements are governed by the color of the chip which each player selects from a cup as she reaches her turn. Selection of a white chip entitles the player to move her piece to the white stripe and a yellow chip to the yellow stripe. To complicate the play, the black stripe on the board never serves as an end-point, and there is a red chip in the cup whose selection loses the player a turn.

[Experimenter instructions as game begins:] This is a game played with these two animals—lion and leopard. They're going to take a race from where they are to the end of this board and then back to where they started from. But the one that will first get back to where they started from becomes the winner.

Transcript 1: Skimpy instruction[2]

I called you to inform you about something. There are two animals here that made a bet, lion and leopard. This one says he can outrun this one. O.K., then after the race, how can they find out who will outrun the other? There is a thing here that the race is taken on. When you leave here then come and get like here, then come and get like here, then start back and get here, then you've outrun the other person. It seemed that's what I want to show you.

Transcript 2: Full instruction

Boima, I called you to come for us to play this game. But before we play, I'll explain to you how the game is played. There are two animals that made a bet: lion and leopard. These are the two animals that are taking a race. But the race is taken on a card that has yellow, white, and black stripes. The colors on this card, some are marked on pieces of paper and put in a red plastic cup.

That's the cup we'll shake, without looking in it, put your hand in, and pick only one. When you pick yellow or white, you set the animal on that color on the card, then put the paper back in that cup. That's how they'll continue to race till we get to the other edge of the card; then return them around and come back to where we started from. But the first person to get to where we started from wins the game. In the game, when you pick the red paper, then you fail, and when you pick two at the same time, then you fail. So you must always pick only one from the cup and the person does not look in the cup while picking from in there. You hear? That's how we'll play.

Our analysis was based on English translations, so we could not make any fine-grained evaluation of the linguistic devices informants used in the Vai language, but we developed reliable means for scoring the informational content and organizational form of the communications.[3]

We used three measures of assessment. First, we enumerated all items of information about the game that could be communicated, amounting to 48 in all. These items were grouped into three categories—information pertaining to game materials (board, cup, chips); to general rules of the game (players alternate turns); and to rules of a turn (pick a chip from the cup). For each item mentioned at least once in a communication, we assigned one information point. Here is how we scored one of the sentences in Transcript 2:

That's the cup / we'll shake / without looking in it / put your hand in /
    (0)   (1)   (1)   (1)
and pick only one.
    (1)

Mention of "cup" did not receive credit in this sentence because this term had been credited in the previous sentence ("and put in a red plastic cup"). Information about shaking the cup, and about other activities involved in taking a turn, was new and was scored for 4 units. (As it turns out, all information items in this sentence are classified as rules of a turn.) Note that the higher the total number of information items in a protocol, the more explicit the message. Compare "There is a thing here that the race is taken on" from Transcript 1 (scored 0 since "thing" did not inform and "race" was previously mentioned) with "But the race is taken on a card that has yellow, white and black stripes" from Transcript 2 (scored 5 for "card," "yellow," "white," "black," "stripes"). Out of a possible 48 points, we made an ad hoc judgment that 28 items were sufficient for adequate performance; in practice, 26 was the highest score achieved.

Additional measures were concerned with qualitative characteristics of the communication. The first was a binary score, *description,* which indicated whether the speaker ever (yes/no) provided information about game components outside of a narrative reconstruction of play. Statements such as "The race is taken on a card that has yellow, white, and black stripes" (Transcripts 2) count as descriptive. A reference to the card made while explaining how to play, "You move your animal on the colored stripes," was not credited as descriptive. We were attempting to capture some distinction between "exposition" and "narrative," guided by the notion that orienting the listener to the components of the game was a more efficient and planful organization of instruction than talk that merely reproduced play.

The third measure indicated whether a speaker ever gave a general *characterization* of the game or of his task. Statements such as "I am coming to teach you a game" or "This is a game like *ludo*" were scored as satisfying the characterization requirement. They provided context which the listener could use to interpret subsequent information. This measure was our attempt to capture use of framing statements such as those we had observed in Vai script letters ("I am writing to ask you a favor").

Results, analyzed for the thirty-eight speakers in each pair of subjects, are presented in Table 12.1. Scores are for oral production 1 and for the written (or dictated) letter.[4] As predicted, Vai script literates gave fuller, more informative instructions about the game (total information score) than either nonliterate group, although they lagged behind the students.

Superiority of literate groups in amount of information transmitted is evident in both the oral and letter-writing conditions and is confirmed by statistical analysis ($F = 11.69$, $df = 3/34$, $p < .01$). The same rank ordering applied to all subcategories of information (physical features of the game, information about general rules, and rules of play), indicating that literates' superiority was not restricted to any one class of situational elements.

In general, students and Vai script literates maintained their expected advantage over nonliterates on the organizational as well as the information measures, but performance here shows exceptions to the rule. In the oral condition, Vai literates have no greater tendency toward descriptive exposition than men nonliterates; both students and Vai script literates frame their oral communications with game characterizations, but their use of this device drops off in the letter condition, while for nonliterate men it increases. A more detailed analysis might have revealed substitute ways literates signaled the nature of the communication in their letters, but we did not undertake such an analysis in this preliminary study.

We were, of course, interested in a comparison of the information supplied in the face-to-face and written (or dictated) versions of the task. Such differences were difficult to assess for a number of reasons: written instructions always followed oral instruction and playing of the game so the speaker had greater exposure to the materials of the game and more practice in explaining it than in the initial trial. We also have to consider the greater physical effort required to write a description than to dictate it.

Keeping these qualifying conditions in mind, Table 12.1 shows that letters contained more information than spoken messages among all groups. Other evidence suggests higher letter information scores reflect true changes in the communication, not a general practice effect. Comparing subcategories of information across oral and letter conditions we find higher letter information scores are due to an increase in the information category "physical features of the game." And, if we look at *exposition* in Table 12.1 we find people making more descriptive statements in their letter instructions than in their face-to-face communications. Since the hypothetical recipient of the letter could not know much about the game components (as compared to the "listener" recipient of the face-to-face communication), the inclusion of descriptive statements and of more information about game materials was responsive to recipient needs and an in-

Table 12.1 Group means on pilot communication study

	English students (N = 10)	Vai script literates (N = 10)	Nonliterate men (N = 8)	Nonliterate women (N = 10)
Total information (number of items)				
Oral	13.90	10.90	5.38	3.63
Letter	16.10	11.90	8.63	8.51
Average	15.00	11.40	7.00	6.07
Exposition (percent describing)				
Oral	60	40	50	13
Letter	90	80	63	63
Average	75	60	56	38
Framing (percent characterizing)				
Oral	100	70	38	50
Letter	50	60	75	25
Average	75	65	56	38

dication that participants were able to tailor what they had to say to the situation.

Many questions remained. The fact that performance measures showed a cleavage between the two literate groups and the two nonliterate groups furnished support for the general proposition that literacy might enhance oral instruction, but it did not directly support our effort to link communication performance to the specific practice of letter writing. We could surmise that English school students in the grades represented in our sample (grades 5–9) engaged in some expository writing, and possibly letter writing in school, but other features of school instruction might also be operative (we will consider effects of schooling on this and other tasks fully in our final chapter). But in this line of research we were not concerned with predicting student performance. Our focus was on the Vai script group and we were troubled by the fact that with data in this study we could not pin down *their* performance to letter-writing activities. Perhaps some literacy-related experience was at work. Perhaps we were dealing with a "general literacy" factor after all. Perhaps Arabic literates would be as good as Vai script literates on this task even though letter writing is not as common an activity among them. We designed a second and more controlled study with a full array of literacy subpopulations, including Arabic monoliterates and Vai script–Arabic biliterates, to address these questions.

FULL-SCALE COMMUNICATION EXPERIMENT

We incorporated a version of the game task in the replication survey (described in Chapter 9), which included 105 men in all the basic literacy subgroups.[5]

We used the same materials as in the first study, but changed the conditions of communication. The experimenter and speaker played the game as before, but the materials were removed when a new person was brought in. Under these conditions, the speaker had to represent to himself what the listener needed to know to play the game and make sure to include this information in his oral instructions. After the speaker and listener played the game, materials were again removed and the speaker dictated his letter of instruction. In contrast to the first study, literate as well as nonliterate instructors used dictation to compose their letters.

Performance measures are summarized in Table 12.2. Students and Vai script literates display superiority over nonliterates on all measures of information and organization, thus replicating results of the first study under changed experimental conditions. Amount of information transmitted by all groups is higher in this study than in the first, and it is reasonable to attribute this difference to the fact that explanations in the present case were always made without game materials present.

Arabic monoliterates and biliterates have higher scores than nonliterates on two measures, information and exposition. But these two groups of Arabic literates also differ from one another; those who are biliterate look more like Vai script monoliterates than they look like Arabic monoliterates.

Regression equations helped clarify these apparent group differences. In the equations we included standard literacy measures (reading scores, variables on script use, years of knowledge, and the like) and other experimental variables that were linked to cognitive outcomes in our major survey or other tasks. Results were clear-cut. Whether we analyzed oral and letter productions separately or together, we secured the same basic equation, and the equation remained stable for the two measures, total information and exposition. We present them here for the oral and letter modalities combined.

Total information = $17.2 + 2.2$ Vai script reading score
$(R^2 = .20)$ (3.4)
$+ 3.5$ modernity of occupation $+ 6.3$ schooling
(2.9) (4.1)

Exposition = $.82 + .17$ Vai script reading score
$(R^2 = .19)$ (3.6)
$+ .25$ modernity of occupation $+ .43$ schooling
(2.9) (3.8)

These equations, taken on their face, support the facilitating effect of Vai script literacy on verbal communication in this task. The analysis also confirmed that it is experience with the Vai script, and not some other factor, that makes for better performance. Without going into all the details of how we arrived at these equations, we would like to convey some of the evidence on which our notion of the solidity of Vai script effects rests. Consider the first equation, total information, for example. An alternate version of this equation could have been written with the group status variables, Vai script monoliterate and Vai-Arabic biliterate, both contributing to the informativeness of the communication. But Vai script reading score substituted for both these groups. This outcome tells us that it is proficiency in the script that lies behind the groups' high standing. We now know that the similar levels of performance for Vai mono- and biliterate groups found in Table 12.2 is accounted for by a common skill—reading Vai script. And we know that the more proficient the reader is in Vai script, the better he is at conveying necessary information. Although average scores suggest that Arabic literacy enhances performance, no factor associated with it entered the equation; the apparent group differences seem to be accounted for by occupational differences (for example, more nonliterate men report farming only as an occupation than others). English schooling, however, makes a major contribution to communication adequacy.

As can be seen from Table 12.2, in this study, unlike the first, there was

Table 12.2 Group means on full-scale communication study

	English students (N = 18)	Vai script monoliterate (N = 22)	Vai-Arabic biliterate (N = 24)	Arabic monoliterate (N = 19)	Nonliterate men (N = 22)
Information (number of items)					
Oral	16.00	14.23	14.08	12.58	9.86
Letter	17.44	13.95	14.63	12.95	9.23
Average	16.72	14.09	14.35	12.77	9.54
Exposition (percent describing)					
Oral	100	86	83	68	45
Letter	94	86	83	74	45
Average	97	86	83	71	45
Framing (percent characterizing)					
Oral	83	82	58	58	55
Letter	78	86	58	68	55
Average	81	84	58	63	55

little overall difference in performance for the oral and letter versions of the task. Recall, however, that in the first study the oral description occurred with game materials in front of sender and recipient, while the letter was written with the game materials out of sight. In the present study, materials were not available when oral instructions were given. Under these conditions, the recipient is as ignorant of the object of communication as if he were in an other town. The sender thus has to provide the (visually) missing data. On the face of it, then, there should not be much difference between the oral and letter conditions in Study 2.

Despite the overall lack of difference in mean scores for the oral and letter conditions, we carried out regression analyses to see if any combination of background variables contributed to letter performance, over and above the initial oral performance. We entered oral information scores into the equation as a control, and found that over and above oral communication, number of years a person knew Vai script made an independent and significant contribution to performance, and this was the *only* factor that did.

Finally, we point out that in this sample Vai reading score was almost perfectly correlated with a variable reflecting multiple uses of the script; reading score can, with justification, be considered an indicator of the literacy practices we believe constitute the learning activities facilitating communication skills.

Modernity of occupation, the one nonliteracy-related measure entering the information equation, bears a plausible relation to communication performance. Those engaged in more modern occupations are people who are likely to spend more time away from home, and thus to write more letters to recipients who may never have shared their living circumstances. However, the fact that occupation is independent of Vai reading score and yet adds to performance suggests that some influences on communication skills are independent of writing per se, and are more likely the result of new forms of social interaction which require specialized kinds of verbal exchange.

Qualitative differences in communication, indexed by the exposition (description) score, also show a direct effect of Vai script literacy, upholding earlier results. The outcome with respect to framing (characterization) is less clear-cut. We were not successful in predicting a great deal of variance ($R^2 = .09$), and we could not get beyond the group status marker "Vai monoliterate" to implicate script usage more directly.

Characterization = 1.17 + .51 Vai monoliterate + .30 school status
($R^2 = .09$)   (2.9)   (2.5)

GIVING DIRECTIONS TO THE FARM

In the preceding studies, we assessed adequacy of instructions in an unfamiliar context (experiment) and with unfamiliar material (a game people had not known before). Our ethnographic observations indicated that it is not customary for Vai people to teach a new game by verbal instructions only, and we knew it was distinctly unlikely that any of our subjects had ever written a letter about how to play a game. Our generalizations about literacy-related communication skills were thus restricted; we did not know whether they would manifest themselves on instructional tasks in other contexts. We needed a task closer to the real-life letter-writing situation than the communication game, yet one in which all participants, including nonliterates, would have roughly comparable knowledge. To accomplish this goal, we commissioned informants to write letters giving instructions on how to reach their farms. To test for sensitivity to information needs of different readers, we secured two letters from each correspondent. One letter was to be addressed to Michael Cole of the Vai Project (then in New York): "Michael Cole has never been in this town and does not know where your farm is. Make the letter clear so when he reads it he will be able to get to your farm without the least difficulty." Another letter was to be given to the writer's wife, telling her how to get to the farm. The order in which people were asked to write the two kinds of letters was counterbalanced, and writers were unaware that they would be asked to write a second letter when writing the first. We arranged matters so that some literates actually wrote out the instructions in Vai script while others dictated their instructions, as did the nonliterate people; this procedure allowed us to compare literates and nonliterates under exactly the same conditions (dictation) while securing some indication of the independent effect of the writing activity itself (write versus dictate among literates). There were three ten-member groups of correspondents: Vai script literates who wrote the letters in script, Vai script literates who dictated letters, and nonliterates who dictated letters. None of the participants had previously been in the communication game; we used the same research assistant to elicit and translate the letters.

Farm Letter Analysis

Sixty letters, two from each subject, are included in this analysis.[6] The letters varied enormously in the explicitness of instructions; in general it would be difficult to consider many of them sufficiently explicit to get a stranger to the farm. Two of the letters to Michael Cole illustrate the range of information given:

Dear Michael Cole,

This is my farm road, I am directing it to you. When you leave from here in Boloma Town, you'll first reach a swamp. But there's a road here they call Wolako road. That's what you'll go with. When you reach the swamp, you cross it and get to the old farm. You'll be walking in the old farm till you get on the main road. When you get on the main road, go for a while, then you'll leave the town's road on your right and you'll branch on your left-hand side. When you branch on your left-hand side, you walk for a while till you reach a farm. That farm has a swamp at the middle. You walk through that farm, cross the swamp, go into the bush, continue to walk till you reach to another farm again. In that farm, the farm hut is built right by the road. When you reach there and meet someone there, you ask the person to show you my farm road. But if you do not meet anyone there, when you get there the road is right ahead of you in front of the farm hut. People's footprints are on that road. You go with it, don't branch out, and it's not far to my farm. Then you'll reach my farm.

Michael Cole, my farm is right behind my coffee farm. So when you come, just ask for my coffee farm then go with that road. It will not be too far, then you'll see the farm.

In the dictated letter condition, which allows for the most straightforward comparison between literates and nonliterates,[7] literates transmit substantially more information about getting to their farms than do nonliterates (average of 16 items per letter compared to 10). These results are clearly in line with those obtained in the communication game, although the contents and formats for transmitting the information are markedly different across the two tasks.

Nonliterates as well as Vai script literates distinguished between informational needs of stranger and wife. In all groups, more information was given to the stranger (average of 6.9 items) than to the wife (average of 5.4 items), and stranger letters included more orienting information (starting points and locational markers) than did wife letters.

If we consider that directions to a farm, like the playing of a game, follow a natural temporal sequence (the phenomena being talked about impose an organization in which certain elements come first, others second, and so on), we would expect all letter senders to adhere to such a pattern in their communications. However, in the communication game we had found that Vai script literates tended to move outside of the temporal narrative to provide the listener with a description of game materials at the beginning of their instructions; such exposition served an orienting function. Opening a letter by "locating" the person's farm and its nearby town (providing starting points) is an analogous orienting strategy. Vai script literates provided starting information in half of their letters overall, (twenty out of forty) and 70 percent of their letters to strangers; nonliterates provided starting-point information in only four out of twenty letters.

We also characterized the style of openings, dividing them into greetings and formulaic openings, such as we found in spontaneously written script letters ("This is your information"), and framing statements or characterizations of what the letter was about ("I am now describing the road to my farm. This is it"). Formulaic openings were concentrated in *written* letters of Vai script literates (fourteen out of twenty) and were almost always used in communicating with strangers; in dictated conditions, literates used these phrases rarely.[8] Characterizations were not common in these letters, but where they occurred they were found almost exclusively in literates' letters. Only two nonliterates used this framing device and each adopted it for the stranger letter only. This outcome, too, paralleled prior experimental findings with the communication game. Again we see specific links between letter-writing experiences and communication effectiveness in a contrived task.

Judging Farm Letters

Our final step was to determine whether Vai script literates had some common set of standards for evaluating "good writing" and "clear instructions," and if so, how these might compare with the criteria we applied in our analyses. We had been present on many occasions when sharp differences of opinion arose among script literates about whether a particular letter or document was "good Vai"; but we needed more systematic information about what distinguished "good Vai" from "bad Vai" and whether communication effectiveness figured in these evaluations.

We arranged individual interviews with Vai script literates in upcountry towns who were expert in uses of the script and asked their help in judging the adequacy of a sample of the farm letters we had commissioned. We selected six written letter pairs in which stranger and wife letters were of approximately equal length and replaced the original openings (to remove cues) with the standard form used to begin letters: "My greetings to you. This is your information." We divided the six letter pairs in half, and gave three pairs each to ten script experts for evaluation, giving us a corpus of sixty judgments from twenty literates. Interviews were recorded and transcribed. We told each informant how the letters had been produced and asked him to select the letter intended for the stranger. Then we probed for reasons for the choice, going over the text line by line until the informant pointed out specific passages in either or both letters which were the basis for his choice. We followed up with questions about differences between the two letters and asked for judgments on the adequacy of directions. Could the stranger make his way to the farm from what was said in the letter to him? Could the wife, on the basis of the letter to her?

Many of the informants found it difficult to make a decision and in general tended to claim that both letters of a pair were good enough to get anyone to the farm, because they were written clearly or in correct Vai. Nonetheless, when pressured to make a judgment about which letter would be more appropriate for a stranger, people did quite well: the rate of correct judgment was 77 percent for pairs on which a choice was made.[9]

This high rate of concordance indicates that judges were responding similarly to some features in the stranger letter, answering in the affirmative our first question about the existence of shared indigenous criteria for communication effectiveness.[10] But what features were decisive? Most judges took great care in answering this question, many of them reading and rereading the two letters, both silently and aloud, advancing one explanation and then another. For some letter pairs, there was high agreement on the specific feature used to differentiate stranger and wife letters; on others, considerable diversity. The most frequent single criterion used to determine the intended recipient was the starting point, the way in which the writer oriented the recipient to the general location of his farm—the feature we have used as an indicator of expository skill. The starting point was often mentioned as the determining criterion for one writer's pair of letters:

> Letter 1 (wife letter):
> When you're going to the farm, you go with the big road.

> Letter 2 (stranger letter):
> When you come to Kobolia, you go to the waterside, going to my farm.

Momakai's response is typical: "I pick number 2 for the stranger because of that phrase, 'When you come to Kobolia.' Maybe the same idea is in number 1 but in writing to your wife you will not tell her, 'When you come to Kobolia.' He will tell his wife, 'When you are coming,' or 'When you are going,' not, 'When you come to Kobolia.'" Sixteen selections of stranger letters were made on the basis of different starting-point information, and no errors were made when the judgment was based on this criterion.

Although our analyses stressed total amount of information as a measure of effectiveness, Vai judges did not concentrate on overall informational content in making their judgments. Only seven judgments used quantity of information as a determining factor, and six of these referred to the inclusion of location or landmark information—for example, instructions to look for a particular tree or branching road. One respondent who made a choice on the basis of locational information explained his decision: "The man made everything explicit . . . That person doesn't want the stranger to catch any difficulty. He does not hide anything from the stranger in order to locate him."

Linguistic criteria, often inaccessible to us in translation, formed the basis for the largest group of judgments. The phrase *a tēka*, which informants translated as "explicit," tended to recur. And there was often a consensus about critical stylistic features. Occasionally, however, the same stylistic feature would serve as the basis for assignment of a letter to the stranger by some and to the wife by others. Presence of possessives—for example, "my farm" versus "the farm"—was considered by some to be more appropriate for a stranger. (One respondent indicated that "my" tells you about the farm whereas "the" means you know about it already.) Several people said that "my" implies joint ownership and thus signals the wife as intended recipient. Another criterion was the distinction between the terms "show" and "direct" ("I will *show/direct* you the road to my farm"). Judges believed that one can only show a person something if that person is present—thus one might show a farm road to one's wife but would have to direct a stranger to it. (This rule of usage, however, failed to conform to that of all the writers, since some used "direct" for the wife.)

A handful of informants based their judgments on orthographic or spelling excellence, failing to adopt criteria for communicative effectiveness. But the readiness with which most judges engaged in content evaluation and their high accuracy in distinguishing between intended letter recipients indicate that criticism of communicative features of letters may be an ongoing aspect of Vai script literacy. While our emphasis on total amount of information was not matched in their judgments, it might be argued that Vai literates caught in more precise terms what we were forced to measure globally. They highlighted locational and orienting information as critical, and stressed the need for explicitness in the way information was conveyed.

Our stress on the usefulness of framing or contextualizing a statement was nicely expressed by one middle-aged informant who had strong ideas about how to write letters. He said it is well to start by telling the person the gist of the thing: "This person wrote this very fine. He said, I send many greetings to you. This is your information . . . In this sentence you first make the person to understand that you are informing him words. Then he will give his attention there. It is the correct way of writing the Vai script."

These studies provide converging evidence that Vai script literates have an advantage in certain instructional tasks. This advantage was demonstrated consistently over nonliterates in all three studies (two communication game studies and one farm letter study) and over Arabic literates in the largest communication study. It was demonstrated consistently for two features we had singled out as aspects of effective instructions—amount of explicit information and expository (descriptive or orienting) statements. On some occasions, Vai script literates showed a greater tendency to use framing or contextualizing statements than did nonliterate or Arabic literate groups. We have also demonstrated that a concern for communicative effectiveness is widely shared among Vai script literates; moreover, their criteria for what is a clear and appropriate instruction do not differ widely from ours.

How does this evidence relate to theories about written communication which stimulated this line of research? The theory is that written speech, more than face-to-face speech, must explain the situation fully in order to be intelligible. As a framework for our discussion we can distinguish among three sets of skills involved in making the situation intelligible: (1) assessing informational needs of the listener; (2) expressing this information clearly; and (3) organizing the information so that it lightens the listener's task of reconstructing the situation the writer wants to communicate.

As for the first set of skills, all our studies indicate that literates hold no special position. In the first game study we found that both literates and nonliterates increased the amount of information they communicated when instructions were being given to a distant recipient and when game materials were not in sight for ready reference (letter condition). In giving directions to the farm, nonliterates as well as literates discriminated in type of information they gave to stranger and to spouse, and also, appropriately, gave more information to the stranger. Thus all groups demonstrated the capacity to consider listener needs for information and to modify their communications accordingly. Vai script literates, however, were considerably better at fulfilling these needs than nonliterates. We used seven different contexts of communication in these studies, and in all but one (written farm letters), literates were more informative than nonliterates, and were especially outstanding in transmitting more items of "sensitive" or "critical" information—descriptions of game materials, landmarks to be used in following directions.

The distinction between sensitivity to special informational needs of different listeners and success in making accurate assessments of these needs and meeting them is an important one. It suggests that one way writing may improve instructional communication is not so much in improving ability to take the listener's perspective, but in equipping a person with techniques to meet the informational demands of the particular communicative situation.[11]

What might some of these techniques be? We do not know all the specific skills accounting for Vai script literates' superiority in providing more information about the game than other unschooled groups. But we have some indication that one of their effective communication techniques consists of extracting certain information from the flow of the narrative and presenting it in an expository mode. We are referring here to Vai script literates' use of static descriptions of game components as compared to mere mention of these components in action statements about how the game is played. In all conditions in which game materials were not present (letter condition in study 1, oral and letter conditions in study 2), Vai script literates more commonly used expository descriptive techniques than nonliterates. Providing this orienting information enhances the listener's ability to make sense out of the action statements in the sequential narrative. Even if bit for bit the amount of information contained in descriptive statements was no more than the information scattered throughout the entire communication, we would be inclined to consider it a more efficient and effective way to introduce someone to a game he had never seen. But in the present case, organizing descriptive information in this way goes along with providing more information. Although the evidence is less consistent, we have some suggestions that characterization is another technique used effectively by Vai script literates. Characterizations, like descriptions, are a way of organizing and presenting information outside of a narrative sequence. Students especially make good use of this technique.

We have made the strongest case our evidence permits for the causal role of Vai script literacy practices in fostering effective instructional communication. But there are obvious restrictions on the range of appropriate claims. For one thing, we are not dealing with skills that are uniquely dependent on these practices. English students always surpassed Vai script literates on all measures, and we cannot reduce their varied and complex educational experiences to literacy per se. What we can claim, using the formulation with which we began this enterprise, is that in communication tasks of the kind described here, Vai script literacy *is* a surrogate for schooling. The magnitude of effects was smaller for script literacy than for schooling, but effects were equally consistent and general across the indicators we selected for analysis.

Not all out-of-school literacy experiences, however, cultivate this specific set of communication skills. We had no indication in our analyses that Arabic literacy contributed to performance on instructional tasks. Differential Vai-Arabic outcomes lend support to our leading hypothesis that specific Vai script literacy practices are at work. We put forward the proposition that the crucial practice is letter writing, and the form letters take and communication tasks they serve among Vai script literates. While we could demonstrate by selected examples that certain Vai script letters impose rather rigorous communication requirements, we cannot leave the impression that letter writing is a highly developed expository art. Most letters have limited content and many presuppose a good deal of shared knowledge between writer and recipient. We would not expect great expertise in communication to result from this set of circumstances, so it is not surprising that Vai script literates' superiority over other groups is a matter of degree only.

In the course of our work, however, we became impressed with another activity involved in Vai script literacy that is superordinate to letter writing and calls for well-developed expository skills—that is the common practice of arguing about letters and applying criteria of communication adequacy to them. Our letter judges put forward definite evaluation standards. With a few exceptions, these were very much like the standards we applied: telling the gist beforehand; making everything clear; using the right words and expressions. All of this implies that, along with the practice of letter writing, Vai script literates have created a practice of criticism and standards for writing that they are in a position to and do apply to their own performance. While the research we have reviewed here cannot establish specific cause and effect links, it strongly suggests that practices surrounding Vai script communication by letter have useful consequences for other communicative exchanges in which learning takes place.

13

Studies of Memory

In this chapter we would like to change the target group and consider possible cognitive skills related to Qur'anic study. In the way they handled listening, reading, and communication tasks, Arabic literates sometimes seemed indistinguishable from nonliterates, which gave the impression that years of practice in memorizing the Qur'an might have had no impact on the individual whatsoever. But it must be remembered that each of these experimental tasks was modeled on practices of Vai script literacy, not Arabic reading or Qur'anic recitation. Applying the logic reflected in previous work, we would expect consequences of Qur'anic practice to make themselves visible when our experimental tasks model the circumstances of Qur'anic learning.

From our earliest visits to Vai country we had been impressed by the sight and sound of young boys reciting passages from the Qur'an in their early morning lessons. Our initial studies on the possible effects of Qur'anic literacy practice were directed at two hypotheses suggested by our early observations. First, we thought that if Qur'anic learning induces people to put a heavy emphasis on literal remembering, we should find this reflected in more accurate verbatim memory under conditions that ordinarily promote tendencies to remember the gist but forget the words. Second, we reasoned that if Qur'anic students undergo years of training in remembering things in order, holding to every word, they ought to be good at rote memory tasks in which they are asked to remember things in a fixed order.

Our first study was designed to test the literal memory hypothesis using an experimental paradigm devised by Paris and Carter (1973) and widely applied in developmental research in the United States. This study suggests that when people hear a set of meaningful and related sentences, they unconsciously and automatically integrate information from the individual sentences to construct the meaning of the set. The result of this integration will be new information consistent with what was said in the individual sentences but never stated explicitly. Paris and Carter demonstrated this phenomenon in a memory task. They presented subjects with sets of three related sentences to remember. One of the sentence sets we used, based on their model, is the following:

> The monkey is inside the cage.
> The cage is under the table.
> The monkey is friendly.

After receiving several such sets and being told to remember them, the subject is presented with a list of sentences and asked to judge whether or not each sentence had been given in the original presentation sets. In the case of the monkey story, the sentences presented for recognition judgment were:

> The monkey is inside the cage. (Previously heard.)
> The cage is on the table. (A distortion of what was previously heard.)
> The monkey is under the table. (A true inference from what was previously heard.)
> The monkey is on the table. (A false inference from what was previously heard.)

Over a wide range of subject populations (including young children and retardates as well as college students), Paris and Carter and other investigators have found a strong tendency for subjects to claim that they had actually heard sentences that were true inferences. In other words, subjects had difficulty in distinguishing between information expressed in the sentences and information implied in the sentences. For example, in the set above, the greatest number of errors occurred on the sentence "The monkey is under the table," a true inference from the information presented. Performance for all the other types of sentences was excellent.

We speculated that men who had gone through several years of Qur'anic training in which exact repetition of presented material is highly valued might, by virtue of practice in literal recall, be less prone to make this inferential recognition error. To check on this possibility, we conducted a replication of the Paris and Carter study with several groups of Vai people: nonliterate men, Arabic literate men, young Arabic students, and children with from two to twelve years of school education in English.

Contrary to our speculations, Arabic literates, along with all other populations, made false recognition errors on true inference sentences while correctly accepting or rejecting other recognition items. While this result is impressive evidence for the universality of a tendency to make sense of what one is hearing by constructing an integrated representation of incoming information, it was a disappointing failure to anticipate a specific effect of practice in the kind of Arabic literacy encountered among the Vai.

SERIAL ANTICIPATION

Next we turned to tests of hypotheses that Qur'anic memorizing practices preserve serial order, and promote remembering when serial order is important. If rote learning of word lists can be considered a reasonable gloss for the activity that young Qur'anic scholars engage in, a direct test of the outcome of this practice would be their performance in recalling lists of meaningless words as compared to those who have not had such practice. Since nonliterates have no knowledge of writing, we could not conduct a study using written words as stimuli. We could, however, present lists of common words orally, or we could present line drawings of common objects, thereby bypassing the first phase of the learning process and getting directly to the point where individuals have to memorize lists.

One version of such a task was part of our test battery in the initial survey (Chapter 8). We had presented a set of twenty-four items, asking for recall after the individual had surveyed them for a while. That trial of free recall was followed by a second on which names of the twenty-four items were presented orally one at a time. This second trial represents a very crude model of serial learning of a list of disconnected (if meaningful) items. It is a poor model because the material had been laid out for the subject to inspect as a set prior to the time it was presented serially, yet we might have expected Qur'anic learning to improve performance on the serial recall trial if its effects were strong enough. Slight evidence for such an effect was found; biliteracy entered the regression equation predicting recall performance, and we know that biliterates in general are practiced readers of the Qur'an. Direct evidence that Qur'anic practice was the crucial factor was weak in this case, because within the biliterate group we could find no variation in recall related to years of Qur'anic study or any other variable designating Arabic literacy—nor did we see any tendency of Qur'anic scholars to recall items in the same order in which they were presented.

In our serial learning studies, we tried to model the procedures more closely on Qur'anic remembering. We used pictures of common objects so that nonliterates could participate and so that remembering would involve encoding of symbolic material, however rudimentary.

Our first method was the method of serial anticipation: we presented one item at a time the first time through the list and then on the second trial asked the subject to name item 2 when item 1 was presented, to name item 3 when item 2 was presented, and so on until the list was completed. Each time the subject failed to name an item, the experimenter supplied it, so that over trials each participant would have the possibility of learning and remembering all the items. This procedure was repeated for five trials. These were followed by a trial in which the subject was permitted to rearrange the order of the picture cards if he wanted to, "to make them easier to remember." Three additional trials were then given using each person's own arranged list orders. We contrasted four groups in this study, each represented by twelve individuals: Arabic literates, Vai script literates, students attending an upcountry junior high school (grades 7–9), and nonliterate men.

224 Testing Consequences: Functional Paradigms

The results are easily summarized. For both the first (trials 1–5) and second (trials 7–9) segments of the study, Arabic and student groups showed numerical superiority over Vai script and nonliterate groups in amount recalled. For example, on the final three trials, students averaged 13 items correct, Arabic literates 12, Vai script literates 11, and nonliterates 10. But the only statistically significant comparison involving Arabic literates was their superiority over nonliterates.

In addition to scoring for number of correct items remembered, we used various measures to assess the extent to which people accurately reproduced the serial order of the items. On these measures crucial to our hypothesis, we could find no differences among groups. Plotting conventional serial position curves, we found that nonliterates and Arabic literates exhibited the same pattern of performance, and we could find no evidence that would allow us to attribute the slight numerical superiority of Arabic literates to better serializing strategies. No striking differences in behavior were observed on the trial when subjects were allowed to recall in any order they chose.

At this point in our work we faced a choice: we could follow the wisps of evidence from this serial anticipation study and attempt more refined procedures to bring out hypothetical consequences of Qur'anic practice, or we could look more closely at Qur'anic practice to see if we could produce a better model of everyday practice. We chose the latter course, motivated by the fact that our various serializing measures—which constituted the best evidence for serial anticipation as a model of Qur'anic remembering—had yielded negative findings.

AN INCREMENTAL MODEL OF QUR'ANIC REMEMBERING

One of the first hints we had concerning a more adequate model of the process of learning the Qur'an came from interviews with young men who were in the process of learning or who had recently been through it. One young man told us:

> My teacher G. wrote the alphabet on a wooden tablet. He took my finger and made me point to the letters, saying Aleph, Beh. We took the first four letters. I had to point to each one and say it. When I knew these four, I went to the next three. When I knew these three I went back to the beginning and said all seven. Then we added three more. And I went back to the beginning until I knew all ten.

Almost exactly the same description was obtained from another young man who was an assistant teacher in a Qur'anic school.

> Each new boy gets a board with the alphabet. I read the alphabet to them one at a time. I say it, pointing, boy repeats it. I do three or four letters at a time until the boy knows them . . . Then I go on to a new group of letters. He learns the new letters by starting from the beginning with the old and coming to the new.

This teaching/learning style is not entirely restricted to Qur'anic teaching. In one of the Vai script literacy classes which we set up, we saw a man who earns his livelihood as a Qur'anic teacher carrying over his Qur'anic teaching style into the teaching of the script. This scene is unrepresentative of the way that Vai script is usually taught or learned; there were a dozen students and the man was working on a blackboard. But the fact that the teacher was using a blackboard and eraser and that Sylvia Scribner was there to record the lesson made it a particularly good example for motivating our studies.

The Vai script teacher (a man who knew Arabic, had finished the Qur'an and taught it) was working at the blackboard with a group of about twelve beginning students learning the Vai script. He put a list of ten words on the board in script. They were in list order, one under the other. Boys recited in unison, going down the list. The teacher then erased the first word and called on a student to come to the board and write it in. The first two words were then erased, and another student was asked to come forward and write in the missing two. The teacher proceeded in this way until the board was blank and the whole list had to be recapitulated from the beginning, which it was—with much laughter and group teaching and effort.

It turns out that exactly this format—trial with a single element, then element 1 + element 2, then 1 + 2 + 3, and so on—has been studied by Mandler and Dean (1969) as part of a program to discover general laws relating to the storage and retrieval of verbal information. In Mandler and Dean's procedure the elements are not letters of the alphabet or words in a foreign tongue, but common nouns. On the first trial a single noun is presented, on the second another noun is added, and so on until an entire list has been presented. The striking similarity of this "1 + 1" method to procedures Qur'anic students reported as part of learning to memorize the Qur'an and Scribner's observations of a Qur'anic teacher teaching Vai led us to hypothesize that if we used it we would find a marked, positive effect of Qur'anic literacy on remembering.[1]

A PILOT STUDY

We began this line of research using materials already familiar from our work on free recall—a list of sixteen nouns from four categories (clothing, food, tools, and utensils). The purpose in using potentially classifiable items was to see if category relations would intrude into recall that would otherwise be organized in a sequential manner.[2] To simplify our exploratory work, we compared incremental memory for two groups—a group of Arabic literates with several years of experience in reading from the Qur'an, and a group of nonliterate men.

We used a Vai translation of instructions similar to those in the original

Mandler and Dean study. In translation back into English they went like this: "I'm going to start reading you words. First I'll read one, then I'll read two, then I'll read three. Each time I say a word to you, or I say a set of words to you, I want you to tell me back every word you heard." These instructions were not particularly explicit, but rather than elaborate on them we instructed by example. We began with the first word ("chair," for example) and if the subject did not repeat it, we instructed him to say "chair." On the second trial, when "chair" and "file" were given, the subject was asked to repeat them. By this point, all subjects understood the idea, and the procedure went on smoothly for sixteen trials.

Measures of Remembering

Since we undertook this study as a model of Qur'anic teaching and learning practices, we sought measures of performance that would reflect the processes we thought the original practice might require. After experimenting with different versions of assessing serializing activity, we settled on two measures that seemed to capture what we were looking for. First, we counted the maximum number of words recalled on any trial in which all the words were in correct order, even if one or more words were omitted from recall. Second, we counted the maximum number of words recalled in correct order with no missing items—that is, perfect recall of some segment of the list. As a general performance measure, we included the maximum number of words recalled on a trial, irrespective of order. This measure allowed for the possibility that subjects might recall a large number of items on later trials (trials with 12–15 items) by reorganizing them into categorical clusters, a very real possibility given the relatively high degrees of clustering that we had observed in the free recall task that was part of our initial survey study.

Results of this pilot study are summarized in Table 13.1 which gives the average performance for fourteen Arabic literate and eleven nonliterate men on each of the three measures of recall. As indicated in the table, the groups differed with respect to each of the three measures; in all cases, Arabic literates recalled more than the nonliterate comparison group.

These results suggested that we had indeed hit upon a useful model for studying the effects of Qur'anic learning, but the outcomes were still mainly suggestive. We were not entirely happy with our procedures as a model of the actual learning setting. In Qur'anic study several people are involved and presentations are less systematic; in actual practice, moreover, people learn sign-sound correspondences, while in our experimental procedure all words were presented orally. We were also quite aware that we needed to extend the range of our subject populations to include other literacy groups if we were to pin down memorizing strategies to practices in a specific (that is, Arabic) literacy.

Table 13.1 Incremental recall comparing Qur'anic and nonliterate men
(study 1)

Literacy group	Max recall (any order)	Max recall with order	Max perfect recall
Qur'anic literates	10.3	7.1	5.8
Nonliterates	8.3	5.4	4.7
t^a	4.0	2.8	2.7

a. A t of 2.7 with 23 degrees of freedom is significant at $p \leqq .02$.

The next experiment in this series moved to remedy some of these short-comings. First, we included all our basic comparison groups, for a total experimental population of 100 men. We included Vai script literates, expecting that they would not be as likely to lean heavily on sequential organization in their recall. We included a group of biliterates, assuming that their practice with the Qur'an would facilitate recall in ways closely tied to the sequential organization of the task, but entertaining the notion that their knowledge of Vai script might either facilitate or impede performance in ways that would make for interesting comparisons with the Arabic monoliterate group. We also included a group of students in English schools. A fair amount of rote remembering goes on in Liberian schools, and we thought it possible that this group would perform quite well in the task, although we knew that the specific "1 + 1" procedure was not prominent in school instruction. Our attention, however, was centered on Vai script and Arabic literates. Could we replicate the superiority of the Arabic literates over nonliterates, and would it be maintained over Vai script literates who had experienced, as far as we knew, no "1 + 1" practice?

Our procedural variation took the following form. We maintained the previous oral presentation procedure for half the subjects in each population group, but for the other half we accompanied the oral presentation of the words with presentation of an easily identifiable line drawing of the object named. In essence, we were making each presentation a "sign + word" trial. These materials differed from those in Qur'anic learning in that the signs represented objects, referents of the words, rather than words themselves; thus they were not "arbitrary." We did not want to require subjects to deal with arbitrary sign-word relations at this point in the research. Stimulus materials were essentially the same as those used in the previous study, except that three furniture items were substituted for foods (as more clearly representable in line drawings), and a picture of an axe was added to the list.

In the oral + visual condition, the experimenter went through the deck of cards asking the subject to name them (and naming them himself when the subject was uncertain). Then the cards were laid face down in a row. For the first trial, the experimenter turned over the first card (moving from left to right), named it, and turned it face down again, and the subject repeated the name. For each successive trial, the experimenter turned over and named the cards included in the previous trial *plus* the next card in the row, always following the order of the pictures on the table. Each picture was shown and named by the experimenter before the next was turned over, and all the pictures included in a trial remained face up until the last picture in that trial was named by the experimenter. After the experimenter named all the pictures, all were turned face down (beginning from left to right and proceeding as rapidly as possible) and the subject was asked to repeat. This procedure continued for sixteen trials, until all the pictures were included in the list.

Results

For all recall measures, the oral + visual procedure produced superior remembering, and in no case did we obtain an interaction between procedures and population groups. Consequently, in presenting the results we combine performance under the two conditions. Table 13.2 compares groups on the three recall measures. Although the magnitude of the differences is not great, an interesting pattern is discernible. First, for the measure of overall recall, there is no significant difference among groups. Only when we move to measures of recall that incorporate serialization—either a weak form that maintains order but permits omissions, or a strong form that requires perfect recall—do we see group differences emerging. The or-

Table 13.2 Incremental recall (study 2)

Literacy group	Max recall	Max recall with order	Max perfect recall
Nonliterate	12.7	7.6	6.0
Vai monoliterate	13.5	8.3	8.1
Arabic monoliterate	13.6 } 13.6	9.0 } 9.6	8.6 } 8.6
Biliterate	13.7	10.3	8.7
Schooled literate	13.1	9.3	8.5
F ratio	1.28	3.10[a]	3.64[b]

a. $p \leq .05$.
b. $p \leq .01$.

dering of the groups is consistent for these latter measures; those who have studied the Qur'an (Arabic monoliterates and biliterates) perform best (this contrast is represented in the table by the entries combining their performances). The schooled subjects come next, followed by the Vai script literates and then the nonliterates. While rank ordering is consistent with our hypothesis, group differences are small and it appears that the various literate groups contrast more strongly with the nonliterates than they do with each other. In this instance, however, we suspected that possible covariates of the literacy groups might be giving us spuriously *small* effects. In this experimental population, our crucial variable, years studied Qur'an, covaried with age. Biliterates who had studied Qur'an for the longest period were also the oldest population group. And we knew from the original survey that age contributes a decrement to recall. In the present study we could not properly disentangle these variables, since background data on the subjects had not been collected with sufficient care to allow us to apply our usual multiple regression techniques of analysis. We felt the matter of sufficient importance to place trust in a replication rather than statistical manipulation of the original results.

We conducted our new study as part of the replication survey described in Chapter 9. We used only the oral + visual condition of the study just reported. Materials were sixteen black-and-white line drawings representing the following objects: chair, file, pot, shoe, bed, hat, cutlass, stick, hoe, hammer, shirt, spoon, axe, trousers, cup, and table. The items were arranged in a random order (list 1) and this order was alternated with its reverse (list 2). Drawings had been pretested for recognizability, and were the same as those used in the second incremental memory study reported earlier.

The experimenter laid the picture cards face down in a row in the predetermined order as he explained the procedure: "Here I have sixteen cards with different pictures on them, face down on the table. First I'll show you one and name it to you. Then, when I put it face down on the table, you name the picture you saw. Then I'll name and show you two. When I turn their faces down on the table, you name the pictures but starting from the first one up to the picture I last named and showed to you. That's how you'll continue to name them until we get to sixteen. But always remember to start naming from the first picture to the last named and shown to you."

This procedure was followed for the sixteen trials. Recall was recorded by hand in English and was scored both for item and order accuracy.

Results, reported in Table 13.3, replicate the pattern of performance secured in the previous study, lending credibility to our conclusions from this general line of experimentation. Again, the largest group differences appeared on measures of recall which include preservation of word order information. In this study we have the additional advantage of a full set of background variables which we can use to rule out the possibility that

Table 13.3 Incremental recall replication (study 3)

	Max recall	Max recall with order	Max perfect recall
Nonliterate (N = 22)	14.4	11.6	9.8
Vai monoliterate (N = 22)	14.9	11.7	10.9
Arabic monoliterate (N = 19)	15.2	14.2	13.2
Biliterate (N = 24)	15.1	12.6	12.2
Schooled literate (N = 18)	14.9	12.4	11.5

group membership defined by literacy status is fronting for some other factor in producing the pattern of group means. Using the three measures of recall previously described and applying regression analysis, we find one basic form of equation predicting each measure: amount of time spent studying Qur'an improves performance while Vai script variables cancel each other out. The surprise in this equation is that schooled subjects were not superior to other groups. Here is the equation for perfect recall.

$$\text{Max perfect recall} = .14 + .30 \text{ years Qur'an} - .09 \text{ age}$$
$$(R^2 = .12) \qquad\qquad (3.2) \qquad\qquad (2.7)$$
$$- 7.94 \text{ Vai monoliterate} + .20 \text{ age} \times \text{Vai monoliterate}$$
$$(2.1) \qquad\qquad\qquad (2.3)$$

We labor under no illusions that one should attach great significance to the fact that practice in Qur'anic learning improves performance on a specific kind of memory task. This result is important within the overall context of our research because it demonstrates that very careful specification of original practice may be necessary to show cognitive consequences. Our set of studies attempting to capture effects of Qur'anic practice on memory included a task in which literal remembering would have aided performance, but we did not find evidence that Arabic literates were more literal than others. With the insight of all post hoc explanations, we can easily argue that our initial expectation was simply wrongheaded. The Paris and Carter false recognition phenomenon depends upon people using their real-world knowledge to make unconscious and automatic inferences as they take in verbal information. These conditions are almost the antithesis of those involved in Qur'anic study, in which, at least in initial stages, people can make little or no sense of the incoming information.

The serial anticipation study moved a step closer to a model of Qur'anic learning, but even here we were wide of the mark in important respects. In particular, we failed to take account of the fact that Qur'anic students are given new items for remembering a few at a time, gradually building up to recalling entire chapters.

Our last series of experiments began to capture the incremental nature of the learning process, but our research stopped short of providing a really detailed model of actual practice. For that we would have required individuals to learn a new symbol system and to use rhythmic recall of partially mastered material and other devices which observation shows are a part of everyday Qur'anic learning. Although we clearly did not follow this work through to completion, we did accomplish one of our major aims by demonstrating that we could devise an experimental model that captured some critical features of Qur'anic learning practices and differentially affected the performances of Vai script and Qur'anic literates. It is particularly important to our argument that it is years of Qur'anic training that predicts performance for both the Arabic monoliterates *and* the biliterates. Vai script literacy was essentially irrelevant to performance, even when individuals were literate in both Vai and Arabic scripts. While we would wish for the opportunity to pursue this line of research to its logical conclusion, the demonstration of differential effects of practice which, in this specific case, promotes the performance of Arabic literates, makes the crucial point that is central to the overall research effort.

This point is reinforced by the only study we conducted in which we did not expect different forms of literacy or education to make a difference in recall. We expected an absence of such effects if the materials presented for remembering were meaningfully organized narratives with familiar content and style. Folk stories seemed to provide an appropriate vehicle for testing such a notion, because such stories are a natural part of Vai social life and the structure of folk stories has been shown to possess certain organizational features that are common, if not universal, in human societies (Propp, 1958).

Our investigation of recall for folk stories was conducted in two phases. First, we presented a sample of five stories, including some extensively analyzed in connection with recall performance in the United States (Mandler and Johnson, 1977) to eighty subjects representing nonliterate adults, adults literate in Arabic or Vai (no distinction was made in this first study), unschooled children ranging in age from six to eleven, and students or educated adults who ranged in age from fourteen to fifty, with from four to twelve years of schooling (the average number of years of schooling was 6.5).

With the exception of the unschooled children, there were only minimal, and statistically nonsignificant, differences among the various adult groups. Furthermore, analysis in terms of the story grammar scheme worked out by Mandler and her associates showed no qualitative group differences in the relative recall of different parts of the stories, suggesting that similar recall processes were at work in all groups. (This study is described in Mandler et al., 1980.)

We followed up this study by incorporating a story recall task in the replication survey (in which we administered the last-reported incremental memory study). We used two of the stories which had been shown to differ in difficulty level—one a structurally simple story about a water witch, another a story about a boy whose literal interpretation of adult instructions led to woe.

Story 1: Jinna story

Once there was a woman who had twelve sons and twelve daughters. One day she met the jinna walking in the forest. The jinna had no child. The woman laughed at the jinna because she had no child. This thing made the jinna vexed. Then the jinna tied the woman on a big rock. The woman cried for ten years. She cried until her tears made a river that still passes by that rock today.

Story 2: Boy story

Once there was a small boy who lived not far from here. One day his mother told him to carry some bread to his grandmother in one of the nearby villages. The boy wrapped the bread in a leaf and tucked it under his arm, then carried it to his grandmother's house. When he got there the bread was all broken or crumbled into pieces. His grandmother got vexed, and told him he should have put the bread on his head to carry so it would not get crumbled or broken up. Then the grandmother gave him some butter to carry back to his mother. The boy wanted to take good care of the butter so he put it on his head and carried it home. The sun was very hot. By the time he got home all the butter was melted. The mother was vexed and told him that he should have wrapped the butter in a leaf so he could get it home safely.

Respondents' versions of the stories were tape-recorded and translated into English. Analysis was carried out on the translated stories.

Each sentence in the story was parsed for information units and assigned a score. For example, a sentence containing one unit ("The jinna had no child") was scored 1; a sentence containing two units ("Once / there was a small boy") was scored 2. Multiple regression analyses were run on total content scores for each story.

Results of this survey study counter any notion that we might discover a general "memory ability" related to any of the literacies in Vai country. Incremental memory and story recall were associated with different factors in a factor analysis of the overall survey results; and the stories themselves appeared on separate factors.

Just as important to our overall argument is the fact that literacy experiences related differently to performance on each memory task. As we have seen, Qur'anic literacy was the main factor improving performance on the incremental memory task. For story recall, this kind of literacy influence disappeared and there is a suggestion that it was even reversed. The basic equations for stories 1 and 2 are:

Story 1 = 14.3 + .94 Vai reading score + .30 last grade − .08 age
$(R^2 = .30)$ (4.2)   (3.3)   (3.4)
                + 2.0 ever concession
                        (2.0)

Story 2 = 14.3 + .57 story 1 − years Qur'an − 3.5 nonliterate
$(R^2 = .35)$ (5.3)   (2.3)   (3.4)

As the equations show, amount of time spent studying the Qur'an did not influence recall of story 1 (the short, simple narrative) and it depressed performance on story 2 (the longer, complex tale). Other literacy influences on story recall were similarly variable: English education and Vai script literacy were positive influences on story 1 recall, but did not make an independent contribution to story 2 recall. (Since story 1 was always given first, we held performance on story 1 constant in story 2 equations.) With this variability between stories, we prefer to interpret results conservatively as indicating that memory for oral stories is not affected by literacy education (an interpretation consistent with the outcome in the Mandler et al., 1980, study of structural components of narrative memory).

These results highlight the limited nature of transfer arising from literacy experience. Qur'anic practice enters into the picture consistently only when the format and sequencing of the to-be-remembered materials model previous learning habits.

14

The Practice of Literacy

In this book we have made a seemingly relentless descent from the general to the specific. We began with grand and ancient speculations about the impact of literacy on history, on philosophy, and on the minds of individual human beings; we ended with details of experiments on mundane, everyday activities that would, under other circumstances, probably escape our notice or our interest. Instead of generalized changes in cognitive ability, we found localized changes in cognitive skills manifested in relatively esoteric experimental settings. Instead of qualitative changes in a person's orientation to language, we found differences in selected features of speech and communication. If we were to regard only general consequences as worthy of serious attention, we would have to dismiss literacy activities among the Vai as being of little psychological interest.

It seems obvious that we do not hold this view. However modest and specialized the outcomes, our studies among the Vai provide the first direct evidence that literacy makes some difference to some skills in some contexts. In terms of concerns with which the research began, we believe it is important that we have identified skills that are associated with literacy learning and that are not byproducts of general learning experiences in the classroom. We can summarize and describe these differences in a straightforward fashion (and this is one of the functions of this chapter), but the critical question is: What do we make of them? Can we bring our evidence of localized and specific changes into relation with scholars' grand speculations about literacy and thought? Or is there no meeting ground between the two sets of terms?

Here is the heart of the problem. To give a satisfactory account of the nature and significance of the differences we found—and failed to find—we would need to draw on some well-specified theory of cognition, especially a theory spelling out the mechanisms by which social factors affect cognitive variation. No such theory was at hand when we commenced our work, and none is at hand today to help us interpret it.

Within anthropology and sociology, we encounter theories of the "Great Divide" variety that look upon literacy as a key ingredient in the packet of social change which separates primitive from civilized, concrete from abstract, traditional from modern thought. Nor do we receive much help from current psychological theories. As we have sketched them in previous chapters, psychological theories of cognitive change have taken two disparate stances with respect to the power of literacy. A dominant trend is to consider cultural inventions, such as literacy, as unrelated to basic processes of intellectual development; literacy may influence how society does its work but not the structures of mental operations (Piagetian theory represents such a position; Piaget, 1977). Those psychologists who consider cultural inventions instrumental to cognitive development (Bruner and Olson, 1979; Greenfield, 1972) tend to see in literacy an "emergent force" that brings into existence entirely new mental structures or processes.

Neither position fits our theoretical predilections and neither will account for our evidence. We cannot describe our results in either a "no difference, all thought is the same" position nor in terms of a Great Cognitive Divide. But one of the more important outcomes of our long trips to Vai country was that we made progress in finding terms more suitable for specifying culture-cognition relationships than the antimonies offered by existing theory. In part this change was brought about by the messy give and take involved in coming to grips with the realities of Vai literate practices and the life of the Vai people in contemporary Liberia. Between the start of the research and the writing of this chapter we had seven years in which to go through cycles of hypothesis testing and to reflect on the implications of our findings. At the same time, we had an opportunity to deepen the scope of our theoretical ideas through intensive study of work by Vygotsky and his students (Luria, 1979; Vygotsky, 1978) that was unavailable to us when the work began. We also benefited from more recent writings of Jack Goody (1977) and a brief period of work with him in Liberia (see Goody, Cole, and Scribner, 1977).

Through these activities we developed a framework for interpreting our findings that we believe is helpful for assessing the significance of the Vai research and more generally for understanding how socially organized activities may come to have consequences for human thought. We call this framework "a practice account of literacy" to emphasize that it is neither a formal model nor a grand theory but a preliminary attempt to bring new questions to our enterprise (Scribner, 1977b). We will present the main features of this framework and then we will apply it, first to an evaluation of the social conditions of Vai literacy and then to an assessment of our experimental findings of literacy-related cognitive skills.

THE CONCEPT OF PRACTICE

We have used the term "practice" informally throughout our report, relying on the context of the discussion to carry its meaning. Now we have to deal more precisely with this concept along with the concept of cognitive skill, which we want to link with it.

By a practice we mean a recurrent, goal-directed sequence of activities using a particular technology and particular systems of knowledge. We use the term "skills" to refer to the coordinated sets of actions involved in applying this knowledge in particular settings. A practice, then, consists of three components: technology, knowledge, and skills. We can apply this concept to spheres of activity that are predominantly conceptual (for example, the practice of law) as well as to those that are predominantly sensory-motor (for example, the practice of weaving). All practices involve interrelated tasks that share common tools, knowledge base, and skills. But we may construe them more or less broadly to refer to entire domains of activity around a common object (for example, law) or to more specific endeavors within such domains (cross-examination or legal research).[1] Whether defined in broad or narrow terms, practice always refers to socially developed and patterned ways of using technology and knowledge to accomplish tasks. Conversely, tasks that individuals engage in constitute a social practice when they are directed to socially recognized goals and make use of a shared technology and knowledge system.

This notion of practice guides the way we seek to understand literacy. Instead of focusing exclusively on the technology of a writing system and its reputed consequences ("alphabetic literacy fosters abstraction," for example), we approach literacy as a set of socially organized practices which make use of a symbol system and a technology for producing and disseminating it.[2] Literacy is not simply knowing how to read and write a particular script but applying this knowledge for specific purposes in specific contexts of use. The nature of these practices, including, of course, their technological aspects, will determine the kinds of skills ("consequences") associated with literacy.

We can illustrate these concepts by considering letter writing among the Vai as an example of a literacy practice. As we have seen (Chapter 12), letter writing satisfies the condition of a socially evolved and patterned activity. Implementation of this activity requires a multifaceted technology: a particular script (the Vai syllabary), materials to write with (once leaves, now pencil and paper), a means of transmitting messages (once foot or canoe, now taxi). It requires shared cultural knowledge: how the Vai language is represented in the syllabary, conventional rules of representation (writing from left to right, for example), and conventions of form and style appropriate to personal correspondence ("Greetings. This is your information"). On any particular occasion the writer must also have information about the topic to be communicated and the reader's knowledge of that topic. To apply this knowledge, the writer must use a complex set of skills on many levels—sensory-motor, linguistic, cognitive. Each skill we might enumerate is, in turn, composed of many different component processes. Encoding language into graphic symbols, manipulating a pencil to form legible characters on a page, retrieving the representation of a word from memory, planning and organizing the message, and taking into account the informational needs of the reader are a plausible subset of what writing a letter demands.

If we move on to another literacy practice among the Vai—keeping a personal diary, for example—we see that it shares a common technology with letter writing and some, but not all, the knowledge and skills that letter writing requires. (For one thing, in writing for ourselves as contrasted to writing for others, we can take the reader's knowledge for granted.) If now we compare the practice of record keeping to letter writing, the set of common components shrinks and new knowledge and skill systems become prominent. For a farmer to keep a ledger of crop sales, he not only needs to know how to use the script, but also how to use another notational system (Arabic number system); he has to be able to record information in a systematic way and to classify it so it is useful for the business at hand (for example, make separate entries for rice sales and coffee sales). These skills are not essential to the composition of an intelligible letter.

All the literacy practices we have described among the Vai may be analyzed in this way. We discover that all, even the most rudimentary (keeping a family album), involve many different types of knowledge and multiple sets of skills.[3]

In this book our interest has been in analyzing psycholinguistic and cognitive skills. We have not been concerned with visual processes involved in decoding written language, nor with the motor processes involved in forming graphic symbols. But as our conceptual model implies and our evidence confirms, cognitive skills, no less than perceptual or motor or linguistic skills, are intimately bound up with the nature of the practices that require them. Thus, in order to identify the consequences of literacy, we need to consider the specific characteristics of specific practices. And, in order to conduct such an analysis, we need to understand the larger social system that generates certain kinds of practices (and not others) and poses particular tasks for these practices (and not others). From this perspective, inquiries into the cognitive consequences of literacy are inquiries into the impact of socially organized practices in other domains (trade, agriculture) on practices involving writing (keeping lists of sales, exchanging goods by letter).

With these concepts in mind, we can seek to place Vai literacy in a broader perspective. We are not concerned with locating it on some "scale" of literacy development, but rather in understanding the social factors that operated in the past and that operate now to shape the contexts and nature of Vai literacy practices. We concentrate on the Vai script and the constraints that have limited its scope.

VAI SCRIPT: A CASE OF RESTRICTED LITERACY

While there can be no doubt on the basis of the historical and ethnographic record that Vai script literacy is a significant feature of Vai cultural activities, it is equally clear that literate practices among the Vai are far more restricted than in technologically sophisticated societies. Vai literacy has maintained itself in the countryside for well over a century but it has not become a mass literacy. Participation in script activities remains restricted to a minority of self-selected men. In spite of the many different uses of script literacy we have cataloged, basic productive activities and the workings of the social order do not seem to depend in any critical way on writing. Although histories of Vai people are recorded in the script along with cautionary tales, proverbs, and aphorisms, these works are privately owned and do not function as authoritative texts for the community at large. Cultural heritage is transmitted orally in a way that does not depend upon texts (we have in mind here secular Vai script texts); technical knowledge such as that required by a tailor or carpenter is transmitted without the aid of written materials in a manner not obviously different from knowledge transmission among neighboring people who possess no writing system. We do not know if the script is ever used in bush schools or secret society activities, since we do not have access to information about how these institutions conduct their affairs. But we do know that their affairs are not conducted *through* writing and reading. In fact, we can think of no educational activity that is mediated by standardized written materials in Vai script. This negative generalization even applies, as we have seen, to teaching of the script itself, which proceeds in most cases with no written aids other than those provided on an ad hoc basis by teacher or student (except for those rare occasions when a syllabary chart is at hand).

Having stressed the usefulness of the Vai script to those who know it, we must place equal stress on the other side of the coin: those who do not know it can get along quite well. We see no evidence that they are barred from leadership roles in the social system or from traditional occupations because they cannot read and write. Vai script is not essential either to maintain or to elaborate customary ways of life.

Even less debatable is the fact that Vai script literacy is not a vehicle for introducing new ways of life. We have called it literacy without education because it does not open doors to vicarious experience, new bodies of knowledge, or new ways or thinking about major life problems. At best, Vai script literacy can be said to engage individuals with familiar topics in new ways.

Although the Vai invented an original writing system and a social mech-

anism for transmitting it, Vai society has not gone beyond the kind of restricted literacy described for northern Ghana by Goody (1968) or "craft
literacy" discussed by Havelock (1976). Vai script literacy does not fulfill
the expectations of those social scientists who consider literacy a prime
mover in social change. It has not set off a dramatic modernizing sequence;
it has not been accompanied by rapid developments in technology, art, and
science; it has not led to the growth of new intellectual disciplines. Two
classes of factors, technological and social, have to be considered in accounting for the restricted spread of Vai literacy.[4]

Technological Factors

By technological factors we mean properties of the writing system and the
means for reproducing it. In a series of publications Havelock (1976, 1978)
has emphasized that the orthography of a writing system has a major impact on its uses and possible cognitive consequences. He argues that nonal-
phabetic systems permit only limited exploitation because they are "ineffi-
cient." Their inefficiency comes about because of the way they represent
the spoken language. While an alphabet represents minimal sound units, a
syllabary maps larger, incompletely analyzed linguistic units. As a consequence, a single character in a syllabary may have several alternative phonetic interpretations. Without a representational system that approximates
a one-to-one mapping between sounds and graphic units, the reader must
rely on contextual information to disambiguate the message. This disam-
biguation process takes work and work takes time. Preoccupied with figur-
ing out the semantic units in the text, the reader finds it difficult to grasp
the message in the sentences and paragraphs. The same dilemma occurs for
the writer, who must choose from among several alternatives the representation of a sound packet (syllable) that best fits an (incompletely represented) piece of speech. The result of pressure from the work involved in
decoding or encoding is to reduce greatly the variety and novelty of written
messages. Writing is used to represent statements that will be expected and
easily recognized by readers. Statements are restricted to what is known
and do not commonly explore what is new.

Havelock's analysis was carried out with respect to prealphabetic syllabaries and may not accurately characterize contemporary scripts. His concept of script inefficiency, however, can be applied to what we have learned
about reading and writing in Vai. We described reading as a complex
problem-solving process (Chapter 10) because of many indeterminacies in
written messages. Writers differ in the way they select characters for certain
sounds (the way they spell) and also in the way they form certain characters. Tone is not represented in the script, which leads to the problem of
multiple interpretations for a single graphic unit in different lexical contexts. The result of these and other uncertainties is slow reading speed, even

for familiar materials. And, as we illustrated, such reading often involves oral "sounding out." Consistent with Havelock's predictions for writing systems with many representational ambiguities, we found that the content of Vai letters largely concerns topics that draw on the recipient's background knowledge of the writer's circumstances. We also found little in the way of original expository text or text written for more than an audience of one.[5]

However, we certainly do not want to ascribe the principal restrictions on Vai literacy to the fact that the script is a syllabary. It is sufficient to note that Japan's two syllabary systems are considered model scripts because of the regularity of their sound-symbol correspondences (Sakamoto and Makita, 1973); some claim that syllabaries fit the sound system of particular languages better than alphabets (as Klingenheben, 1933, did for the Vai; for an interesting case of an alphabet converted to a syllabary, see Riesenberg and Kaneshiro, 1960); others (Gleitman and Rozin, 1973, for example) claim that syllabaries are easier to learn. No orthographic system preserves all the features of spoken language (Haas, 1976; Glushko, 1979); some are selected for representation while others are neglected (tone and stress are often omitted, for example). Whether or not sufficient information is preserved to make the script efficient (in Havelock's sense) seems to depend on factors in addition to the particular linguistic features a script selects for representation.

Here a second aspect of the technology of Vai writing needs to be taken into consideration: the technology of its production and storage. In the nineteenth century the Vai wrote on leaves using dyes from local trees. They have long used paper and pen or pencil. However, only in recent times, and for very limited material, has there been quantity production of any piece of text (the YMCA newsletter, for example). Since there is no type font for the syllabary, reproduction of text by any process is enormously difficult. Even when low-technology devices such as mimeograph machines are available, the master copy must be cut by hand, a time-consuming task that produces fuzzy and wobbly characters. But without some form of quantity production and circulation of texts, conventional standards of graphic representation cannot readily come into existence. Circulating texts help to establish consistent rules for the way letters and characters should be formed as well as the way particular lexical units should be represented (spelled). Although English literacy rests on the efficiency of the alphabet, popular literacy would hardly be conceivable in the absence of the printing press and widespread circulation of texts (Chaytor, 1945; Eisenstein, 1979).

A theory based on simple technological determinism would lead us to expect that if potentially useful technological innovations were introduced in Vai country, rapid changes would occur in literate practice. The evidence contradicts this expectation. Almost twenty years ago a group of scholars, including prominent script literates, produced a standard syllabary that included all permissible Vai syllables. Some script writers familiar with the conventions of English tried to introduce word spacing and punctuation. But these attempts at standardization and reform did not take hold. For the explanation of this fact we have to look beyond the properties of Vai script technology to the social processes operating within Vai society and Liberia that have limited the press for a greater instrumental role of the script in social and intellectual affairs.

Social Sources of Restriction

Three interrelated social factors operate to restrict the spread and development of Vai literate practices. First, the Vai, despite their involvement in small business and trade, remain largely a subsistence agricultural group. As Goody (1968) points out in his study of restricted literacy in northern Ghana, the functions of literacy under such circumstances are limited. Second, the Vai are by no means the dominant ethnic group within Liberia, which is ruled by an elite composed largely of Americo-Liberian descendents of free slaves. The existence of the Vai script has been a source of political friction on the national level as well as a source of pride among the Vai.[6] Finally, and crucially, two other scripts, each a world-scale alphabet, may have contributed to narrowing Vai script's range of operation. In each area where Vai script might find an avenue for expansion, one or the other of these scripts is well entrenched.

Arabic, of course, dominates Vai religious life insofar as Vai religion consists of Islamic practices. The advent of Islam among the Vai dates back at least to the early years of the nineteenth century, approximately the time when the Vai script came into use. Historical evidence about early relations between the two modes of literacy is scant. We heard stories of competition between the two scripts, but at present they display a functional accommodation in village life. Vai script is used primarily for secular or pragmatic tasks, while Arabic is used primarily for liturgical and religious practices. Each script intrudes on the other's territory but in ways that serve to emphasize their restrictions. Arabic is almost exclusively a written language among the Vai, one that is comprehended by very few. The close tie to Islamic religious and sub-Saharan magic practices keeps such literacy under the control of a small circle of experts who interpret the word (Goody, 1968). Thus, the mere existence of an alphabetic script does not undo the restrictions on Vai literate activities.

Relationships between Vai script and English, the official national language of Liberia, are also quite complex. Vai country was nominally under the control of Liberia's central government at the time the script came into use. The government understandably pushed for the use of English in its dealings with local Vai officials. Again the evidence is scant, but we spoke with Vai elders who had acted as civil and legal officers of the government. They reported that court records were kept in Vai prior to World War II. Such practices are now legally unacceptable. In all official dealings with Monrovia, for taxation, laws, elections, and in commercial dealings with non-Vai, English is the official medium of communication, in writing as well as speaking. The hegemony of English in government and civil affairs beyond the regional level places very real restrictions on the utility of the Vai script.

Keeping the restrictions on socially organized practice in mind, we now turn to a review of the facts obtained in our experimental studies of literacy's consequences. In keeping with the social realities of Vai literacy, our review will cover the scripts individually, emphasizing the effects of practice in each. It will also consider interrelations among the scripts, seeking areas where they may have common effects.

EXPERIMENTAL FACTS IN REVIEW

To help us summarize and display our accumulated experimental evidence, we have resorted to a literacy device. The entries in Table 14.1 summarize results of all multiple regression analyses, dividing them into tasks conventionally defined as those tapping general higher-order skills and tasks we devised or adapted to examine functional skills in Vai script and Arabic literacies. The contributing variables to each prediction equation are ordered in terms of their relative magnitude.[7]

In the next sections, when we describe effects of schooling and traditional literacies, our frame of reference will be performance on these tasks and we will temporarily set aside observational evidence. Later, when this assessment is completed, we will consider what experimentally demonstrated cognitive effects might mean in the world in which the Vai carry on their daily pursuits and confront their changing future.

Consequences of Schooling

English school stands out as an important influence on performance across a wide spectrum of tasks.[8] However, there is no across-the-board superiority for Vai men who have been to school. This checkered pattern of results presents problems for prevailing notions about how attendance at formal school contributes to cognitive skills.

A convenient way of grasping the role of school is to consider first those tasks on which it was the highest ranking determinant of performance. These were: explanation of sorting, logic explanation, explanation of grammatical rules, game instructions (communication), and answers to hypothetical questions about name switching. All of these are "talking about" tasks. Topics being talked about are quite diversified—from rules of language to the person's own cognitive operations—but it is a reasonable assumption that they all require some common set of component skills in verbal exposition or, borrowing Olson's terminology for the moment, skills involved in the logical functions of language.[9]

Once we move away from verbal exposition, we find no other general patterns of cross-task superiority. Schooling exerts some selected effects on story recall (story 1) and on behavioral measures in tasks taken to indicate higher-order skills: abstraction (choice of form or number as a sorting principle); recall memory for a list of object names (recall 2); and correct solution of logic problems. These results are consistent with earlier cross-cultural studies among traditional rural populations. But while schooling improved performance, it often proved a less important determinant than other experiential factors or, in the case of memory, age. Schooling also improved performance on three tasks devised to test for generalization of functional skills involved in Vai script literacy (rebus reading and writing tasks, communication game). We shall discuss the implications of this fact below.

Next, consider negative outcomes—tasks on which there were no school effects. These, too, are varied. Contrary to most studies, schooling did not lead to a greater use of taxonomic clustering in free recall or to a preference for grouping objects by class membership. Urban experience, rather than schooling, was a major determinant of taxonomic classification. Failure to find school experience enhancing a person's flexibility in sorting (number of dimensions used in sorting task) is also out of line with previous studies using the same materials. Schooling did not affect performance on several metalinguistic tasks (longest word, word definitions) nor on incremental recall nor on auditory integration of syllables. Whether we group tasks in terms of general cognitive skills versus specific skills, or whether we group them simply by target domain (for example, memory), schooling presents a mixed picture: it enhances performance on some measures and tasks and not on others.

It is possible to point to a wide variety of factors that could account for those cases where we failed to obtain increments in performance as a function of experience in school. Prior research with free recall tasks, for example, has demonstrated that differences in procedures markedly modulate the size of school-nonschool differences. The procedures we finally settled on involved only two trials, each presented in a different way, the second of which suggested an effect of schooling. Considering the fact that school effects on such tasks have often appeared most clearly on later trials in a multitrial procedure (see, for example, Sharp et al., 1979) and even then only for relatively advanced levels of schooling, we might invoke this aspect of our population or our procedures as the source of failure to obtain a schooling effect.[10]

Similar considerations apply to other tasks where we might expect, but failed to obtain, school effects. Had this been a study of the effects of formal schooling in English, we would have devoted considerable time and energy sorting out the conditions that related school attendance to these kinds of cognitive performance. But this was not our purpose. Rather, we set out to study Vai script literacy, using schooling effects as our baseline.

Nonetheless, our data on schooling are significant in their own right. Perhaps because our tasks and methods were eclectic, they are especially relevant to theories that attempt to specify effects of schooling in terms of general competencies or skills. Some investigators have concluded that "attendance at school stimulates growth of overall cognitive competence" (Stevenson et al., 1978, p. 47), but school effects in our studies are not consistent enough to support that generalization, even if it is qualified to refer to cognitive competence as measured in experimental tasks only. For similar reasons, it is difficult to match up our results with accounts invoking general causes (for example, school promotes familiarity with experimental tasks; summarized in Rogoff, 1980). Why does school improve performance on some tasks and not on others that presumably qualify as tasks of the same type? The one hypothesis about schooling effects that escapes these difficulties is the observation that school fosters abilities in expository talk in contrived situations (Scribner and Cole, 1973). All primary influences of schooling in the present research fit this description.

Consequences of Nonschooled Literacies

Vai script literacy was the focus of our attention, and we can quickly review what this literacy meant in terms of performance on our experimental tasks (see Table 14.1). Reading and writing the script was associated with specific skills in synthesizing spoken Vai (auditory integration task), in using graphic symbols to represent language (picture reading and writing tasks), in using language as a means of instruction (communication board game, farm letters), and in talking about correct Vai speech (grammar task). In all cases except the last, these script-related skills were displayed on tasks we devised or adapted on the basis of our functional analysis of everyday practices of script literacy. And with respect to grammatical explanations, on a post hoc basis, we recognized a close link between the discourse about Vai language elicited in our interviews and ordinary conversation among script literates about the quality of writing specimens.

Vai script literacy was also associated with modest contributions on three general ability tasks: experts who taught the script showed a preference for form or number in sorting geometric figures; Vai script reading score contributed to performance on story recall and language objectivity tasks in one of their administrations; Vai script letter writing was associated with more categorical choices of food items but not utensils. We have no principled explanations of these spotty effects.

In our research, Arabic literacy served essentially as a foil to strengthen the comparative case for differential effects of Vai script and schooled literacies. Here, too, the strongest effects were on the task we adapted to mirror a specific literacy practice. A direct measure of time spent in memorizing the Qur'an was associated with greater recall in the incremental memory task. Within this task, the strongest effect of Qur'anic practice appeared on the measure reflecting retention of both word and order information (maximum perfect recall). Arabic literacy, like schooling and Vai script literacy, also conferred an advantage over nonliterates in auditory integration of words, in writing with pictures, and in preference for form or number on the sorting task (among biliterates). In contrast to incremental memory, superiority on these tasks was limited to those literates who understood Arabic as a language and wrote or taught it. With the exception of the sorting task, neither Qur'anic nor true Arabic literacy made any difference on other standard tasks tapping higher-order or metalinguistic skills.

This outcome should be interpreted within the limits of our research program. Since our focus was on the Vai script and schooling, we were not prepared to investigate the full range of Arabic literacy systematically. We did not, for example, devise experimental tasks modeling the advanced literate practices of Qur'anic teachers and others learned in Muslim theology and law. We have to take seriously the possibility that their reading and writing activities have intellectual implications that the tasks we used did not capture. Like others before us, we were repeatedly impressed by the theoretical interests and conversational acumen of the Qur'anic experts with whom we worked. Writing in the 1920s, the French scholar Marty (quoted in Goody, 1968b) praised the intellectual worth of Muslims in West Africa, linking it to their knowledge of writing: "The reading and explanation of texts has refined their minds and one is amazed to see certain mallams [teachers] explain difficult texts with a real feeling for exegesis and grammar" (p. 221).

Our practice framework suggests that participation in disputation and commentary on the Qur'an may be the crucial activities underlying this "feeling for exegesis." To explore this possibility we would want to design experiments that test for transfer of skills involved in critical exposition. We cannot project at this point what such a model would look like, but we believe it would be radically different from our metalinguistic tasks in at least one way: these tasks emphasized abstract, relational features of language (grammatical principles, logical functions); but interpreting the word of the Prophet is likely to involve critical reasoning which proceeds by fine discriminations in meaning. Such reasoning might lead Qur'anic scholars to heightened awareness of semantic distinctions and contextual implications of linguistic expressions.

Table 14.1 Summary of factors affecting performance. (Rankings are based on t values. Rankings for verbal explanations use performance measures as controls. The symbol • indicates that results were replicated. Note that there was no schooled population in the metalinguistic survey.)

Performance (dependent variables)	R^2	Background characteristics (explanatory variables)			
		Rank 1	Rank 2	Rank 3	Rank 4
ABSTRACTION					
Sort-resort (number dimensions)		– – – – – – – unpredictable – – – – – – –			
Form/number	.08	+ in school now	+ Vai-Arabic biliterate	+ teach Vai script	
Verbal explanation	.48	+ last grade	– in school before		
CLASSIFICATION					
Common objects					
Category choices (food)	.17	+ live in Vaitown	+ write Vai letters		
Category choices (utensils)	.05	+ years urban residence	+ teach Arabic	– years studied Qur'an	
Verbal explanation (food)	.16	– special role in bush school	+ years urban residence		
Verbal explanation (utensils)	.12	– special role in bush school	+ years urban residence		

MEMORY					
Free recall (major survey)					
Recall 1	.08	+ (upcountry residence × last grade)	− age	− (Vaitown residence × last grade)	+ speak tribal languages
Recall 2	.05	− age	+ Vai-Arabic biliterate	+ (age × last grade)	
Cluster scores		– – – – unpredictable – – – – –			
• Incremental (replication survey)					
Max words recalled	.19	− age	+ (age × Vai monoliterate)	+ years studied Qur'an	− Vai monoliterate
Max words in order	.11	− age	+ (age × Vai monoliterate)	+ years studied Qur'an	− Vai monoliterate
Max perfect recall	.12	+ years studied Qur'an	− age	+ (age × Vai monoliterate)	− Vai monoliterate
Story recall (replication survey)					
Story 1, content	.30	+ Vai reading score	− age	+ last grade	+ concession
Story 2, content (control, story 1)	.37	− nonliterate status	− years studied Qur'an		
LOGIC					
Number correct					
Major survey	.12	− farmed last year	+ English reading score	− special role in bush school	
Metalinguistic survey		– – – – unpredictable – – – – –			
Replication survey		– – – – unpredictable – – – – –			

Table 14.1 (continued)

	R^2	Rank 1	Rank 2	Rank 3	Rank 4
Theoretical explanations					
Major survey	.52	+ last grade	+ in school now		
Metalinguistic survey	.79	+ procedure			
Replication survey		– – – – – – – – – – – – unpredictable – – – – – – – – – – – –			
GRAMMAR EXPLANATIONS					
• Metalinguistic survey	.12	+ Vai reading score			
• Replication survey	.19	+ in school before	+ Vai reading score	– last grade	– (Vai monoliterate × farm only)
• Integration survey	.25	+ last grade	+ Vai reading score		
LANGUAGE OBJECTIVITY					
Major survey	.80	+ (Vaitown residence × last grade)	+ Vai-Arabic biliterate	+ in school before	+ writes English letters
					– (age × last grade)
Metalinguistic survey	.16	– farm only	+ Vai-Arabic biliterate	– (age × Vai-Arabic biliterate)	
Replication survey	.12	+ English reading score	+ (Arabic monoliterate × speak English)	+ number of places lived	+ Vai reading score

• COMMUNICATION GAME					
Replication survey					
Information score	.20	+ school status	+ Vai reading score	+ modern occupation	
Exposition score	.19	+ school status	+ Vai reading score	+ modern occupation	
Framing score	.09	+ Vai monoliterate	+ school status		
• AUDITORY INTEGRATION					
Words	.20	+ Vai reading score	+ last grade	+ advanced uses of Arabic	− age
Syllables	.18	+ advanced Vai reading score	− age		
Syllables, with word control	.46	+ advanced Vai reading score			
• REBUS READING AND WRITING					
Sentences read	.32	+ Vai reading score	+ last grade	+ number of tribal languages	
Sentences written	.28	+ Vai reading score	+ last grade	− age	
Number features changes, written sentence (with control)	.48	+ advanced Vai reading score			+ advanced uses of Arabic + number of tribal languages

LITERACY EFFECTS: A COUNTERARGUMENT

All our evidence for literacy effects comes from group comparisons. These groups were not constructed on the basis of random assignment of individuals to groups, an essential requirement in experimental demonstrations of cause-effect relationships. Aware that possible preexisting differences between groups might be confounded with literacy experiences, we administered most of our tasks in survey format so we could assess the contributions of as many background characteristics as possible. As results indicate, we were successful in capturing a number of literacy covariates (for example, occupation, age) and taking them into account in our analyses. But this kind of statistical control is always problematic, and one set of possible covariates, personal aptitudes, cannot be addressed in this way.

It is therefore possible to advance a selection-by-ability interpretation of our findings: performance differences among the literacy groups result not from different educational experiences but from differential abilities that led individuals to become members of these groups in the first place. We are most familiar with this selection-by-ability argument in relation to schooling. Because of consistent correlations between IQ scores and school achievement in industrialized societies, the claim has been made that findings of school effects in traditional cultures might be spurious, masking differences in IQ or "smartness" between children attending and not attending school, or children advancing through the grades and those dropping out. The extent to which prior aptitude as measured by IQ tests might act as a filter in determining school populations is under active investigation (Fahrmeier, 1975; Irwin et al., 1978), but there is also evidence to indicate that other factors—family's cash resources, location of schools—play a more important role. Moreover, even where selection factors may be operating, their magnitude cannot generally account for the size of school effects (Sharp, Cole, and Lave, 1979).

Setting aside the controversy with respect to school, the claim for general intelligence as a causal factor cannot be directly extended to Vai script or Arabic literacies. The selectivity of the cognitive effects associated with these literacies and their non-interchangeability argue against a general intelligence interpretation; a selection argument, accordingly, has to posit special abilities such as memory, verbal fluency, and the like.

Here is how such an argument might be applied to Qur'anic learning: "You claim that when an individual spends many years studying the Qur'an, he learns how to memorize in a particular way, and these acquired skills help him do well in a task similar to the original practice. But for all we know, this person's good memory might be the reason why he took up studying the Qur'an in the first place or the reason why he persists. So your correlation between years of Qur'anic study and number of words remembered may make more sense turned around: people who can remember more were more successful in studying the Qur'an." The argument may sound plausible, but it cannot account for the pattern of our results. If it is true that good memories distinguish Qur'anic students from others, why is it only on the incremental memory task that their superior mnemonic abilities are manifest?[11]

Or consider Vai script literates. One might account for their superior performance on auditory integration of syllables by arguing that they were able to learn Vai script because they had abilities in phonic analysis, but then how can we account for their adeptness in teaching others how to play a board game, for example? If skills in phonic analysis will not account for that, some other skills must be invoked. A selectivity argument can be maintained by calling upon increasingly specific aptitudes, or clusters of aptitudes. But as special abilities proliferate, the thesis becomes both inelegant and unconvincing.

We do not dismiss selectivity arguments in their entirety. Propensities and aptitudes may play a part in decisions to start or stop literate activities and they may interact with learning achievements. But the stronger the evidence for specific literacy-related skills and the clearer the linkages between literacy practices and experimental performance, the less important ability arguments become to our general understanding of the way in which socially organized experiences influence individual cognitive functioning. Taken as a whole, our evidence justifies the position that literacy, as well as schooling, has identifiable cognitive consequences.

WHAT ABOUT NONLITERATES?

Our results are in direct conflict with persistent claims that "deep psychological differences" divide literate and nonliterate populations (see Maheu, 1965). On no task—logic, abstraction, memory, communication—did we find all nonliterates performing at lower levels than all literates. Even on tasks closely related to script activities, such as reading or writing with pictures, some nonliterates did as well as those with school or literacy experiences. We can and do claim that literacy promotes skills among the Vai, but we cannot and do not claim that literacy is a necessary and sufficient condition for any of the skills we assessed.

Another way to approach the matter is to question whether we secured any evidence for general deficiencies among nonliterates. To support a deficiency position, we would need a pattern of results in which all literacies contributed an increment to performance vis-à-vis nonliteracy. We have identified only three such tasks and have noted that they all call on encoding skills. It is hardly surprising that people with absolutely no experience in using graphic symbols to represent language find it more difficult than literates to undertake such activities; it is more surprising that nonliteracy per se failed to confer a general disadvantage on other tasks.

One explanation for the variegated pattern of nonliterate performance is that other life experiences besides school and literacy were potent influences on some of our tasks. Principal among these was urban residency. Living in cities was a major influence in shifting people away from reliance on functional modes of classification to use of taxonomic categories—a shift which Luria years ago took as a sign of the conceptual restructuring brought about by literacy and participation in collective farming. Jobs in the modern sector were associated with better communication skills. A cluster of factors indicating the obverse of cosmopolitanism (farming only, playing a special role in bush school) retarded a formal approach to verbal problems (or, in another interpretation, adequacy of verbal explanations). Multilingualism also influenced performance in a way that we can readily interpret—it enhanced ability on tasks requiring some competencies with language (transforming picture symbols into a meaningful sentence).

Evidence for these facilitative influences cautions us against considering literacy and schooling as the only vehicles for the promotion of the cognitive skills we have studied. When both literacy-related and nonliteracy factors contribute independently to a skill, we have to consider the possibility that they are functionally equivalent. We have little in the way of theoretical concepts that might help us understand such equivalence, but the educational import is nonetheless clear: nonliterate populations are not a homogeneous mass, nor are they likely to require explicit tutelage in literacy to acquire some of the skills demonstrated by those who "know book."

COMPARING LITERACIES

The evidence we have summarized in this chapter strongly favors the conclusion that literacy is not a surrogate for schooling with respect to its intellectual consequences. This conclusion does not rest on the fact that schooling more often produced a difference in cognitive performance for the tasks that we investigated. Rather, crucial evidence is supplied by the different patterns of consequences observed for each of the literacies and the fact that these patterns map onto our analysis of the different socially organized domains of practice characteristic of each script.

Figure 14.1 presents these patterns as we see them. It represents our best judgment of what our experimental results add up to; we might consider it a confidence score in the significance of study outcomes. We have chosen to be liberal in assigning school effects, since many other research undertakings have demonstrated similar influences. But with respect to Vai and Arabic literacies, we have chosen to be conservative, since our studies stand as sole evidence of literacy-related skills. The literacy effects presented in Table 14.1 have been rearranged according to script and kind of cognitive skill involved. Each row of the figure represents one of the three scripts for

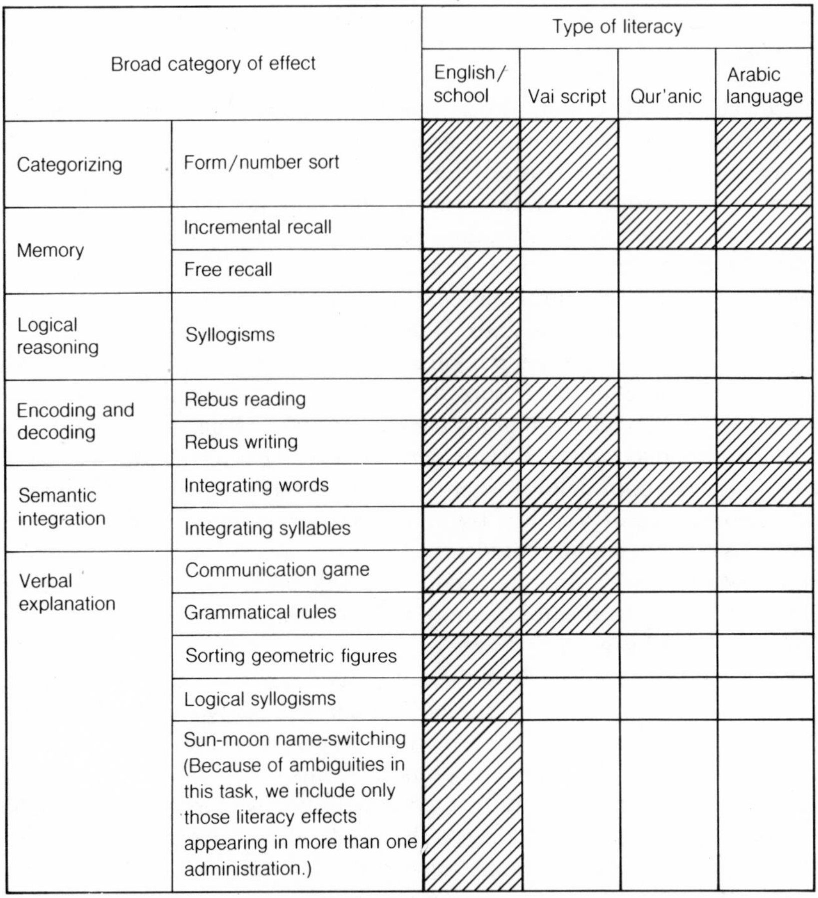

Broad category of effect		Type of literacy			
		English/ school	Vai script	Qur'anic	Arabic language
Categorizing	Form/number sort	▨	▨		▨
Memory	Incremental recall			▨	▨
Memory	Free recall	▨			
Logical reasoning	Syllogisms	▨			
Encoding and decoding	Rebus reading	▨	▨		
Encoding and decoding	Rebus writing	▨			▨
Semantic integration	Integrating words	▨	▨	▨	▨
Semantic integration	Integrating syllables		▨		
Verbal explanation	Communication game	▨	▨		
Verbal explanation	Grammatical rules	▨	▨		
Verbal explanation	Sorting geometric figures	▨			
Verbal explanation	Logical syllogisms	▨			
Verbal explanation	Sun-moon name-switching (Because of ambiguities in this task, we include only those literacy effects appearing in more than one administration.)	▨			

Figure 14.1. Schematic representation of effects associated with each literacy

which we studied literate practices—English (school), Vai script, and Arabic. Each column represents a cognitive task or aspect of a cognitive task that was used to tap cognitive skills. Wherever the intersection of script and task is shaded in on the figure, our results have indicated that the designated cognitive skill has been enhanced by practice in the corresponding script. In scanning the columns of Figure 14.1, we note an asymmetry between school and script effects: English schooling contributes to performance on most tasks that we devised to model Vai script practices (significant exceptions are discussed below). But script literacy shows no such similar spread to the general ability tasks that historically have demonstrated the influence of schooling.

Script-associated skills are also more localized. Both schooling and Vai script literacy enhance ability to give clear instructions on playing a board game, and both contribute to grammatical explanations. But students go on to offer more adequate explanations on logic, sorting, and language objectivity tasks, whereas Vai script literates are not distinguishable as a group in these tasks.

Our observation about Vai script's specialization in relation to English schooling applies with equal or greater force to Arabic literacy and reinforces the general conclusion that under literacy circumstances in Vai country, knowledge of reading and writing does not have the same intellectual consequences as schooling. Nor do the consequences of schooling completely subsume the consequences of nonschooled literacies. The auditory integration task illustrates conditions under which school and script literacy promote different skills. When the task is to integrate word units into a meaningful sentence, schooling and Vai script literacy operate similarly, but when syllables are substituted as the units from which a sentence must be constructed, schooling confers no advantage; only expert Vai script knowledge contributes to performance. Schooling and Vai script knowledge are both helpful when a person has to put pictures together to make a sentence in Vai; but the sentences that students compose do not display the same sophisticated transformation of picture names into Vai homonyms as do Vai literates' sentences. Schooling did not confer an advantage in the incremental memory task which showed clear-cut effects of Qur'anic learning.

On a handful of tasks, schooling and the two nonschooled literacies make similar contributions to performance: choice of form or number in sorting (biliteracy appears here); using pictures to compose a sentence; and sentence integration with words as units. It seems immediately obvious that these tasks are dependent on the type of skills involved in decoding, encoding, or comprehending language—the mechanics of reading and writing. Our findings thus provide some support for the position (see, for example, Downing, 1973) that some common component processes may be involved in reading and writing whatever the characteristics of the script or teaching method.

Summing up the evidence with respect to the substitutability of indigenous literacy and schooling, we see the following pattern: where tasks involve highly specialized skills involved in learning or using a particular script, school drops out as a determinant of performance. "General competencies" or general familiarity with experimental-type tasks, if these factors are operative, do not compensate for lack of experience with certain specific operations required by Vai script and Arabic literacy. Reversing the picture: as tasks move away from specific script-related skills, Vai script and Arabic influences on performance disappear. But this is not an even trade-off: schooling goes considerably farther in encompassing functional literacy-related skills embodied in our experimental tasks than script knowledge does in capturing school-related skills.

One of our goals in studying Vai script literacy was to gain evidence for or against the proposition that literacy is the crucial learning that goes on in school from the point of view of cognitive consequences. Since the nonschooled literacies do not yield the same pattern of performance on experimental tasks as schooling, we might be inclined to conclude that literacy is an unimportant factor in producing school effects. We need some caution here, since nonschooled and schooled literacies among the Vai involved different languages and writing systems, but insofar as a single piece of research allows conclusions about this tangled set of questions, our studies indicate that school effects are not brought about through the ability to read and write per se.

The practice framework that guides our interpretations permits a more articulated view of the relation between literacy and schooling. The asymmetry between them may arise from several different sources. For one thing, school and nonschool contexts of use may set different tasks for the reader and writer, even within the "same" practice. Writing a letter to earn a passing grade in English poses different requirements from penning a note to a friend, although for some purposes we can refer to both acts as letter writing. The range and variety of literacy practices will also differ in the school and the community. And, most important to the interpretation of our findings, schooling consists of many other practices and activities in addition to those involving writing.

The most pervasive effects of schooling in our studies were in the ways people handled verbal explanations. We have no reason to believe that skills required to explain why problems were answered in a certain way are fostered by knowledge of a written language. Rather, they strike us as being exactly those skills that are required in teacher-pupil dialogue in the classroom. Teachers ask questions very much like those we asked: "What made you give that answer? How do you know? Go to the board and explain what you did." Similarities in functions served by explanations in our tasks and in classrooms are not merely hypothetical; recent studies of classrooms (Mehan, 1979) show that teacher-student exchanges commonly invoke talk about mental operations or the procedures for accomplishing various intellectual tasks. We have little direct evidence for this interpretation in Vai country (and, indeed, what observations we do have suggest that such interchanges, while present, are a less common feature of schoolrooms there). But the major point is that in school, literate activities are part of other practices, the sum total of which constitutes "schooling." The set of such practices is relatively large and only partially overlaps with the nonschooled literacies. It is to variability in the practices in which reading and writing are embedded that we look for an explanation of the asymmetry of schooled and nonschooled literacy effects.

The same need exists to understand each of the nonschooled literacies as a set of practices in which only some of the relevant skills and operations depend directly on reading and writing.

HOW VALID ARE OUR EXPERIMENTAL FINDINGS?

In research attempting to relate cultural experience to cognitive outcomes, contrived situations such as experiments are useful devices only if they inform us about knowledge and capabilities individuals may have available for action in other situations—learning about world events, explaining a new method of seeding rice, planning a building or a road. The great appeal of the grand theories of transformational effects of literacy lies just in the fact that they see in writing a means of enlarging the power of the human intellect in many fields of endeavor, both mundane and extraordinary. Even modest claims for limited and specialized cognitive skills require a demonstration that such skills are operative in nonexperimental situations if they are to be considered consequences of any importance. In short, we have to make a case for their external validity (Cronbach, 1970) or ecological validity (Bronfenbrenner, 1979).

With respect to Vai script and Arabic literacies, we can make the strong claim that the skills we assessed in our functionally derived tasks are operational in naturally occurring situations because the tasks were designed to be models of those situations. Whether we were sudying conversations about language or memorization techniques, we were building on prior knowledge of the ways people engaged in these behaviors as part of their literacy activities. Observations of what people did without research intervention helped us design the experiments. Patterns of performance across variations in the tasks served as tests of the degree to which known skills transferred to performance situations differing in various ways from those ordinarily encountered.

Taken together, the situations we identified in everyday life and the experiments modeled after them provide a starting point for mapping the range of application of literacy-related cognitive skills. Had the research continued, we could have constructed detailed models of other literacy activities (list making, for example) to generate new experimental tasks assessing transfer of literate skills. Equally important, we could have used experimental results and analytic schemes to sharpen our ability to conduct studies of ongoing behavior.

An important question our research left untouched is the extent to which literacy-related cognitive skills function in everyday situations outside the context of literacy practice. For example, we learned from experimental studies that Vai script literates were better able to carry out a contrived oral instruction task in a more informative and planful way than nonliterate men; but we do not know whether they would also be more effective in oral communication situations that arise in the course of daily life, such as giving out work instructions or delivering information through a messenger. Would these communications also show Vai literates conveying more information? Would the conditions of interaction that occur normally ever demand such added explication? Prior experimental analysis would help us pursue this inquiry by pointing to certain features of performance where literacy-associated differences might be located (exposition, for example). The specification of skills we achieved through experimentation would put us in a better position to identify and analyze skills in naturally occurring, uncontrolled situations. Through a continual interplay between observation and experimentation we could, in principle (limited in practice by the technical means at hand), acquire an understanding of how restricted or widely applicable particular literacy-associated skills are in Vai society.

While the logic of the research is clear, actual implementation of such an ideal program is enormously complicated. Work on devising methods for identifying component skills in everyday behavior is still in beginning stages (Ginsburg, 1978; Cole and Traupman, 1980; Lave, 1980; Scribner, 1980), but we now know enough to know that there are no short and easy ways to tackle big questions about formative influences on intellectual behavior.

The interpretive problem with respect to consequences of schooling is less straightforward. For one thing, the experiments which historically have been used to examine intellectual consequences of schooling, and which formed our initial cognitive batteries, were not designed as tests of skills transfer[12]—for the simple reason that in most cases we cannot point to the activities in school which fostered them. Inadequate analysis of intellectual work in the school means that, with respect to formal education, we are a step behind in carrying out the mapping program we proposed above for nonschooled literacies. Our inability to specify in detail the learning and use contexts of experimentally demonstrated skills in the school environment hampers our ability to locate occasions outside of the school which entail these same skills.

A further difficulty arises from the theoretical status of the experimental tasks, a recurring theme in our discussion. To the extent that these tasks are considered indicative of some general mental abilities, the question of how experimental evidence can be brought to bear on statements about cognitive functioning in everyday life does not tend to arise as an empirical question. It is assumed by definition that general abilities will have a wide range of operation.

It should be clear that our practice framework requires us to view the range of application of school-based skills as problematic in the same way that we viewed nonschooled literate skills as problematic. Determining that range is as much a matter for empirical work as mapping the cognitive implications of nonschooled literacy. We are under no illusion that the framework we have presented here can do more than serve as a cautionary statement and one among many general orientations to that work. But insofar as we can identify recurrent activities in school which qualify as a practice (in the sense we have defined it), we can search for similar activities in a nonschool domain and compare the tasks presented, the knowledge involved, and the skills shared or unique to each setting. In this respect, literacy practices represent a strategically useful target for investigation. A piece of writing, whatever its form, serves as a flag to signal activities in the ongoing stream of behavior that may have some component skills in common. When we describe various forms of engagement with written material, we are laying the basis for defining tasks and for working out principled ways of tracing relationships among tasks. Rather than trying to isolate literacy from schooling, our present framework suggests the usefulness of using literacy activities to examine the cognitive implications of one set of important school practices for the individual's later functioning in society.

VAI LITERACY IN PERSPECTIVE

The cognitive skills that we found in our research among traditional Vai people have been shaped by the range of literacy practices in Vai society. Our ethnographic data show this range of practices to be limited when compared with literacy functions in modern, technologically sophisticated societies. If uses of writing are few, the skills they require are likely to be limited. They may be used to accomplish only a narrow range of tasks in a few content domains. Such a pattern can be expected to give rise to specialized or specific literacy-related skills—the pattern we found in our studies. As the repertoire of functions increases, existing practices may come to embrace more complex tasks or be extended to new content domains. For example, it might become more commonplace among the Vai to write letters to strangers as well as friends. Two practices formerly carried separately might combine. We might find a Vai elder writing a letter to distribute proceeds from a funeral feast, merging list making with letter writing. Co-occurrence of requirements specific to each practice in a common task might provide the opportunity for application of monitoring or planning skills (for example, planning the organization of the communication) and promote their use in other tasks.

As the technology of a society becomes more complex and it becomes more closely integrated into world affairs, we can expect the number and variety of literacy practices to increase, bringing with them new skills or more complicated versions of old skills. Thus, the fact that we found specialized literacy-related skills among the Vai does not preclude the possibility of finding more generalized skills, or different skills in other societies. On the contrary, if our argument that particular practices promote particular skills is valid, we might expect future studies to demonstrate some literacy-related skills that developmental psychologists predicted and that we failed to find among the Vai—but only under conditions evoking these skills.

Wherever technological, social, and economic conditions furnish many purposes to be served by literacy we would expect the skill systems involved in literacy practices to become varied, complex, and widely applicable. Individuals engaged in a number of practices will have an opportunity to acquire this variety of skills. Under these conditions, the functional and general ability perspectives—which we have up to now presented as contrastive approaches—will converge in their predictions of intellectual outcomes. Whether we choose to interpret these acquired functional skill systems developmentally is a matter of theoretical predilection, the discussion of which lies outside the present argument. But the core of the argument is that a framework which situates cognitive skills in culturally organized practices provides one way of moving beyond the antonymic terms that dominate much thinking about thinking: general versus specific, higher order versus lower order—terms that offer little guidance to our search.

It appears, too, that the concept of practice-based skill systems can help us achieve a balanced and informative way of characterizing the kind of difference that cultural differences make to individual thinking. Following a long tradition, sustained in part by the nature of multivariate statistical analysis, we have tended to speak of cultural factors as "antecedent" to individual intellectual skills which are "consequences." This is an acceptable shorthand but misrepresents the unitary nature of intellectual activity. It tends, as Geertz (1973) points out, to represent culture as a "power" to which behaviors or processes can be causally attributed, rather than as a context in which they can be intelligibly described. It also tends to split the study of behavior and process between those social scientists who label their phenomena of interest "cultural" and those who label theirs "psychological." If, however, the topic of inquiry is a configuration of practices, cultural and psychological approaches do not stand in relation to each other as concerned with different sets of phenomena (some considered "antecedent" and others "consequent") but rather as two different perspectives that can be brought to bear on the same set of phenomena. We have seen that Vai culture is *in* Vai literacy practices: in the writing system, the means used to transmit it, the functions it serves and contexts of use, and the ideologies which confer significance on these functions. But literacy activities are carried out by individuals, and our research has shown that psychological skills are also *in* Vai literacy practices: in properties of the writing system, in its method of acquisition, and in its uses. We can, of course, continue to ask questions about cause and effect, but we do not need to conceive these as requiring us to shift from one level of analysis to another. Rather, we can look upon the endeavor as a search for relationships among various sets of practices which can be analyzed in terms of both their cultural and their psychological components.

We are a long way from a grand synthesis of culture and cognition. We doubt very much that we will achieve one, if by synthesis we mean that one single interpretive framework will provide all the answers or raise all the significant questions. But each new way of looking at the problem and each case study cannot help but enlarge our view of the way humans shape their skills through their socially patterned activities.

Appendixes   Notes

Bibliography   Index

Appendix to Chapter 3:
History of the Vai Script

The Vai script was one of the first indigenous writing systems in West Africa to be discovered by Europeans. News of the script's existence reached England in 1849 in a lecture presented to the Royal Geographical Society by Mr. Edwin Norris, a British Naval Officer just returned from antislavery patrol duty in Cape Mount County, Liberian home of the Vai.

Norris's report and script specimens aroused astonishment and some incredulity. In the climate of opinion current in mid-nineteenth-century Europe and America, industrial nations and white people were often held to represent superior cultures whose distinguishing feature included literacy in the Roman alphabet. The clearly sophisticated characteristics of the Vai script raised a disturbing question: "how these natives . . . pursuing an unobtrusive existence in the seclusion of the primeval forest far from the course of the world's traffic, came to possess a cultural treasure of so high a quality, one usually met with only among people of ancient and rich culture" (Klingenheben, p. 158). Articles in the mid-1800s (see, for example, Creswick, 1868) suggest that one source of this persistent questioning was disbelief that a "Negro race" should have shown itself capable of joining Europeans in this most "civilized of all the arts."

Today, with greater knowledge of the contributions of African civilizations to world history, the Vai script no longer appears an exotic curiosity requiring explanation. Fascination with the script rests on solid linguistic and sociological grounds. Not many societies have given rise to an original system of writing; on that score alone, Vai script qualifies as a significant topic for inquiry. But in addition, the script's intrinsic properties and unusual social features command more widespread scholarly interest. The script is far from rudimentary; it ranks among advanced writing systems of the world because of its systematic representation of the sound stucture of the language and the originality of its graphic symbols. It is advanced as well in having taken root among broad sections of the people and generating a level of popular literacy rare among agrarian societies in any part of the world.

These features of the Vai script—which are important to our own inquiry into intellectual consequences—suggest questions to be posed to historical accounts of the script's invention and dissemination. What factors influenced the characteristics of the script? What conditions helped to spread and perpetuate it in the face of competition from the already available Arabic and Roman alphabets? Historical reports offer no definitive answers to these questions, but they contribute to our understanding of the contemporary social context of Vai literacy.

ORIGIN OF THE SCRIPT

One famous origin story derives from the account of a German-born philology student (Koelle, 1854) who came to Cape Mount immediately after the script's discovery was announced and stayed to prepare the first grammar of the Vai language. Koelle reported that one Dualu Bukele "was the real inventor of [the script] assisted by five of his friends. The first impulse to attempt it was given him in a dream, which he narrated to me as follows: About fifteen years ago, I had a dream, in which a tall, venerable-looking white man, in a long coat, appeared to me saying: 'I am sent to you by other white men ... I bring you a book'" (1854, p. 235). The messenger showed Dualu a number of signs, but when he awoke, he could not remember all the signs which had been shown him by night, so he gathered a number of his young friends and together they made new signs. "And on this ground," says Koelle, "we are fully justified in speaking of a real *invention* of the Vei [*sic*] mode of writing" (p. 237).

English-educated Vai scholars today substantially accept Koelle's account (see Johnson, 1975; and publications of the Liberian Ministry of Information, Culture and Tourism), but in the towns and villages some elders recount different stories about the invention and early development of the script. These stories and related oral histories suggest that the Koelle account portrays only one set of important events in the script's history. Other evidence indicates that the script may have undergone a number of partially independent developments at different times and places in Vai country. But there is little controversy about the fact that a small group (or groups) of Vai men, in the early part of the nineteenth century, elaborated a graphic system exemplifying consistent phonetic rules. Nor does it detract from this accomplishment to point out that Vai society had witnessed the use of writing systems for a number of centuries previously. Portuguese traders are known to have reached Cape Mount in the mid-fifteenth century, establishing extensive and lasting trade relations with the Vai who had migrated to the coastal areas (Holsoe, 1967). According to their own historical accounts, the Vai owe their origin to migrations from Mande areas along the upper and middle Niger to the coastal areas—events currently thought to date from the late fifteenth and early sixteenth centuries. The Vai and other Manding peoples maintain close linguistic and cultural ties to this day—a relationship important to our current topic because of the known role Manding scholars played in spreading Islam throughout the region. Thus, books and writing, and the instruments producing them, were known to some Vai from both African and European contacts for at least three centuries before the Vai script's reported invention.

In the 1820s and 1830s, these two foreign literacies, the Roman and Arabic alphabets, began to impinge more directly on village life. By this time, Islam had become strongly established throughout Vai country, with the conversion of many leading persons and the building of mosques and lodging houses for itinerant Manding teachers in practically every sizable town (Hair, 1963). Another major event of this decade was the founding in 1822 of the Colony of Liberia at Cape Mesurado, some fifty miles to the southeast of Vai country. The founders were free American Negroes who elected repatriation to Africa to establish their own society and were supported by a joint U.S. government and church colonization effort. These English-speaking colonists, some of whom were literate and were also Christian ministers, made contact with Vai leaders at Cape Mount. Simultaneously, Christian missionaries began to move into Liberia from Freetown, Sierra Leone, and in some country towns set up schools that provided the rudiments of an English education. During this same period, European traders dealing mainly in slaves became especially active on the Vai coast. Thus, at the time of systematic development of the script, the Vai were in intensive contact with four literate groups, two alphabets, and three domains of literacy practices: the Americo-Liberian colonists using the Roman alphabet for governance and military purposes; European coastal traders using the Roman alphabet and inland Muslim traders the Arabic alphabet for commercial purposes; Christian missionaries with their Bible and Muslim scholar-missionaries with the Qur'an practicing literacy for primarily religious purposes.

The Vai script, however, cannot simply be dismissed as a borrowed innovation. Since the foreign scripts in use were alphabets and the Vai script is a syllabary, we know that whatever external influences were active in creating pressure for an indigenous writing system, the form and articulation of that system represented an original production. According to Massaquoi (1911) and other scholars (see Olderogge, 1966; Dalby, 1968, 1970), script inventors were building on a preexisting system of graphic signs long in use among the Vai and some of their neighbors. Massaquoi, a member of a leading Vai family, made this claim directly, basing it on an analysis of the resemblance of certain script characters to pictograms used for communicative purposes for many generations (see Figure A3.1).

Dalby (1968) finds Massaquoi's claim plausible since indigenous graphic

V. Hiero.		Eng. Equivalent.		Meaning.		Present forms.
	=	Mo	=	man	=	
	=	Ku (n.)	=	head	=	
	=	ta	=	fire	=	
	=	lba	=	{ mother, large }	=	

Figure A3.1. Vai script pictograms (from Massaquoi, 1911)

symbols are known to have figured prominently in the traditional culture of a number of West African peoples. Early travelers, writing before the invention of any of the known West African scripts, commented on the widespread use of graphic symbols in ritual and ceremony in this region. Symbols were also used for interpersonal communication, especially in love affairs and in war (see Dalby, 1968, p. 179). Some West African societies developed these symbols into elaborate graphic systems with well prescribed and regulated uses. The Bambara of Mali are famous for two such systems. One, consisting of over 259 ideographic symbols, was used primarily for ritual and magical purposes and was available only to those at high levels of initiation in secret societies. Alongside this system existed another that was extended to some secular uses and was associated particularly with blacksmiths and other artisans.

In addition to this evidence that visual symbols making up the script had indigenous roots, a claim has been made that the concept of using syllables as the basic unit of language analysis was an attribute of West African language communities from earliest times. Traditional language games, still widespread among the Vai and other local cultures, play off the syllabic structure: in one such game, for example, nonsense syllables are inserted between constituent syllables composing words. It has even been speculated that awareness of syllables lies behind African drum-language and that different drum beats correspond to different syllabic tones (Olderogge, 1966).

These strands of cultural history suggest a long period of evolution for the Vai script during which pictograms gradually acquired a phonetic character. Some evidence for this transformational process is found in early Vai script manuscripts in which certain characters stand for words and concepts rather than sounds directly. Stewart (1972) has identified sixteen of these logograms in the "Book of Ndole," written sometime before 1850, one of the earliest script specimens available to Western scholars. While many of these logograms have disappeared in the modern script, replaced by their phonetic equivalents, some are in use; for example, a logographic symbol is commonly used for "death" and is displayed on tombstones. In the "Book of Ndole," a few logograms were used in a purely phonetic way. For example, the character for "be finished," *ɓañ*, was used as the initial character in the word for "sky," *ɓanda* (Stewart, 1972, p. 12). The existence of these logograms and their subsequent elaboration by sound extension lends credence, if not direct support, to the view that the Vai script had a developmental history which carried it from a pictographic to a phonographic system.

Whether or not these historical reconstructions receive further confirmation, it seems clear that pictographic symbol systems in older days served a variety of social functions, and that cultural activities involving symbols provided numerous settings which might have encouraged the organization of a systematic writing system. The close connection of these symbols with animistic ritual and magical practices makes it seem unlikely that all indigenous sources of the script will be completely uncovered. Even today, its ties with older uses of symbols do not appear entirely severed. While modern ethnographers do not find Vai women wearing silver ornaments around their necks in which proverbs are engraved in script characters (reported in Creswick, 1868), the script today is still used for inscriptional purposes (door lintels, personal possessions) suggesting a historical continuity with some of its earliest functions.

SPREAD OF THE SCRIPT

All reports agree that the Vai people seized on the new invention with enthusiasm. Koelle, on the spot some fifteen years after the reported invention, gained the impression that a majority of men in the towns he visited could write the script. In later decades, others reported that most of the men, and some women, could read script characters (Creswick, 1868; Massaquoi, 1899; Johnston, 1906). If these impressions and reports were correct, there may have been a greater spread of popular literacy in Cape Mount County in the nineteenth century than in many areas in Europe and the United States during that period. On the other hand, some scholars have questioned whether the script spread as rapidly or as extensively as others have suggested (Delafosse, 1899).

It is a fascinating historical fact that when we visited Vai country in the 1970s, in an era of modernization and spread of schooling, Vai script was taught tutorially and with no formal institutionalization. But Koelle reported that 150 years previously the Vai had functioning schools whose purpose was to spread the script among the population. According to this account, a school had once been established in the town of Jondu (a slave-trading center); it was equipped with benches and wooden writing tablets on which script characters were drawn with reed pens and juice from an ink plant. In warfare with the Gola people, the town was captured and the schoolhouse and manuscripts destroyed by fire. Vai "bookmen" subsequently gathered together to build the town of Bandakolo as a new site for a Vai script school, but this town, too, was destroyed in intertribal warfare. After a third attempt, the Vai abandoned efforts to establish these schools, but other informal and formal modes of transmission were used to maintain literacy in the script.

The rapid spread of the script and the repeated organized efforts to disseminate it indicate that it served important societal needs. Our comments here take on an even more speculative character, but what is known about the history and activities of the Vai people in the nineteenth century fits well with observations social scientists have made about the economic and social conditions accompanying the spread of literacy in other societies (see, for example, Goody and Watt, 1963, and Gelb, 1963). One condition closely connected with the incorporation of written technology into social life is the existence of large-scale trading and commercial networks. Characterizing Vai society as agrarian is only partially accurate, since we know that from their first arrival on the coast, trading activities were an important feature of their economy and have remained so to this day. As Holsoe (1967) chronicles, the Vai conducted a vigorous seaward trade with Portuguese and Dutch merchant seamen as early as the fifteenth and sixteenth centuries. Acting as middlemen between these traders and the people of the interior, they first exchanged items such as gold, camwood, and ivory for salt, tobacco, and various metals, and then became increasingly involved in the sale of slaves. Slave trade increased in importance during the eighteenth century, but it was only after the British and American governments prohibited it in 1807 that the Vai coast gained widespread notoriety as the "haunt of slavers." For a variety of reasons, the period from 1807 to 1850, after the trade was declared illegal, records a sharp increase in the number of slaves exported from this region (Holsoe, 1977, gives estimates of annual shipments ranging from three to fifteen thousand—p. 295.) Organizational activities required for the procurement, containment, and exchange of large numbers of slaves under circumstances in which such activities were ostensibly "unlawful" (and the British Royal Navy was patrolling the coast to suppress the trade) would clearly have been facilitated by a writing system available for record keeping and transmission of messages. We do not mean to suggest here that there is anything special about trading in slaves that promotes literacy, but rather that the large-scale nature of trading enterprises in which the Vai engaged, including but not confined to slaves, and their expansion at this time, created a pressure for the utilization of written technology. It may well be, however, that because some trading activities concerned slaves, and the Vai people were engaged in recurrent intertribal warfare and hostilities with the Liberian government over these activities, a powerful stimulus existed for the adoption of a writing system that no one else but the Vai knew. These were the years, too, when the Americo-Liberian colonists were buying land in Vai country and seeking to establish hegemony over the indigenous peoples living in the territory. More than one observer has been struck by the dual functions served by the Vai script: it met practical record keeping and communication needs while at the same time keeping Vai business "secret" and protecting the community from outside forces (Hair, 1963; Johnston, 1906).

If the exigencies of commerce and politics created external pressures for the development and use of a private writing system, Vai social organization seems at the very least to have provided crucial supports. Holsoe (1977) describes Vai society during the nineteenth century as stratified and with various forms of domestic servitude (some of which characterized other neighboring cultures in Liberia, including the Americo-Liberian culture). One is tempted to speculate that the existence of an agricultural labor force supporting a number of free-born families played a role in constituting a social group with the time available to invest in systematization and teaching of the script. No direct evidence supports this speculation. Smith (forthcoming) convincingly argues that the script's enthusiastic adoption by the Vai was due to the complexity of the economic and social transactions the people engaged in, and the dispersal of kin groups, friends, and trading partners across Liberia and Sierra Leone. By the 1820s to 1830s, he maintains, these affairs demanded the organization of such diversified groups of people separated by sufficiently great distances in all directions that oral communication was under great strain.

The historical accounts we have briefly reviewed here remove some of the "mystery" of Vai literacy. While outsiders have found the origin and maintenance of the script astonishing, we have seen that a conjuncture of material and social forces produced and maintained it. The script served ideological values through its role in traditional activities, pragmatic values in trade, and political values in maintaining the autonomous interests of the Vai in a region beset by local colonization and foreign penetration.

BIBLIOGRAPHIC NOTE

Vai script has attracted the attention of scholars in a number of countries. Vai scholars include Massaquoi (1911) and Johnson (1975). Foreign scholars include Dalby (1967, 1968, 1970), Delafosse (1899), Hair (1963, 1968), Klingenheben (1933), Koelle (1854), Migeod (1909), Stewart (1967, 1972), Stewart and Hair (1969). Dalby's accounts are especially thorough and place the script in a comparative and historical perspective. Stewart and Hair provide a bibliography. Only fleeting references are made to the Vai script in classic works on the history of writing, but see Gelb (1963, p. 208) and Diringer (1968, p. 130). The present account is indebted to Dalby's articles and the other sources cited. Raum (1943) discusses origins of graphic symbolism in African societies.

Holsoe (1967, chap. 2), provides a brief history of the Vai people. History of the colonization movement and the role of repatriated slaves in Liberia can be obtained from any of the following secondary sources: Fraenkel (1964); Liebenow (1969); *Area Handbook of Liberia* (1972). Holsoe (1971) has a bibliography of largely primary sources.

For histories of Islamic learning in West Africa, see Wilks (1968) and articles in Allen and Johnson (1970). Hopewell (1958) examines Muslim penetration into Liberia and neighboring areas before 1850.

Appendix to Chapter 5:
Reading Tests and Questionnaires

READING TESTS

Tests for all three literacies were constructed along the same lines. The first item consisted of three simple questions which the informant was asked to read aloud and answer. This was followed by one or more prose passages which were also to be read aloud. Probes for comprehension of the passages varied with the particular literacy: for English and Arabic, comprehension was assessed by reader's ability to translate the passage into Vai; the Vai script literate was asked to explain the passage in his own words.

I. Testing
  1. *English literacy*
     a. Have informant read aloud and answer the following questions:
        1. Where do you live now?
        2. Where were you born?
        3. I would like to know your name.
     b. Have him read aloud the following passage and translate it into Vai:
        "Three aged citizens of the County of Grand Cape Mount have closed their books and laid down the sword in the battle of life when they were severally summoned by the High Sheriff during the course of the last fortnight." (First paragraph of article in the *Ys' Men's Review,* March 19, 1973. The *Review* is a local mimeo newsletter produced in Robertsport, Cape Mount County. It circulates widely among the Vai because it carries a page in Vai script in each issue.)
        Alternate passage:
        "The Ministry of Public Works on Wednesday, March 14, 1973, threw a picnic for its work force handling the construction of the

Robertsport-Madina Road. The picnic, which began in the afternoon lasted until late that evening near the historic town of Toso,
at the lakeside estate of the late Hon. Roland Tombekai Demp-
ster, a natural beauty in the Tombe Chiefdom of Grand Cape
Mount County." (First paragraph of article in the *Ys' Men's Review*, March 19, 1973.)

2. *Vai script literacy*
   a. Have informant read aloud and answer each of the following
      questions:

(Where do you live now?)

(Where were you born?)

(I want to know your name.)

   b. Have informant read aloud the following passage. Ask him if it is a
      letter or an announcement. Then ask him to explain it in his own
      words.

Translation: "This is to inform you the Vai in general that last Wednes-
day was decoration day. That day is the day the government chose so that
we can pay respect to the dead."

—Passage from the *Ys' Men's Review*, March 19, 1973.

3. *Qur'anic literacy*
   The following materials were prepared by a Qur'anic scholar.
   a. Have informant read aloud and answer each of the following
      questions:

(Where do you live now?)

اي بلدولد

(Where were you born?)

اريد ان اعرف اسمك

(I want to know your name.)

b. Have the subject read Chapter 1 of the Qur'an and ask him to translate it into Vai.

بسم الله الرحمن الرحيم

الحمد لله رب العلمين الرحمن الرحيم مالك يوم
الدين اياك نعبد واياك نستعين اهدنا الصراط
المستقيم صراط الذين انعمت عليهم غير
المغضوب عليهم ولا الضالين آمين

Translations of Chapter 1

In the name of Allah the Gracious, the Merciful
All praise belongs to Allah, Lord of all the worlds
The Gracious, the Merciful
Master of the Day of Judgment
Thee alone do we worship and Thee alone do we implore for help
Guide us in the right path
The path of those on whom Thou hast bestowed Thy blessings, those
who have not incurred Thy displeasure, and those who have not gone
astray

c. Have the subject read Chapter 108 from the Qur'an and ask him to translate it into Vai.

قل اعوذ برب الناس ملك الناس اله الناس
من شر الوسواس الخناس الذي يوسوس في
صدور الناس من الجنة والناس

Translation of Chapter 108

In the name of Allah, the Gracious, the Merciful
Surely we have given thee abundance of good
So pray to thy Lord, and offer sacrifice
Surely, it is the enemy who is without issue

II. Rating literacy performance
   1. Note speed of subject's performance reading all parts of the test.
   2. Note how accurately he answers the questions or makes the translations.
   3. Assign a score in accordance with the literacy scale.

III. Literacy Scale
   0—Person cannot read at all.
   1—Person reads slowly and comprehends little or nothing.*
   2—Person reads rapidly and comprehends little or nothing.
   3—Person reads slowly and comprehends most or all.
   4—Person reads rapidly and comprehends most or all.

   * Note: To judge comprehension, do as follows: For English or Arabic, have the person translate what he is reading into Vai. For Vai, have him answer the questions he has read.

QUESTIONNAIRES FROM MAJOR SURVEY

We present below the texts of the three survey instruments: Part I—demographic questionnaire; Part II—questionnaire on how each script was learned; Part III—questionnaire on uses of each script. Part I was administered to every individual selected as a member of the sample population. Parts II and III were administered to respondents who reported reading or writing knowledge of any of the three scripts. Separate forms were completed for each script known.

   Interviews were conducted in Vai in colloquial language. English versions follow. Selected items or somewhat modified items were included in the interviews conducted in the metalinguistic and replication surveys described in Chapter 9.

Part I. Demographic Questionnaire

An asterisk indicates an item on modernity scale.
   House # _____ Respondent # _____ Town: _____
   Interviewer: _____ Date: _____
   Ask first: Is this the town where you usually live? (If no, stop the survey, unless the place of residence is included in the survey list.)
   1. Name: _____ 2. Sex: _____ 3. Age: _____
   4. Tribe: _____ 5. Clan: _____
   6. How big is your family? _____
   7. How many children do you have? (were born to you) (enter number) _____ 8. How many of your children live with you here? (enter number) _____

*9. Which is most important for the future of this country? (Have person choose one, and circle the one he chooses.)
   A. The hard work of the people.
   B. Good planning on the part of the government
   C. God's help
   D. Good luck
10. How long have you lived in this town? _____
11. Where were you born? (town and county) _____
12. Have you ever lived anywhere else? Yes _____ No _____
   (If yes, complete the following)

	Name of town	County (Country)	When did you go there?	How long did you stay?
1.				
2.				
3.				
4.				

13. What have you been doing most of the time the past twelve months?
   Working _____
   Not working _____
   If working, which describes person best:
   Self-employed _____
   Paid Employee _____
   Employer _____
   Unpaid family worker _____
   If not working, get a description of what person has been doing and check one of the following:
   Housekeeping _____
   Student _____
   Retired _____
   Temporarily out of work _____
      (ex.: unemployed)
   Other (specify) _____

   _____

14. A. (For those temporarily unemployed, ask:) What was your last job? (Fill out under column 1. Then go to C.)
   B. (For those presently working, say:) I'd like to know about your work. What work do you do most of the time now? (enter in first column of table.) Then ask, "Do you do any other kind of work now?" (Enter in column 2 and indicate that it is present work by marking "Present" in the "how long" column.)
   C. Continue by asking, "Did you ever do anything else?" (Enter any other work in remaining column.)

	1	2	3	4
Kind of work (be specific)				
For whom?				

Where

What kind of business?

How long did you do it?

---

15. (If trade, salary or professional work is reported now, continue. If not, check here: DNA_____)
    A. Tell me what you do in your work (try to get a description of job duties).

    B. About how many days a week do you work at this? _____
    C. How many months did you work last year? _____
    D. How much money do you earn a month on the average? _____
    E. About how much money did you earn all last year? _____
    F. Do you get paid anything besides money? YES _____ NO _____ If yes, what? _____
    G. Did you have any special training for this work? YES _____ NO _____ If yes, what? _____

16. (If farming is reported now, continue. If not, check here: DNA _____)
    A. What do you grow? _____
    B. Did you sell anything you grew last year? YES _____ NO _____
    C. (If yes) What did you sell? _____
    D. About how much money did you receive from your farming last year?

    ---

17. (If person reports selling anything, or owning a shop or business, continue. If not, check here: DNA _____)
    A. What kind of business (or shop) is it? _____
    B. Are you the (check one) OWNER? _____ or PART OWNER? _____
    C. Do you have any *paid* workers? YES _____ NO _____ (If yes) How many? _____

18. (Ask everyone) Did you receive any other cash income last year? YES _____ NO _____ (If yes) About how much? _____
    From what? _____

19. What work or trade did your father do most of the time? _____

---

*20. Two twelve-year-old boys took time out from their work in the rice fields. They were trying to figure out a way to grow the same amount of rice with fewer hours of work.
    1. The father of one boy said: That is a good thing to think about. Tell me your thoughts about how we should change our ways of growing rice.
    2. The father of the other boy said: The way to grow rice is the way we have always done it. Talk about change will waste time but not help. Which father said the wiser words? (Circle one.)

21. Marital status: (Check one—A, B, or C. If B or C checked, complete). Are you:
    A. Single, never married? _____
    B. Married now? _____
       (If yes, ask)
              A. How many spouses do you have now? _____
              B. How many spouses have you had? _____
    C. Married before, but not now? _____
       (If yes)

A. (Check those that apply)
Widowed _____
Divorced _____
Separated _____
B. How many spouses have you had? _____

22. A. What is the farthest place you have ever traveled to? _____
    B. What was the reason for your trip? _____
    C. How long did you stay? _____

23. When were you last out of _____ (name of survey town)?
    _____ Where did you go _____
    What was the reason for this trip? _____
    How long did you stay? _____
    About how many times do you make trips out of_____ (name of survey
    town)? _____
    What are the reasons for your trips? (Get full explanation)

    _____

    _____

24. Have you any houses? YES _____ NO _____
    (If yes) How many? _____
    Where are they? _____

    _____

25. What was your father's tribe? _____
    What was your mother's tribe? _____

26. Do you believe in water people (jinna)? YES _____ NO _____

27. Were you ever in bush school? YES _____ NO _____
    When bush school is in session, do you have a special part to play?
    YES _____ NO _____

28. Which is it more important for children to learn (check one):
    society business? _____ or church business? _____

29. Do you have any children who are in school now or who were ever in
    school? YES _____ NO _____ (If yes, fill out the following table for every
    child who has *ever* been to school—include all children the respondent is
    putting through school. Put an "O" beside the names of his own children
    and an "S" beside the name of a sponsored child.)

Name	Sex	Age	In school now? (yes, no)	Last school attended	Kind of school	Last grade com-pleted	No. of years alto-gether
1.							
2.							
3.							
4.							
5.							

30. (If person has children, ask the following. Otherwise check DNA _____)
    How many of your children serve you?
    A. Schoolchildren: ALL _____ SOME _____ NONE _____
    B. Unschooled children: ALL _____ SOME _____ NONE _____

31. (Only for people with children *under 20*. Otherwise check DNA _____)
    A. What kind of work do you *think* your children will do?
    BOYS _____ GIRLS _____
    B. What kind of work would you *like* your children to do?
    BOYS _____ GIRLS _____

*32. Have you ever been so concerned about some public problem that you really wanted to help do something (such as building a road)?
    A. Frequently   B. A few times   C. Never

33. What languages do you speak? _____

34. A. Do you read Vai? YES _____ NO _____
    B. (If yes) in Vai script? YES _____ NO _____ In alphabet?
       YES _____ NO _____
    C. (If no) Did you ever want to learn the Vai script?
       YES _____ NO _____ Why didn't you learn it?
    _____

35. What is the name of the man who invented the Vai script? _____

36. How many characters are in the script? (If person doesn't know, write "doesn't know") _____

37. (For people who say they know Vai script) About how many characters do you know? _____

37. Have you seen anything in your town written in the script?
    YES _____ NO _____ Describe _____
    _____

38. (If person says he reads Vai, ask the following. If not, check DNA _____)
    A. Some people have a book name. Do you? Yes _____ NO _____
    B. (If yes) What is your book name? _____

39. Do you read any other language? YES _____ NO _____ DNA _____
    (If yes, ask for each language:
                    Language   Read?   Write?   Where did you learn it?
    ARABIC _____
    ENGLISH _____
    OTHER _____
              Record literacy test score here for each language
                         Language   *Score*
                    1. _____   _____
                    2. _____   _____
                    3. _____   _____

40. (For people who don't write any language. Otherwise check DNA _____)
    Did you ever ask someone to write something for you?
    YES _____ NO _____
    (If yes) Who was that? Name _____ Sex _____ Town _____
    What did he write for you? _____
    Language? _____ Does he write for others? YES _____ NO _____

41. A. Do you think it is important for people to know the Vai script?
       YES _____ NO _____
    B. (If yes) Who? Why?
       1. · _____
       2. _____
    C. (After getting person's free responses, if the following are not mentioned, ask:)
       The chief? YES _____ NO _____ Why? _____
       _____

       Poro or Sande officials? YES _____ NO _____ Why? _____
       _____

       Women? YES _____ NO _____ Why? _____
       _____

Children? YES _____ NO _____ Why? _____

42. Should Vai script be taught in the government schools?
    YES _____ NO _____ Why? _____
43. Who knows Vai script best in this town? (IDK _____)
         Name   *Sex*   *Identification*
    A. _____
    B. _____
    C. _____
44. Do you think more people knew Vai script (check one):
    in the olden days _____ or today _____
    Why is that? _____
*45. If you were to meet a person who lives in another country a long way off
    (thousands of miles away), could you understand his way of thinking?
    YES _____ NO _____
46. Have you ever been to school? (Check one)
    In school now _____ (fill out table)
    In school before _____ (fill out table)
    Never in school _____ (go to question 47)
    For anyone ever in school, fill out names of all schools attended and iden-
    tify them as government, mission, private (not mission), mosque, techni-
    cal.

Name of school	Kind of school	Where is it	Last grade attended	No. years attended
1.				
2.				
3.				
4.				
5.				

A. After last school has been named,
   For person in school before: Why did you stop school then?

   _____

   For person still in school: How far do you want to go in school? _____
   Do you think you will be able to? YES _____ NO _____
B. Considering everything, do you think school helped you in any way?
   YES _____ NO _____ How? (Write all reasons. Encourage full an-
   swer.) _____

47. Did you ever study Qur'an or Arabic? YES _____ NO _____ (If yes, con-
    tinue) For how many years? _____ At what point (in the Qur'an) did you
    stop? _____

    (Give number or name of last chapter completed.)
48. Did your father go to school? YES _____ NO _____ IDK _____ (If yes, fill
    out all schools attended.)
       Name of school   *Kind of school*   *Last grade attended*
    1. _____
    2. _____
    3. _____

49. Did your mother go to school? YES _____ NO _____ IDK _____ (if yes, fill out all schools attended.)

    Name of school   *Kind of school*   *Last grade attended*
    1. _____
    2. _____
    3. _____

50. Does (or did) your father write Vai script? YES ____ NO ____ IDK ____
    (If yes) Do you know who taught him? YES _____ NO _____ IDK _____
    (If yes) Names: _____ Relationship to father _____
    _____
    Does anyone else in your family write Vai script? YES _____ NO _____
    IDK _____ (If yes, fill out)

    Name   *Sex*   *Relationship to respondent*
    1. _____
    2. _____
    3. _____
    4. _____
    5. _____

51. Does (or did) your father know the Qur'an? YES _____ NO _____
    IDK _____
    Does (or did) he know how to write Arabic? YES _____ NO _____ IDK
    _____ Does anyone else in your family write Arabic? YES _____
    NO _____ (If yes, fill out)

    Name   *Sex*   *Relationship to respondent*
    1. _____
    2. _____
    3. _____

52. (If person has children *under 20*, ask the following questions. Otherwise, check here: DNA _____)
    A. How much schooling do you want your children to get? _____
    _____

B. How much schooling do you think they will get? _____
   _____

   C. If a family can only send *some* of their children to school but not *all* of them, who do you think it would be most important for them to send? (Try to get the full answer _____
   _____

*53. Learned men (scientists, scholars) in the universities are studying such things as what determines whether a baby is a boy or a girl and how it is that a seed turns into a plant. Do you think that these investigations are:
   A. All very good _____
   B. All somewhat good _____
   C. All somewhat harmful _____
   D. All very harmful _____

54. In olden days, did anyone work for your family? YES _____ NO _____
    IDK _____
    In olden days, did your family work for anyone else? YES _____
    NO _____ IDK _____
    (If yes) For whom? (Identify position, not name) _____
    _____

55. In olden days, were your people Vai? YES _____ NO _____ IDK _____
    (If no) Who were they? _____

56. (If yes) Were they old Vai? YES _____ NO _____ IDK _____

57. Who were the families that established this town? (IDK _____)
    A. _____
    B. _____
    C. _____
    D. _____
58. Who are the elders in this town? (IDK _____)
    A. _____
    B. _____
    C. _____
    D. _____
    E. _____
*59. Some people say that:
    1. Men will someday understand what causes such things as floods, epidemics, and droughts. Other say:
    2. Such things can never fully be understood by man. Which opinion do you agree with? 1. _____ 2. _____ (Write any comment or explanation person gives. Encourage him to give one by asking, "Why do you agree with that opinion?") _____

    _____
*60. Which of the following reasons should carry the most weight in determining the honor that a man receives?
    1. Coming from an important family _____
    2. Having a lot of money _____
    3. Having a high education _____
*61. 1. Some people say that it is necessary for a man and his wife to limit the number of children to be born so that they can take better care of the children they already have.
    2. Others say that it is wrong for a man and his wife purposely to limit the number of children to be born.
    Which of these opinions is the correct one? _____
*62. Which source of information do you trust the most to learn about what is going on in this country?
    1. The word of your friend
    2. What the paramount chief tells you
    3. What you hear on the radio
*63. Do you think a man can be truly good without having any religion at all?
    1. Yes _____
    2. No _____
    3. Maybe _____
*64. Have you ever talked with a government official to tell him your opinion about some public issue such as what the government should do about building schools or carrying the road to your town?
    1. Many times _____
    2. A few times _____
    3. Never _____
*65. What are the biggest problems facing the town where you live?
    1. _____
    2. _____
    3. _____
*66. Where is the town of Gbarnga? _____
    In what country is the city of Conakry? _____
    In what country is the city of London? _____
*67. How often do you listen to the radio?
    1. Every day _____

      2. A few times a week _____
      3. Rarely _____
      4. Never _____

*68. Have you ever been so concerned about some problem that you really wanted to help do something?
      1. Frequently _____
      2. Few times _____
      3. Never _____

69. Suppose that everyone in the world got together and decided that from now on we will call the sun the moon and the moon will be called the sun. All we are going to do is change the names. Could we do that if we wanted to?

_____

_____

_____

Now, when you go to bed at night, what will you call the thing that you see up in the sky? _____
What will the sky look like when you go to bed if this is so?

_____

_____

_____

_____

Part II. Learning Vai/Arabic/English Scripts

House # _____ Respondent # _____ Town: _____
Interviewer: _____ Date: _____
Name of person being interviewed: _____
1. At what age did you begin to learn _____ script?
2. Did someone encourage you to learn it? Yes _____ No _____
   (If yes) Why? _____
Relation to respondent, if any? (specify genealogical relationship) _____
3. Did you yourself want to learn it? Yes _____ No _____
   (If yes) Why? _____
4. Did anyone in your family know it? Yes _____ No _____ (If yes, fill in the following)

Name	Sex	Age	Exact genealogical relationship to respondent	Taught by whom?	Where?

5. Did you learn _____ in school? Yes _____ No _____ (If no, go to Question 6) What type of school was that? (government/mission/Qur'anic) _____ Where? (town and country)

_____

6. Which teacher did you start with? Name _____ Age _____ Sex _____ Relation, if any, to the respondent (be exact) _____ How long did you study with this person? _____

7. How did you come to choose this person as a teacher? _____
_____ (after free responses, ask) Did you choose him/her because you are related (if so, how?) or because of his/her reputation as a Vai scholar?
_____

8. Did you have any other teachers? Yes _____ No _____ (If yes, ask)

Name	Genealogical relation, if any	Where was this?	For how long?

9. When studying, did you meet your teacher every day? Yes _____ No _____
How often? _____

10. How long was each lesson? (Obtain range of variation)
_____

11. Did you meet your teacher alone? Yes _____ No _____ (If no, How many others were learning with you? _____
Can you remember their names? (Give list of names, plus genealogical relationships, if any) _____

12. Can you briefly explain how the script was taught? Teachers teach in different ways—some give the names of things, some give the signs one by one, some do both—what did your teachers do? _____

13. Was there any order in the way in which you learned the characters? Did your teacher group them by appearance, by sound, by words (meaning) or was there no apparent order?
_____

14. If your teacher began with single characters, did he then move on to teaching whole words? _____

15. Some teachers use different things to show students the script; did your teacher ever show you a chart of all the characters? Yes _____ No _____
(If yes) Did he write it himself? Yes _____ No_____ IDK _____ Could you describe it?
_____

Did he ever show you some letter he'd received? A book of some kind? or anything else? If so, could you describe it/them? _____

16. Did you ever study without your teacher ? Yes _____ No _____ (If no) How many others studied with you when teacher wasn't there? _____ (For both yes and no) How did you teach yourself?
_____

Did you create any practice for yourself? (copying out, reading letters, etc.) What sorts of books or letters were these? (description) _____

17. Did you ever consult other men known to be learned in the script? _____
If so, who?

Name	Age	Sex	Relationship, if any	Where is he/she living now?

18. Was learning the script difficult? _____
Has teacher lost any pupils because of learning difficulties? Yes _____ No

_____ IDK _____ If so, what are these difficulties? (give instances) _____

_____

19. What makes a good student? _____

_____

How long did it take the best student to learn? _____
The worst? _____

20. When does the teacher/student know that he knows enough and can continue on his own? _____

_____

This may sound like the same question, but how do you tell when a man is learned in _____ script? What are the indications of this? _____

21. Is there a common core of characters/number of words? Yes _____ No _____ If yes, approximately how many? _____

22. Is there a continuing relationship between teacher and student such that a student goes back to his former teacher when he has trouble reading or writing something? _____

_____

Part III. Uses of Literacy (in Vai, Arabic, English Scripts)

House # _____ Respondent # _____ Town: _____
Interviewer: _____ Date: _____
Name of person being interviewed: _____
I would like to know what you use the _____ script for.

1. Do you write letters in _____? Yes _____ No _____
   (If yes) to whom? (Relationship) _____
   About how often? _____

2. Do you receive letters in _____? Yes _____ No _____ From whom? (Relationship) _____
   About how often? _____

3. Did you use to write more letters than you do now? Yes _____ No _____
   About how often? _____
   Did you used to receive more letters than you do now? Yes _____ No _____
   About how often? _____

4. Do you use _____ to keep any records or did you once use it to keep records (examples: family, births, deaths, etc., financial or business: money distribution, ordering goods, etc., legal settlement of a dispute or estate, land transfers, etc.) Yes _____ No _____ If yes, complete

Kind of record	Specific description	How often now?	How often before?
A.			
B.			
C.			
D.			
E.			
F.			
G.			

5. Do you now _____ or did you ever _____ use _____ for some technical plans or diagrams? (For example, land, house, or farm plans) Yes _____ No _____
   (If yes) Describe _____

6. Do you now _____ or did you ever _____ use _____ for some work or trade you did? Yes _____ No _____ (If yes) Describe

   (If person used it before but not now, ask) Why did you stop?

7. Do you now _____ or did you ever _____ use _____ to write things of a personal or literary nature (e.g., diaries, proverbs, stories, poetry, historical accounts)? Yes _____ No _____ (If yes) Describe _____

8. Do you now _____ or did you ever _____ use _____ for any religious purposes? (e.g., prayers, hymns, Qur'an, Bible) Yes _____ No _____ (If yes) Describe _____

9. When did you last write something in _____ script? _____ What was that? _____

10. Have you ever used the _____ script to write any other language? Yes _____ No _____ If yes, what language was this? _____ Tell me about the last time you did this _____

11. Have you anything in your house written in _____? Yes _____ No _____ (If yes, list; if many things are reported, describe generally)
    A. _____
    B. _____
    C. _____
    D. _____
    E. _____
    F. _____

12. Do you now _____ or did you ever _____ read any stories in _____? Yes _____ No _____ (If yes,) Describe (what kind, how often, where it was obtained, etc.) _____

    _____

13. Do you now _____ or did you ever _____ use _____ script for some town business? (e.g., minutes of meetings, records of decisions, accounts, etc.) Yes _____ No _____ If you haven't yourself, were you present at any meetings where someone else did this? Yes _____ No _____ In either case, please give full details for both questions. (If person is leading figure in town, try to get as much information as possible about how he uses his knowledge of _____ for town business and in dealings with the government, outside agencies, etc.) _____

14. Have you ever seen anything in the town that was written in _____? Yes _____ No _____ (If yes) Describe _____

15. When did you last read something that was written in _____? What was that? _____

16. Have you ever been asked to do something special because you knew _____? Yes _____ No _____ (If yes) Describe

    Have you ever asked anyone else to do something for you because they could read or write? _____ Yes _____ No _____ If so, could you tell me what this was for and how you chose the person (Was he/she related to you? If so, how? Was he known as learned in the _____ script?) _____

    In either case please could you clearly tell us your relationship with the person involved (genealogical, commercial/trading, official or government business, Poro or Sande business) _____

17. Has knowing how to read and write _____ helped you in any way? Yes _____ No _____ (If yes) How? _____

18. Have you taught anyone how to read or write _____?
Yes _____ No _____ (If yes, complete the following. If no, go to Question 20. If possible, even if it means coming back another day, try to get the following details on all pupils; if not at least a general description of the kinds of individuals)

Name	Identification and relationship	Place of birth	Where taught?	Where is he/she now?

19. How do you teach the script? What do you do first, then what do you do? (Description in detail) _____

Is this the way you were taught? Yes _____ No _____ Do you teach everyone in this way? Yes _____ No _____ (If no) Could you give me some descriptions of how/with whom/and under what circumstances you vary your teaching? _____

20. Do any of your children know how to read and write?
Yes _____ No _____ If yes, please complete following

Name	Age	Teacher (identification and relationship)	Where learned?

(If Question 20 is no) Do you want them to read and write _____? Yes _____ No _____ If yes, why don't they learn it? _____

Appendix to Chapter 6:
A Technical Note on Literacy Estimates

No reports are available from government or private sources on the full extent of literacy in Liberia. The Liberian Census counts as literate only those individuals five years of age or older who have completed three years of English school. This count includes children and youth still in school but excludes English literacy acquired outside of school (or in less than three years), Arabic literacy, and literacy in indigenous or other scripts. Because of these exclusions, we were interested in using the occasion of our survey to arrive at a more adequate estimate of literacy among the Vai people.

Our general procedure was to determine the proportion of the total residential population in the survey towns who were literate in any script. "Survey towns" included all towns in Cape Mount County in which we conducted systematic interviewing with sample populations. We used population reports of the 1974 Liberian Census as the source for total population counts for these towns. We also used Census figures on English literates (for reasons discussed below). Our own survey interviews provided counts of Vai script and Arabic literates. Since our survey towns were selected to be representative of the various clans and chiefdoms in Cape Mount County, we believe that this procedure resulted in a reasonable estimate of the level of literacy in the county at large.

Literacy in the Total Population

Population base. According to the Liberian Census, the total population of Cape Mount County survey towns in 1974 was 1,564. (Source: Computer run of population totals made available by Liberian Ministry of Planning Affairs.) Since we conducted our interviewing during 1973–1974, this census figure was applicable, and we used it as our base number in calculating percentage of literacy.

Literacy counts. Our survey provided exhaustive enumeration of all residents in survey towns, fifteen years of age or older, who were literate in Vai script, Arabic, and English. The adequacy of these figures for computing proportion of total population who were literate varied for each script.

Vai script: Vai script is rarely learned at an age younger than fifteen. Therefore, our count of Vai script literates, taken as a proportion of the total population including children, is an unbiased estimate of extent of literacy in that script.

Arabic script: The fact that we confined our interviews to adults fifteen years and over resulted in the exclusion of young children enrolled in Qur'anic schools at the time of our survey. Thus our figure for proportion of Arabic literacy in the total population (including children) underestimates its extent. Since no figures were available on Qur'anic school participation from other sources, we could not correct for this bias.

English script: Excluding children under fifteen also underestimated the proportion of English literates in the total population. An alternative was available here in the form of the Census count. The Census Bureau imputed literacy to persons five years and older who went to the third grade or beyond. (Source: Republic of Liberia, 1974 Census of Population and Housing, Population Bulletin No. 2, September 1976, p. vii.) Enumeration of literates was available only for Cape Mount County as a whole; town-by-town counts were not available. We took the proportion of the total county population reported as literate (11.6 percent) and applied it to the total population of our survey towns. (Source: 1974 Census of Population and Housing, Population Bulletin No. 1.)

Literacy in the Adult Male Population

Population base. Preliminary census reports available to us did not give age and sex breakdowns for literates by individual towns. We thus needed to estimate the adult male population of the survey towns. According to the census, Population Bulletin No. 1, 31.8 percent of the total population of Cape Mount County consisted of men age fifteen years or over. We applied this proportion to the total population of survey towns to arrive at an estimated adult population of 497. This figure was used as the base for computing percent of literacy.

Literacy counts. For all scripts, we used the number of people fifteen years and over who reported reading and writing knowledge in our interviews. As we have previously reported, these numbers closely corresponded to literacy counts based on reading tests, and we use them as best approximations to census self-report methods.

To arrive at total percent of literates in Cape Mount survey towns, we added the census count of English literates to our count of Vai script monoliterates, Arabic monoliterates, and Vai-Arabic biliterates. Thus, the total literacy estimate is based on an unduplicated count of individuals. For individual script literacies, however, we added across population groups as follows: for Vai script literates, we added Vai script monoliterates, Vai-Arabic biliterates, Vai-Arabic-English literates, and so on.

Appendix to Chapter 7:
Demographic Characteristics
and Factor Analysis Procedures

SELECTED DEMOGRAPHIC CHARACTERISICS

In the tables below, we present summaries of selected background characteristics for our comparison populations. Summaries are based on interviews conducted around the demographic questionnaire of the major survey. This questionnaire was administered to all adults in a random sample of nonliterate households and to all adults in all households reporting a member literate in one or more of the three scripts.

Population Groups

Total population included in these summaries is 650. This figure represents all survey respondents in the survey towns in Cape Mount County and the sample from Vaitown, the largest Vai community in Monrovia at the time. During the survey, we conducted additional interviews with 64 men and women in Monrovia who were in various salaried and hourly occupations. Our purpose was to enlarge our occupational profiles, but since these respondents were selected in an ad hoc manner, rather than by sampling methods, they were excluded from data analyses presented in this book.

Literacy groups here are defined by affirmative answers to questions (included in the questionnaire) about reading and writing knowledge of the scripts. All those reporting reading knowledge of English were classified as English literates even if they knew another script.

The population breakdown is as follows:

Total population	650
Female	360
Male	290
Nonliterate men	99
Literate men	191
Vai script monoliterates	53
Arabic monoliterates	38
Vai-Arabic biliterates	47
English literates	53

Definition and Explanations of Coding System

Questionnaires were coded by American research assistants, after having been checked out for completeness and accuracy in the field. A great many of the items presented no difficulty of interpretation. Coders were trained to achieve reliability for different items.

On many questions, coding categories simply mapped the actual response classes: for example, "Sex—male, female." Only the less straightforward coding categories and second-order codes are described here.

Survey town

Town size was rated on a scale, taken from the 1962 Liberian Census (the latest available information), starting with a population category of less than 100 and culminating in a category of large city (10,000 and over).

Town road rating

Towns were also scaled according to whether they were entirely off the road, on a spur road, on the main road, or part of a large city (Vai-town).

Places lived

All residences listed by the respondent, including birthplace, were classified as rural, urban with populations between 2,000 and 9,999, or urban with populations of 10,000 and over. This classification followed that of the 1962 Liberian Census. All place names were checked against the census listing and coded accordingly.

Travel

Places visited were checked against the 1962 Liberian Census of urban areas for yes/no determination of whether respondent had ever traveled to an urban area of 10,000 in Liberia. Standard atlas sources were consulted for classifying places traveled to in Sierre Leone and other African countries.

Occupations

Skill ranking—Respondent's descriptions were checked against the list of occupations given in the 1962 Liberian Census. These job titles were then rated against the six-class skill scale of the U.S. Census (where applicable).

Modernity of occupation—Sixty-four of the most common occupations were listed on cards and presented to a panel of ten Vai informants who rated them as traditional, transitional, and modern. These ratings were applied to respondent's principal occupation and father's occupation.

Tabulating Conventions

Response distributions are displayed separately for women, men, and members of literacy comparison groups. Since these subpopulations differ considerably in size, we have converted raw response figures to percentages in order to simplify group comparisons. Percentage totals will not always add up to 100 percent. In some cases (indicated by notes), a portion of the population was excluded from the analysis if the question did not apply (for example, skill rating of occupation was not applied to persons reporting their occupation as Muslim medicine or other traditional nonclassifiable role). "Missings" are not reported, but they also reduce the total in some cases. In the six tables presented here, categories are (from left to right): total population (T), total female (F), total male (M), nonliterate men (NL), Vai monoliterate men (V), Arabic monoliterate men (A), Vai-Arabic biliterate men (VA), and English literate men (E). All numbers are percentages.

Table A7.1   Personal characteristics

	T	F	M	NL	V	A	VA	E
Age								
Under 20	11	13	12	7	—	18	—	37
20–29	29	33	24	28	9	39	9	34
30–49	36	34	37	42	38	31	51	15
50 and over	24	20	27	22	53	11	40	14
Marital status								
Single	16	5	29	25	6	50	4	64
Widowed/divorced	10	13	6	10	8	11	3	0
Married	75	83	65	66	87	39	94	36
Head of household								
Respondent is head	20	8	37	28	58	21	64	17

Table A7.2 Family and resources

	T	F	M	NL	V	A	VA	E
Number of houses owned								
None reported	50	56	42	46	19	55	15	70
One	39	36	43	45	49	32	64	19
More than one	12	8	15	8	32	14	21	10
Number of spouses								
None reported	25	18	34	34	13	61	4	64
One	64	82	43	53	53	29	49	21
More than one	10	1	22	13	35	10	46	15
Number of children								
None reported	30	23	39	44	13	58	6	62
One and two	29	36	20	26	17	18	20	14
Three and four	33	40	27	20	38	16	51	12
Five and over	7	2	15	9	32	8	23	12
Number of children in school								
None reported	73	81	80	89	65	89	64	75
One	10	11	9	4	8	8	17	15
Two and more	17	8	12	7	27	3	19	10
Total income								
None reported	32	—[a]	27	27	19	37	31	21
Under $100	44	—	33	43	49	45	31	39
$101–$500	15	—	17	11	19	6	15	34
Over $500	10	—	14	18	12	11	24	6

a. Frequency distribution for women not determined through oversight.

Table A7.3 Residence and mobility

	T	F	M	NL	V	A	VA	E
Number of places lived								
One	15	16	14	19	8	21	4	15
Two and three	54	59	46	36	44	55	68	44
Over three	32	25	40	44	49	24	28	41
Number of years in survey town								
Under 3 years	11	8	12	14	8	11	4	21
3–12 years	32	13	22	24	13	32	15	32
12–20 years	26	11	18	19	11	26	9	27
20 years and over	32	68	47	42	68	32	73	19
Number of trips per year								
Less than 1 per year	15	19	12	9	17	13	6	13
1 per year	25	25	24	19	26	18	30	28
More than 2 per year	59	55	62	71	56	68	63	58

Table A7.3 (continued)

	T	F	M	NL	V	A	VA	E
Work and education related travel[a]								
Work travel reported	41	31	54	61	60	61	42	40
Education travel reported	6	1	12	2	9	32	11	21
Number of years in towns 2,000 and over								
None	41	43	38	38	34	63	41	19
6 mos. to 2 yrs.	12	14	12	14	10	11	15	10
2–8 yrs.	23	23	24	25	28	21	18	20
8 yrs. and over	23	20	27	22	28	6	25	51
Number of years in cities 10,000 and over								
None	51	55	46	43	49	71	55	31
6 mos. to 2 yrs.	14	14	15	22	12	6	8	10
2–8 yrs.	19	18	21	20	20	16	15	29
8 yrs. and over	17	14	18	15	20	6	21	30
Ever live in concession?								
Yes	19	15	24	25	28	5	28	23

a. Duplicated count; individuals could report travel for both work and education.

Table A7.4 Occupations

	T	F	M	NL	V	A	VA	E
Farming last year[a]								
No farming reported last year	31	31	30	28	28	29	13	70
Subsistence only	40	37	45	51	45	53	60	15
Some cash farming	15	12	18	17	27	14	28	8
Craft								
One or more crafts reported	15	2	30	31	42	39	43	57
Modernity of occupation[b]								
Traditional	56	66	44	55	40	50	53	17
Transitional	15	3	31	21	55	26	40	21
Modern	6	1	13	18	4	8	2	25
Skilled rating of principal occupation[c]								
Unskilled—manual	46	53	36	46	34	47	30	15
Semiskilled and skilled— manual	19	1	41	36	55	39	45	30
White collar—clerical up to managerial professions	14	16	12	9	10	—	21	19
Son's (respondent's) skill compared to father's (principal occupation)								
Lower	—	—	19	14	15	39	19	15
Equal	—	—	27	38	28	13	30	13
Higher	—	—	33	34	49	21	34	21

Table A7.4 (continued)

a. This analysis excludes respondents who replied on a previous question that they had never farmed.

b. This analysis covers the sixty-four most common occupations which were rated with respect to modernity by ten Vai judges.

c. Occupational titles were obtained from the 1962 Liberian Census. These were classified according to the U.S. Census Bureau's six basic skill categories. Reported work activities that could not be mapped into these systems (for example, drummer) were excluded from this analysis.

Table A7.5   Knowledge of languages

	T	F	M	NL	V	A	VA	E
Number of languages spoken in addition to Vai								
None other	23	29	15	16	23	13	19	2
One other	39	44	32	42	32	37	15	26
Two or more	37	26	52	41	46	49	66	71
Speak English								
Yes	48	39	60	55	53	47	51	96
Breakdown of additional languages spoken (tribal and English)								
Neither English nor tribal	23	29	15	16	23	13	19	2
Tribal, no English	23	31	24	26	25	39	30	4
English, no tribal	16	16	16	20	19	5	4	26
Both English and tribal	32	23	44	35	34	42	47	70

Table A7.6   Traditionalism

	T	F	M	NL	V	A	VA	E
Belief in water people								
Yes	60	67	52	46	72	50	57	38
Special role in bush school								
Yes	15	17	12	9	23	11	6	11
Elder								
Yes	5	1	11	5	23	5	17	8
Ever in bush school								
Yes	93	98	87	94	94	79	91	70

DESCRIPTION OF FACTOR ANALYSIS PROCEDURES

This summary is based on a report provided by David Burns, who carried out the analyses described here.

Classification of Variables and Data Reduction

Two classes of variables comprised the set of descriptive characteristics of the population obtained from the survey questionnaire, Part I:

   a. Historical-demographic characteristics (parental education, family status, personal characteristics, work experience, travel, and the like). Ninety-two variables were represented in the initial codings.

   b. Literacy and education (such as amount of schooling; reading proficiency in Vai, Arabic, and English; whether or not individual was named as a script expert or scribe). Eight variables were coded in this category.

Preliminary data reduction was accomplished by excluding uninformative variables. A variable was excluded if:

   a. the information was contained in another variable;

   b. 95 percent or more of the respondents received identical scores; or

   c. the variable was nominally scaled and could not be transformed into a meaningful indicator variable.

Of the ninety-two variables originally contained in the class of historical-demographic variables, seventy-four remained after preliminary screening. When the eight education and literacy variables were included, we ended up with a set of eighty-two variables which were used to describe the population in terms of our survey questions.

Factor Analysis Methods

A useful introduction to factor analysis is provided by Child, 1970. Here we report our technical decisions.

Method of solution. In factor analysis, factors may be constructed so that the correlations among factors are either (a) zero (that is, factors are orthogonal); or (b) nonzero (that is, factors are oblique). For descriptive purposes, the two methods of construction are equally useful; orthogonal solutions are reported here.

Exclusion of sampling error. Although the sampling error associated with factor scores is minimal, the fact that two variables may be spuriously correlated implies that "spurious factors" may occasionally be constructed. However, because the probability of spurious correlations among N variables quickly diminishes to zero as N increases, the factors formed as a result of spurious correlations are likely to account for relatively small proportions of total variance. The amount of variance accounted for by a factor is reflected in the factor's eigenvalue. Thus, spurious factors can be excluded by including in the factor solution only the factors whose eigenvalues are sufficiently high. We included only those factors whose eigenvalues exceeded 1.0 (Harris, 1975).

Rotation to simple structure. The interpretability of each factor is facilitated when the factor solution is "rotated to simple structure," that is, when the number of significant loadings for each variable and factor is minimized. In the analyses reported here, the "varimax" rotation was applied (see Harris, 1975).

Choice of significance level. Interpretability is also affected by choice of significance level. With sample sizes larger than 100 (our sample size for male population was 290), factor loadings in the range from .1 to .2 are significant at the .05 level. However, for exploratory studies of the kind reported here, a more conservative significance level is recommended (Child, 1970). In the present analyses, the criterion for treating a factor loading as significant was varied in order to determine the most interpretable solutions. The most interpretable factor solutions were obtained when the minimum value for a significant factor loading was set at the conservative level of .3.

Appendix to Chapter 8: Further Information about the Survey Tasks

SORTING AND GEOMETRIC STIMULI

Stimulus materials used in this task—eight cards with figures varying in color, form, and number—were described in the text (Figure 8.1). We used two equivalent sets of cards. One was made up of red or green squares or triangles, with two or four figures per card. The second set consisted of black or green squares or triangles, with three or five figures per card.

The procedures we used departed somewhat from previous research. The experimenter displayed the eight cards to informants in a haphazard array, saying, "Here are eight cards and I want you to pick out four that are alike in some way." If the subject asked a question that required divulging a correct answer ("Do you mean according to how they are made?"), the experimenter answered noncommittally ("Any way that they seem alike to you").

The subject was then permitted to arrange the cards into two piles and the experimenter recorded the arrangement. If the grouping arrived at corresponded to a classification by color, form, or number, the experimenter asked (pointing to one of the groups), "How are they alike?" Then he pointed to the second pile and asked, "How are these different from the first group?"

The cards were then shuffled and laid out again on the table, with the following remarks: "That is fine. There are other good ways to do it. Can you find another way to pick four cards that are alike?"

As long as the subject experienced no difficulty, this procedure continued through the three classification rules. If the subject repeated a previous classification, the experimenter said, "That is fine, but you did it before. Try a new way." After two repetitions of the same classification, the experimenter provided a correct classification not yet offered by the subject and asked the subject how they were alike. If the subject produced a grouping that corresponded to none of the predefined classifications, the experimenter demonstrated a correct classification, asked for a justification, and permitted the subject to try again.

At each step, the subject was given as much time and flexibility in responding as he/she seemed to need. At each step where a failure occurred (according to our predefined criteria), the experimenter completed the classification and sought to determine if the subject could continue.

We used three indicators of performance: (1) Number of dimensions classified prior to obtaining assistance; (2) whether either number or form was ever used as a classification dimension; and (3) adequacy of explanations, summed over successful classifications.

Explanations were scored on a five-point scale. Failure to offer any explanation was scored 0, an explanation containing no reference to a dimension used in the sort was scored 1, ambiguous reference implying a correct dimension was scored 2, reference to one of the specific attributes of the correct dimension was scored 3, and specification of the correct dimension was scored 4.

Breakdown of performances by population group and grade are shown in Table A8.1. Averages in the table suggest immediately that there are no large differences in average performance among populations on any of the three geometric sorting measures. However, results of the regression analysis indicate some small differences associated with literacy for the second two measures. The regression analysis produced the following results:

a. Number of dimensions. Unpredictable.

b. Sorting on form and/or number. On first inspection of average group scores, we were surprised to find that the schooled group ranked behind biliterates and Vai monoliterates (in that order). This picture was modified by the regression analyses; schooling effects were present but were confined to that part of the English literate population still in school. The basic equation is:

Sorting on form or number = 1.05 + .11 teach Vai script
$(R^2 = .08)$ (2.2)
+ .28 Vai-Arabic biliterate + .36 in school now
(3.2)   (3.2)

Students with three years of schooling (the minimum period for attaining even rudimentary competency in English) showed the greatest percent of form and number choices, but ex-students dropped to a level indistinguishable from that of monoliterates. Since in our population the number of ex-students is greater than the in-school population, combined means are pulled toward the lower end of the scale, producing the average result contained in Table A8.1.

The contribution of Vai script literacy is shown in the specialized function of teaching Vai script. Although teaching is an activity normally car-

Table A8.1 Average performance for geometric sorting task

	Performance measure		
	Number of dimensions sorted (max 3)	Use of number and/or form (max 2)	Verbal explanation adequacy (max 12)
By literacy group			
Nonliterate	1.6	1.1	5.3
Arabic monoliterate	2.0	1.1	5.8
Vai monoliterate	2.0	1.1	5.1
Vai-Arabic biliterate	1.9	1.4	5.6
English schooled	1.7	1.2	5.6
By grade completed (schooled group)			
Under grade 4	1.4	1.1	4.0
Grades 4–9	1.6	1.1	3.6
Grade 10 and over	1.9	1.2	9.3
By school status (grade 4 and over)			
In school	1.7	1.3	7.5
Out of school	1.7	1.1	4.7

ried out by individuals proficient in reading and writing and Vai reading score would substitute for it in the Vai monoliterate file, teaching was a better predictor of performance for this subgroup and the only Vai script variable functioning in the full equation for the population as a whole.

Biliteracy entered the equation in a positive direction. We attempted to determine, within the group, which particular script or combination of scripts was influencing performance, and we turned up evidence for effects of both. Vai reading score enhanced performance, while low Arabic reading scores, reflecting Qur'anic memorizers, depressed it. Two Arabic script variables requiring comprehension of Arabic language (writing letters to strangers and keeping records in Arabic) contributed positively to performance among biliterates.

The results were different for explanation of sorting:

Verbal explanation
(with number classif.
held constant) $= -.21 + 3.14$ number classif. $+ .03$ (last grade)^2
$(R^2 = .47)$ $\qquad$ (15.1) $\qquad$ (4.5)
$\qquad$ $- 2.25$ in school before
$\qquad$ (3.6)

CONSTRAINED CLASSIFICATION

Nine pairs of items were constructed from the stimulus set by random selection. Six pairs were composed of two items from the same category (for example, two food items) and are referred to here as intracategorical pairs; three pairs were composed of two items from different categories (for example, a food and a utensil), referred to as intercategorical pairs. Pairs were presented in nine different random sequences. When each pair was presented, the subject was asked to choose an object from the remaining set; "Pick one thing that is like —— [experimenter named one item of the pair] and also like —— [experimenter named second item of the pair] and put it between them." After the person made his choice, the experimenter asked, "Why did you choose the ——? [referring to the selection]." Analyses are presented only for the intracategorical pairs.

As in the geometric sorting task, we developed separate behavioral and verbal measures. For the former, we scored whether the item selected to complete the triad was a member of the same category; for the latter we developed a scale for verbal explanations ranging from 0 to 7 in which the use of a generic class term ("they are all foods") represented the high point of the scale and a non-task-related or nonspecific reason was given a low score. Scores were summed across all pairs for a maximum score of 42. Results are displayed in Table A8.2.

The following four regression equations show the effect of literacy variables and urban residence on each of the four performance measures contained in Table A8.2:

Number of categorical
choices (food pairs) = .80 + .15 frequency of Vai letter writing
$(R^2 = .17)$ (2.6)
           + 1.16 live in Vaitown
              (7.7)

Number of categorical
choices (utensil pairs) = 2.23 + .22 teach Arabic − .03 years studied Qur'an
$(R^2 = .05)$ (2.3)   (2.2)
          + .05 years urban living
              (3.2)

Verbalization (food)
(with no. of categorical
choices held constant) = 10.80 + 1.01 number of categorical choices
$(R^2 = .16)$ (6.0)
          − 1.63 special role in bush school
              (3.10)
          + .17 years urban living
              (2.8)

Verbalization
(utensils)
(with no. of categorical
choices held constant = $8.42 + .99$ number of categorical choices
$(R^2 = .12)$ (4.5)
                                      − 1.70 special role in bush school
                                               (3.3)
                                        + .15 years urban living
                                               (2.6)

The only firm result to emerge from these analyses is that urban living (either in the form of residence in Vaitown or in the variable labeled in the equation "years urban living," that is, number of years lived in a town of 2,000 or more people) enhances performance on this task. Taking a special part in bush school is associated with a decrement in the adequacy of one's verbal explanations. We have no theoretical reason to think that playing a special role in bush school makes one less articulate; rather, this experience seems to stand in as a marker of relative lack of involvement in experiences occurring outside the traditional culture.

Nonschool literacy effects are spotty and difficult to interpret. A marker of increased use of Vai script (frequency of letter writing) and sophistication of Arabic knowledge (teaching Arabic) both enhance performance, but each occurs on only one of the two subcategories of items. Thus, even if we had a strong rationale for expecting literacy effects on categorizing, we would be hard pressed to explain why they are so localized. The negative effect of Qur'anic learning is also restricted to one subset of items.

On balance, categorizing in this constrained manner using real-world objects does not seem to be greatly affected by literacy factors of any kind.

MEMORY

Items included in the free classification and free recall task, listed by category, were: foods—eddo, bitterball, banana, lime, orange, cassava; kitchen utensils—spoon, pan, plate, stick, pot, knife; tools—saw, cutlass, axe, hoe, hammer, file; clothing—trousers, shoe, headtie, belt, hat, shirt.

In the first task these objects were arrayed on a table for one minute and then covered with a cloth. Each person was asked to name as many objects as possible in any order he chose. When the informant had recalled as many items as he or she could (with the objects still covered), the experimenter read their names in random order. We used two different random orders prepared with the restriction that no two items belonging to the same taxonomic category occurred in succession. The informant was again asked to recall the names in any order. Performance measures included the number of words recalled, a statistic called the Z score (see Frankel and Cole, 1971) that estimates the extent to which items from the same category were recalled in clusters and a statistic estimating the tendency to re-

Table A8.2 Average performance for constrained classification task

	Number of categorical choices			Verbalization		
	Food pairs (max 3)	Utensil pairs (max 3)	Total (max 6)	Food pairs (max 21)	Utensil pairs (max 21)	Total (max 42)
By literacy group						
Nonliterate	1.1	2.3	3.4	12.5	10.0	22.4
Vai monoliterate	1.2	2.4	3.5	12.0	9.9	21.9
Arabic monoliterate	0.8	2.2	3.0	11.1	8.6	19.7
Vai-Arabic biliterate	1.1	2.4	3.5	12.1	8.8	20.9
English schooled	1.4	2.4	3.8	12.9	10.2	23.1
By grade completed (schooled group)						
Under grade 10	1.3	2.4	3.8	12.3	9.5	21.8
Grade 10 and over	1.5	2.4	3.9	14.1	11.6	25.7

Table A8.3 Measures of free recall memory

	Task 1		Task 2	
	Recall	Z score	Recall	Z score
Literacy group				
Nonliterate	16.2	2.1	16.9	2.5
Arabic monoliterate	16.2	2.7	17.2	2.5
Vai monoliterate	16.0	2.2	16.8	2.3
Vai-Arabic biliterate	16.2	2.4	17.9	2.8
English schooled	17.1	2.4	17.7	2.1

call the items in the order presented. Neither the index of categorical clustering nor of serialization produced any differences associated with population variables, so we restrict our discussion to number of items correctly recalled.

The average performance levels for the two recall tasks are shown in Table A8.3. Different subgroups show considerable uniformity of recall; the range of scores amounts to only 1.1 words out of 24 on both recall tasks.

Recall Task 1

The best fitting equation for amount recalled was the following:

Amount recalled = 16.4 + .30 last grade × live upcountry
$(R^2 = .08)$ (3.1)
$- .02$ (last grade)^2 × live in Vaitown
(2.5)
$- .0004$ age^2 + .84 speak tribal languages
(2.7) (2.0)

Age^2 (a transformation indicating that age is nonlinearly related to performance) and knowledge of other tribal languages had straightforward effects on performance, but schooling effects (indexed by "last grade") were surprising—they were both negative and positive, depending on where schooling took place. In further analyses designed to untangle this finding, we found that upcountry students have the highest recall scores, not only of all schooled groups but of all groups in the survey. Performance declines among those out of school, but they still exceed other groups. Vaitown's "peculiarity" is not in the out-of-school population, which compares favorably with its upcountry counterpart, but in the student population, whose performance is the lowest of any group in the survey. We have no indication of what factors may have been at work to produce this result.

Recall Task 2

Preliminary analyses within the data files set up for each of the literacy groups again suggest that last grade was positively related to performance while performance decreased with increasing age, but the regression coefficients clearly show these effects to be slight.

Amount recalled
$$(\text{task 2}) = 17.6 + 1.27 \text{ Vai-Arabic biliterate}$$
$$(R^2 = .05) \qquad\qquad (2.4)$$
$$+ .00001 \text{ age} \times (\text{last grade})^2 - .0004 \text{ age}^2$$
$$(2.1) \qquad\qquad (3.2)$$

Within the biliterate file, Arabic reading score predicted higher recall, giving some substance to the notion that practice in reading Arabic may affect recall when items are presented verbally one at a time, as they were in this second recall task.

LOGIC

The six logic problems were presented to informants in various orders in a single set. Instructions stressed the nature of the problem, using colloquial expressions to try to make clear that the questions could be answered on the basis of what the words said: "I have some questions to ask you. These questions can always be answered yes or no. To answer them all you have to do is to listen carefully to the words and assume that they are true." After answering the question, the informant was asked to explain why he answered as he did. Informants' responses were recorded verbatim as they were given.

Empirical reasons were scored 0 and theoretical reasons 1. Our scoring system gave more credit for correct answers to ambiguous and counterfactual problems than to factual problems, resulting in a scale from 0 (none correct) to 10 (all correct).

Mean performance in terms of both number correct and number of theoretical reasons are given in Table A8.4. Entries in the table clearly indicate that the groups perform almost alike except for the educated group which is superior to all the others.

Multiple regression analyses confirm this observation. Looking first at the measure of number of correct solutions we see that the English literacy effect is manifest through English reading score. We experimented with simple school variables and combinations of variables, attempting to capture any possible Vaitown-upcountry differential, but none of these succeeded in displacing English reading score as the best predictor for overall accuracy in syllogisms. Two experiential factors—personal involvement in farming during the previous year and special role in bush school—are neg-

Table A8.4   Responses to logical syllogisms

	Number correct (max 6)	Number of theoretical justifications (max 10)
Nonliterate	1.6	6.1
Arabic monoliterate	1.3	5.7
Vai monoliterate	1.7	6.2
Vai-Arabic biliterate	1.5	5.7
English schooled	3.0	7.6

atively related to solution. Both of these activities are associated with the "traditional Vai" factor in our demographic factor analysis.

Number correct = 6.83 + .36 English reading score
$(R^2 = .12)$ (3.4)
                    − 1.03 farmed last year
                         (3.8)
                    − .68 special role in bush school
                         (1.9)

A similar equation predicted the nature of people's justifications of their responses. In order to control for the fact that people who give correct answers are in a better position to give theoretical justifications for their answers, we calculated regression equations with and without the prior correctness of responses held constant. The effect that remained in the equation in both cases was schooling; it is interesting to note here that last grade was a stronger predictor variable in these equations than English reading score, although this was not the case for other dependent measures. The difference between the two equations is interesting, so we report it here. When we simply predict performance on the explanation measure, the best equation is:

Explanation score = 2.42 + .01 (last grade)^2 + .61 in school now
$(R^2 = .25)$ (4.7)   (2.1)
                    − .52 special role in bush school
                         (2.4)
                    − .69 farmed last year − .16 travel large city
                         (4.3)   (2.3)

Only the schooling factors survive as predictors when we hold constant the number of correct responses:

Explanation score
(with number correct
    held constant)   = − .63 + .36 number correct + .01 (last grade)^2
$(R^2 = .52)$ (13.9)   (5.0)
                    + .52 in school now
                         (2.2)

Table A8.5 Language objectivity results

	Answer at least first question "yes" (percent)	Total score (Max 3)
Nonliterate	39	.68
Arabic monoliterate	39	.47
Vai monoliterate	49	.91
Vai-Arabic biliterate	66	1.24
English schooled	62	1.31

LANGUAGE OBJECTIVITY

Procedures are given in the text.

Table A8.5 displays the percentage of correct answers to the question about reversing the names of the sun and the moon. The most striking feature of the results is the relatively low performance of all groups. The most common explanations for judging the names to be nonchangeable involved real-world pragmatic considerations and distinctly unchildlike answers. Thus "no" answers for the most part did not indicate confusion between names and things, but rather the respondent's refusal to accept the presuppositions of the question—that people of the world could agree to do anything together, or, if they could agree, that they should undertake actions that rightfully belong in God's domain.

Our first regression analyses were based on raw scores expressing how many items in the sun-moon question were answered correctly before an unacceptable answer was given (total score). These ranged from 0 (refusal to agree that names of the sun and moon could be changed) to 3 (correct description of the sky at night after names were changed). Schooled individuals clearly have the edge, but the distance of their mean score (1.31) from the completely correct score of 3 indicates that even this group favored an interpretation of the question quite different from the conventional interpretation in Geneva and the United States.

When we partialed out different influences on total scores, we found that schooling did indeed exert the most powerful effect but did so in complicated ways. Items entering the equation reflect the varied characteristics of the schooled population, including the now familiar distinction between Vaitown men and those upcountry. On this occasion, however, attending school in Vaitown *adds* to performance. Here we also have a functional variable related to English literacy: writing for others, an activity that is primarily undertaken to meet personal needs of fellow townspeople. Biliteracy has a positive effect which subanalyses showed was closely related to frequency of letter writing. Among biliterates, Arabic script uses contribute both positively and negatively to scores. Because these literacy effects are expressible in alternative ways that are not easily summarized, we mark them in the equation by the group label "biliterate." No other personal attribute or experience approaches significance as a contribution to performance. The most reasonable summary is contained in the following equation:

Language objectivity = 6.98 + .65 writes letters for others in English
$$(R^2 = .08) \qquad\qquad\qquad\qquad (2.2)$$
$$+ .50 \text{ biliterate} + .01 \text{ (last grade)}^2 \times \text{ live in Vaitown}$$
$$(2.9) \qquad\qquad\qquad (2.9)$$
$$+ 5.4 \text{ out of school now} - .00001 \text{ age} \times \text{ (last grade)}^2$$
$$(2.4) \qquad\qquad\qquad (1.9)$$

Enough variables enter this equation to make it confusing for the reader (as it was for us as analysts!). The major thing to note is that there is an effect of schooling that depends on the informant's age and place of residence. Active use of English in writing letters and some aspect of being a biliterate in Vai and Arabic are associated with improved performance. We will not try to explain more about this complex set of relations here, because we included this task in later studies so that replication of the effect rather than statistical argument could be used to decide among alternative explanations.

Appendix to Chapter 9:
Forced-Choice Longest-Word Study

To overcome some of the ambiguities in examining concepts of word length solely through linguistic means, we developed a task using graphic materials. This task was incorporated in our final survey investigation, the integration survey (see Table 9.1).

We selected eighteen words differing in the number of constituent syllables; all were names of common objects, which we depicted in simple black-and-white drawings. We gave each respondent practice naming the pictures until we were certain they could name all without error. We presented the pictures two at a time and asked which picture had the longest name. These modifications in the conditions for making judgments about words entailed others, which again bring out the special problems involved in studies about language understanding. As soon as we introduced pictures as the things we were talking about, it became inappropriate to designate their labels with the term *koali kulē,* just as it would be inappropriate for us to insert the term "word" in the sentence, "Tell me which pictured thing has the longer word." English requires the use of "name" in that sentence frame, and the Vai language has the same requirement. In this instance, Vai—which has no unambiguous term for "word"—has a term, *tōn,* which seems a direct equivalent for the verb "to be named." This change in terminology had the effect of restricting our investigation to a particular class of words.

In this task we also tapped into our continuing interest in nominal realism. To determine whether judgments about word length were affected by object size, we systematically varied the relationship between name length and referent size; in some pairs the smaller object had the longer name; in some the larger object had the longer name; and in some the longer name and shorter name applied to objects of equal size.

Picture pairs were as follows (both Vai names and their English equivalents are given):

1. *keñ*, foot   *b̄o-lo*, hand
   one syllable   two syllables
2. *b̄i-nda*, spoon   *fo-ki-a*, fork
   two syllables   three syllables
3. *kpa-to-lo*, cutlass   *ka-li*, hoe
   three syllables   two syllables
4. *mē-sē-li*, needle   *keñ*, house
   three syllables   one syllable
5. *ja-mba*, leaf   *kōñ*, tree
   two syllables   one syllable
6. *liñ*, ring   *lo-ma*, shirt
   one syllable   two syllables
7. *jii*, key   *jen-di-a*, window
   one syllable   three syllables
8. *ta-wa-la*, pipe   *ka-la*, snake
   three syllables   two syllables
9. *ja-kpō*, eye   *b̄a*, goat
   two syllables   one syllable

In pairs 1–3, the size of the referents in each pair is approximately equal but the number of syllables in their respective names varies in length (for example, spoon and fork are about the same size but the Vai name for fork has one more syllable than the name for spoon). In pairs 4, 5, 8, and 9, the smaller object has the longer name, and in pairs 6 and 7, the larger object has the longer name. Pairs were presented in random order.

Instructions began with a discussion about Vai names: "Vai language has all kinds of names. Some are long names; some are short names. For example names of people—*Bai* is a short name; *Abdullai* is a longer name than *Bai; Famata* is a longer name that *Jebe.* Some things to eat have short names; some have long names. *Lumbōkpōmēsē* is a long name; *jowo* is a

---

Table A9.1 Group means for forced-choice longest-word task

	Number judged correctly (max 9)
Nonliterate	6.70
Qur'anic	7.60
Arabic	7.00
Beginning Vai script	7.55
Advanced Vai script	7.45
Schooled	8.35

shorter name than *lumbōkpōmēsē.*" When the person understood, the experimenter continued by saying he would show two pictures and would ask the informant to name them as he showed them. After the informant named both pictures, he was asked to tell which name was longer.

This procedure was followed for all pairs. If the informant made a mistake in naming a picture, the experimenter supplied the correct name.

Table A9.1 presents groups averages for number of correct longest word judgments. All groups performed at a high level of accuracy. Literacy groups appear to have some advantage over nonliterates but regression analyses do not confirm this impression; the only variable improving performance is one indicating whether or not the respondent had ever worked at a foreign concession. The regression equation was:

Number correct judgments = 1.7 + 1.3 ever concession
$$(R^2 = .07) \qquad\qquad (2.5)$$

We also tape-recorded responses and systematically scored for elongation of vowels or "stretching" of words, such as, to use an English example, pronouncing "key" as "ke-e-ey." We found very few instances of such word stretching, and thus we can rule out this childlike response as a characteristic of adult performance. When we divided the stimulus pairs into critical pairs (longer names associated with smaller objects) and noncritical pairs (objects of equal size, or word length and object size consistent with each other), we found no differences in accuracy or reaction time between these sets for any group. Even the lowest performers showed greater variability within a set than between sets. The evidence suggests two conclusions. First, when the notion of word length is operationalized as "name" and people are presented instances from which to make a choice, they can perform the necessary analysis into component syllables to make correct judgments of length. Second, these judgments are unaffected by the relationship between word size and referent size.

A fascinating sidelight on this task is that in certain cases Vai script literates erred because they were basing their judgments on the number of characters used in writing the names rather than on the time it took to say them. A script literate was given the pictures for cutlass (*kpatolo*) and hoe (*kali*) and was asked which had the longer name. In Vai *kpatolo* is spoken as three units and may be written as two or three units; *kali* is spoken as two units and written as two units. (See Chapter 11 for a discussion of optional use of L+ vowel syllables in pronouncing and writing certain words.)

The informant said the two names were equal in length. When asked why, he said, "Because it takes two characters to write each one." The interviewer then asked, "Are they equal in sound?" "No," replied the man, "*kpatolo* is longer in sound."

In these cases we have a clear example of metalinguistic awareness that is linked specifically to writing, and an early indication of a point made in Chapter 11: Vai script literates may make mental reference to the written form of their language when asked to deal with a verbal task.

After we presented all the picture pairs, we repeated the question used in the metalinguistic and replication surveys to say the "longest word you can think of." Our analyses of these results indicated that previous practice with longest names did not transfer to tasks involving longest words. Nonetheless, results of this study provide the strongest evidence we have that Vai adults are not victims of nominal realism.

Notes

1. WRITING AND THOUGHT

1. A classic work on communication among bees is Von Frisch (1967). For birds, see Marler and Tamura (1964); and for chimpanzees, Rumbaugh and Gill (1976).

2. Others who have drawn conclusions about differences in oral and literate thought largely on the basis of analysis of differences in the modes of communication most typical of each are Innis (1951); Ong (1958, 1971); and, in part, McLuhan (1962).

3. Significant exceptions to this generalization are reviewed in Cole and Scribner (1974).

2. SCHEMES AND DESIGNS

1. During the course of our work we became increasingly critical of this antecedent-consequent model of culture-cognition relationships and developed an alternative conception (see Chapter 14), but we present the original model here since it organized our research planning efforts.

3. VAI PEOPLE AND THEIR SCRIPT

1. The description of Vai life given in this chapter is not intended to be an ethnography. For more details see Johnston (1906); Ellis (1914); Holsoe (1967); and Smith (forthcoming). Our description of Gohn is taken from Mike Smith's project reports.

2. Some reports are Harley (1941); Bellman (1975).

3. This is a modified version of the modern syllabary prepared at the University of Liberia by a group of indigenous Vai script experts and a for-

eign linguist. Several earlier syllabaries exist, including one prepared by the Vai diplomat and scholar Momolu Massaquoi in 1911. While important differences are evident between the University of Liberia syllabary and characters in early specimens of Vai script writing, the structure is basically unchanged. Stewart (1972) discusses the relationship between early and contemporary Vai script.

4. We should note here that the syllabary chart is an idealized document prepared by linguists. It is not used in the countryside to teach or learn the script. Our field experience leads us to conclude that it is not a representation of what all Vai literates know or use. Characteristics of the script figure prominently in some of our experimental studies, and more detailed information is presented in Chapters 10 and 11.

4. DOING THE WORK

1. The staff decided that they could record more accurately and better preserve the sense of what was said by using English rather than attempting to reproduce the original Vai in the phonetic alphabet for later translation.

2. Refusals amounted to 6 percent of the initial sample population. To put this figure into some perspective, we report that it compares to a 9 percent refusal rate in a well-known modernity interview survey in rural areas of East Pakistan (Schuman, 1967).

5. SURVEY GOALS AND METHODS

1. A large town was defined as a town with an adult population of two hundred or more, according to the 1962 Liberian Census, the most current census available at the time.

2. We modified this procedure in Diaa, the town which was the site of the ethnographic study. The ethnographer, with the aid of informants, interviewed *all* adult members of this town.

3. Vai people do not routinely mark off years of birth, although, as we discovered among literates, a popular function of writing is to record major family events such as birth dates. Ages are therefore estimates; we used a procedure for estimating ages recommended by the designers of the 1962 Liberian Census.

4. Among the Vai people, English literacy, with few exceptions, is acquired in government or missionary schools where reading instruction follows a year or more of instruction in English as a second language.

5. See Holsoe, 1977, for an analysis of domestic servitude among the Vai. Background information is available in *Area Handbook for Liberia*

(1972), pp. 16–18; Fraenkel (1964), pp. 25–27; Liebenow (1969), pp. 65–70; and Wilson (1971), pp. 115–127. See also Smith (forthcoming) for a critical review of Holsoe's analysis.

6. We present evidence for the statistical significance of intercorrelations among items in our discussion of outcomes of factor analysis, Chapter 7.

6. LITERACY AND ITS CHARACTERISTICS

1. To our knowledge there have been no other systematic attempts to determine the extent of literacy in the Vai script. On the basis of her own observations and occasional interviews, Stewart (1967) estimated that "Vai literates constitute 20% to 25% of all Vai speakers" (p. 73). This informal estimate is within the range of our survey figures.

2. A comparison of our rate of English literacy (6.2 percent) with that reported by the Census (11.6 percent), which includes all students in school, indicates that English will have a much greater share of total Cape Mount literacy in years ahead as school attendance increases and more graduates maintain residence in the county.

3. See Goody (1968b) and Ferguson (1971) for accounts of multiscript usage in other nonindustrialized societies. In a number of these societies, certain scripts seem to be functionally restricted to priestly or elite populations, and utilization of one or another writing system relatively fixed by status and/or religious affiliation. In others (for example, Ethiopia), popular literacy involves more than one script, as it does among the Vai.

7. SOCIAL CORRELATES OF LITERACY

1. A variable indicating student status at the time of the interview also entered the equation with a slight negative contribution. We attribute this to the particular characteristics of our school sample (discussed in Chapter 8).

2. After weeding out unsuitable or duplicate questions we had a set of seventy-four items concerning people's backgrounds or current circumstances for analysis. Initially we considered separation of these variables into two subsets—facts antecedent to the acquisition of literacy that would help us address the selectivity problem, and facts that were coincident to or consequences of literacy (that is, simple covariates). Our efforts to select facts that were clearly antecedent proved disappointing. Since Vai script literacy is acquired in adulthood, not childhood, we often could not rule out the possibility that certain experiences were simply coincident with literacy rather than prior, determining factors. We also found that questions about parents' lives elicited many "I don't know" responses; informants

often were unable to state the extent of their parents' education work experience, travel, and so on, especially if the informants had not been raised in their parents' houses. Because of these difficulties, we ended up with few reliable questions about antecedents, and we confined ourselves to a single factor analysis that included all possible covariate information from the questionnaire.

8. DOES LITERACY SUBSTITUTE FOR SCHOOLING?

1. We followed certain standard rules of procedure in conducting experiments and interviews. We describe them briefly here, but it should be kept in mind that they apply not only to experiments in the major survey but to all studies discussed in this book.

We used the Vai language in all interviews and experiments with only minor exceptions for the schooled group. Students, especially those in higher grades and in Monrovia, sometimes preferred to handle the questions about personal history in English, since this had become the language in which they were most fluent. For some members of this group, the requirement to explain grammatical errors, give instructions, and carry out other tasks in Vai put them at a linguistic disadvantage relative to others.

Instructions were prepared in English, translated into Vai, and back-translated. This reiterative procedure was carried out several times for interview topics that were especially dependent on preserving fine distinctions of meaning. We were fortunate in being able to enlist the services of several Vai men with backgrounds in linguistics and social sciences to help in this process, but, as we describe in the text, we could not satisfactorily resolve all problematic conceptual areas.

Studies were conducted by Vai men with at least some high school education. They worked in teams or singly, in all cases in close collaboration with a full-time member of the project staff.

2. Some evidence in the cross-cultural psychology literature suggests that difficulties in abstrcting a single dimension or in shifting criteria are associated with the particular stimuli used. Irwin and McLaughlin (1970) found that Liberian (Mano) rice farmers were better able to sort varieties of rice than geometric figures. A later study by Irwin, Schafer, and Feiden (1974) found that exactly the opposite was true of American college students. However, Gay and Cole (1971) found no differences among the Kpelle between sorting of geometric figures and line drawings of familiar scenes; Greenfield (1974) found no facilitative effect of presenting familiar (flower) stimuli; and Sharp et al. (1979) found that sorting of corn kernels and geometric shapes among Yucatecans were equally difficult. Because of these uncertainties and our interest in stimuli that had the "abstract" features said to be a part of schooling and writing systems, we employed only geometric shapes for this task.

9. LITERACY AND METALINGUISTIC KNOWLEDGE

1. Fifty people of the seventy-five interviewed were included in regression analyses. Some schooled men in these towns also knew Arabic or Vai script, and the resulting group of English monoliterates was too small to include in the analysis. This survey, therefore, does not have a schooled comparison group. In these towns, all Arabic literates also knew the Vai script so the survey lacks an Arabic monoliterate group.

2. This criticism does not apply to English reading score since only one survey included a schooled population.

3. We conducted a series of studies on Vai script literates' skill in using syllables as units of language; these are described in Chapter 10.

4. Mohamed Nyei, who is literate in Vai script, English, and Arabic, prepared materials for this study and carried out the analysis.

5. The term used here is *kpololeñ*, which literally means "book child," the expression used to denote script characters.

6. We have no explanation as to why this effect was limited to this particular range of Vai script literates.

7. Failure to find effects of schooling and English literacy may be due to the fact that all our studies were conducted in the Vai language and were about the Vai language. It is unfortunate that time did not allow us to follow up on the possibility that English literates who acquired their knowledge of English through formal instruction in school might have displayed a grasp of the concept of word in that language.

10. MAKING SENSE OF SOUND AND SYMBOL

1. The Vai script is said to have had rebuslike features in its early days; as we went along, it soon became clear that our reading task was not culturally inappropriate nor unrecognizable as a reading task.

2. Vai language scholars (Klingenheben, 1933; Welmers, 1958, 1976) differ in their analyses of the tonal and vowel systems. We relied on the judgments of Mohamed Nyei working with Stephen Reder.

3. In work with American children, integration has been typically assessed by requiring the child to act out instructions presented in the sentence (as in the example above, "JUMP OVER THE BLOCK"). We did not choose to follow this procedure. We were working with adults who took these interviews seriously and were concerned lest they make themselves appear foolish or do the wrong thing. Asking them to act out a sentence appeared inappropriate. In addition, we could not find ways of representing suitable action statements in easy-to-decipher pictures.

4. In addition to this reading task, we experimented with various practice and test procedures for a sentence construction or writing task which was included in our follow-up studies.

5. Stephen Reder's analysis of the functional skills involved in reading Vai script was the basis for these studies, and he contributed importantly to their conception and design.

6. This analysis is based on a population of twelve Vai script literates and ten nonliterates whose protocols were complete.

7. This was the same study in which we piloted the reading task.

11. THE WRITTEN AND THE SPOKEN WORD

1. This chapter briefly presents research more fully developed in Reder (1977).

12. COMMUNICATION: MAKING MEANING CLEAR

1. See also the letters reproduced in Chapter 6.

2. Vai script literates produced both Transcript 1 and Transcript 2—a reminder that the skills with which we are concerned cannot be linked to literacy in any deterministic way.

3. For a fuller description of coding systems and tests of coder reliability, see Pratt, Scribner, and Cole (1977).

4. Analyses of the second oral presentations are omitted because the results were similar in all essential respects to those for the first oral productions.

5. Information on background characteristics is in Table 9.2.

6. Recorded letters and Vai script letters were transcribed and translated into English. Analyses were carried out by a research assistant who had also rated some of the communication game protocols. The communicative features that were used as the basis for group comparisons were arrived at inductively—through inspection of the letters, conversations with Mohamed Nyei and others, and analogical comparisons with the communication game.

7. Written letters were considerably shorter than dictated letters. As the text indicates, they contained more conventionalized stylistic elements and less information.

8. Five nonliterates also used the stock "this is your information" phrase—a small but interesting sign of their familiarity with letter-writing conventions.

9. Out of fifty-nine letter-pair judgments (one was omitted by experimental error), informants made no choice in fourteen instances.

10. Deborah Malamud performed this analysis.

11. This view is consistent with recent interpretations of developmental changes in communication performance (Gelman, 1978).

13. STUDIES OF MEMORY

1. Mike Smith's more detailed observations of Qur'anic learning suggest that while the incremental method is popular, it is not an exclusive instructional technique, and is likely to be most prominent in early learning stages.

2. The actual items were: clothing—hat, trousers, shirt, lappa; utensils—pot, pan, plate, spoon; food—banana, cassava, eddc, orange; tools—cutlass, file, saw, hammer.

14. THE PRACTICE OF LITERACY

1. We are reminded of Barker's (1968) treatment of the nested character of purposeful behavior; smaller behavior units are nested within larger units as boxes within boxes. How the investigator chooses to slice up activities—in this case, the size or level of the unit of practice—depends upon the purpose of the analysis.

2. We use the term "technology" broadly here to embrace characteristics of the graphic symbol system as well as the material means of its representation.

3. We find Vygotsky's concept of functional system a useful way to refer to the assembly of skills involved in a practice. Luria (1966, p. 24) defines this concept in biological terms, but with slight adaptations it can be taken as a general definition: "A functional system is directed toward the performance of a particular task and consists of a group of interconnected acts that produce the effect." We discuss a cognitive approach to functional systems in Cole and Scribner, 1974.

4. We are highlighting what we consider to be major factors; our analysis is not intended to be exhaustive.

5. Havelock (1976) considers the requirement that texts be written for an audience to be an important determinant of full literacy.

6. For example, during World War II the Vai were suspected of using the script to send coded messages to the Germans, a rumor fueled by the fact that early linguistic study of the Vai script was carried out by the Germans.

7. The highest-ranking variable in the prediction equation is the variable with the largest t ratio.

8. Because of the near-perfect correlation of English reading score with schooling, we have interpreted this variable as a schooling variable. Other school variables include last grade and school status (student now or before).

9. Only one "talking about" task—constrained classification—failed to

show an overall influence on schooling, but higher levels improved performance (see Chapter 8).

10. In our pilot work we obtained some evidence of a schooling effect using a multitrial procedure. The switch to the procedures used was a calculated risk designed to obtain more information about the relation between classification and recall.

11. Four other memory tasks were studied. These include two free recall tasks in the major survey, story recall, and Paris and Carter sentence recognition (see Chapters 8 and 13).

12. We are using the notion of transfer here in an informal sense.

Bibliography

Ach, N. 1905. *Über die Willenstätigkeit und das Denken.* Göttingen: Vandenhoeck & Ruprecht.

Allen, C., and R. W. Johnson, eds. 1970. *African perspectives.* New York: Cambridge University Press.

Anderson, R. C. 1977. *Schema-directed processes in language comprehension.* Technical Report No. 50. Urbana, Ill.: Center for the Study of Reading.

Anderson, R. C., R. S. Spiro, and W. E. Montague, eds. 1976. *Schooling and the acquisition of knowledge.* Hillsdale, N.J.: Lawrence Erlbaum Associates.

Area Handbook for Liberia. 1972. Washington, D.C.: American University.

Armer, M., and R. Youtz. 1971. Formal education and individual modernity in an African society. *American Journal of Sociology* 76: 604–626.

Asher, S. R. 1978. *Referential communication.* Technical Report No. 90. Urbana, Ill.: Center for the Study of Reading.

Barker, R. 1968. *Ecological psychology.* Stanford: Stanford University Press.

Bartlett, E., and S. Scribner. 1981. Text and context: Referential organization in children's narratives. In M. Whiteman, ed., *Writing: The nature, development, and teaching of written communication,* vol. 1. Hillsdale, N.J.: Lawrence Erlbaum Associates.

Basso, K., and N. Anderson. 1973. A Western Apache writing system: The symbols of Silas John. *Science* 180: 1013–22.

Bateson, G. 1972. Social planning and the concept of deutero-learning. In G. Bateson, ed., *Steps to an ecology of mind.* New York: Ballantine Books.

Bellman, B. L. 1975. *Village of curers and assassins: On the production of Kpelle cosmological categories.* The Hague: Mouton.

Bernstein, B., ed. 1971. *Class, codes and control.* Vol. 1: *Theoretical studies toward a sociology of language.* London: Routledge & Kegan Paul.

Berry, J. W. 1976. *Human ecology and cognitive style.* New York: Sage-Halsted.

Bronfenbrenner, U. 1979. *The ecology of human development.* Cambridge, Mass.: Harvard University Press.

Brown, A., and L. A. French. 1979. Commentary in D. Sharp, M. Cole, and C. Lave, *Education and cognitive development: The evidence from experimental research.* Monographs of the Society for Research in Child Development, 44 (1–2, Serial No. 178).

Bruce, B. C., A. Collins, A. D. Rubin, and D. Gentner. 1978. *A cognitive science approach to writing.* Technical Report No. 89. Urbana, Ill.: Center for the Study of Reading.

Bruner, J. Introduction. In J. Bruner et al., 1966. (See below.)

Bruner, J., R. Olver, P. Greenfield, J. Hornsby, H. Kenney, M. Maccoby, H. Modiano, F. Mosher, D. Olson, M. Potter, L. Reisch, and A. Sonstroem. 1966. *Studies in cognitive growth.* New York: Wiley.

Bruner, J. S., and D. R. Olson. 1977–78. Symbols and texts as the tools of intellect. *Interchange* 8 (4): 1–15.

Cazden, C. 1974. Play with language and metalinguistic awareness: One dimension of language experience. *Urban Review* 7: 28–39.

Charbonnier, G. 1973. "Primitive" and "civilized" peoples: A conversation with Claude Lévi-Strauss. In R. Disch, ed., *The future of literacy.* Englewood Cliffs, N.J.: Prentice-Hall.

Chaytor, H. J. 1945. *From script to print: An introduction to medieval vernacular literature.* Cambridge, Eng.: W. Heffer and Sons.

Child, D. 1970. *The essentials of factor analysis.* New York: Holt, Rinehart & Winston.

Cicourel, A. 1964. *Method and measurement in sociology.* New York: Free Press.

Clammer, J. R. 1976. *Literacy and social change: A case study of Fiji.* Leiden, The Netherlands: E. J. Brill.

Cohen, J., and P. Cohen. 1975. *Applied multiple regression/correlational analysis for the behavioral sciences.* Hillsdale, N.J.: Lawrence Erlbaum Associates.

Cole, M., J. Gay, J. Glick, and D. W. Sharp. 1971. *The cultural context of learning and thinking.* New York: Basic Books.

Cole, M., and S. Scribner. 1974. *Culture and thought: A psychological introduction.* New York: Wiley.

Cole, M., and S. Scribner. 1977. Cross-cultural studies of memory and cognition. In R. V. Kail, Jr., and J. W. Hagen, eds., *Perspectives on the development of memory and cognition.* Hillsdale, N.J.: Lawrence Erlbaum Associates.

Cole, M., and K. Traupmann. In press. *Comparative cognitive research: Learning from a learning disabled child.* 1979 Minnesota Symposium on Child Development, vol. 12.

Creswick, H. C. 1868. On the syllabic characters in use amongst the Vey negroes. *Transactions of the Ethnological Society* (London) 6: 260–263.

Cronbach, L. J. 1970. *Essentials of psychological testing.* New York: Harper.

Dalby, D. 1967. A survey of the indigenous scripts of Liberia and Sierra Leone: Vai, Mende, Loma, Kpelle, and Bassa. *African Language Studies* (University of London) 8: 1–51.

———— 1968. The indigenous scripts of West Africa and Surinam: Their inspiration and design. *African Language Studies* (University of London) 9: 156–197.

———— 1970. The historical problems of the indigenous scripts of West Africa and Surinam. In D. Dalby, ed., *Language and history in West Africa.* New York: Africana.

Delafosse, M. 1899. Les Vai: Leur Langue et leur système d'écriture. *L'Anthropologie* (Paris) 10: 129–151, 294–314.

Diringer, D. 1962. *Writing.* London: Thames & Hudson.

———— 1968. *The alphabet: A key to the history of mankind.* (3d ed., 2 vols.) New York: Funk & Wagnalls.

Downing, J., and P. Oliver. 1973–74. The child's conception of "a word." *Reading Research Quarterly* 9: 568–582.

Ehri, L. C. 1979. Linguistic insight: Threshold of reading acquisition. In T. G. Waller and G. E. Mackinnon, eds., *Reading research: Advances in theory and practice,* vol. 1. New York: Academic Press.

Eisenstein, E. L. 1979. *The printing press as an agent of change.* New York: Cambridge University Press.

Ellis, G. 1914. *Negro culture in West Africa.* New York: Neale. (Repr. New York: Johnson Reprint Corp., 1970.)

Fahrmeier, E. D. 1975. The effect of school attendance on intellectual development in Northern Nigeria. *Child Development* 46: 281–285.

Farnham-Diggory, S. 1967. Symbol and synthesis in experimental reading. *Child Development* 38: 221–231.

——— 1970. Cognitive synthesis in Negro and white children. *Monographs of the Society for Research in Child Development* 35: 1–84.

——— 1978. On the logic and pitfalls of logograph research. *Journal of Experimental Child Psychology* 25: 366–370.

Farnham-Diggory, S., and H. A. Simon. 1972. *Cognitive synthesis of auditory and visual symbols.* Complex Information Processing Paper No. 217, Department of Psychology, Carnegie-Mellon University.

Ferguson, C. 1971. Contrasting patterns of literacy acquisition in a multilingual nation. In W. H. Whitely, ed., *Language use and social change.* Oxford: Oxford University Press.

Flavell, J., P. Botkin, C. Fry, J. Wright, and D. Jarvis. 1968. *The development of role-taking and communication skills in children.* New York: Wiley.

Fraenkel, M. 1964. *Tribe and class in Monrovia.* London: Oxford University Press.

Frankel, F., and M. Cole. 1971. Measures of category clustering in free recall. *Psychological Bulletin* 76: 39–44.

Frankfort, H., H. A. Frankfort, J. A. Wilson, and T. Jacobsen. 1972. *Before philosophy.* Baltimore: Penguin Books. (First pub. 1946.)

Gay, J., and M. Cole. 1967. *The new mathematics and an old culture.* New York: Holt, Rinehart & Winston.

Geertz, C. 1973. *The interpretation of cultures.* New York: Basic Books.

Gelb, I. J. 1963. *A study of writing.* Rev. ed. Chicago: University of Chicago Press.

Gelman, R. 1978. Cognitive Development. *Annual Review of Psychology* 29: 297–332.

Ginsburg, H. 1978. Poor children, African mathematics, and the problem of schooling. *Educational Research Quarterly* 2: 26–44.

Gleitman, L. R., and P. Rozin. 1973. Teaching reading by use of a syllabary. *Reading Research Quarterly* 8: 447–483.

——— 1977. The structure and acquisition of reading, I: Relations between orthographies and the structure of language. In A. Reber and D. Scarborough, eds., *Toward a psychology of reading.* Hillsdale, N.J.: Lawrence Erlbaum Associates.

Glushko, R. J. 1979. Cognitive and pedagogical implications of orthography. *Quarterly Newsletter of the Laboratory of Comparative Human Cognition* 1 (2): 22–26.

Goldstein, K., and M. Scheerer. 1941. *Abstract and concrete behavior: An experimental study with special tests.* Psychological Monographs 53 (2, Whole No. 239).

Goody, J. 1968a. Restricted literacy in northern Ghana. In J. Goody, ed., *Literacy in traditional societies.* New York: Cambridge University Press.

Goody, J., ed. 1968b. *Literacy in traditional societies.* New York: Cambridge University Press.

Goody, J. 1977. *The domestication of the savage mind.* New York: Cambridge University Press.

Goody, J., M. Cole, and S. Scribner. 1977. Writing and formal operations: A case study among the Vai. *Africa* 47: 289–304.

Goody, J., and I. Watt. 1968. The consequences of literacy. In J. Goody, ed., *Literacy in traditional societies.* New York: Cambridge University Press. (First pub. 1963 in *Comparative studies in society and history* 5: 27–68.)

Gough, K. 1968. Implications of literacy in traditional China and India. In

J. Goody, ed., *Literacy in traditional societies.* New York: Cambridge University Press.

Gray, W. S. 1969. *The teaching of reading and writing.* Paris: UNESCO Monographs on Fundamental Education, No. 10.

Greene, W. C. 1951. The spoken and the written word. *Harvard Studies in Classical Philology* 60: 23–59.

Greenfield, P. M. 1972. Oral and written language: The consequences for cognitive development in Africa, the United States, and England. *Language and Speech* 15: 169–178.

———— 1974. Comparing dimensional categorization in natural and artificial contexts: A developmental study among the Zinacantecos of Mexico. *Journal of Social Psychology* 93: 157–171.

———— 1976. Cross-cultural research and Piagetian theory: Paradox and progress. In K. F. Riegel and J. A. Meacham, eds., *The developing individual in a changing world.* Vol. 1: *Historical and cultural issues.* Chicago: Aldine.

Greenfield, P. M., and J. S. Bruner. 1966. Culture and cognitive growth. *International Journal of Psychology* 1 (2): 89–107.

———— 1969. Culture and cognitive growth. In D. A. Goslin, ed., *Handbook of socialization: Theory and research.* New York: Rand-McNally.

Gundlach, R. 1981. On the nature and development of children's writing. In J. Dominic and C. Fredericksen, eds., *Writing: The nature, development and teaching of written communication,* vol. 2. Hillsdale, N.J.: Lawrence Erlbaum Associates.

Haas, W. 1976. Writing: The basic options. In W. Haas, ed., *Writing without letters.* Manchester: Manchester University Press.

Hair, P. E. H. 1963. Notes on the discovery of the Vai script, with a bibliography. *Sierra Leone Language Review* 2: 36–49.

———— 1968. An ethnolinguistic inventory of the Lower Guinea coast before 1700: Part I. *African Language Review* 7: 47–73.

Harley, G. W. 1941. *Notes on the Poro in Liberia.* Papers of the Peabody Museum of Archeology and Ethnology, Harvard University, 19 (2).

Harlow, H. F., and M. Kuenne. 1962. Learning to think. *Scientific American* 207: 136–146.

Harman, D. 1976. Nonformal education and development. In D. Harman, ed., *Expanding recurrent and nonformal education.* San Francisco: Jossey-Bass.

Harris, R. J. 1975. *A primer of multivariate statistics.* New York: Academic Press.

Havelock, E. A. 1963. Preface to Plato. Cambridge, Mass.: Harvard University Press.

———— 1976. *Origins of Western literacy.* Toronto: Ontario Institute in Education.

———— 1978. *The Greek concept of justice: From its shadow in Homer to its substance in Plato.* Cambridge, Mass.: Harvard University Press.

Higgins, E. T. 1977. Communication development as related to channel, incentive, and social class. *Genetic Psychology Monographs* 96: 75–141.

Hill, S. A. 1961. A study of the logical abilities of children. Ph.D. dissertation, Stanford University.

Hodge, C. T. 1975. *Ritual and writing: An inquiry into the origin of Egyptian script.* Lisse: Peter De Ridder Press.

Holden, M., and W. H. MacGinitie. 1972. Children's conceptions of word boundaries in speech and print. *Journal of Educational Psychology* 63 (6): 551–557.

Holsoe, S. E. 1967. The cassava-leaf people: An ethno-historical study of the Vai people with a particular emphasis on the Teewo Chiefdom. Ph.D. dissertation, Boston University.

———— 1971. *A bibliography on Liberia, Part II: Publications concerning colonization.* Newark, Del.: Liberian Studies Association in America.

———— 1977. Slavery and economic response among the Vai. In S. Miers and I. Kopytoff, eds., *Slavery in Africa: Historical and anthropological perspectives.* Madison: University of Wisconsin Press.

Hopewell, J. 1958. *Muslim penetration into French Guinea, Sierra Leone, and Liberia before 1850.* Ann Arbor: University Microfilms.

Horton, R. 1967. African traditional thought and Western science. *Africa* 32: 50–71, 155–187.

Hsu, F. L. K., ed. 1972. *Psychological anthropology.* 2d ed. Cambridge, Mass.: Schenkman.

Hunter, C. St. J., and D. Harman. 1979. *Adult illiteracy in the United States.* New York: McGraw-Hill.

Huttenlocher, J. 1964. Children's language: Word-phrase relationship. *Science* 143: 264–265.

Hymes, D. 1963. Review of M. McLuhan, *The Gutenberg Galaxy. American Anthropologist* 65: 478–479.

Inkeles, A. 1969. Participant citizenship in six developing countries. *American Political Science Review* 63 (4): 1120–41.

———— 1973. The school as a context for modernization. *International Journal of Comparative Sociology* 40 (14): 163–178.

Inkeles, A., and D. H. Smith. 1974. *Becoming modern.* Cambridge, Mass.: Harvard University Press.

Innis, H. 1951. *The bias of communciation.* Toronto: University of Toronto Press. (4th ed., 1971.)

Irwin, M. H., and D. H. McLaughlin. 1970. Ability and preference in category sorting by Mano school children and adults. *Journal of Social Psychology* 82: 15–24.

Irwin, M. H., P. L. Engle, C. Yarbrough, R. E. Klein, and J. Townsend. 1978. The relationship of prior ability and family characteristics to school attendance and school achievement in rural Guatemala. *Child Development* 49: 415–427.

Irwin, M. H., G. N. Schafer, and C. P. Feiden. 1974. Emic and unfamiliar category sorting of Mano farmers and U.S. undergraduates. *Journal of Cross-cultural Psychology* 5: 407–423.

Johnson, S. J. M. 1975. History and development of the Vai script. Paper presented before Liberian Research Association, May.

Johnston, H. S. 1906. *Liberia.* New York: Dodd Mead. (Repr. 1969 by Negro Universities Press, a division of Greenwood, New York.)

Karpova, S. N. 1966. The preschooler's realization of the lexical structure of speech. *Voprosy Psikhol.,* 1955, 4: 43–55. Abstracted in D. I. Slobin, Abstracts of Soviet studies of child language. In F. Smith and G. A. Miller, eds., *The genesis of language.* Cambridge, Mass.: MIT Press.

Keeton, A. 1977. Children's cognitive integration and memory processes for comprehending written sentences. *Journal of Experimental Child Psychology* 23: 459–471.

Kilpatrick, J. F., and A. G. Kilpatrick. 1965. *The shadow of Sequoyah.* Norman: University of Oklahoma Press.

Klingenheben, A. 1933. The Vai script. *Africa* 6: 158–171.

Koelle, S. W. 1854. *Outlines of a grammar of the Vei language.* London: Church Missionary House. (Repr. Farnborough, Eng.: Gregg International Publishers, 1968.)

Laquer, T. 1976. The cultural origins of popular literacy in England 1500–1850. *Oxford Review of Education* 2: 255–275.

Lave, J. 1977. Tailor-made experiments and evaluating the intellectual consequences of apprenticeship training. *Quarterly Newsletter of the Institute for Comparative Human Development* 1 (2): 1–3.

Leichter, H. J., ed. 1976. *The family as educator.* New York: Teachers College Press.

Lefevre, L., and H.-J. Martin. 1976. *The coming of the book.* London: NLB.

Lerner, D. 1958. *The passing of traditional society.* New York: Free Press.

Lévi-Strauss, C. 1966. *The savage mind.* Chicago: University of Chicago Press.

———— 1973. See Charbonnier.

Liberman, I. Y., D. Shankweiler, F. W. Fischer, and B. Carter. 1974. Explicit syllable and phoneme segmentation in the young child. *Journal of Experimental Child Psychology* 18: 202–212.

Liebenow, J. G. 1969. *Liberia: The evolution of privilege.* Ithaca, N.Y.: Cornell University Press.

Lilley, S. 1966. *Men, machines and history.* New York: International Publishers.

Litowitz, B. 1977. Learning to make definitions. *Journal of Child Language* 4: 289–304.

Lord, A. B. 1960. *The singer of tales.* Cambridge, Mass.: Harvard University Press.

Luria, A. R. 1966. *Higher cortical functions in man.* New York: Basic Books.

———— 1976. *Cognitive development: Its cultural and social foundations.* Cambridge, Mass.: Harvard University Press.

———— 1979. *Making of mind.* Cambridge, Mass.: Harvard University Press.

Maheu, R. 1965. Address, World Conference of Ministers of Education on the Eradication of Illiteracy. Teheran: UNESCO.

Malinowski, B. 1965. *Coral gardens and their magic,* vol. 2. Bloomington: Indiana University Press.

Mandler, G., and P. Dean. 1969. Seriation: The development of serial order in free recall. *Journal of Experimental Psychology* 81: 207–215.

Mandler, J. M., and N. W. Johnson. 1977. Remembrance of things parsed: Story structure and recall. *Cognitive Psychology* 9: 111–151.

Mandler, J. M., S. Scribner, M. Cole, and M. DeForest. 1980. Cross-cultural invariance in story recall. *Child Development* 51: 19–26.

Marler, P., and M. Tamura. 1964. Culturally transmitted patterns of vocal behavior in sparrows. *Science* 146: 1483–86.

Massaquoi, M. 1899. The Vey language. *Spirit of Missions* (New York) 64: 577–579.

———— 1911. The Vai people and their syllabic writing. *Journal of the African Society* 9: 459–466.

Mattingley, I. G. 1972. Reading, the linguistic process, and linguistic awareness. In J. F. Kavanagh and I. G. Mattingley, eds., *Language by ear and by eye.* Cambridge, Mass.: MIT Press.

McLuhan, M. 1962. *The Gutenberg galaxy.* Toronto: University of Toronto Press.

———— 1964. *Understanding media: The extensions of man.* Toronto: McGraw-Hill. (Paperback ed., 1965.)

Mehan, H. B. 1979. *Learning lessons.* Cambridge, Mass.: Harvard University Press.

Migeod, F. W. H. 1909. The syllabic writing of the Vai people. *Journal of the African Society* 9: 46–58.

Moorhouse, A. C. 1953. *The triumph of the alphabet.* New York: Henry Schuman.

Naroll, R. 1970. Cross-cultural sampling. In R. Naroll and R. Cohen, eds., *A handbook of methods in cultural anthropology.* New York: Random House.

Ogden, C. K., and I. A. Richards. 1923. *The meaning of meaning.* London: Kegan Paul, French, Trulner.

Olderogge, D. A. 1966. Ancient scripts from the heart of Africa. *The UNESCO Courier* 19: 25–29.

Olson, D. R. 1975. Review of *Toward a literate society*, ed. J. B. Carroll and J. Chall. *Proceedings of the National Academy of Education* 2: 109–178.
—— 1977. From utterance to text: The bias of language in speech and writing. *Harvard Educational Review* 47 (3): 257–281.
—— 1978. The languages of instruction. In R. Spiro, ed., *Schooling and the acquisition of knowledge*. Hillsdale, N.J.: Lawrence Erlbaum Associates.
Olson, D. R., and N. G. Nickerson. 1978. Language development through the school years: Learning to confine interpretation to the information in the text. In K. E. Nelson, ed., *Children's language*, vol. 1. New York: Gardner Press.
Ong, W. J. 1958. *Ramus, method and the decay of dialogue.* Cambridge, Mass.: Harvard University Press. (Repr. Octagon Books, 1974.)
—— 1971. *Rhetoric, romance and technology: Studies in the interaction of expression and culture.* Ithaca: Cornell University Press.
Osherson, D. N., and E. Markman. 1974–75. Language and the ability to evaluate contradictions and tautologies. *Cognition* 3 (3): 213–226.
Papandropolou, I., and H. Sinclair. 1974. What is a word? Experimental study of children's ideas of grammar. *Human Development* 17: 241–258.
Paris, S. G., and A. Y. Carter. 1973. Semantic and constructive aspects of sentence memory in children. *Developmental Psychology* 9: 109–113.
Piaget, J. 1929. *The child's conception of the world.* London: Routledge & Kegan Paul (Repr. New York: Littlefield, Adams, 1960.)
—— 1977. *The development of thought: Equilibration of cognitive structures.* New York: Viking Press.
Plato. 1928. *Phaedrus.* In I. Edman, ed., *The works of Plato.* New York: Modern Library.
—— 1945. *The Republic.* Trans. with introduction and notes by F. M. Cornford. London: Oxford University Press.
Pratt, M. W., S. Scribner, and M. Cole. 1977. Children as teachers: Developmental studies of instructional communication. *Child Development* 48: 1475–81.
Propp, V. 1958. *Morphology of the folk tale,* trans. L. Scott. Publication 10. Bloomington: Indiana University Research Center in Anthropology, Folklore and Linguistics.
Rafe-uz-Zaman. 1978. Why literacy? *Literacy Discussion.* Teheran: UNESCO.
Raum, O. F. 1943. The African chapter in the history of writing. *African Studies* 2: 179–192.
Reder, S. 1977. The functional impact of writing on Vai speech. Ph.D. dissertation, Rockefeller University.
Republic of Liberia. 1962. *1962 Census of Population.* Monrovia: Ministry of Planning and Economic Affairs.
—— 1974. *1974 Census of Population and Housing.* Population Bulletin No. 2. Monrovia: Ministry of Planning and Economic Affairs.
Resnick, D. P., and L. B. Resnick. 1977. The nature of literacy: An historical exploration. *Harvard Educational Review* 47: 370–385.
Riesenberg, S. H., and S. Kaneshiro. 1960. *A Caroline Islands script.* Bulletin 173, Anthropological Papers No. 6. Smithsonian Institute: U.S. Bureau of American Ethnology.
Rogoff, B. 1981. Schooling and the development of cognitive skills. In H. C. Triandis and A. Heron, eds., *Handbook of cross-cultural psychology*, vol. 4. Allyn & Bacon.
Rumbaugh, D. M., and T. V. Gill. 1976. The mastery of language-type skills by the chimpanzee. In S. R. Harnad, H. D. Steklis, and J. Lancaster, eds.,

Origins and evolution of language and speech. New York: New York Academy of Sciences.

Sakamoto, T., and K. Makita. 1973. Japan. In J. Downing, ed., *Comparative reading.* New York: Macmillan.

Sapir, E. 1921. *Language.* New York: Harcourt, Brace & World.

Savin, H. B. 1972. What the child knows about speech when he starts to learn to read. In J. F. Kavanagh and I. G. Mattingley, eds. *Language by ear and by eye.* Cambridge, Mass.: MIT Press.

Scardamalia, M. 1981. How children cope with the cognitive demands of writing. In J. Dominic and C. Fredericksen, eds., *Writing: The nature, development and teaching of written communication,* vol. 2. Hillsdale, N.J.: Lawrence Erlbaum Associates.

Schallert, D. L., G. M. Kleiman, and A. D. Rubin. 1977. *Analysis of differences between oral and written language.* Technical Report No. 29. Urbana, Ill.: Center for the Study of Reading.

Schmandt-Besserat, D. 1978. The earliest precursor of writing. *Scientific American,* June, 50–59.

Schofield, R. S. 1968. The measurement of literacy in pre-industrial England. In J. Goody, ed., *Literacy in traditional societies.* New York: Cambridge University Press.

Schuman, H. 1967. *Economic development and individual change.* Center for International Affairs, Harvard University. Republ. New York: AMS Press, 1973.

Schuman, H., A. Inkeles, and D. H. Smith. 1967. Some psychological effects and noneffects of literacy in a new nation. *Economic Development and Cultural Change* 1: 1–14.

Scribner, S. 1968. The cognitive consequences of literacy. Unpublished paper, Albert Einstein College of Medicine.

—— 1974. Developmental aspects of categorized recall in a West African society. *Cognitive Psychology* 4: 475–494.

—— 1975. Recall of classical syllogisms: A cross-cultural investigation of error on logical problems. In R. Falmagne, ed., *Reasoning: Representation and process.* Hillsdale, N.J.: Lawrence Erlbaum Associates.

—— 1977a. Modes of thinking and ways of speaking. In P. N. Johnson-Laird and P. C. Wason, eds., *Thinking: Readings in cognitive science.* New York: Cambridge University Press.

—— 1977b. Cultural practice and cognitive skills. Paper presented at annual meeting of the American Anthropological Association, Houston.

—— 1980. Studying literacy at work: Bringing the laboratory to the field. Paper presented at NIE Conference on Basic Skills, Washington, D.C.

Scribner, S., and M. Cole. 1973. Cognitive consequences of formal and informal education. *Science* 182: 553–559.

Sharp, D. W., M. Cole, and C. Lave. 1979. *Education and cognitive development: The evidence from experimental research.* Monographs of the Society for Research in Child Development 44 (1–2, Serial No. 178).

Smith, M. R. Forthcoming. The social background of literacy in a Vai town. Ph.D. dissertation, Cambridge University.

Snell, B. 1953. *The discovery of the mind.* New York: Harper & Row.

Stevenson, H. W., T. Parker, A. Wilkinson, B. Bonnevaux, and M. Gonzales. 1978. *Schooling, environment, and cognitive development: A cross-cultural study.* Monographs of the Society for Research in Child Development 43 (3, Serial No. 175), 1–92.

Stewart, G. 1967. Notes on the present-day usage of the Vai script in Liberia. *African Language Review* 6: 71–74.

—— 1972. The early Vai script as found in the Book of Ndole. Paper presented at Conference on Manding Studies, School of Oriental and African Studies, University of London, June 30–July 3.

Stewart, G., and P. E. H. Hair. 1969. A bibliography of the Vai language and script. *Journal of West African Languages* 6: 109–124.

Sticht, T. G., L. Beck, R. Hauke, G. Kleiman, and J. James. 1974. *Auding and reading: A developmental model.* Alexandria, Va.: Human Resources Research Organization.

Tambiah, S. J. 1968. The magical power of words. *Man* 3: 175–208.

UNESCO Regional Report on Literacy. 1972. Teheran: UNESCO.

U.S. Census of Occupations. 1960. Washington: Government Printing Office.

University of Liberia. 1962. *The standard Vai script.* African Studies Program, August.

Von Frisch, K. 1967. *The dance language and orientation of bees.* Cambridge, Mass.: Harvard University Press.

Von Humboldt, W. 1971. *Linguistic variability and intellectual development.* Coral Gables, Fla.: University of Miami Press. (First publ. 1863.)

Vygotsky, L. S. 1962. *Thought and language.* Cambridge, Mass.: MIT Press.

——— 1978. *Mind in society: The development of higher psychological processes,* ed. M. Cole, V. John-Steiner, S. Scribner, and E. Souberman. Cambridge, Mass.: Harvard University Press.

Welmers, W. E. 1958. *The Mande languages.* Georgetown University Monograph Series in Languages and Linguistics 11: 9–24. Washington: Georgetown University Press.

——— 1976. *A grammar of Vai.* Berkeley: University of California Press.

Werner, H. 1948. *Comparative psychology of mental development.* Repr. New York: Science Editions, 1961.

Whiting, J. W. M. 1971. Socialization process and personality. In F. L. K. Hsu, ed., *Psychological anthropology.* Homewood, Ill.: Dorsey Press.

Wilks, I. 1968. The transmission of Islamic learning in the Western Sudan. In J. Goody, ed., *Literacy in traditional societies.* New York: Cambridge University Press.

Wilson, C. M. 1971. *Liberia: Black Africa in microcosm.* New York: Harper & Row.

Index